Spurgeon Susanah

Ten Years of My Life in the Service of the Book Fund

Spurgeon Susanah

Ten Years of My Life in the Service of the Book Fund

ISBN/EAN: 9783337302986

Printed in Europe, USA, Canada, Australia, Japan

Cover: Foto ©ninafisch / pixelio.de

More available books at **www.hansebooks.com**

TEN YEARS OF MY LIFE

In the Service of the Book Fund:

BEING

A GRATEFUL RECORD OF MY EXPERIENCE
OF THE LORD'S WAYS, AND WORK,
AND WAGES.

BY

MRS. C. H. SPURGEON.

SECOND EDITION.

LONDON:
PASSMORE & ALABASTER, PATERNOSTER BUILDINGS.
1886.

LONDON:
ALABASTER, PASSMORE, AND SONS, PRINTERS,
FANN STREET, E.C.

PREFACE.

I GRATEFULLY adore the goodness of our heavenly Father in directing my beloved wife to a work which has been to her fruitful in unutterable happiness. That it has cost her more pain than it would be fitting to reveal is most true; but that it has brought her a boundless joy is equally certain. Our gracious Lord ministered to His suffering child in the most effectual manner when He graciously led her to minister to the necessities of His servants. By this means He called her away from her personal griefs, gave tone and concentration to her life, led her to continual dealings with Himself, and raised her nearer the centre of that region where other than earthly joys and sorrows reign supreme. Let every believer accept this as the inference of experience: that for most human maladies the best relief and antidote will be found in self-sacrificing work for the Lord Jesus.

If I said a word in praise of the worker herself my Preface would not be acceptable to the author of these Reports; and therefore I must content myself with expressing my conviction that the work was sadly needed, has been exceedingly useful, and is still urgently called for. How can many of our ministers buy books? How can those in the villages get at them at all? What must their ministries become if their minds are starved? Is it not a duty to relieve the famine which is raging in many a manse? Is it not a prudential measure, worthy of the attention of all who wish to see the masses influenced by religion, that the preachers who occupy our pulpits should be kept well furnished with material for thought?

By the Book Fund not less than 12,000 ministers of all denominations have been supplied with at least a few fresh books. Sometimes men have been aided in somewhat unusual studies, for which they had a special predilection: not long ago I had to become adviser to the Fund as to a grammar, and so forth, for the study of Syriac, for the use of one who had a call in that direction. The Fund does not profess to grant works other than those needed for the special work of the ministry, but even this gives a wide range, especially in the case of missionaries. I think great discretion has been used in the distribution of the bounty: I am sure it has been blended with the utmost sympathy and Christian love.

From this date the beloved worker feels that she must slacken. The business has overpowered her: the waggon is running over the horse. A measure of this ministry *must* pass into other hands, for, to my great sorrow, I have seen that over-pressure is now causing a growing sense of weariness. It cannot long be possible to wake up every morning with a dread of that pile of letters; to sit all day, with scarce an interval, writing and book-keeping; and to go to bed at night with a sigh that the last stroke has hardly been made before the eyes have closed. However brave an invalid may be, love will not always allow such incessant toil to grind down a willing spirit. As the embodiment of loving prudence, I feel that I must place an urgent veto upon the continuance of this labour *at its present rate.*

Especially the Report-writing has been dreadful drudgery. I think the outcome of the drudgery is most memorable, and I do not wonder that the Reports have commanded a host of interested readers; but they cost too much of the life-blood of their author, and are to me like the water from the well of Bethlehem, whereof David refused to drink when he knew at what a price it was procured. I trust our many friends will henceforth be content with brief Reports of a somewhat diminished work, and will believe that the matter is so arranged *because it must be.*

Oh for a blessing on the thousands of books which have gone out from our beloved "Westwood"! Prayer never ceases on this account. May the Lord lead others of His servants to carry on such part of this ministry as may cease from our doors, and doubly bless that portion which remains with us!

C. H. SPURGEON.

WESTWOOD, BEULAH HILL,
 March, 1886.

TEN YEARS OF MY LIFE

IN THE SERVICE OF THE BOOK FUND.

How the Fund became a Fact.

IT was in the summer of the year 1875 that my dear husband completed and published the first volume of his "Lectures to my Students." Reading one of the "proof" copies, I became so enamoured of the book, that when the dear author asked, "Well, how do you like it?" I answered, with a full heart, "I wish I could place it in the hands of every minister in England." "Then why not do so: *how much will you give?*" said my very practical spouse. I must confess I was unprepared for such a challenge. I was ready enough to *desire* the distribution of the precious book; but to *assist* in it, or help to pay for it, had not occurred to me. But "John Ploughman" "drives a straight furrow" to one's heart, and knows how to turn over the thick clods of selfishness which lie there choking up the useful growths; and very soon his words set me thinking how much I could spare from housekeeping or personal matters to start this new scheme. I knew it would necessitate a pressure somewhere, for money was not plentiful just then; but to see dear John's face beam so radiantly, at the idea of my scattering his books far and wide, was worth any effort; and love, even more than obedience, constrained me to carry out the suddenly-formed plan. Then comes the wonderful part: I found the money ready and waiting! Up-stairs in a little drawer were some carefully hoarded crown-pieces, which, owing to some foolish fancy, I had been gathering for years whenever chance threw one in my way; these I now counted out, and found they made a sum *exactly* sufficient to pay for one hundred copies of the work! If a twinge of regret at parting from my cherished but unwieldy favourites passed over me, it was gone in an instant, and then they were given, freely and thankfully, to the Lord, and in that moment, though I knew it not,

THE BOOK FUND WAS INAUGURATED!

Notes from "The Sword and the Trowel."

BY PASTOR C. H. SPURGEON.

July, 1875.—Mrs. Spurgeon, our beloved and afflicted wife, begs us to say that she has been so much interested in reading the book entitled "Lectures to my Students," that she would like to bear the cost of giving a copy to each of a hundred poor Baptist ministers, who would accept it from her. She mourns that she can do so little personally for her Lord, and hopes that this little gift may be owned of God, to the stirring up of some of His ministers to yet more earnest labour for His glory. We cannot deny our dear sufferer anything which causes her pleasure, and therefore willingly give publicity to this her own spontaneous desire. To prevent disappointment, from the applications being too numerous, we, for this month, invite only Baptist ministers to apply.

* * * *

August, 1875.—Mrs. Spurgeon very speedily distributed the hundred copies of the "Lectures to my Students," and so numerous were the applicants, that she felt bound to give another hundred. These also have all been seized upon, and many other claimants are left unsupplied. It has been a great pleasure to our beloved wife to give a book to so many needy servants of the Lord; but it is a sad fact that there should be so many needing such a present. Cannot something be done to provide ministers with books? If they cannot be made rich in money, they ought not, for the people's sake, to be starved in soul. Some of the applicants say that they have not been able to buy a new book for the last ten years! Does anybody wonder if preachers are sometimes dull?

* * * *

September, 1875.—Mrs. Spurgeon is every day sending out books to needy brethren whom we have selected for her, and it gives her intense pleasure to be thus of use to the Lord's people. She suffers very greatly, and this holy service cheers the tedium of sickness, and affords her much comfort. Those who have sent the means have made us both very happy, and we earnestly pray the Lord to reward them. Very cruel is the poverty of many Baptist ministers. How can they feed the people when they never see a new book? To supply them with mental food is a boon, not to them only, but to all their hearers. We trust this beneficent service will be continued. We have named the work,

"Mrs. Spurgeon's Book Fund,"

and we believe that it will not soon come to an end, but will do great good.

* * * *

October, 1875.—Mrs. Spurgeon has been able to distribute a large number of parcels of books to ministers whom she knew to be in need. Several friends have sent sums of money; to these she tenders her sincere thanks.

We trust that from time to time others will do the same. One gentleman has sent a number of exceedingly good books for the same object. We have on several occasions in days past received parcels consisting of old magazines and the sweepings of libraries, and we have concluded that the donors thought we kept a butter shop; but this friend has sent really standard volumes, which will, we trust, be a boon to some poor preacher. This good work of providing mental food for ministers ought never to cease till their incomes are doubled. May "*Mrs. Spurgeon's Book Fund*" become a permanent source of blessing to ministers and churches!

* * * *

November, 1875.—During Mrs. Spurgeon's extreme illness the work of distributing books to ministers has been delayed, but she has now resumed it. The delight with which the volumes sent out have been received is a great joy to the poor invalid, and to us it is a matter of supreme satisfaction. We have met with brethren who have only four books, and others who have but few more, all of a worthless character; for hardly one out of the number would be worth buying for sixpence at a bookstall. There is an absolute famine of books among poor Baptist ministers, and the work of supplying them is one of the most needful which Christian charity can undertake. We are feeding the church when we feed the minister's mind. God the Holy Spirit must teach him to profit; but, by supplying instructive books, we have at least used the means. So long as funds last, Mrs. Spurgeon will continue the distribution, and it is not supposable that she will be left without the needful money, while so many of our Master's stewards are increasing in wealth.

A few Words concerning the Book Fund.*

By Mrs. C. H. Spurgeon.

From "The Sword and the Trowel," February, 1876.

ALL last winter, in the sunniest corner of the south window of our especial sanctum, there stood a common garden flower-pot containing a little plant which we deemed a marvel of grace and beauty. We had sown some lemon pips the preceding autumn with a lively hope that one or more of them might possess the wonderful life-germ, and we were well rewarded for our confidence. In due time a frail little stem and two of the tiniest leaves that ever coaxed their way through the dark mould made their appearance, and from that moment it was watched, and watered, and tended with assiduous care. So frail at first, and delicate, that a drop of dew would have overwhelmed it, it nevertheless soon gained courage, the tender stem strengthened, one by one other and larger leaves unfolded themselves, and the little plant stood perfect and complete. It was a very little thing; but it gave great pleasure; and though some of the younger members of the household would occasionally ask, with just a suspicion of sarcasm in their tone, "If there were any lemons yet?" we cherished our little plant even more lovingly, and thanked God who, with infinite tenderness towards His suffering children, often deepens and intensifies their enjoyment of daily mercies, throwing a special charm around their common comforts, and causing a leaf, a flower, or the song of a bird, to whisper sweet "comfortable thoughts" in their hearts.

But this winter our Heavenly Father has given us a better

---

* The beloved writer, with profound reverence for our editorial authority, placed this paper in our hand with a great deal of diffidence, and coaxingly entreated us to alter and amend it, and make it presentable. It is not in our heart to touch a word of it; we could not improve it, and we do not want to partake in the honour of it. Every line cost the suffering writer pain, and gave her joy, and it shall speak for itself. We cannot, dare not, alter it.

plant to care for. The little tree of the "Book Fund" sprang from as small a beginning as the lemon plant itself and we fondly hope it is as surely a creation of the Lord's hand. Great was the lovingkindness which brought *this* plant into our sick chamber, and gave us the loving commission to "dress and keep it." With what joy we received the charge, and how happy the work made us, words fail to tell; but since the little tree has grown rapidly under the sunshine of the Lord's blessing, we thought our friends would be interested to know how much and what manner of fruit it bears.

At first we intended only to distribute one hundred copies of Mr. Spurgeon's "Lectures to my Students," but we received so many kind donations from friends who sympathized with our wishes, that we soon became ambitious, and, without discontinuing the distribution of "Lectures," we longed to supply needy ministers with the precious volumes of "The Treasury of David," "Sermons," etc. This we have been enabled to do, and the work goes on daily. Without any solicitation, friends have sent in £182, and though our dear Mr. Editor thinks they might not like their names to be published, yet if he should one day change his mind, they are all ready for him, faithfully registered, and would look very nice in his *Sword and Trowel*. We keep also a strict debtor and creditor account, in which said dear Mr. Editor takes great interest, being quite as delighted as ourselves when any increase to the fund is announced. Better still, the Lord's "book of remembrance" is open, and therein assuredly the names of all those who aid his toiling servants will be recorded. We are still prepared to give the "Lectures" to all ministers who apply direct to us. Up to this date we have sent out *five hundred and fifty* "Lectures," each one with an earnest prayer for God's blessing, and we have had many delightful proofs that this has been bestowed. One minister thus writes:—

I may also say, for your encouragement, that after I received your copy ("Lectures") Mr. Mayers kindly sent me one, which I gave to a poor brother in the neighbouring village, who has not been to our College, and the effect on his heart has been most blessed; after reading it he went to prayer, like myself, and next Lord's-day he and his congregation were in tears.

As yet, with three or four exceptions, "The Treasury of David" has been given only to Pastors once students of the Pastors' College; but as our work prospers, we may hope to extend the boon to others also.

How greatly these gifts of ours are needed, and how thoroughly they are appreciated, will be best seen by some extracts from letters, which we here subjoin :—

Your great gift to me came safely to hand this morning. I cannot command language that will adequately convey to you the thanks I desire to offer. You will believe me when I say that the gift, and the way in which it came to me, thoroughly broke me down, and tears of joy flowed freely.

My salary is £60 a-year. I have a wife and family. You will be able to conceive my feelings on receiving four volumes of "The Treasury," when I tell you that these are the only new books I have had for three years past.

I was not educated at the Pastors' College, and fear, therefore that I have no claim; but if mistaken in this, I shall be most thankful for any help of the kind you may be able to render me. My library is small, and minus several books which I am daily thirsting to possess, but thirsting in vain, inasmuch as there are nine of us to subsist upon £100 per annum. It costs so much to clothe and feed my boys and girls, that I have nothing left for the clothing and feeding of my bookshelves. If it is not in your power to assist me, I will not murmur, for I have become accustomed to disappointment, but will labour on as hitherto with the Master's help.

Through the long illness of my dear wife . . . I have been unable to add a single book to my very small stock for the last two years; therefore any present of a book is most thankfully accepted. . . . May the Lord raise up many other friends, so that you may be able to help poor ministers yet more and more.

The prospect of having a new book seems to put new life into me. I have often longed to have "The Treasury of David," but could not afford to purchase it. After buying necessary things, there is nothing left for buying books.

I have long desired the whole of "The Treasury of David." Mr. Spurgeon gave me the first volume (which is all I possess); but I had given up all hope of possessing the remaining volumes. You will understand this when I tell you I have a wife and five little ones to support, also aged parents, one of whom is now in his eighty-sixth year, and £100 is my only income to meet all, so that out of it I dare not attempt to buy such a valuable work as "The Treasury."

Perhaps, in closing this short statement, my dear Mr. Editor would graciously accord me the privilege of laying aside for a moment that formal and perplexing "we," and allow me to say how deeply I am personally indebted to the dear friends who have furnished me with the means of making others happy. For me there has been a *double* blessing. I have been both recipient and donor, and in such a case as this it is hard to say which is the "more blessed." My days have been made indescribably bright and happy by the delightful duties connected with the work and its little arrangements, and so many loving messages have come to me in letters, such kind words, such hearty good wishes, such earnest, fervent prayers have surrounded me, that I seem to be living in an atmosphere of blessing and love, and can truly say with the Psalmist, "My cup runneth over." So, with a heart full of gratitude to God, and deep thankfulness to my dear friends, I bid them for the present a loving farewell.

A Letter to her Friends.

By Mrs. C. H. Spurgeon.

From "The Sword and the Trowel," August, 1876.

Dear Friends,

My "Few Words" in the February number of *The Sword and the Trowel* were received with so much tender sympathy and consideration, that I feel encouraged to present you with another slight sketch of the work which the Lord's love and your kindness have made so prosperous. I then told you from how small a matter the fund rose, and how pitifully and graciously the Lord dealt with me in giving me so blessed a work to do for him when all other service was impossible. *Now* I have the same song to sing, but the notes are higher and more assured, and the accompanying chords deeper and fuller; for the "little one has become a thousand," and the mercy which was so great before has grown exceedingly, until my heart echoes the poet's words :—

> "For if thy work on earth be sweet,
> What must thy glory be?"

I have very much to tell you, and I shall do it in the best way I can; but as all my friends know that my pen is "unaccustomed to public speaking," I think I may crave special indulgence for all failures and shortcomings.

We will discuss money matters first, because I want you to sing "*Laus Deo*" with me. John Ploughman says that "Spend, and God will send, is the motto of a *spendthrift*." Now, I must not dispute this, for dear John is always right, and, moreover, knows all about everything, but I may say I consider it singularly inappropriate to the spendthrift, and should like it handed over to me at once and for ever for my Book Fund; for again and again has it been proved most blessedly true in my experience. I have "spent" ungrudgingly, feeling sure that the Lord would "send" after the same fashion, and indeed he has done so, even "exceeding abundantly above what I could ask or even think." I have received now upwards of £500, and the glory of this is that it is *all spent*, and more keeps coming! I never tell you, dear friends, when my store is slender, but I am sure the Lord does, and opens your hearts to give just when it is most needed; for never since I first began the work have I had to refuse an application for want of funds. I must tell you, too, that this £500 represents quite £700 or £800 in books; for Mr. Spurgeon's good publishers let me purchase on such liberal terms that by their delightful magic my sovereigns turn into thirty and sometimes forty shillings each! This, also, is of the Lord, and I bless Him for it. I often look with intense pleasure on the long list of subscribers' names spread out before the Lord, and before Him only; for your kind deeds, my dear friends, are unpublished to the world, but are, perhaps, for this reason all the more precious in his sight, who "seeth not as man seeth." It is, indeed, pleasant to look down the long columns and note how many strangers have become dear friends, and former friends have grown dearer through this loving link of sympathy for Christ's servants between us.

But it is time I gave you some details of the work accomplished. The number of books given up to this moment is 3,058, and the persons receiving them have been pastors of all denominations. But ah! dear friends, when I look at the list of names, I see the only shadow of sadness that ever rests upon my Book Fund. It is the grief of knowing that there exists a terrible necessity for this service of love; that without this help (little enough, indeed, compared with their wants) the poor Pastors to whom it has been sent must have gone on famishing for lack of mental food, their incomes being so wretchedly small that they scarcely know how to "provide things honest" for themselves and their families, while money for the purchase of books is absolutely unattainable. Hear what one says, who like Paul, can thank God he is "chargeable to none":—

Dear Mrs. Spurgeon,—In this month's *Sword and Trowel* ministers are kindly invited to apply for a grant of books from your Book Fund. I should be glad of a grant if ever so small. . . . . I have a wife delicate in health, necessitating the keeping of a servant; we have had twelve children, six the Lord has taken home, and six are with us here. Not a year has passed since our marriage (twenty-five years ago) without the doctor being in the house; I am but now slowly recovering from illness, the effect of an overwrought mind and frame; the eldest of our children living is the only one earning anything, and he but a trifle more than sufficient to clothe him; we hardly make the two ends meet, and were it not for the extras the Lord is ever and anon sending us, we could not do so at all. . . . . I take in *The Sword and the Trowel*, *Baptist Messenger*, and Mr. Spurgeon's "Sermons"; am extravagant enough *sometimes* to buy a two shilling or two shilling and sixpenny book: but the whole of my library would scarcely fetch thirty shillings. . . . The Lord is good to us; though often lacking, there is help at last, and I trust, if it is his will, the lack which I feel for books he will kindly supply, to some extent, through your Book Fund.

After having received a nice box of books this tried brother writes:—

I know not how to express my gratitude for the choice and valuable books you have sent me. I do not think I could ever have dreamed of having the four volumes of "The Treasury of David." May the Lord grant, indeed, that it may be a "treasure" to myself and others. Bless

His name, He has indeed done all things well, and has again and again showed us "He is good, a stronghold in the day of trouble, and He knoweth them that trust in Him." In that He has through you sent me such valuable aid, He has shown again how mindful He is of the least of His children.

Their very gratitude for the boon conferred often makes my heart ache in the midst of its gladness; for the sense of need must have been sorely felt, since relief is received with such rapture. Here are one or two more selections from scores of similar epistles.

I have a family of eight children, four of whom are now grown up. My stipend at first was £60, it is now £70; my wife for seventeen years has managed the house without the assistance of a servant, and our expenditure, with the utmost thrift and economy, always exceeds my stipend; but through a kind Providence we are enabled to do, and pay ready cash for everything.

My salary is £80 per annum; with a wife and three children into the bargain. I have a few books, and among them the first five volumes of Mr. Spurgeon's "Sermons," which I purchased before I was married; and a short time since I invested £2 17s. in the purchase of Brown and Fausset's "Commentary," and my wife thinks it will be a very long time before we recover the shock which this outlay has given to our finances.

It is most touching to hear some tell with eloquence the effect the gift produced upon them. One is "not ashamed to say" he received his parcel with "tears of joy," wife and children standing around and rejoicing with him. Another, as soon as the wrappings fall from the precious volumes, praises God aloud and sings the Doxology with all his might; while a third, when his eyes light on the long-coveted "Treasury of David," "rushes from the room" that he may go alone and "pour out his full heart before his God."

Now this is very beautiful and admirable, but is there not also something most sorrowfully suggestive to the church of God? Surely these "servants of Christ," these "ambassadors for God," ought to have received better treatment at our hands than to have been left pining so long without the aids which are vitally necessary to them in their sacred calling. Books are as truly a minister's needful tools as the plane, and the hammer, and the saw, are the necessary adjuncts of a carpenter's bench. We pity a poor mechanic whom accident has deprived of his working gear, we straightway get up a subscription to restore it, and certainly never expect a stroke of work from him while it is lacking; why, I wonder, do we not bring the same common-sense help to our poor ministers, and furnish them liberally with the means of procuring the essentially important books? Is it not pitiful to think of their struggling on from year to year on £100, £80, £60, and some (I am ashamed to write it) on less than £50 per annum? Many have large families, many more sick wives, some, alas! have both; they have heavy doctors' bills to pay, their children's education to provide for, are obliged to keep up a respectable appearance, or their hearers would be scandalized; and how they manage to do all this and yet keep out of debt (as, to their honour and credit be it said, the majority of them do) only they and their ever-faithful God can know! I never hear a word of complaint from them, only sometimes a pathetic line or two like this: "After upwards of sixteen years' service in the Master's vineyard, I am sorry to say that, with a small salary, and a wife and five daughters to provide for, my library is exceedingly small, and I am not in a position to increase its size by purchasing books." Or again like this: "My salary is small (£60), and if I did not get some little help from some benevolent societies, I should have very great difficulty in keeping the wolf from the door." Are these men to be kept in poverty so deep that they positively cannot afford the price of a new book without letting their little ones go barefoot? "The labourer is worthy of his hire;" but these poor labourers in the gospel field get a pittance which is unworthy both of the workmen and the work, and if their people (who ought to help them more) either cannot or will not do so, we at least, dear friends, will do all in our power to encourage their weary hearts and refresh their drooping spirits. This is a digression, I dare say, from my authorized subject; but I was obliged to say what I have said, because my heart was hot within me, and I so earnestly want to do these poor brethren good service. Now I return to the details of my work.

I have been doing a brave business in Wales through the

magnificent generosity of a stranger, whom now we count a friend. This gentleman first introduced himself to us by sending £100 to Mr. Spurgeon, £50 of which was for my Book Fund. I was greatly gratified at receiving so large a sum all at one time, and set about " spending " it as quickly as possible, and here you will see how grandly true my " motto " proved; for, about six months after the first gift, the same kind friend called at our house one evening, and to our sincere admiration and astonishment, announced his intention of giving a copy of "Lectures to my Students" to *every* Calvinistic Methodist minister, preacher, and student in North Wales (of whom there are five hundred) if I would undertake the "trouble" of sending them. Trouble!! The word was inadmissible! With intense joy and deep gratitude to God I received the charge, and *another* £50 to meet expenses! This was on the 18th of March, 1876. Since then, to this day, the work there has flourished; for as soon as 400 copies had been given in the northern part, I received authority from the same noble donor to continue, at his expense, the distribution throughout South Wales also. The books are very eagerly accepted by our Welsh brethren, and on May 16th, the Quarterly Association sent copies in Welsh and English of a resolution passed at their meeting at Ruthin, of "Cordial thanks to the kind brother, *whoever he may be*, to whose liberality we are indebted, etc., etc., and grateful acknowledgments to Mrs. Spurgeon, for her kindness in forwarding the books." Nor does the matter rest here; other ministers besides Calvinistic Methodists coveted the precious volume, and wrote to me asking why they should be left out? I have supplied all who have written, and at this present moment I have promised copies to all the Wesleyan ministers of South Wales, and when they are satisfied, I doubt not their northern brethren will request the same favour. These copies, of course, are provided by my Book Fund, our friend's gift being confined to his own denomination; but you see, dear friends, I never *can* be the least troubled at a large expenditure, because I have the firmest possible faith in my motto, "Spend, and God will send."

Some weeks since, a gentleman sent me a splendid lot of second-hand books, so well selected and suitable, that they have proved most valuable in making up parcels; but usually I would prefer that help did not come to me in that shape; for I find, as a rule, that Mr. Spurgeon's works are more eagerly sought after, and more joyfully welcomed than *any* others. "His words are like the dew-drops of heaven to my soul," writes one pastor; and to most "The Treasury of David" seems to have been a possession long coveted and ardently desired.

Am I not happy to have been able to send forth seven hundred volumes of this veritable "Treasure"? I have given also a goodly number of Mr. Spurgeon's lesser works. This arises from the fact that many evangelists, colporteurs, and lay preachers apply to me for books; and, although my fund is chiefly for the aid and comfort of poor *Pastors*, I find this other class so sorely needing encouragement and help, that I cannot pass them by. Denied the blessing of a solid education in their youthful days, they find it difficult to pick up knowledge in middle life, and when called upon to conduct cottage-meetings or open-air services, they painfully feel the strain on their mental powers. To such the "Morning and Evening Readings" are an inestimable boon; for, open the book where they will, they may find sermons in *embryo* in every page, and nuggets of thought only waiting to be picked up and appropriated. The following letter from one who left the Colportage for the ministry will confirm my statement:—

Dear Madam,—Pardon the liberty I am taking, but I think I may say if anyone needed a little help in the book line I do. I am labouring in three country villages, preaching to and visiting the people. I am receiving £60 a-year, and have five children to provide for. I cannot find money to purchase books, and my stock is limited to a few works—old sermons, etc. I can assure you Mr. Spurgeon's "Lectures to my Students" would be thankfully received. I dare not ask any further, having no claims whatever on your generosity. Your kind letter in *The Sword and the Trowel* has encouraged me to make this application. I don't know what I should do sometimes but for Mr. Spurgeon's "Evening by Evening," which not only helps us in our family devotions, but provides me with many a subject for my congregations.

Some books were sent, and this grateful answer received:—

> I beg to acknowledge your kind present, which reached me on Saturday evening. My children could not have been more delighted if they had received a parcel containing toys than I was when I saw the contents of the package. I cannot find words to express my heartfelt thanks to you; I could only exclaim, "How good is my Father in heaven!" Like the poor negro, I might say, "Bless the Lord; me hab all kind o' commodations, like Joseph in Egypt." May the Lord reward you by sending in abundantly the help you need to carry on your work of love.

Next to "The Treasury of David," the "Sermons" of our very dear Editor are the objects of desire on the part of those who know their worth, and happy is he who has the set complete! I have helped very many to attain their wishes in this matter when they have already possessed many volumes; others have to be content for the present with three, four, six, or eight volumes, as the case may be. I cannot speak of the blessing these Sermons carry with them wherever they go; God owns and blesses them so mightily that eternity alone will reveal their power and value.

And now, dear friends, though I have by no means exhausted my information, I think I have told you all I can remember of *special* interest. What do you think of *your* work? It is yours as much as mine; for without your kind and loving aid I could not carry it on to so large an extent. Does it satisfy and please you? To me, as you know, it brings unalloyed joy and comfort, and to the Lord's poor servants it carries new life, and light, and vigour; but I want most of all that it should promote *God's glory*, and have for its chief aim and object the uplifting of His holy name. Do, dear fellow-workers, pray *very* earnestly that a rich blessing may rest upon every book sent out, so that first the minister, then his church, and next of all the unsaved in the congregation, may be the better, and the Lord may receive "the thanksgiving of many."

I cannot close my letter without reference to my little lemon plant; for its history interested many, and it will ever be tenderly associated in my mind with my God-given work. It has thriven in its way as gracefully and grandly as the

Book Fund, and is now an ambitious, healthy young tree, preparing itself, I hope, for future fruit-bearing. One of John Ploughman's "boys" (such a *dear, good* boy according to his mother) can use his pencil deftly, and handle the graving tool with some skill (though John's wife says she *knows* his father's heart is set upon his following the *old plough* some day); so I asked him to make me a little sketch of my pretty tree, and here it is, dear friends, for you to see, though I can assure you the grace of its form and the glossy beauty of its leaves cannot be depicted. I have always cherished the fanciful idea that each leaf must represent £100; so now you can count them, and smile at the magnificent future I anticipate for my Book Fund. Twenty-one, are there not? That must mean £2,100, and *plenty of strength to grow more!* Well, it seems a great deal of money, certainly; but what a trifle it must be to the God who made all the silver and the gold! Ah! I believe that some day,

> "When grace has made *me* meet
> His lovely face to see,"

the subscription list of the Book Fund will record its thousands of pounds; the once tiny plant will be a tree bearing fruit to perfection, and the dear old motto, "Spend, and God will send," will be found true and unfailing to the end.

With the utmost loving gratitude, dear friends, I am, on the behalf of Christ's poor servants, your happy almoner.

How the Book Fund prospers.

By Mrs. C. H. Spurgeon.

From "The Sword and the Trowel," January, 1877.

"A RECORD OF COMBAT WITH SIN, AND LABOUR FOR THE LORD." These words on the cover of our magazine startled me the other day as I sat thinking over my work, and what I should say about it. I felt almost ashamed of my audacity in presuming to ask a place again amidst its pages, seeing that I am not strong enough to bear a "sword," and my "trowel" is such a very little one that it can only hope to gather enough mortar to supply some few of the labourers who build up the living stones. But I remembered with exceeding comfort that, when the wall of Jerusalem was repaired, in Nehemiah's time, the work of the daughters of Shallum was as faithfully recorded as the labour of the princes and the priests.

So I take courage to tell again of the Lord's great goodness to me, and how marvellously He has continued to help and bless the Book Fund. As certainly as if He had stretched forth His hand from the heavens and given me a written commission for the service, so surely do I know that this work came to me through His indulgent love, and from the first moment of its existence to the present, He has guided, and supported, and blessed it, and every atom of the glory shall be His. *He* sent me the needful funds to carry it on, by moving the hearts of His people to help me; for *not one penny* of the £926 received from August 11th of last year till now was solicited except from Him. And He has heard and answered the prayer that a great blessing might follow the books into the homes of His dear servants, comforting their hearts and refreshing their spirits, as well as aiding them in their preparation for the pulpit. I have *two great heaps* of letters from them, so heavy that I lift them with difficulty; and if all the joy and gratitude to God therein expressed could be written out, it would fill some volumes. Knowing how deeply interested in these letters the readers of *The Sword and the Trowel* have hitherto been, I propose in this paper to give a series of extracts from them,* a set of word-pictures as it were, which I shall call

A GLIMPSE AT SOME ENGLISH INTERIORS.

Years ago, when I had the felicity of sharing my dear husband's annual holiday, one of our chief pleasures consisted in visiting the picture gallery of every continental town we entered. There "walking circumspectly" over the shining, treacherous floors, we spent many happy hours, and enjoyed to the full the works of the grand old masters; but I am not ashamed to confess that I at least used to linger longer and more lovingly over a "Dutch Interior," by Teniers or Ostade, than I cared to do over any "Madonna and Child" that Raphael or Rubens ever painted. These latter never stirred any *devotional* feelings within my soul, and failing this, they ceased to interest, and even grew tiresome by constant repetition. But it was charming to be absorbed in the "little beautiful works," as an authority on painting calls them, which the Dutch masters loved to draw with such wonderful and tender minuteness of detail. The interior of a fisherman's hut, with its quaint wooden cradle, and its basket of freshly-caught fish, would, on close inspection, reveal unsuspected objects of interest, and the picturesque farm kitchens, with their glittering array of bright pans, their wealth of delf ware, their chubby children, and their comely Vrows, were so homelike, and so natural, that the more one gazed at them the more vividly real they became, and it was an easy task to weave a tale of family joy or sorrow around each glowing canvas.

But now I want to show my friends, by pen in lieu of pencil, some scenes in English home-life where the tale of gladness or of suffering is even more plainly pictured, and needs no effort of the imagination to unfold it. A hasty glance into a parlour, at the moment when a gift from the

---

* When the writers of these letters recognize their own compositions, they need have no fear of betrayed confidence; for with my own hands I have prepared all the copy for the printer, so that their names might be unknown.

Book Fund has arrived; a peep into a study where the four portly volumes of "The Treasury of David" have just enriched the scanty store of books; a glimpse of a figure with bowed head and clasped hands, pouring out a heart full of gratitude before his God—these, and such as these, tell their own story, and as we pass from one picture to another, will only need a word or two from me to introduce them. I could show some where tearful faces gather, and a little coffin occupies the foreground; but these are *veiled*, and my hand dares not withdraw the covering.

The first "Interior" which I point out to you is shining with the brightness of domestic love. The little room may be poorly furnished, and the bookshelves, *I know*, are sadly bare (how can they be otherwise, when the minister's income has the very uncomfortable habit of oscillating between £40 and £60 a year?); but you can see with what intense delight that kind and happy wife is assisting to unpack the treasure of new books which will cheer her husband's heart, and make him feel a richer man for some time to come. There is a *Sword and Trowel* lying on the table, and . . . . but you shall look for yourselves :—

The receipt of your communication this morning was a surprise. A pleasing and agreeable surprise; for I had no idea that my kind, good wife had written to you. Often have I seen "The Treasury of David" advertised, and have secretly desired to have it. But in order to be happy I am compelled to nip my desires in the bud, lest they should grow to be troublesome. My soul's desire for books has to be slain, which is wearisome work, so that some passages of Scripture, in an improper sense, have a secret meaning to my soul. "My soul is weary because of murderers." "Happy is he that taketh and dasheth thy little ones against the stones"; but in this case I have to thank you and my dear wife that my desire for "The Treasury of David" has not perished with the rest; a little Moses saved, and I trust will prove a blessing. Please accept my *hearty thanks*. May the Lord abundantly bless you in your mission, and move the hearts of His children to contribute. Much pleased to see a sketch of your lemon plant, and to find it flourishing: I have often thought and wondered whether the little thing was still alive. . . . . No one but the Lord, and the partner of our joys and sorrows, know the struggles of a minister. Thank God for a good wife. Minster churchyard, in Kent, has a monument to the wife of a minister, of whom it is recorded, "She cheered him with her smile, sustained him with her counsel, and aided him in his ministry for thirty-six years." And she is not the only one. . . . . After examining the work. I am constrained to write again and express my high appreciation of it. I am impressed with the immense amount of labour which must have been expended in its production—the mines of truth it contains. It is indeed a treasury of things new and old—to me a treasure indeed. Others have laboured, and I am favoured to enter into their labours. It is the most valuable work I have, the Bible, of course, excepted. The whole church owes Mr. Spurgeon a debt of gratitude, not only for his own thoughts, but also for bringing up from the past the thoughts of the thoughtful of other ages. It will, it must, be a lasting benefit to thousands, and ought to be on the shelf of every minister. Yours is a noble work, to distribute to those who cannot afford to purchase. Pardon me for writing a second time. If I were to hold my peace the stones would cry out.

There is so much homely, yet pathetic grace in the next picture, that it must attract all eyes, and hearts also, I hope. How true to nature, and how touching is the chief incident—the evening stroll down the brightly-lighted streets of the town, the unmistakable *gravitation* of the poor minister's mind and body towards the fatal bookstall, and the overwhelming anxiety of the tender wife to avert the threatened peril to her scantily-filled purse !

Being the wife of one of those ministers whom God has put it into your heart to help, I feel that I owe you a debt of gratitude, and as my heart is too full to hold all it feels, I pour it out before God and you whom He has chosen to carry out a work so noble. A thousand thanks for your timely aid. . . . . I am the mother of seven children—six are yet with us—the eldest is fifteen, the youngest is just over eight. While rearing these children up to now, mine has been a life of hard work and self-sacrifice. Our salary in the past has been much lower than it is now, but still we have to struggle to make ends meet as family wants increase year by year. My husband is a great lover of books, and I am almost ashamed to confess that when walking in town with him I have very carefully avoided going into the streets where the book stores were kept, *knowing it would be hard work for him to pass them by*. Many times after receiving our quarter's salary it has puzzled me to know how to divide it—the quarter's school bills nearly due, one must have a new suit of clothes, another a dress, the twin boys must have new boots, caps, etc. I assure you that to spare a little for my husband's library I have had to be servant, tailor, and dressmaker, and very frequently have my hands been in the dye-pot in order to send my family out respectable.

We cannot help saying, "Well done! good wife, good mother; the Lord reward thee 'in that day'!"

Now we come to a small but choice picture. The minister sits in his study (a cosy one), and we rejoice to see his shelves moderately stocked with books ; he has just had the pleasure of adding "The Treasury of David," and Watson's "Body of Divinity" to his store; he is writing rapidly, and this is what he says:—

> This evening I have received the four much-desired volumes. Heartily I thank you, and unfeignedly bless the Lord, joining in the prayer so kindly recorded in Vol. I. that the precious contents may avail me. Here is a mine of gold—I hope to dig up nuggets for my people. How the cream of the gospel stands thickly on this unadulterated milk! Prayer and meditation shall churn it into butter; nay, shall I not give them butter and honey till they *all* know how to refuse the evil flesh-pots of Egypt, and choose the good things of the land where David dwelt, where milk and honey flow? Your noble efforts for ministers will be a blessing to both mind and body. It *is* rather trying to the nerves to be clearing the ground with a borrowed axe, carving wood with one's fingers, and working at the pump when the sucker is dry. But now, through Mrs. Spurgeon's loving work, poor men whose thoughts stand still for want of gear-oil will have heart and mind set spinning like the "Chariots of Amminadib"!

There is one difficulty I experience in arranging this little gallery of home scenes, which arises from the loving gratitude of the sketchers themselves. Some of the most interesting and touching letters I receive contain so many gentle and gracious *personalities*, that I am obliged to conceal them from public view, and for this reason many a bright picture enshrined in the privacy of my "sanctum" can never leave it to touch other hearts as it has touched mine. I hope, however, that those I am able to present to my friends will interest them greatly, and next in order I place one which has two aspects—winter and summer; for, thanks to the kindness of dear friends, I was able, for a time at least, to make the sun shine on the hitherto cheerless prospect. Would to God I could do more, not only for this "good wife," but for the many others who I know have terrible reason to be "afraid of the snow for their households." Just think of the dear little children patiently lying in bed while their scanty clothing was being washed!

> Forgive me for troubling you with a statement of our poverty. Many times I have felt prompted to ask if you have a fund for supplying poor ministers' wives and children with clothes. If so, I sincerely trust you will have compassion on us, for we are in great need. My husband has been in the ministry more than twenty-six years, and has never received more than £5 per month. We are seven in family, and I am such a sufferer from rheumatics that I cannot do the house-work;

and as we cannot pay for hired help, our eldest girl, who was in a situation, is obliged to come home again. If you can help us in any way, it will be very, very acceptable; for the winter is near, and firing and house-rent are high, and my dear husband's clothes are getting as bare as our own.

* * * *

I am going to try to drop you a few lines, but do not know how sufficiently to thank you and dear friends for your great kindness to us. We were all of us overjoyed; it is an old saying that it is always darkest before the dawn, and we found it so; for when your present came to hand the dear little ones *were in bed, that we might wash their clothes*, as we had not change of raiment for them. But you may depend there was no more sleep for that day when they were told that Mrs. Spurgeon had sent money to buy them new warm clothes. Since then we have received a cheque from Mr. ———, and a box of very valuable clothing from Mr. ———, which we feel sure is through your sympathy. . . . We sincerely hope that none of the kind friends who have helped us will ever know one-tenth of the trouble that we have had; yet we never had so much joy as this week has brought us!

Although I have *scores* more of such letters, I am afraid I must close my collection here, lest I tire my reader's patience, and trespass too far on my Editor's precious pages. It has been a joy inexpressible to minister, even in the least degree, to the crying needs of the pastors who have sought the aid of the Book Fund; but I cannot forget that there are hundreds still unsupplied, and if the Lord permit and spare me, I hope to do more this year than was accomplished in the past. I depend *wholly* on the Lord to move the hearts of His people to help me, and I know He "will not fail me," nor "forsake the work of His own hands." 4,967 volumes have been distributed, 701 ministers have received grants of books, and as I am *corresponding secretary*, as well as treasurer, manager, etc., my friends can imagine I have had full employment. The only part of the work delegated to another is the *packing* of the parcels, and this service is always performed as a "labour of love" by the willing hands of the dear friend to whose devoted affection I already owe so much. Who should be my "director in chief" and my "referee" in all perplexities but my dear Editor? To him I run in search of counsel, comfort, or wise advice, and need I say I always find it?

Dear friends, farewell. As on former occasions, so now, I

must beg that the effort to place before you some details of my work may be viewed with lenient and indulgent eyes. "John Ploughman's Wife" may well be forgiven when she humbly acknowledges that the "pen of a ready writer" is not to be wielded by her feeble fingers; yet, notwithstanding conscious inability and weakness, she confidently hopes that some "honour, and glory, and blessing" will be laid at the Lord's feet by this tribute to His wonderful lovingkindness, shown so manifestly in the continued prosperity and vigour of the Book Fund.

"REMEMBER ME, O LORD, FOR GOOD."

How the Book Fund prospers.

BY MRS. C. H. SPURGEON.

FROM "THE SWORD AND THE TROWEL," AUGUST, 1877.

FOR many weeks past I have had a great desire in my heart to write out the gracious details of the Lord's dealings with the Book Fund during the present year; but almost constant pain has fettered both head and hand, and rendered the fulfilment of the heart's wish well-nigh impossible. But even the "school of affliction" has its "holidays," true holy-days these, and as the "good Master" has granted me one such to-day, I will consecrate it to His honour and glory by telling what great things He hath done for me and my work since I wrote last. The commencement of the new year was marked by an offer of six volumes of the Metropolitan Tabernacle Pulpit to every minister who had formerly been a student of the Pastors' College; and so enthusiastically was it responded to, that in three months' time 164 of our own old students had received 980 volumes! I had intended this effort to be an *extra* one, and to extend over the entire year; but the Lord had more work for me to do than I knew of, so

He would allow of no lingering, but graciously gave me strength to accomplish easily what at first sight seemed a formidable task. During this time the usual work of the Book Fund was not neglected, but applications were cheerfully responded to.

For a short time during the months just flown by, it seemed as if the Lord were trying my faith by sending me more "needs" than "supplies;" but I am almost ashamed to speak of fears which then possessed me. Now I see that the Lord only brought a cloud over the sun to veil its brightness, lest the heat of labour should overpower His weak child, and cause her to faint under the burden of the day. So, blessed be His name, He "leads on softly" as "we are able to bear it." Turning over the pages of my "day-book," I cannot but rejoice to know that already nearly 3,000 volumes have been distributed since the beginning of this year; and though this number falls wofully short of supplying the need which exists, yet I thank God and take courage. The following extracts from letters will show that the intense appreciation and loving eagerness with which these gifts were at first received has not abated one whit.

My dear Mrs. Spurgeon,—Though I have watched with interest and pleasure the birth, growth, and usefulness of your Book Fund, I little thought I should ever be so deeply indebted to you as I find myself to-day. The nice parcel you so kindly sent came as "cold water to a thirsty soul," and judging from the feelings of gratitude and delight produced in my own breast, I feel your work of love has made not a few pastors' hearts to "sing for joy." I rejoice also to know that the work yields such sweet solace of joy to you in your affliction; I really think it must be *one* rose at least on this sin-blighted earth *" without a thorn."*

What this dear brother says is perfectly true. The Book Fund is the joy of my life, and ever since the Lord gave the sweet service into my weak and unworthy hands He has led me by green pastures and beside still waters, and crowned me with lovingkindness and tender mercies. The next letter is from a much-tried servant of God, who, with a wife, invalid daughter, and four young children to support (there are nine children living) on eighty pounds per annum, may well be "unable to buy books."

My dear Madam,—Most gratefully do I beg to acknowledge the receipt of the four volumes of "The Treasury of David." The gift, I can assure you, is a most acceptable one. Often when at the homes of my brethren I have seen the work, and longed for its possession, deeming the desire, however, quite Utopian, seeing that the purchase of such books is altogether beyond the limit of my slender income. Ten years have elapsed since my return from ———, where for a long time I laboured, and those years have been one long protracted struggle for bare existence. Blessed be God, that is not *all*; for if my tribulations have abounded, so also have my consolations, "Hitherto the Lord hath helped me." The Psalms of David are ever a tower of comfort to tried saints, and your honoured husband's work is to my mind the best book that I have seen, in that it brings out the marrow and fatness of the text. Again, I thank you most deeply and sincerely for the gift, as also for the good wishes by which it was accompanied.

The two letters which follow are from a "Methodist" preacher and a "Baptist" minister, both being charming expressions of a glad and grateful heart. When I receive such epistles I always wish they could be passed round to every kind friend who has contributed to the "Fund," that they might catch glimpses of the abounding happiness which they thus bestow on others.

My dear Mrs. Spurgeon,—The parcel containing four volumes of "The Treasury of David" arrived all safe yesterday. I had been rejoicing over my good fortune in getting, as I supposed, one volume of Mr. Spurgeon's great work; but the receipt of such a gift was a surprise for which I was unprepared. I am entirely at a loss to express all I feel respecting such kindness; but I beg to offer my heart's deepest gratitude, and my earnest prayers that heaven's richest blessings may come down upon yourself, and upon all through whose disinterested generosity you are able to carry on such a work of love.

This is a gift indeed! May God help me to use it for His glory. One may, I think, be justly proud of having four such volumes in his library, and the aid they will afford in my work no one can fully realize but myself. Probably there are hundreds of grateful hearts lifted up from day to day in prayer for yourself and your indefatigable husband. If my feeble prayers can be of any possible advantage, most gladly will I pray daily that in your affliction the Lord will impart a large measure of His soothing grace, that your soul may always be filled with the brightness and peace of the Saviour's presence, and that you may long be spared to continue the noble enterprise, which has already sent relief, joy, and light into hundreds of homes, and brought blessings into probably thousands of minds.

Madam,—The very handsome present which you have so kindly sent me (Mr. Spurgeon's "Treasury of David," four vols.) arrived quite safely about half-an-hour ago. It has come upon me as a pleasant surprise, for your kindness has much exceeded my expectations. I thought you might send me *one* volume—I never even hoped, so far as I remember, for more than *two;* and yet here are the whole *four!* A valuable present, truly, in more senses than one. I have already been tasting its quality with relish, and feel certain that I shall find it, as you kindly wish, "a treasure indeed." Thank you very, very, very much for it; and for your letter with all the kindness of heart which it reveals. Whatever may be the needs and privations of some village pastors, you, at all events, are trying to minister to their joy, and to make them more efficient in the service of the Master. And you know, without my suggesting it, that He will give you your reward. Again I thank you with an earnestness which increases as I continue to look into the volumes.

The Book Fund has received this year some splendid additions, as gifts, to its stores of works by other authors, and I have rejoiced greatly to have at my disposal such standard volumes of divinity as the works of Haldane, Dr. Hodge, and others. But the fact becomes more and more evident to me every day, that *unless already possessed of "The Treasury of David,"* our pastors look upon no other volumes as *my* gift with *complete* satisfaction, and that in applying to me for books, they fix their heart's desire upon "The Treasury," or the "Sermons," as the *summum bonum* of their happiness. And I think this is very natural and very proper, so long as the management of the Book Fund rests entirely in these feeble hands; but I trust that some day, when all the churches awaken to a sense of the urgent need there is that "the poor minister's bookshelf" should have plenty of books upon it, many a noble volume, both ancient and modern, will take its place beside "The Treasury of David."

As to old books, which sometimes come to me troublously fast, I am obliged to smuggle them in with the coveted works of my dear husband, and but a very faint echo of any welcome they receive ever reaches my ear. I really fear that some people think that *anything in the shape of a book* will do for a minister, or they would scarcely send such things as "Advice to Wives and Mothers," "Essays on Marriage," or "Letters to a Son," as aids to pulpit preparation!

On looking over the list of contributors for the last year, I find a falling-away of *some* old friends, which somewhat grieves me, for the work is more deeply needed than ever.

The famine is sore in the land—not a famine of bread, nor a thirst for water, but a deeply-felt and widespread need of mental food, by those under-shepherds who have to "feed the flock of God"; and I had hoped that all the friends who had so generously aided me at the commencement of my work would have "continued with me." To the *many* who have done so I tender my most heartfelt thanks. "God bless you," dear friends, and return into your own bosoms some of the joy, and gladness, and gratitude with which you have filled mine. New friends, too, are cordially welcomed to co-operation in the blessed work, and every gift that comes for the Book Fund is offered to the Lord as a sacrifice of thanksgiving. I am just now rejoicing over the fact that the Lord has inclined the heart of a dear friend, to whom I am already greatly indebted, to give me a large donation for the purpose of supplying all the Presbyterian ministers in Argyleshire with " The Treasury of David," and I have another sum of money given by one who is a great sufferer, set apart for the distribution of the same precious volumes in Ireland. For the next few months, dear friends, you may know that the "Work of the Book Fund" will be in the full swing of business; and I pray you to remember that you can truly and tenderly help me by asking the Lord to set the seal of His blessing on every book sent out.

Does any one care to know that my lovely lemon tree is in vigorous health and perfect beauty? I have not dared to count its leaves lately, because I feel it has far outstripped the proportions with which my fancy fettered it; yet I never look upon it or think about it without blessing God for making it grow so wonderfully in my sick room that winter, where it heralded, and illustrated, helped forward, and finally became the emblem of the Book Fund.

A Song of Thanksgiving.

Y very dear Mr. Editor,—Among your "Notes" for the coming month, will you kindly sound one, clear and jubilant, of grateful blessing on behalf of the Book Fund? Nay, a "note" will scarce suffice me, I need psalms of praise, and symphonies of sweetness wherewith to make melody unto the Lord for His great goodness. Tell the dear friends who read *The Sword and the Trowel* that "my mouth is filled with laughter, and my tongue with singing" at the remembrance of the gracious love which continues to give support, and sustenance, and success to me in my beloved work. I am impatient to speak of His mercy, and feel constrained *now* to call on all who love the Lord to rejoice in my joy, and to aid me in magnifying His dear name. It is only two years since this sweet service was gently and graciously laid on my heart and hands, and yet during that time the Lord has enabled me, though compassed with infirmity, to send forth, like seed corn, *many thousands* of volumes to aid the toiling labourers in the gospel field. More than £2,000 have been received and expended; the money coming "fresh from the mint of heaven," for God has sent it all; as the dear friends through whom it reaches me must very well know, seeing that *I* never ask them for their loving gifts. Just as the olive trees in Zechariah's vision constantly and silently yielded their rich streams to feed the lights of the golden candlestick, even so, as divinely and mysteriously, does the Lord send me the means to provide "oil, beaten oil, for the lamps of the sanctuary."

Ah! dear Mr. Editor, sound the notes of praise for me! I want God's people to know how *very* good He is to unworthy me, that they may take comfort and courage from my experience of His tenderness and love. I would I had Miriam's timbrel in my hand to-day to "sing unto the Lord" withal, and lead out others to sing also; but as that cannot be, I pray you, lift up your voice for me, and "praise the Lord before all the people."

Yours with true love and "reverence,"

S. SPURGEON.

First Report of the Book Fund.

1876.

BY MR. G. H. PIKE.

A SHORT PREFATORY LETTER BY C. H. SPURGEON.

To the Subscribers of the Book Fund.

My dear Friends,

PERSONALLY I thank you all for aiding my most precious wife in the work of furnishing books to poor bookless ministers. Not only have you been doing immense service to the pulpits of our land, and also in the most efficient manner benefiting many congregations, but you have incidentally supplied my dear suffering companion with a happy work, which has opened channels of consolation for her, and imparted great interest to the otherwise monotonous life of an invalid. She has entered into this most gracious work with great zest, and continued in it with unflagging perseverance, and, while it has frequently cost her exertion beyond her strength, it has also relieved her weary hours, and helped her to forget a portion of her pains. Such an alleviation of her affliction is the most suitable and effective that could have been devised by the wisest affection; for it destroys the horrible suspicion of being useless, which, to a heart full of zeal, is as a sword in the bones. No woman has ever more readily entered into all her husband's plans for the extension of the

Redeemer's kingdom, nor more readily spared him from her side when called away upon "the King's business." Incessant occupations demanded by my sphere of labour give me but scanty opportunity to pay the attentions which are the natural due of a sickly wife; but so far from complaining because of this, she surrenders me with real heroism. Nor is this all, nor the ten thousandth part of what I could write, but I forbear; for if I say more, I fear that my prefatory letter will be "declined with thanks."

Before starting for the Continent, the little Report for the Book Fund was talked over, and I persuaded my beloved one not to attempt to write the account herself; for I have seen, with much pain, at what cost every line of her writing is produced. Readers of *The Sword and the Trowel* will regret the loss of an article from her pen, for she writes admirably; but their sympathy with a painful sufferer will lead them to agree with me that the pleasure of reading is too dearly bought when it costs the writer great anguish. I requested one of the staff of the magazine to prepare materials for the little history which follows this note, and I submit it to the kind subscribers as the best substitute which it is in our power to offer for the acknowledgments which Mrs. Spurgeon would gladly tender from her own pen, if she were able to do so. In her name I earnestly thank every donor.

You have wrought a good work in aiding this fund; a work which Christians will appreciate in proportion to their intelligence. The least educated see the benefit of distributing bread and garments, but the more spiritual and thoughtful know that to preachers of the gospel books are quite as much a necessity. The mind, like the soil, needs feeding. The thought which springs from an unaided intellect may be for a time as fresh and vigorous as the first growth of virgin soils, but this cannot last long. To produce crop after crop, especially for fifty-two harvests in a year, if these are to be of any value, something must be put into the man's soul upon which his brain can feed. Without reading on the part of the sermonizer, discourses must sooner or later become stale and unprofitable. How can a man make bread without flour, or build houses without bricks?

Instead of finding fault with a bookless preacher, who has to beat his brains for new subjects, and then finds it hard to treat them with any freshness, it would be far wiser to send him a present of suggestive volumes. To whip the horse is both unjust and unwise when a feed of corn is really wanted.

It may be said that good men should rely upon the Spirit of God. So they should; but He works by means, and full often while perusing "the books and the parchments" the Lord's poor servants are conscious of the divine influence. Man does not live by bread alone, and yet we give the hungry man a loaf; and even so, while the mind must be spiritually instructed by the Holy Ghost, it is ours to furnish books by which the Word of God may be better understood.

Nor is this all; for in scattering the volumes supplied by *The Book Fund* much happiness has been created, and other useful purposes have been answered. Little can it be told, with paper and ink, how much joy this donation of helpful books has caused, and how much of generous feeling towards poor ministers has been incidentally evoked thereby. Anything which turns the attention of Christian people to the pressing poverty of many of our preachers of the gospel is a good thing, and must tend to remedy the crying evil. The Book Fund, from its peculiar character, has excited special interest in this direction, and hundreds of pounds have found their way to the homes of the Lord's ministers which else would never have come there.

Dear friends, I pray you help Mrs. SPURGEON still, and she will be gratified to be your happy almoner.

I am, yours gratefully,

C. H. SPURGEON.

Mrs. Spurgeon's Book Fund and its Work.

1876.

THE BOOK FUND, with which the name of Mrs. SPURGEON is intimately associated, originated in a very simple and unexpected manner. On the day of its birth nobody suspected that so promising a child was born into the world; its growth has far surpassed its parents' expectation. The Fund sprang up as suddenly as Jonah's gourd, and under its shadow many a man of God has found refreshment; but no worm is at its root, and therefore it has not in the same speedy manner passed away. It was time that some generous agency should endeavour to lessen the grievous book famine now existing among poor Nonconformist pastors, and this came at the nick of time to alleviate the distress at once, and perhaps to open up for the future a large and permanent source of supply. Who knoweth? No company of sympathetic philanthropists drew up the programme, appointing, as they would have been bound to do, a committee, a treasurer, and a secretary; but with twain, who are truly one, it commenced, and by one it has been carried on. The suggestion to distribute books to ministers arose out of the casual pleasantries of a summer day, to be at once adopted as though it had been a message direct from heaven.

No sooner was the work of distribution commenced than gifts flowed in, and, at the same time, unexpected evidence of the vast need to be met excited greater ardour in the invalid worker into whose hands the task had fallen. In the sick chamber there was a delicate, carefully nurtured lemon plant, which had sprung from a pip which had been sown in the preceding winter. While it was very, very small it was the object of many pleasantries, and its apparent non-progressiveness was the theme of many a merry remark, against which the invalid always protested. It did grow, and it would grow, she was quite sure. Somehow or other this lemon plant came to be looked upon as the emblem of the Fund. First came the shoot, then the fragile stem, next the tiny leaves. The health of the tree was good from the first, and at last its development could not be doubted. A wish was expressed that the Book Fund and the exotic might thrive together, that indeed every leaf should presage a hundred pounds' worth of literature dispensed among needy Pastors. The Fund has prospered beyond expectation; still it has not kept pace with the robust vigour of the growing lemon tree, which has now no less than forty leaves to match with less than twelve hundreds subscribed for ministers' books.

Donations continued to be sent unsolicited, so that the originally confined area of operation was necessarily widened. Students as well as Pastors were supplied with the "Lectures"; and after a little experience more costly volumes, such as "The Treasury of David," were included in the presents. The interest which the work of Book donation excited was both keen and widespread; for Pastors whose scanty stipends hardly allowed of even an occasional volume being added to their bare shelves saw that a door of hope was opened, and that at least for once they might feed in fresh fields and pastures new. Men who had preached the gospel according to their ability with a Bible, a Concordance, and sundry volumes collected in earlier and perhaps happier years, hailed the promised boon with a fervour which necessity alone could enable us fully to understand. A supply of books to these needy, thoughtful men, was like giving mulberry leaves to silkworms, or feeding a fire with fuel. No one can tell the hunger of the heart for books but those whose tastes are literary, whose occupations are mental, and whose purses are bare. Strong is the temptation to set prudence on one side and purchase a volume of which the reviewers speak so highly; but no, the children must have shoes, and the threadbare coat must be replaced by a fresh Sunday's best. The books must go and the brain must starve, yet there must be sermons made and fresh matter brought forth. Is not this hard—this making of bricks without straw? Yes, it is hardest to those who least deserve to suffer it, and would best repay abundant help.

Necessitous as they were, numbers of Pastors hesitated before sending in their applications; but modesty was at length so far overcome that at last they not only asked for the books, but frequently made a confidante of their new friend, heart and soul seeming to find relief in speaking of life trials or family sorrows to one who would heartily sympathize, and, where possible, relieve. Though poverty was known to abound among ministers of all denominations, its extent was under-estimated, and we shall not now incur the charge of writing a sensational story by giving that full, unadorned revelation which the materials in hand would allow. The case is bad as bad can be. To generous hearts there was something depressing in the eager joy, as well as in the vehemently expressed thanks, with which the gifts were received. Coming from professional men, who are expected to walk abroad in gloves and broadcloth, the language used was terribly indicative of that grinding economy which is only another name for continual self-denial and concealed want. It was a new experience when gifts of small pecuniary value were magnified in such terms as have abounded in many an acknowledgment. One is completely broken down, melted into tears, at the sight of the "great gift." Another acknowledges with "ten thousand thanks" "The Treasury," for which he had long sighed in vain. One recipient has not had a new book come across his threshold for three years; while others speak of sick wives and impoverishing doctors' bills as absorbers of their small means. Salaries small enough are spoken of as unpaid for months after they are due, and wives are described as keeping no servant, washing, and making all the clothes, and yet as not having enough for housekeeping to allow of the purchase of meat, except as a luxury. In such cases the purchase of even a cheap magazine has necessitated self-denial at the scanty table, and the thought of a new book has been far away. What are rich Christians thinking of, that they allow the Lord's servants thus to be mentally starved? Do they expect men to work without tools? Do they hope to reap where they have not sown?

The position of Nonconformist pastors in sparsely inhabited country districts is extremely difficult, and ought to command the sympathy and help of all their brethren. On account of their position appearances have to be studied, and much of their scanty means must thus be expended. Even their rustic audiences would hardly bear to see the pastor in a smock frock and his children barefooted. Such is the consummate art with which home poverty is often concealed that friends on the spot are not aware of their pastor's necessities. If they would but think a little they would soon perceive how hard the pinch must be; but that is exactly what many hearers are not anxious to do. Where ignorance saves their pockets, they think it folly to be wise. Because he enjoys apparent health they conclude that their minister has a well furnished table; and while his sermons are of tolerable quality no one suspects that he suffers from scarcity of literature. The art of concealing one's family privation may be even more strikingly exemplified. We have known of a good man—a Baptist pastor—whose example of liberality would have delivered him from the ordeal of being pinched and worried, had it only been copied by those around him. Sinners were converted through his earnest evangelical sermons; the young revered him as a father, not seldom crowding his tea-table on Sabbath afternoons; elderly people valued his ministry more than they suspected until death abridged their privileges; and yet this zealous teacher of the church never had a pound to spare for books during the later years of his life. His course was an unceasing warfare with adverse circumstances, a rugged, thorny, uphill path of daily self-denial, in which flesh and blood at length succumbed, worn out with cares which he concealed, crushed with burdens of which he never spoke. The Book Fund, which could have supplied the dire needs of his thoughtful mind, did not then exist; and the case is only quoted as an example of hundreds of others that the Fund now seeks to relieve. If we cannot lift all burdens from the hearts of our brethren, nor even supply all their urgent needs, let us at least keep them going with fresh thought. Let us furnish the library if we cannot fatten the larder. By other deficiencies the good man is made lean himself, but want of books starves the congregation. Perhaps if the worthy brother reads more, he will by God's blessing preach better, and then the people will love him more, and do more for him, and so the full book-shelves will lead to the filling of the pantry and the coal cellar. At any rate, *the Fund* aims at this, and it has an ambitious programme, which, with God's blessing, it means to carry out.

From August, 1875, to the second week in December, 1876, the donations amounted to £926, the sum having reached £1,000 before the close of the year. This money represented the free gift of over five thousand volumes, three thousand one hundred and sixteen of which were the larger works by Mr. Spurgeon, the remainder having been books of a miscellaneous kind—new and second-hand, while a few were the pastor's smaller productions. Seven hundred and ten applicants have received grants of from four to eight volumes each; and, meanwhile, the working expenses have been reduced to a minimum; for the postmaster and the carrier are the only servants employed who receive remuneration. Beyond postage and carriage there are literally no expenses incurred, Mrs. SPURGEON combining in one person the offices of corresponding secretary, treasurer, and manager in general. What has been already accomplished has given abundant cause for gratitude to God, but greater things remain to be done in the future.

The work is capable of indefinite enlargement so long as the strength of the suffering one shall hold out. May it be greatly increased and long preserved is the prayer of all who perceive the great value of that fountain in the desert which is opened in

MRS. SPURGEON'S BOOK FUND.

Record of Book Fund Work.

1877.

By Mrs. C. H. Spurgeon.

IN giving an "account of her stewardship" during the past twelve months, the writer is actuated by an intense desire that every word she writes may reveal the infinite tenderness and love which the Lord has displayed towards her. She wishes above all things to call attention, not to her own doings, but to God's dealings with her; and she earnestly prays that no word of hers may in the least obscure the lovely radiance of that mercy and grace of which the following pages are a record. If any heart shall be filled with holy admiration and praise, at the wonderful condescension of the Lord to one of the least of His children, in giving her this work to do, and strengthening her to perform it; if any feeble faith shall find fresh life and power in the consideration of His unfailing faithfulness to one of the poor dependents on His bounty; if any honour and glory shall be gotten to the Lord through this little Report, her "labour will not have been in vain in the Lord."

The Great Master could not have chosen a "weaker vessel" by which to convey the treasure of knowledge to His servants; nor could he have selected to minister to the wants of His toiling messengers one more needing the ministry of love on her own account; but it is sometimes His good pleasure by His choice of servants to manifest His strength and wisdom, making the very feebleness and foolishness of

His chosen instruments to redound to the greater glory of His sacred name. " Make known His deeds among the people, talk ye all of His wondrous works," sings David ; and truly, if David's God will help His child to tell in fitting words the story of His great mercy and love to her, the lips of some of His saints shall be set singing fresh psalms of praise.

Into this dear home of mine, as anyone may easily imagine, the tide of periodical literature flows pretty freely. Dailies, weeklies, monthlies, quarterlies—papers and pamphlets of all sorts and descriptions, pour in like a flood, and for a season overwhelm the Pastor's study table. From thence, at ebb tide, they drift lazily into my sanctum, and, cast up upon my coast, they yield me pleasant spoils of amusement and information. From their pages I have lately gathered, with some surprise and much pleasure, the knowledge that a very large number of God's people are seeking to accomplish, by individual effort, those works of benevolence and Christian love which in days gone by were attempted only by fully constituted agencies, and societies with vast resources. A special form of need seems to strike some particular heart with pity, and forthwith the hand is stretched forth to relieve it, not with fitful or capricious charity, but with a wise tenderness and determined constancy which lead at last to an entire consecration to the chosen service. Some of the religious periodicals above alluded to contain long lists of such " works of faith and labours of love," and in many I note that, while they confide in a human head for management, they lean wholly on the hand of the Lord for maintenance. A fellow-feeling for these workers prompts me to watch their course with loving interest, and often leads me to breathe a prayer for their prosperity and success. I know that the world's great need necessitates the church's organized efforts on the largest scale, and therefore I bid "God speed" with all my heart to the grand societies which are the glory of our land; but yet I turn to the solitary sower of the seed, or to the lonely gatherer-out of stones, with the most vivid and loving sense of kinship and communion, because our experiences so well agree.

My own work, so feeble and insignificant in comparison with that of others, can claim but the most modest mention among the numberless schemes for the glory of God and the good of man to which reference has been made, and yet I may assert that its origin is as divine, its object as beneficent, its support as certain, and its success as assured as the most glorious of them all. Though but a rill among the rivers, it sprang from the same heavenly source as the greatest of them: though as yet only a sapling among the trees of the wood, it "giveth goodly boughs" and grateful shade in its measure; and though it be but one note in the never ceasing song of "Glory to God in the highest, peace on earth, and goodwill to man," it will one day help to swell the shout of rapture which shall rise when the "glory of the Lord shall cover the earth as the waters cover the sea!"

Hoping that this little book may fall into the hands of some who have hitherto been strangers to my work, I propose to give full information concerning it, and, yielding to that habit which I suppose is inherent in us all, of trying to imitate those we love most, I shall divide my little discourse into four "heads" after the following fashion :—

THE BOOK FUND.

I. Its Origin; II. Its Object;

III. Its Sustenance; IV. Its Success.

I.—ITS ORIGIN.

The "Fund became a fact" in the most natural manner possible to all outward seeming; for, as the kind writer of the first report says, "the casual pleasantries of a summer's day suggested the distribution of books to poor ministers;" but faith traces the true rise and spring of this "brook by the way" to a higher source, and humbly dares to ascribe the origin of the Book Fund to the kind hand of the loving Father Himself, who is revealed to us as the "God of all comfort." No loving relative, however earnestly bent on discovering a fresh source of alleviation for constant pain, or a compensating joy for a life of comparative seclusion, would for a moment have imagined that the desired solace would have been found in this most blessed work. "God, that comforteth those that are cast down, comforted us," after His own peculiar manner, by putting a delightful work into our feeble charge. Tenderly, too, and gradually, as His poor weak child was able to bear it, did the Lord "lead on softly," until "He brought her out into a wealthy place and established her goings."

An intense desire took possession of me, after reading my dear husband's "Lectures to his Students," to place a copy in the hands of every minister in England, and consulting with the dear author on the matter, he approved my wish, and we decided to devote a few pounds to the partial gratification of it. Before the distribution of the copies thus purchased was completed, friends heard of and appreciated the scheme, and sent gifts, some of 100, some of 50 volumes, some of money, to help in the work, so that very quietly and silently, but most surely, as the months rolled on, it came to be a matter of established fact that a Book Fund existed and prospered.

One day, in my husband's study, the four comely volumes of "The Treasury of David" caught my eye, and the question instantly sprang to my lips, "Why could I not send these also to poor ministers? Only think what a boon they would be!" Conjugal love feared the task would be too heavy, and the responsibility of such a work too burdensome for the often weary one; but the Lord knew better, for He fostered the desire till it became too strong to be repressed, and then He graciously gave the power and means to fulfil it. Blessed be His name, I feel that it cannot be presumption to believe that this sacred charge was given me from the Lord Himself, because the fact has been abundantly proved, both by my own weakness and the manifestation of His gracious strength.

It is not the first time He has "given power to the faint," or chosen a "thing of nought" to do Him service, and I rejoice with exceeding joy over my work, because it is His from beginning to end; all the good, and the grace, and the glory, are His, His wholly and only! He has reminded His stewards of a need which they are far too apt to overlook, and He has supplied for many of His ministers a necessity which they had scarcely the courage to mention. Preachers without books are as the Israelites when required by Pharaoh to make bricks without straw; but hundreds of such poor oppressed workers are toiling on from year to year, without sympathy from any one. Some little help was needed for these servants of the Lord to give them "a little reviving," and that aid has come by an unlooked-for hand. It was unlikely that one who is neither bookworm nor theologian should be raised up to supply poor preachers with books; and yet so it has been, and the matter is from the Lord.

II.—ITS OBJECT.

The Book Fund aims at furnishing the bare bookshelves of poor Pastors of every Christian denomination with standard works of Theology by various authors; books full of the glorious gospel of Jesus Christ, the study of which shall enrich their minds, comfort their hearts, quicken their spiritual life, and thereby enable them to preach with greater power and earnestness "all the words of this life." How deeply needed this service of love has long been, what an urgent and painful necessity it has become, is fully proved by the intense eagerness shown on every hand to obtain the proffered boon. The writer could point to many a faithful servant of the Lord, who, toiling on in secret poverty for years, has not even *seen* a new book (except in the shop windows), till a grant from the Book Fund filled his heart with joy and his lips with thanksgiving. "These books have brightened my hope, and quickened my faith," writes one such pastor, "I will not trouble you with my difficulties for want of a commentary to stimulate and guide my poor thought, *they are too sad to tell*, but they have helped me to appreciate your gifts." Those whose resources enable them to enjoy, without stint, the luxury of a "new book," can scarcely realize the longing and craving which gnaws at the heart of a poor minister when he sees—beyond his reach—the help and refreshment he so sorely needs. His brain is weary with producing unaided thoughts; his mental powers are flagging for want of stimulus and encouragement; his spirit is burdened with the pressure of cares, which stern poverty brings upon him; and yet, though a few sterling, solid books would be a specific for much of this misery, the purchase of such blessed potions is as impossible to him as would be the acquisition of the "Elixir of Life" itself! Many a one has told me that the books sent seemed to "put new life" into him, and it is not difficult to read in those three words a sad and sorrowful story of mental faintness and famine. "Read good suggestive books," says the President of the Pastors' College, in his "Lectures to Students," "and get your minds aroused by them. If men wish to get water out of a pump which has not been lately used, they first pour water down, and then the pump works. *Reach down one of the Puritans*, and thoroughly study the work, and speedily you will find yourself, like a bird on the wing, mentally active and full of motion." But what if there is no water at hand to coax the up-springing of the living stream? or, rather, what if the bookshelves are bare, and no Puritans can be reached down? This is a question which the Book Fund seeks to answer in the only satisfactory manner, by placing as a free gift in the hands of poor Pastors that nourishment for their brains which is as absolutely necessary to mental vigour as food for their bodies is essential to physical existence. "Ten thousand thanks," said a dear brother, writing lately, "for sending the books *when you did*. Their coming brought deliverance and salvation to my mind. I was in an agony of spirit—at my wits' end for a text. I opened one and found, 'The Lord liveth, and blessed be my rock.' This was just what I wanted; it took hold of me, and the Lord helped me to take hold of it." "I have very little to spend in books," says another. "My salary is only £60 per annum; so that when a new book comes, it is like bread to the hungry. I do not say this to make you think I am a martyr—if so, I am a very happy one, for I have chosen willingly Christ's service, and my very wants are a means of grace to me." Again another pastor writes, "I cannot tell you how much the receipt of these useful and suggestive volumes cheered me. The sight of a refreshing spring never more gladdened a weary traveller."

No one who knows anything of the position and means of our country Pastors can doubt that the "object" of this Fund meets, and, as far as it is able, alleviates a sadly overlooked evil. After more than two years' daily correspondence with ministers all over the land, the writer feels that she speaks with sad and serious certainty on the matter, and she is grieved to know that everywhere the want is felt, and the same cry is heard. "Oh, for some books to help me in my pulpit preparation!" says one; "I have to preach before the same people three, perhaps four times a week, and though the Lord has promised that my 'branch shall not wither,' it sometimes gets *very dry*." "I know we should depend upon the Spirit's aid, " says another, "and so I do; but if I could read some of the burning thoughts which are recorded by God's earthly seraphs, my lips, too, might glow with holy rapture, and give forth 'goodly words.'" "I never dare now to *think* of a new book," writes a third, "two or three times I have begun to save a little money towards the purchase of a long-coveted work, but every time it has gone for something else; Johnny, and little Harry, and Walter, *must* have boots; or mother is ill; or the girls' frocks are getting shabby; and so the precious volumes are still unattainable." And yet a fourth most touchingly says: "When I witness the self-denial, and hard unremitting labour to which my wife so cheerfully submits herself to keep our household moving comfortably in the sphere God has given, I cannot with any pleasure add to her difficulty by purchasing the books I often covet, though this doubtless hinders the freshness and variety of my ministry."

Dear Christian friends, these are no fancy pictures which I am painting, these are no silly tales of fiction, told for the purpose of exciting emotions as worthless as they are weak; but I write of living, suffering realities of flesh and blood— our brethren in Christ, and men, moreover, who claim and bear the title of the "King's ambassadors"—and I ask, "Ought they to be thus treated?" I want you to ponder for a moment the sad *fact* that throughout the length and breadth of this dear England of ours there are *hundreds* of Christ's ministers so poor that they can scarcely find proper food and clothing for themselves, their wives and their little ones, out of the miserable pittance which is called their "*salary!*" Books, which ought to be "common things" with them—littering their rooms in "most admired disorder," crowding each nook and corner with mute but matchless companionship—are, through their poverty, unattainable luxuries, vainly-coveted blessings, the very thought of which must be laid aside, lest the longing should lead to repining, and the desire deepen into distress. Such things ought not to be, but unhappily they *are*, and till the churches of Christ shall awaken to a sense of their responsibility in this matter, and their moral obligation to provide their ministers with mental food, I will rejoice that my Book Fund does, at least, lighten a little of the darkness, and relieve somewhat the pressure of the famine.

III.—ITS SUSTENANCE.

"The silver is mine, and the gold is mine, saith the Lord of hosts."

The Book Fund has been nourished and fed from the King's Treasury, and I must "make my boast in the Lord" that all needful supplies for the carrying on of the work have plainly borne the stamp of Heaven's own mint. I say this because I have never asked help of any one but *Him*, never solicited a donation from any creature, yet money has always been forthcoming, and the supplies have constantly been in due proportion to the needs. Once only during the year did the Lord try my faith by allowing the grants of books to outnumber the gifts of money, and then it was only for a "small moment" that a fear overshadowed me. The dark cloud very speedily passed away, and fresh supplies made me more than ever satisfied with the resolution I had formed to draw only on the unlimited resources of my heavenly Treasurer. None of the friends whose hearts have "devised liberal things" on behalf of my work will reproach me with ingratitude towards them when I lay my *first* loving thanks at His feet; they will rather join me in praising Him for so sweetly inclining their hearts to help His needy ones, and will joyfully say, "O Lord, of Thine own have we given Thee!"

I recall with very glad satisfaction the first donation which reached me, "for sending books to ministers." It came anonymously, and was but five shillings' worth of stamps, yet it was very precious, and proved like a revelation to me, for it opened up a vista of possible usefulness and exceeding brightness. The mustard seed of my faith grew forthwith into a "great" tree, and sweet birds of hope and expectation sat singing in its branches. "You'll see," I said to my boys, "the Lord will send me *hundreds of pounds* for this work." For many a day afterwards mother's "hundreds of pounds" became a "household word" of good-humoured merriment and badinage. And now "the Lord has made me to laugh," for the hundreds have grown into thousands; He has done "exceeding abundantly above what I could ask or even think;" and faith, with such a God to believe in and depend upon, ought surely to "smile at impossibilities, and say, 'it shall be done.'"

After praising Him "from whom all blessings flow," my loving thanks are due to the friends who, by their generous gifts, have co-operated with me in this blessed work. Money has come to me from all quarters, and always with congratulations and good wishes. Many dear personal friends have liberally aided me; some of my dear husband's constant and devoted helpers have been pleased when sending him a cheque, to make it a *little larger* for the Book Fund; while quite a number of strangers (though strangers no longer), whose names were previously unknown to me, have sent very considerable donations to my beloved work. *God bless them all!* And if only a tithe of the happiness their gifts have secured to me and my poor pastors be returned into their own hearts, their cups will be full to overflowing, and their joy will abound. Oh! how sweet some of these sums of money have been to me! Real "God-sends" I may truly call them; for the gold has seemed to lose its earthly dross when consecrated to Him, and has often shed a light as from Heaven's own "golden streets" upon my pathway! Coming sometimes in seasons of great pain and suffering, these gifts have been like precious anodynes to soothe my weary spirit, and hush my restless thought; for they plainly showed the Lord had not "forgotten to be gracious." They have almost charmed away my sorrow by teaching me to plan for others' joy, and ofttimes they have been truly "means of grace" to me, leading to blessed commerce with heaven, by supplying frequent occasions of prayer and praise. Surely, after so much mercy past, if I did not bless His name, "the very stones would cry out."

The twelve hundred and eighty odd pounds which stand recorded for this year in the balance-sheet do not include all the moneys which I have received from the Lord through the hands of His loving people. Herein lies a *secret*, very precious, and hitherto very safely guarded, but now to be revealed for the honour of God and the good of His needy ministers. The thought will naturally occur to any one who has so far read this little book, that such an intimate acquaintance as I have made with the sorrows and trials of poor pastors must have many a time caused me a sad heartache, unless means were at hand to relieve their earthly wants and woes as well as their mental necessities; and here another note of praise to the Lord must be sounded on a very tender string; for in His goodness and lovingkindness He has provided pecuniary help for exceptional cases of extreme poverty and urgent need. Without this, I think sometimes I should have felt crushed beneath the burden which my knowledge of many pressing needs has laid upon me. The tried ministers never complain; I do not remember having ever read a solitary sentence which could be construed into a murmur; but sometimes a chance word on my part leads them to confide in me, and then the sad fact is revealed, that other shelves beside the bookshelf are in pitiful need of replenishing.

At the commencement of 1877, a generous friend placed at my disposal a sum of money, and thus founded a private

PASTORS' AID SOCIETY,

from which I could draw such sums as occasion required and prudence directed. This money has been further supplemented by gifts from my dear husband and others; and though not attaining any vast proportions, it has sufficed to solace many a suffering one, and has lifted very heavy burdens from care-laden hearts. Full details of this little branch of my Book Fund are withheld from motives of delicacy and tenderness to the dear brethren whose poverty, though honourable, is as jealously concealed as if it were a hidden treasure; but could I dare to tell of the sickness and sorrow, the straits and the struggles which have come to my knowledge during this year, many of my readers would think I was romancing, and that such a state of things could not exist in this Christian land. But alas! dear friends, the evil is deep and wide-spread, very real, and very saddening, and I would that those of God's people, to whom He has given liberally of the "precious things of the earth beneath," would bestow some of their overflowing wealth upon their poorer brethren. I could promise them that from "golden grains" thus sown they should reap a hundredfold harvest of blessing and sweet content.

IV.—ITS SUCCESS.

Judged by the benefits and blessings the Book Fund has conferred, its success will be best told by extracts from letters received in acknowledgment of gifts; and as it has become entirely unsectarian in its operation, it will, perhaps, be interesting and pleasant to introduce some "kind words" from ministers of different denominations who have joyfully accepted this service of love. It has been no easy matter to restrain my hand in making these selections from the many hundreds of letters I possess; I have felt a veritable *embarras de richesses*, and most unwillingly have omitted many a passage brimful of joy and gladness, lest I should weary my readers; but when they have perused with delight these thankful, loving words, they may rest assured the "half has not been told" them. Having commenced the year by offering six volumes of Mr. Spurgeon's "Sermons" to all ministers formerly students of the Pastors' College, first speech is accorded to one of their number:—

My dear Mrs. Spurgeon,—I feel deeply grateful to you for the six volumes of sermons which reached me this morning. When I opened the parcel, I experienced such a rush of emotion as made me kneel down instantly and thank God for His goodness to me, as well as to pray for His blessing to descend upon you. Many times when a few brethren have met together at my house, or I have gone to theirs, have we mentioned your work in our prayers, and the best expression of my gratitude, I feel, will be in the fervency and faith of my petitions. I trust you will accept my thanks, though they were so imperfectly conveyed. My heart glows, but my pen fails.

The extract next subjoined is also from an old student, but it claims special notice because the writer is labouring in a far distant land, and a gift of books to him is truly "as cold water to a thirsty soul." It is not often that the opportunity is afforded of ministering to the necessities of brethren in foreign lands, on account of the heavy expense of transit; but when friends are found to take charge of a parcel, we have the rare pleasure of receiving in due time such an answer as this:—

Dear Mrs. Spurgeon,—I have to acknowledge, with gratitude and pleasure, the receipt of six volumes of Mr. Spurgeon's "Sermons," which you so kindly forwarded by Mr. ——— of this village. May the Lord reward you a thousandfold for this great, and I might almost say, unexpected kindness to a stranger in a strange land. . . . . When settling here rather more than three years ago, I often found an American volume of the "Sermons," well worn, and highly appreciated; and I assure you they made me feel more at home than otherwise I should have done in this rugged country. One old man, nearly 90, whom I buried a few months since, had a volume of that kind, and he had read it perhaps hundreds of times, until it was almost worn to pieces. It was nearly his sole companion for several years before his death, and none can tell how much he was cheered and comforted by reading it. You can scarcely imagine the joy I felt in receiving the sermons fresh from England; but this you may rest assured of—both yourself and your dear husband were prayed for that night with more than usual fervour and feeling, and special thanks were given to Him "from whom all blessings flow."

If space permitted I could give extracts of letters from France, Sweden, Nova Scotia, Nebraska, Cape of Good Hope, Spain, Sydney, Adelaide, Bengal, Jamaica, Barbadoes, and many other "strange lands," which would delight and interest my readers; but I must content myself and them with the following much-prized communications from Church of England missionaries, one on leave of absence for a while from India, the other just starting to his work at Palamcotta (S. India). The first-mentioned writes thus:—

Many, MANY thanks for the four volumes of "The Treasury of David"; I prize them much. I doubt not that, if not already, these volumes will soon become standard works on the Psalms. Every one knew and felt that there must be "a feast of fat things" for mind and soul in the Psalms; but Mr. Spurgeon has dished them up in a way so superior to what anybody else has ever done, that both mind and soul receive much more from his "Treasury" than from any other work. I am thankful to find the books in the libraries of Church of England clergymen at D—— and K—— with less dust on them than Browne "On the Articles," or theological works akin to Den's "Theology," etc. The day of Christ will reveal the great good the Lord has been doing through Mr. Spurgeon's instrumentality. When a student at —— College, I used to visit some of the Irish courts around the neighbourhood. In one of these dens of villainy and iniquity there lived a man who was my terror, and who more than once sent me flying out of the court, pushing me by laying his hand to the back of my neck. My heart sank every time I entered the place if I met this man. He was all that is wicked and iniquitous. One day, to my surprise, instead of cursing me, he asked me to his filthy dark room. I entered it with fear, not knowing what was in store for me; but, thank God, it was to tell me that he had found Jesus, and had resolved in His strength to follow Him. The message of love, and mercy, and peace, had been conveyed to this man's heart by the lips of your good husband. He heard Mr. Spurgeon preach in some public place or other, and there Jesus met him and called him. From that day till his death he lived the life of a Christian, and died glorifying the depths of Jesus' love. I do not think you can have ever heard of this case; and there must be many unknown to you, who on the great day will welcome your dear husband as the one who was the means of leading them to the feet of Christ.

Dear Madam,—The books arrived safely on Saturday night. May God bless you for your kindness and liberality to a perfect stranger. I have long been under deep obligation to your honoured husband, since it was through reading a passage in one of his books in South India, that I was first awakened out of a sinner's natural self-complacency to cry, "What must I do to be saved?" And twice during the last two years have I been greatly cheered and strengthened by two sermons that I had the pleasure of hearing him deliver in Islington. Though we may never meet on earth, though we may differ on minor points, ever shall my prayers ascend to God for you both, and we shall assuredly meet where partings are unknown.

I may just say here that many missionaries of different denominations have, on leaving England, applied to me for "The Treasury" to carry with them to their distant stations, (Damascus, Madrid, China, the Punjaub, Ceylon, Delhi, Lagos, and Timbuctoo recur to my mind at this moment, but there are many more), and it has given peculiar satisfaction to grant the requests of these dear brethren, and to receive from them assurances of the great comfort and refreshment they have derived from the perusal of the precious volumes when toiling far from home and friends and country.

About the middle of the year an unexpected and most delightful impetus was given to the Book Fund by a very kind and generous friend, who desired that all the ministers in Argyleshire should possess "The Treasury of David," and entrusted the writer with funds to carry out his wishes. How heartily the good divines of Scotland welcomed and appreciated this gift, it would take too long to tell.

Returning to home-work, I give a letter from a Congregational Pastor, which could be supplemented by hundreds, for my Book Fund has had the privilege of ministering to very many in the Independent denomination.

Dear Madam,—The four volumes of "The Treasury of David" arrived safely. This thoughtful and most generous gift has filled my heart with real delight. Perhaps the infrequency of such a windfall will account for a little of the pleasure, but I cannot help tracing much of it to the kind manner in which you have presented the gift, and to the intrinsic value of the books themselves. I am a prey to the hunger usual among my brethren for the only kind of communion open to many of us with the richest and noblest minds that have served the Saviour. The possession of your honoured husband's beautiful and valuable volumes makes me feel sensibly richer, and I am sure I shall frequently turn to them, both for private profit, and the enrichment of my ministry.

Being fearful of over-taxing the patience of my readers, I must pass without notice the epistles received from Evangelists and Home Missionaries, some of which would certainly vie in interest and pathos with any that have been already given. I, therefore, introduce but one other letter, making it do duty as the representative of kind and appreciative words from the many divisions of Methodism—Wesleyan, Primitive, and so forth. It is from the pen of a Bible Christian minister, and it tells the same "old story" of deep need of books, and utter inability to procure them.

Dear Madam,—Your very valuable and welcome present came duly to hand, and positively made my heart leap for joy, and outflow with a thousand blessings upon the kind donors. I can never express in words the deep feelings of gratitude I am the subject of, for your great kindness in thus shedding sunshine upon the difficult pathway of one who is trying, amid all his unworthiness, to serve his generation faithfully, and to do the work assigned him by the Master; but what I cannot put into language I can breathe in heart at the heavenly throne—that Jehovah's benedictions in ever-increasing richness may fall upon you and your honoured husband, until taken to the eternal home. The "Psalms" have always been my favourite resort for meditation and exposition, and I should long ago have purchased "The Treasury of David" had I been able; but a salary of £80 a year allows only a very small margin for books, and though my mind often *craved* for them, the luxury was not enjoyed.

As no record of my work could be considered *quite* complete without some reference to the beautiful plant which has always been associated with it, I am happy to say that the lemon tree is in a most prosperous condition. Meeting the gardener the other day, he observed, "Your lemon tree is brought up to the house, ma'am, *it is making a great deal of new wood*," and the Book Fund seems to follow suit with its old friend; for buds and blossoms of unexpected promise are asserting their existence and vitality. This Christmastide has brought me a number of letters from Christian ladies, who are anxious to aid the *families* of poor pastors, by suitable gifts of clothing; and I have had the intense satisfaction of submitting to their loving care and consideration the names of twenty-five ministers, all of whom I believe have been made happier, and undeniably *warmer*, by the reception of seasonable garments for themselves and their little ones. And yet another new branch of my work bears promise of much good fruit to poor pastors; for through the kindness of two thoughtful hearts, *The Sword and the Trowel* is to be sent regularly during the present year to 60 ministers who could not afford to purchase it for themselves. The prospect of this indulgence has greatly cheered many hearts. "I have not been able to take in a religious periodical for five years," said one to whom I made the offer, "the monthly visit of the magazine will indeed be a great boon."

What other work the Lord may have in store for me, or how far He intends graciously to extend that which at present fills my hands, or whether perchance He may think fit to call me away from it altogether, I know not; but this one thing is certain: "There hath not failed one word of all His good promise" from the beginning until now; and for the future I am persuaded that the "Book Fund and its Work" will live and thrive vigorously in its own "little corner" of

God's vineyard, where the sunshine of His blessing shall ever rest lovingly upon it, causing it to bring forth much fruit to His glory.

And now, the "Report" is a "tale that is told;" but I pray that its record of God's infinite tenderness and love may not leave a merely transient impression on any heart. Poor as my words are, and destitute of all literary ability, their very poverty and deficiency should be as foils to the bright deeds of mercy and grace which they endeavour to set forth. Dear Friends who have helped me, the work is yours as much as it is mine, and I hope my little Report will tell you that I am deeply grateful to you for trusting me with some of your substance, and that it may also make you partakers in my joy—the joy of helping the ministers of our Lord Jesus Christ. For the present I bid you a loving and grateful farewell.

> "Another year—*or part*—to serve Thee, Lord ;
> To sleep, to rise, and always leave to Thee
> The precious seed my feeble hands have sown.
> To make it spring and grow is Thine alone ;
> This takes all anxious care away from me.
> I trust *Thee*, Lord, to cause Thy seed to yield
> Full golden sheaves to deck Thy harvest field."

The Book Fund and its Work.
1878.
By Mr. V. J. Charlesworth.

PREFATORY LETTER.

Dear Friends,

ILL you be so good as to read this short letter before you turn to the Report? It is exceedingly needful that you should do so, because otherwise, you may form a wrong judgment of the following pages. My dear wife shrinks from issuing it because it contains a measure of praise as to herself, and this she very sincerely disclaims. Yet I, for one, cannot see how the commendatory paragraphs can be struck out (indeed, I know them to be well deserved), and I believe that they will not be misunderstood if the circumstances under which the Report is written are fully known.

Mrs. Spurgeon has been too ill to write for herself, and her husband, who would rejoice to have undertaken the task for her, has been also under the Lord's afflicting hand. None of our loving friends would wish either of us to have attempted the work, for which we were equally unfitted. Moreover, my dear one has so poor an idea of her own abilities that she has almost always submitted her compositions to my revision; and though my verdict upon her writing so entirely differs from her own that I seldom alter a word, yet she cannot bring herself to the task without me, nor would she lay an ounce weight of labour upon me by asking me to look at her pages, and therefore it was determined that she would this year leave the Report to be written by a friend.

Here is *the friend's* production, which I highly prize; but at the same time, Mrs. Spurgeon feels a great delicacy as to herself sending it out. I am hardly so sensitive, but I fully sympathize with her feeling, and therefore beg the subscribers to accept the Report as *a friend's* generous effort, and not as ours. We cannot, either separately or unitedly, produce the necessary document, nor alter the present one, so as to speak by it ourselves; and I am certain that Christian love will make every necessary apology, and remember that a friend may say, and will say, that of us which we would not dream of saying, or thinking, of ourselves.

Personally, I thank every one who has helped my beloved wife; and though painfully parted from her for a while by a trying Providence, we are so united in heart, that *in her name* I also return most sincere and hearty thanks to each donor of a sum, great or small. This work becomes dearer every month to her who carries it on; she rejoices in the painful exertion which it often costs her, and counts it an honour and a delight to be the channel by which such valuable aid is conveyed to the servants of the Lord.

To feed hungry bodies is a work of common humanity; but as the benefit in this case is mental and spiritual, the beneficence rises into a higher sphere. Fewer are those who sympathize with mental hunger, hence the loftier value which the almoner sets upon the gifts of those who help her in this more elevated form of Christian charity. These donations are not to be expended in bread and fish for the multitude, though this would be most commendable, but upon the means of feeding the souls of ministers who shall afterwards feed others with the bread of heaven. There is in this department of service the more need for prayer, that the end may not be missed, since it is more easy to secure the nourishment of a body by loaves than of a soul by books. We must in this work rely wholly upon the Spirit of God. Pray, then, dear friends, for the Lord's own blessing. The result may be marvellous if God shall favour the work with His grace; let us therefore be the more eager to secure a worthy result by our supplications.

Yours most heartily,
C. H. SPURGEON

Mrs. Spurgeon's Book Fund.

1878.

WHEN the Master bids his servants "stand still"—whether to await, in mute suspense, the command to "go forward," or in earnest solicitude, the anointing, which is at once the secret and the pledge of all true success—there is a moral excellence in the self-restraint which obeys without a murmur, and it is equally accepted with the zeal which asserts itself in heroic deeds, for

> "They also serve who only stand and wait."

In the wide economy of grace there is a place, doubtless, for Mary sitting at the feet of Jesus—

> "Rapt into still communion that transcends
> The imperfect offices of prayer and praise,"

just as truly as there is ample scope for an apostolic ministry, fired by a zeal which impels to unceasing activity till it is quenched in the fires of martyrdom, or is transmuted into the ardour of the seraph. The King must have His remembrancers at home as well as His ambassadors abroad.

In the history of the Book Fund we have an illustration of the blending of these two qualities—the patience which awaits year after year in the narrow sanctuary of a sick chamber, and the zeal which, at length, converts that sick room into an armoury, from which to send forth weapons and instruments for "the good soldiers of Jesus Christ," and "workers together with God," to enable them to carry on the "combat with sin and labour for the Lord."

Again and again has the "crown of life," promised to those who "are tried," appeared within the grasp of the sufferer, during her long years of waiting; but the baptism of suffering proved to be the chosen medium of a divine anointing for a ministry which has caused the "thanksgiving of many to redound to the glory of God." Mrs. Spurgeon received a call from the Master to supply His poor servants with the bullion from which to coin the currency of their sacred ministry, and, with a zest sharpened by long retirement from active Christian service, the mission was commenced, and its existence has been fully justified by the good which it has already accomplished.

The lemon plant, so often referred to by Mrs. Spurgeon, not only served to beguile the tedium of the waking hours occasioned by a painful affliction; it furnished also an emblem of the power of vitality, and proved the symbol of a modest but useful ministry. The Book Fund, designed originally to supply a copy of "Lectures to my Students" to a few poor ministers, has, like the lemon plant, grown to goodly proportions, and hundreds have been cheered and blessed by its instrumentality.

What has been accomplished during the past year the Report will partly show; much, however must remain unrecorded until "the day shall declare it." Anxiety for needed funds to meet increasing demands has prompted to incessant prayer, and solicitude in selecting the right persons to be assisted by the Fund has entailed an enormous correspondence, the labour of which, to an invalid, is not easily estimated. That the work is of the Lord none can deny or doubt. "Sore need have I had," writes Mrs. Spurgeon, "for His tender, pitiful care, and He has never failed me; but, in spite of almost constant ill-health, He has enabled me to accomplish even an increased amount of labour, and has extended the benefits of the Book Fund far and wide. To His name be the praises of my heart!"

To have had any share in the good work will be a pleasing memory and a sacred solace to every donor, and the inspiration of the truest joy will be found in the Master's recognition and reward—"Inasmuch as ye have done it unto one of the least of these My brethren, ye have done it unto Me."

To all who "pray for the peace of Jerusalem" such a work must commend itself to their sympathies, their prayers, and their generous support.

The important ministry of good books is so apparent, that it seems scarcely necessary even to state the fact; but to none have books such a mission as to the preacher, whose usefulness depends so largely upon the utterance of "Thoughts that breathe and words that burn."

To a devout and honest man the possession of a good book is a priceless treasure; its study stimulates thought, which enables him, by the husbandry of reflection and prayer, to reap a harvest, larger and richer, perhaps, than that of the author from whose granary he first obtained the seed-germs of his ideas.

Bearing these facts in mind, who can forecast the issues of the Book Fund, which, during the three years of its existence, has distributed NINETEEN THOUSAND ONE HUNDRED AND FORTY-THREE volumes of sacred literature to ministers, who have derived, from their study, inspiration and help in the work of soul-winning? In the chain of Christian service thus indicated, every link will receive its due share of the honour, and in the Spiritual Harvest Home, when the sheaves are garnered, " he that soweth and he that reapeth shall rejoice together."

When it is borne in mind that hundreds of ministers receive a stipend below the average weekly wage of a skilled mechanic, upon which they are expected to appear in broadcloth, occupy a house suitable to their position, maintain and educate their children in a manner becoming their profession, contribute to the various societies connected with their denomination, and keep abreast of the age in their pulpit ministrations, it will be seen how much they stand in need of the help which the Book Fund affords. Burdened with the anxiety to " provide things honest in the sight of all men," the acquisition of helpful literature is " a consummation devoutly to be wish'd," but rarely attained by those who, in the spirit of Christian heroism, hold their ground as "good soldiers of Jesus Christ." All honour to these brave warriors, who "endure hardness" as lone sentinels, or " die facing fearful odds!" If they have " fought a good fight," they will receive "the crown of righteousness," and it will be all the brighter from the fact that their weapons were the "ox-goad" or the "smooth stones from the brook." Well has the poet said—

"Strongest minds
Are often those of whom the noisy world hears least";

and when "the fire shall try every man's work," the bead-roll of martyrs shall become the muster-roll of heroes, and the "well-done, good and faithful servant" will stamp with eternal fame the conquests of life long obscurity. It is a cause of thankfulness that the Book Fund has armed many of these sturdy warriors with the weapons for their spiritual warfare, and that their triumphs have been all the greater for the equipment. To the Captain of our Salvation be all the praise !

One feature of the mission of the Book Fund must be mentioned : it has furnished an example of liberality to some who, while scarcely paying their minister a sufficient sum to enable him to meet his household expenses, have nevertheless required him to be a very Solon in the pulpit. John Ploughman advises all drivers, who expect their horses to go, to "put the whip into the manger"—in other words, to feed them better—and the Book Fund has urged the moral of the proverb in another direction ; for, while leaving the critics of the pew to complain of the pace of the pulpit, it has put the whip into the minister's study in the shape of goodly volumes of theology. A sparse library, to which the poverty of a minister has doomed him, should not only disarm the unkind criticism in which some thoughtful—we had nearly written *thoughtless*—hearers indulge, but rather furnish an occasion, as it points to the necessity, of supplying the lack. We fear, however, that the Book Fund will not be superseded by individual liberality ; for the money power of the smaller churches is severely strained to provide even the inadequate stipend of the minister. So long as the need exists, the Book Fund will endeavour to supply it, and, we are assured, the means will always be forthcoming. During the three years of its existence the amount expended has reached £3,511 14s. 2d.; and in the brief statement to subscribers, issued by Mrs. Spurgeon before the writing of this Report, the following expression of thanks for their generosity occurs :—" Your gifts are received as from the Lord, often coming as special answers to prayer, and always as tokens of His favour and approval of the effort ; and when they have thus enriched my soul, they carry to the weary, toiling servants of the Master substantial blessings—divine luxuries—the worth of which only a poor 'bookless' pastor can rightly appreciate."

The operation of the Book Fund, discovering so much poverty, has led to the formation of "The Pastors' Aid Fund," by which many a needy minister has received timely assistance. A detailed report of this branch of the work is withheld, for reasons which will be apparent. It is sufficient to say that many a weary heart has been cheered, and many a heavy burden lifted through the medium of this Fund; as much as £200 a year having been received and disbursed. To a faithful minister a pecuniary burden is one of the most painful to bear, and its removal is not only a relief to his mind, but it affects every department of his ministry, and, humanly speaking, increases his chances of success. While the kind donors who thus lovingly contribute to assist the distressed servants of the Lord may cherish the gracious promise—"Your Father which seeth in secret Himself shall reward you openly,"—the thanks of the almoner and recipients alike are hereby tendered, and the fervent "God bless you" of many a grateful heart.

During the past year, village pastors, to whom the works of standard authors are known only in name, and to whom their possession has been a long cherished desire, have, on hearing of the Book Fund, told the story of their struggles and their privations to justify their appeals. Often with much reluctance, always with diffidence, the applicants have ventured to ask for a grant of books in terms which but ill concealed their fears that they would be refused. Their acknowledgments prove that, in many instances, the arrival of the books has surprised their faith; and, as they have peeped into the volumes for the first time, through tears of gratitude, they have administered the self-rebuke—"O thou of little faith, wherefore didst thou doubt?"

The large proportion of Mr. Spurgeon's works which are given is not to be attributed to the partiality of the almoner, but to the choice of the applicants, who express their desire to possess them. When we state that neither authors nor publishers profit by the transactions, this fact should disarm the suspicion that the Book Fund, while benevolent in its intention, is commercial in its operation.

We cull a few extracts from the correspondence, which illustrate the necessity for the operations of the Book Fund, and express the gratitude evoked for the books received.

A Baptist Pastor, with a wife and four children to maintain on £60 per annum, writes thus :—

A few books would be a boon to me, but I am too poor to buy, and, unless some be given, I must go on "making my bricks without straw."

When, in answer to this appeal, Mrs. Spurgeon's gift reached him he says :—

I have not words which can express my heartfelt gratitude to you for the valuable present you have so kindly sent me. I could but go on my knees and bless God for thinking of me, and fervent prayer ascended for you and Mr. Spurgeon, and all who have contributed to the Book Fund. As I look at my few books, I feel that every one of them increases my responsibility,—if my heavenly Father gives me greater help, he will require better service. May your prayers be answered for my increased power and usefulness.

A minister in the far West, on receiving a grant of books, writes :—

I beg to express my heartfelt thanks to you, Madam, for sending me five vols. of "The Treasury of David," a work I have long desired to possess, and great, indeed, was the pleasure I felt when I found the parcel contained such a treasure. I beg also to acknowledge the receipt of a volume of Mr. Spurgeon's "Sermons" for the year 1877, for which I heartily thank you. I would not multiply words to express my thanks. I would only say that I feel truly grateful to our Heavenly Father that He has put such a desire into your heart as to bestow such favours upon His servants with limited means; and I am thankful that you have bestowed such a favour on me.

From the extreme northern country a minister writes :—

Having acknowledged the receipt of the parcel of books, I am utterly lost for want of suitable words and ways to express my intense gratitude. I seem like a person who has suddenly come to an unexpected and valuable possession, and is at a loss what first to admire and enjoy. From the depths of my heart I thank you for the invaluable gift. May God help me so to work in this "mine of sanctified thought and hallowed affection," that my own personal ministry may be more useful, vigorous, and holy than it has ever been. I am thankful to possess "The

Treasury of David," by your beloved husband, and assure you that it will be prized by me as long as I live. I shall place it by the side of his "Sermons" and "Lectures to my Students," and hold their gifted and honoured author in loving remembrance. That the blessing of Him who dwelt in the bush may rest upon yourself, your husband, and all the works of your hands, is my earnest prayer.

When Andrew found the Messiah, his anxiety was aroused for his brother, and "He first findeth his own brother Simon, and saith unto him, We have found the Messias, which is, being interpreted, the Christ. And he brought him to Jesus." Such an example has been copied again and again, and the benefits received by one have led to their extension to others who were the objects of Christian solicitude. In this way the operations of the Book Fund have widened out, to the joy and rejoicing of many hearts. We give one illustration out of many.

A Devonshire minister writes :—

I have realized great help from "The Treasury" in sermonizing, and I have realized great help in my own personal living to God by the consecutive reading of it for devotional purposes. It is natural that I should desire for others the same good I have realized myself. The case I beg very respectfully to submit to you is that of my brother, for whom I ask the gift of Mr. Spurgeon's "Treasury." My brother is a Wesleyan Missionary in the small Island of St. Eustatius, West Indies, the only Protestant minister in the island, and, of course, the advantages there, either of the way or the means of getting such books, are very few.

It is scarcely necessary to add that importunity prevailed in this case, and the volumes were forwarded in due course.

Throughout the country, and from some of the most out-of-the-way places, with names which few people out of Ireland have ever heard, letters come, telling the old story of struggles and privations. One minister writes :—

I have been ministering to the spiritual comfort of a small congregation of Christians, commonly called Baptists, in this village for thirty years, struggling all the time under temporal difficulties beyond what anyone could imagine. The annual average amount of my income during that time is not more than £12. We kept a small shop for some years, until my wife's health, with hard work and privation of even the common necessaries of life, completely broke down, so that for the last six years we have had to give our business up, as she could not help, and my labours for the Lord occupied my own time ; and for the last nine months she has been very little out of bed. You will see by this, and bringing up four children, we must have had a hard time of it, without purchasing books, and therefore that my library must be very small. You will naturally say, How did you get through? I answer—the God who feeds the ravens sent us in little by little, though sometimes our board has been very scant, and our backs but thinly clad; but we can say, "The Lord will provide."

The utter dearth disclosed by these unaffected statements is pitiable in the extreme. How the dear good man has succeeded in teaching the same congregation for thirty years would be an insoluble mystery did we not know that "strength is made perfect in weakness," and that the "foolishness of preaching," when sanctified by faith and prayer, is ordained of God "to save them that believe." Now that the six goodly volumes, sent through the Book Fund, form a cheering oasis in the barren library of the poor pastor, his ministry will, doubtless, yield a more abundant harvest than heretofore; for this law of the kingdom still remains in force—"Unto him that hath, shall be given, and he shall have more abundance."

The donors will be glad to be informed that, when an applicant is able to purchase, books are sent on the most advantageous terms, and thus the benevolent operations of the Fund are restricted to ministers in necessitous circumstances.

The limits of this account prevent the insertion of many expressions of gratitude with which the letters abound, and the hopes which are cherished of future help and cheering testimonies to increased usefulness from the study of the books. While the agent is not overlooked, the "Giver of every good and perfect gift" is not forgotten by the writers, and no fitter words can close this brief memorial of another year's labour for the Lord than those which place the crown of every holy enterprise on His head, who alone is worthy—"Not unto us, O Lord, not unto us, but unto Thy name be the glory."

Record of Book Fund Work.

1879.

By Mrs. C. H. Spurgeon

INTRODUCTORY LETTER.

Dear Friends,

WITH much diffidence this little book is laid before you. It has cost me considerable effort and thought, yet it but feebly represents the progress and prosperity of my work, and very unworthily records the faithfulness and love of our gracious God. I have earnestly tried to do my best; but the preparation of an Annual Report is the only duty connected with the Book Fund which I find burdensome; and were it not that I hope the work will bear the precious fruit of "glory to God," I could not have attempted it. Last year there was no question about the matter, for extreme ill-health and weakness had brought me very low: but during the last few months the Lord has dealt so gently with me, and given me such happy cessation of suffering, that I want to devote the first efforts of partially-renewed strength to the humble and grateful fulfilment of this duty. The Report for 1878 was written by a kind friend who willingly and ably supplied my lack of service, and my hearty thanks are now rendered to him for assistance given in a time of much sorrow and need. Very soon after this good friend had accomplished his task,

I began to wonder how the present year would be provided for: the months roll by so quickly, that no sooner is one record given than it seems time to think about another. Musing one day on this matter, a "happy thought" suggested itself—that, as often as opportunity presented, I should gather material for future use by jotting down, somewhat in diary-form, any subject of interest or thanksgiving pertaining to my work, and so present to my friends a Report, perhaps novel in character, but less difficult for me thus to produce, and, I hope, not more unpleasant to them to peruse.

In the following pages, therefore, I have endeavoured to give frequent details of the special service which the Lord has entrusted to my care, noting down any particularly interesting incident, recording some memorable mercies, and preserving much pleasant correspondence.

Here and there the reader will find, intermingled with *bonâ fide* book-work, a few domestic and more private experiences, which *would* insinuate themselves into the little history, and which, seeing that the dear home-life and the Book Fund are so tenderly "joined together" by the Lord's good pleasure, I had not the heart or the wish to "put asunder."

Imperfectly as I have worked out the idea which in the first instance possessed me, I yet hope the perusal of this little book will interest my friends still further in the work they, by their kindly gifts, are sharing with me. If in any degree it helps them more clearly to perceive that in this sweet ministry I am *acting for them*, being truly and gladly their "servant for Christ's sake;" that the joy, and delight, and reward are not all for me only, but are shared by them most fully, while all the "glory" is given to our faithful God: then my difficult task will not have been undertaken in vain, nor shall I regret that I tried to put on record some of the "goodness and mercy which followed me" during the year eighteen hundred and seventy-nine.

Susie Spurgeon.

Nightingale-lane,
    Balham.

Record of Book Fund Work.

In 1880 the Book Fund enters upon the fifth year of its existence. Very many of the old friends, who saw its formation, have lovingly watched its advance, and generously contributed to its increase; they are as well acquainted with its aims and ambitions as with its origin; but for the sake of the new friends who may be led to sympathize with me in the endeavour to help "poor bookless ministers," I will give a brief account of the nature of the work which has become so dear to many hearts.

The Book Fund makes grants to "poor Pastors of every evangelical denomination, who are in actual charge, wholly devoted to the ministry, and whose income from all sources does not exceed £150 per annum."

These grants consist of seven or eight volumes, and usually comprise "The Treasury of David," or some of Mr. Spurgeon's "Sermons"—not to the exclusion of other books, but chiefly because they are the works most sought after by applicants to the Fund—and, I am not afraid or ashamed to say it, because I know I could not, with the slender means at my command, give any more precious or more helpful. Seldom are requests made for other authors, nor do I profess to supply them; but when opportunity offers I gladly make the addition of new and standard works to my stock. There are several special books for ministers which I would at once add to my list if friends who wish for their circulation would supply me with the means.

It is sad to know that the limit of £150 in income gives me as wide a field as I can compass for the bestowal of these coveted blessings. *Poor* ministers are the rule, not the exception; they are not restricted to the Baptist denomination, nor to our own land, but abound in every connexion, and in all climes—their needs are very urgent, their prospects seldom brighten, and their ranks never seem to thin; my work for them is as great a necessity now as it was at its commencement, nay, I think its importance has increased with its extension, the latent thirst for knowledge has been developed by its gifts, and a keener appetite for mental food has been produced by the provision it has furnished. I need not enlarge on the absolute necessity which exists for a minister to possess books if he would be an efficient teacher and preacher—the mind which is itself not fed, cannot very long feed others; but I would point out the impossibility of procuring these essential helps and appliances, when a man has to provide for himself and a wife and family on a pittance of £60, £80, or £100 per annum.

To such weary "workers with a slender apparatus" my Book Fund stretches forth a helping hand : it fills the empty basket with tools, gives a key to a well-stocked storehouse, replenishes an exhausted brain, supplies ammunition for the combat with evil, makes sunshine in shady places, and by God's own blessing does a vast amount of good wherever its gifts are scattered.

* * * *

It is the joy of my life thus to serve the servants of my Master, and the daily blessings and tender providences which surround my work are more precious to me than words can express. "Some of the subjects of my thankfulness may seem small and inconsiderable to others, but to me they are of constant interest and importance"; my retired life shuts out the usual pleasures of social intercourse, but opens wide a world of glad delight in thus "ministering to the necessities of the saints." I have scores of friends with whose circumstances I am intimately acquainted, yet whose faces I have never looked upon. I hope to know and greet them on the "other shore"; and, meanwhile, their love and prayers are a sweet reward for such pleasant service as the Lord enables me to render to them. In these pages will be found some of the expressive outpourings of grateful hearts, and though the letters here given form but a small portion of the great mass of affectionate correspondence connected with the Fund, they will serve to reveal some of the daily comfort and encouragement I receive through this channel. Ah ! if by His grace we can but win from our Master the approving words, " *Ye did it unto me*," the joy of service is then only "a little lower" than the supreme felicity of heaven!

* * * *

January.—Two years since, a few thoughtful, kindly friends proposed a regular distribution of *The Sword and the Trowel* magazine to a certain number of poor country ministers who could not afford to take it in, and they generously forwarded donations for this special purpose. I find written in the Report for that year that "the prospect of this indulgence has greatly cheered many hearts," and that one to whom the offer was made, remarked, "I have not been able to take in a religious periodical for five years; the monthly visit of the magazine will, indeed, be a great boon." The new work then commenced has been continued, but not increased, though there can be no doubt as to its value and good influence, and I regret that it only comes to my hands as a divergence from the main business which fills my heart. All my time and strength are given to what I feel to be the more urgent work of furnishing empty book-shelves, and the profit and pleasure which would undoubtedly arise from a well-ordered monthly distribution of religious literature by the Book Fund is but partially developed on this account. We must hope for better things by-and-by; meanwhile, I believe that those Pastors now receiving the magazine are greatly pleased and delighted with their visitor, and I hope not only to retain all the names at present on my list, but during the year to add to their number.

* * * *

A curious little incident happened lately during a time of prolonged sickness. At the close of a very dark and gloomy day I lay resting on my couch as the deeper night drew on, and though all was bright within my cosy little room, some of the external darkness seemed to have entered into my soul, and obscured its spiritual vision. Vainly I tried to see the hand which I knew held mine, and guided my fog-enveloped feet along a steep and slippery path of suffering. In sorrow of heart I asked, "Why does my Lord thus deal with His child? Why does He so often send sharp and bitter pain to visit me? Why does He permit lingering weakness to hinder the sweet service I long to render to His poor servants?" These fretful questions were quickly answered, and though in a strange language, no interpreter was needed, save the conscious whisper of my own heart. For a while silence reigned in the little room, broken only by the crackling of the oak log burning on the hearth. Suddenly I heard a sweet soft sound, a little, clear, musical note, like the tender trill of a robin, beneath my window. "What *can* that be?" I said to my companion, who was dozing in the firelight; "surely no bird can be singing out there at this time of the year and night!" We listened, and again heard the faint plaintive notes, so sweet, so melodious, yet mysterious enough to provoke for a moment our undisguised wonder. Presently my friend exclaimed, " It comes from the log on the fire ! " and we soon ascertained that her surprised assertion was correct. *The fire was letting loose the imprisoned music from the old oak's inmost heart!* Perchance he had garnered up this song in the days when all went well with him, when birds twittered merrily on his branches, and the soft sunlight flecked his tender leaves with gold; but he had grown old since then, and hardened; ring after ring of knotty growth had sealed up the long-forgotten melody, until the fierce tongues of the flames came to consume his callousness, and the vehement heat of the fire wrung from him at once a song and a sacrifice. Ah! thought I, when the fire of affliction draws songs of praise from us, then, indeed, are we purified, and our God is glorified ! Perhaps some of us are like this old oak log—cold, hard, and insensible; we should give forth no melodious sounds were it not for the *fire*, which kindles round us, and releases tender notes of trust in Him, and cheerful compliance with His will ! " As I mused, the fire burned," and my soul found sweet comfort in the parable so strangely set forth before me ! Singing in the fire ! Yes ! God helping us, if that is the only way to get harmony out of these hard, apathetic hearts, let the furnace be heated seven times hotter than before.

✱ ✱ ✱ ✱

How opportune and precious is the following letter: —

My dear Mrs. Spurgeon,—I have been much concerned to find from *The Sword and the Trowel* that you, as well as your dear husband, have been again brought into great suffering, and I am constrained to say how deeply and affectionately I sympathize with you and him in these repeated afflictions, and how earnestly I pray that both of you may enjoy to the full the supports of divine grace. I do not know you personally, but that need not forbid my writing to you such a note as this; for we are *one in Christ*, and one member of His body cannot suffer without other members suffering along with it. Besides which, you were wonderfully kind to me a year ago in that gift of books, which I have so greatly prized, and for which I have been, and shall continue to be, so deeply grateful. Those four volumes of "The Treasury of David," how helpful have they been to me in many ways, and with what relish do I always turn to them! They are excellent reading, not only when I want thoughts for the pulpit, but also when I want my own spiritual life to be quickened and cheered. What a wonderful man God has made Mr. Spurgeon to be! Well may we pray that his life may be spared, and that his heart and brain and tongue and fingers may keep the fine rich power with which grace has endowed them.

My sympathy with you and with him is the keener just now by reason of a heavy domestic affliction through which I am passing. . . . Do not take the trouble to acknowledge this letter. I only wanted to let you know how one to whom you have been kind is sympathizing with you, and praying for you and yours.

* * * *

February.—A quaint message comes to me to-day across the sea from Africa. It stirs pleasant memories, and well fulfils the loving commission given to it to encourage and strengthen my heart. Thus it runs: "Tell dear Mrs. Spurgeon to keep inching along, Jesus Christ 'll come by-and-by."

I must explain the nature of this uncommon communication, and why it so interests and touches me. When our two coloured brethren, Messrs. Johnson and Richardson, were on the eve of departure for missionary work in Africa, they came with their wives to our dear home to bid us farewell. A very pleasant and memorable time we spent together, their Pastor encouraging them in the work to which they had devoted their lives, and their love and sympathy overflowing to him and to me (then very sick), in return. At the request of my dear husband they sang to me some of the strange, sweet songs of their captivity, for they had once been slaves; and all who heard these plaintive melodies sung in the Tabernacle at their farewell meetings will agree with me that sweeter, yet sadder melodies could scarcely be imagined. My heart was especially attracted by a peculiar air, to which they sang as a refrain these most curious words:—

> "Keep inching along, keep inching along
> Like a poor inch worm,—
> Jesus Christ 'll come by-and-by."

It is impossible to describe the weird pathos with which they invested these few sentences, and my interest was so aroused that I asked if some special history attached to this strange song. Then they told me how in the sorrowful days of their bondage they would stealthily gather together, night after night, in one of the low miserable huts they called their home, and sitting crouched on the floor, hand clasped in hand, in darkness and terror, they would pray with one another, and in muffled tones would *whisper* this very song. *Sing* it aloud they *dared* not, for fear of their master, who would have exacted full payment by stripes for such an assertion of nature's rights; but rocking to and fro in time to the wailing melody, they found a "fearful pleasure" in the disobedience which brought spiritual comfort to their oppressed souls.

The glorious hope of future deliverance excited and enraptured their hearts. "Sometimes," they said, "one of our number would forget the caution and silence so essential to our safety; and a voice would ring out in the darkness, jubilant and clear, 'Jesus Christ 'll come by-and-by!'" Then all would sit trembling after such an outburst, lest they should be discovered by the shout of anticipated triumph, and angels might have wept for the poor, downtrodden souls, and have longed to bring the sweet chariot, "coming for to carry them home."

"Will you sing to me *in whispers* as you sang then?" I asked, and they very sweetly complied with my wish, though, blessed be God, their surroundings were now so happy that they could give but a faint copy of the terrible reality. I shall never forget that pitiful hushing of their voices. There was not a dry eye in the little company when the song was ended; but we wiped our tears away, soon remembering that the cause for sorrow no longer existed. The "poor inch worms" are now free, noble, educated men and women; they can sing, and pray, and preach as loudly and as long as they please, and are bound for the land of their fathers, with the intention of exercising these privileges to the full, and making known the gospel of the grace of God to their kindred according to the flesh. The Lord go forth with them and prosper them.

The echoes of that singular song have lingered with me ever since, and many a time have they comforted my heart. Day by day the work of the Book Fund has "kept inching along," and though prevented by my weakness from taking giant strides, how gracious is the Lord to allow His unworthy child to creep even inch by inch along the pleasant road of service for Him! I should like to send forth fifty parcels weekly—I should like each parcel to be a complete library of theological lore, so that very soon not a true minister in the land should faint and fail for lack of knowledge; but as my highest aims cannot be fulfilled, I will thankfully and joyfully *do what I can*, and with the Lord's blessing resting on the books sent out in His name, my ten to twenty packages a week will not fail to accomplish His good purpose. Thus, cheerfully, gladly, I "keep inching along," and for me, as surely as for the greatest saint on earth—"Jesus Christ 'll come by-and-by."

* * * *

March.—It is not unworthy of record that a minister of the Society of Friends has sought and obtained the free gift of "The Treasury of David." This is so far the only instance where the help of the Fund has been given to one of that body of Christians, though many Moravians, and brethren of various names, have eagerly accepted my gift of books. In acknowledging the receipt of the parcel, he says, in the pretty, quaint Quaker style:—

"Susie Spurgeon,"—My dear kind friend,—Thy note and the parcel came all right. I am much interested in thy work, and do hope the blessing of the Lord will rest upon it. I should be glad of time to say how I have enjoyed the prospect of a feast over this "Treasury"; but I have only a moment to write, and must simply say how truly obliged I am, and how much I reciprocate the kind wishes expressed in thy note. When I have looked over this gift in my western home, I may send a line. Kind love to thyself and thy husband, Thy obliged friend,

. . . .

* * * *

April.—At the time of the Annual Conference of the Pastors' College the Book Fund usually prepares a little present for the three hundred Pastors who then assemble. This is meant to be both a memorial of a happy gathering, and a pledge of continued interest in their welfare. This year, after due consideration, I have decided to give Miss Havergal's "Royal" books (two to each pastor) as a choice and dainty morsel for their spiritual refreshment and quickening. No commendation is needed to ensure a hearty welcome to a work by this devoted lady. Miss Havergal's pen is guided by a hand fast clasped in that of her Master, and therefore her simple words thrill to the inmost depths of the soul, and touch many a hidden spring of tender, deep, religious feeling. I anticipate not only the pleasure with which our "old students" will receive these delightful little books at my hands; but the abundant blessing they may bring to their hearts and homes. Through the kindness of Messrs. Nisbet, the publishers, I have been able to purchase a thousand copies, and having made it a matter of special prayer that not one of these precious seeds should be unfruitful, I shall hopefully and patiently await the result.

* * * *

To ministers who are not quite so necessitous as those for whom the Book Fund was specially founded, yet who can ill spare the published price of "The Treasury of David," or the "Sermons," I offer these books at a somewhat reduced rate, and I have much satisfaction in knowing that the privilege is warmly appreciated. The following letters are fair samples of the spirit in which the favour is sought, and the warm gratitude evoked by its accordance :—

My dear Mrs. Spurgeon,—In the libraries of my friends I have very frequently perused that most choice and savoury work of your husband,

"The Treasury of David"; and if I have not actually incurred the guilt of breaking the tenth commandment, I fear I have come near to doing so, and from time to time I have been looking how I could contrive to purchase it; but have found as often that my income has been forestalled by family and other claims. I have long known that you have been doing a most valuable work for the Master, by helping poor Pastors to some good books; but hitherto I have not ventured to write lest I should be standing in the way of some brother more necessitous even than myself. This week, however, I was in the library of one of my brethren, and again looking over some parts of "The Treasury," the desire to possess it for myself returned with such strength that I felt somewhat as I suppose a hungry ox would feel, tethered outside, but just in sight of, a luxuriant field of clover! After ruminating over the matter again and again, I came to the conclusion that I could manage part of the price, so I have determined to say to you that I should esteem it a great favour indeed to receive a copy from your hands, if I shall not stand too much in the way of some other poor brother.

It was, indeed, a great joy to *open the gate of the clover field!* May the good brother "go in and out and find pasture."

* * * *

There is also a goodly number of workers for the Lord, evangelists, local preachers and others, who, having no pastorate, are ineligible for the free gift of "The Treasury," yet covet earnestly this precious aid in their work; these, many of them, save up a little money, and sending it to me by degrees, have in time the joy of receiving the longed-for treasure, which, doubtless, they value none the less for the self-denial which has procured it. I often regret that I cannot give books to all Christian workers; but a strict boundary line is absolutely necessary in a work carried on, not by a "Society," but by one pair of hands, and those not over strong or capable.

* * * *

May.—There are some friends of the Book Fund who take great pleasure in sending nice *new* articles of clothing to be placed in the minister's parcel of books as a glad surprise to his wife or children, and much gratification and comfort have resulted from this thoughtful kindness. A lady in Scotland regularly supplies me with soft woollen shawls for this purpose, and I have recently received from another loving hand useful dress pieces, which will prove a great boon to the weary wives and mothers whose unselfish love forbids their attending to their own needs while the little one's requirements are so urgent. Two lonely widows in the midland counties constantly employ their time in working thus for me, making nice strong under-garments, flannels, &c., and twice a-year sending me a large box, tightly packed with the results of their loving, patient industry. I always feel a little choking sensation in my throat when that box comes, and as we lift out garment after garment, *dozens of them*, all well made and neatly folded, my satisfaction is very tenderly blended with sympathy for the two lonely, patient workers, whose fingers must have been so unremittingly active in their self-imposed service. As they sit and sew so assiduously for His servants, may the "God of all consolation" pour balm into their wounded hearts! The reception of one such parcel and enclosure as the above-mentioned is thus described by a worthy pastor:—

> I cannot tell you how delighted my dear wife was when she saw a parcel for her. Do you know the little "s" on the inner address, turning "Mr." into "Mrs." made her eyes sparkle with joy. "Why," she exclaimed, "there's something for *me!* Oh, how kind and thoughtful!" And the shawl was a strangely acceptable present, as you will see, when I tell you that last winter I so much needed a large scarf or plaid, such as Scotchmen wear, that Mrs. G. cut her shawl (of the same kind as the one now sent, only a different colour) to make this said wrap, and now, as the winter is upon us, and she requires such a comfort, *it comes.* How good God is! How kind friends are! The dress material was also received with very much pleasure indeed. Truly, He who clothes the lilies of the field doth not forget His poor servants.

* * * *

June 5.—To-day £200 is mine from the great Testimonial Fund, raised last Christmas; £100 is allotted to the Book Fund, and £100 to the Pastors' Aid Society. My dear husband's kindness secures this splendid help to my work, and I bless God both for him and his delightful gift. If "John Ploughman's" wife might say here what she thinks of "John" in this, and all other matters, it would be an easy task to fill these pages with his praises; but since such a wifely eulogy might be deemed out of place, Mrs. J. P. may at least record in her little book her hearty and appreciative thanks to the hundreds of true friends who have lately done honour to the "Prince of her life," * and furnished him with the means of more abundantly blessing all the poor and needy ones who look to him as their best earthly friend and comforter. If I knew anyone who doubted the truth of that Scripture, "There is that scattereth and yet increaseth," I could bring no more unanswerable proof of its veracity than is found in the unselfish life and loving deeds of the God-honoured man I reverence as my head and husband. I find a graceful appropriateness in the gift of part of this money to Baptist Pastors, seeing that to one of themselves the whole magnificent sum is offered as a tribute of devoted admiration and love. What a joy it will be to use this consecrated gold in their service! What heavy burdens it will lift! What aching hearts will be consoled! What praise to God will be given by joyful lips! When I think of all it will do, I wish it were ten times as much! I get greedy for their sakes—my poor, weary, toiling brethren—but that only lasts a moment, for indeed I am most fully "satisfied with favour" on their behalf, both from the Lord and from man.

* * * *

June 27.—We had a very pleasant visit to-day from the Bishop of Sierra Leone. The story of the Book Fund work had reached him far away in Africa, and he came to solicit the gift of "The Treasury of David" for one of his coloured Pastors. After some gracious and profitable talk with the master of the house, and a turn round the garden, the good bishop accepted the promise not only of "The Treasury," but also some other books, for the workers in Africa. It is noteworthy that the Lord is now constantly giving me opportunities of spreading the good old doctrines of grace in foreign lands, through the distribution of books; this year much seed corn has been thus scattered, and we may look hopefully for the harvest. Before he left us Bishop Cheetham enrolled his name as a subscriber to the Book Fund, and I hope he carried away with him, in addition to the

---

* Name for Mr. Spurgeon suggested by a Welshman.

promise of books, some pleasant memories of his visit to Nightingale Lane.

Following on the above pleasant incident comes the subjoined loving testimony to the worth of "The Treasury of David" from a vicar in the Midland Counties:—

Allow me, as an aged minister of the Church of England, to express my deep sense of gratitude to God (as I have often done upon my knees) for putting it into the heart of your husband to compile such a work for the people of God—a book which will minister instruction to generations yet to come, and gather many harpers to stand before the Throne, and sing the praises of Jehovah Jesus.

* * * *

How sudden and unexpected is the announcement that Miss Havergal has "passed from earth to Heaven!" And yet, had not our eyes and ears been dulled by worldly words and visions, we might have seen the light of the Celestial City shining on her footsteps, and have heard a note or two of heavenly music in her angelic songs. It could be most truly said of her that "her heart was with Him on His throne," and so sweet a singer could not tarry long away from the place "where all his singers meet." We all mourn as for a friend greatly beloved, for those of us to whom she was personally a stranger had made close and tender acquaintance with her through her precious little books. None can read her rapturous and touching words concerning her "King" and "Master" without feeling glad that He "exceedeth the fame which she heard," and rejoicing in the unutterable bliss which she will for ever enjoy in His presence. Those of her writings which have been published since her decease are full of grace and power; but the wonderful little work on "Consecration"* is her swan-like death song, the sweetest and best of all. I intend, as long as I can afford it, to put this pearl of books, as an *extra* blessing, into every parcel I send out from the Book Fund, and may the Lord grant that through its sweet influence many may be led to consecrate body, soul, and spirit anew to His service and His cause!

---

* "Kept for the Master's Use," by the late F. R. H. Messrs. Nisbet and Co.

July 19.—These times of depression and disaster tell heavily on my poor friends the Pastors of country churches. "Burdens grievous to be borne" seem laid on their hearts and lives, and with the universal social troubles, personal trials come in sad fellowship of suffering. Sickness, and consequent doctors' bills, are heavy items in the sum of misery, and even those who do their best to "provide things honest in the sight of all men" are just now bowed to the very earth by the terrible pressure of obligations which they are powerless to avoid, and are equally unable to fulfil. I have had some appeals lately which reveal a state of things among our country Pastors greatly to be deplored, and though immediate relief was given, the problem of permanent amendment is still left unsolved. How is a man (and that man a *minister*) to house, and feed, and clothe himself, his wife, and a varying, I was on the point of writing "unlimited," number of children on £80 a year? I know scores who are trying to do it, but can we blame them if they fail? "I have had but one *new* suit for the last nine years," writes one who knows what Paul meant by "enduring hardness." How can the good man spare £4 or £5 for orthodox broadcloth when meat graces the table but once or twice a week, and the children's clothes are almost too shabby for them to wear in the House of God? I heard of a good man the other day, who is thankfully wearing in the pulpit a second-hand coat of dark bottle-green, the gift of some commiserating friend, who noticed the pitiful seediness of his best suit. I do not suppose that his sermons are deteriorated by the mere fact that he wears a bottle-green garment; but I do think that the man himself would be vastly bettered, and helped to a modest share of self-respect, if he had becoming apparel in which "to minister in holy things." Is it any wonder if sometimes the "cares of this world" choke and cramp the spiritual energies of poor needy Pastors? "We have had a dull enough sermon this morning," says a hearer who has all that heart can wish for; "what can have come to our minister to make him so listless and uninteresting?" If that good brother were to try the effect of a little loving help and sympathy (a £5 note, for instance, delicately and tenderly given), he would see a wonderful lifting and lightening of the clouds and darkness which encompass his pastor's spirit, and be quite surprised at the life and energy infused into his next discourse. "My people do all they can for me," many a distressed pastor writes, and it may be so in some cases; but I question whether in the Master's presence they would themselves dare to say this; for He still "sits over against the treasury," and must note how little even of "their abundance" His people cast in for His servants and His cause. "It is a tale often told to you, I imagine, by such as myself, whose incomes are so pitifully small," wrote a minister the other day, "that to buy books, when there are little hungry mouths and wistful faces at the table daily is an IMPOSSIBILITY." The good man has deeply underlined this last word, and well he may, for his church only raises £80 a year for him, while a grant from the Augmentation Fund barely rescues them from absolute need. Ah! some of us who can not only "make both ends meet," but "have enough over to tie a bow and ends," can scarcely realize the toiling and striving, the anguish of longing, which must tear at the hearts of a poor pastor and his wife, as they try to eke out the scanty store of coin, and make one shilling do the duty of a score! "My wife sends you her heartfelt thanks," says one of "our own" men; "she says you cannot know what good you are doing, or how much you gladden the hearts of poor Pastors' wives, though you cannot feel *as* they feel, for you have never been in the same position."

No, not quite, yet I can tenderly sympathize with them; for well do *we* remember, in the early days of our married life, a time, nay, many times, when "God's Providence was our inheritance," and our mouths were "filled with laughter, and our lips with singing," by the signal deliverances He afforded us when means were straitened, and the coffers, both of college and household, were well-nigh empty.

* * * *

August 4.—Interesting and welcome letters are so abundant that the difficulty is how to make a wise choice from amongst them. To-day I am delighted to receive from a Primitive Methodist minister a request to be allowed to purchase the whole set of Mr. Spurgeon's "Sermons." "I feel it an effort," he says; "but myself and wife do not think we could spend money in anything that would impart a more healthful impulse to our spiritual life, or prompt us to greater zeal in God's service." This has greatly pleased me; and in sending the precious parcel to this good brother, I intend it to contain *more* than the twenty-four volumes he has paid for. What a pleasure it would be to see him unpack his treasure, and watch the tender, reverent handling the books will be sure to receive when he releases them from their wrappings! When a man dearly loves books, it is a treat to see him in his library, and mark his intimacy with them, the peculiar touch he gives them, and the certain knowledge he has of the whereabouts of any one of them! My love for the Book Fund work is frequently stimulated by noting the tender regard my husband has for his books, and the constant and patient use he makes of them; and a glance at the well-filled shelves at home sets my heart a-longing to introduce like blessings into the scantily-furnished studies of our needy brethren.

* * * *

August 14.—Though in these bad times there is not much money coming in for the Book Fund, the supplies have not by any means failed; there is just enough to show that the Lord has not ceased to care for it, and does not mean it to fall to the ground, and yet little enough to make me ask earnestly at His Treasury for more. I feel much encouraged by the steadfast kindness of some dear friends, who seem to have enrolled themselves as monthly, quarterly, or annual subscribers, and so send me constant and regular help. This is manifestly of the Lord; He has thus inclined their hearts to remember my work; for I never ask except from Him, and no articles in *The Sword and the Trowel* this year have brought the Book Fund prominently into notice. More distinctly and blessedly than ever, therefore, the Lord has been my helper, and from His hand have proceeded the stores which have relieved and refreshed His servants.

* * * *

How constantly have I wished and prayed that the brief records given from time to time of the Lord's gracious dealings with me in my small service for Him might help some fainting heart to trust Him more and love Him better! The following letter comes like a breath from the land of fulfilled desire, and rekindles my fervent longing to give to my generous God the glory due unto His name :—

Dear Mrs. Spurgeon,—Since my first letter to you on the subject of your kind presentation of books to my locals and myself, I have been re-reading your various messages in *The Sword and the Trowel* concerning the Book Fund. Its history has cheered me much, and strengthened my unaccountably weak faith in a Father who can send hundreds of pounds as easily as He can produce a lemon plant, and who is as able to do it for one of His children as for another. I am going to try to obtain more faith (and I know I must trust Him even for that), and so attempt a greater work of soul-conversion than I had ever supposed could have been done through me. Oh! to believe that Jesus can use any tool, so skilled a workman is He! I passed over to my friends last evening your gift of "Lectures to my Students." They were very pleased, and in prayer earnestly thanked God, and besought Him to bless you yet more and more. You may be sure that they asked the choicest blessings they could think of, and I doubt not that choicer ones were already in the store-house of grace, packed up to send you, waiting there in their rich fulness, "blaming the shallowness of our request." As for your very kind present to me, I know not how to thank you. But I will try to use it well, and do pray that each volume may be, by the Holy Spirit's power, made useful in winning some souls to Christ, and drawing them into close communion with their Friend. Please accept my hearty thanks, and my earnest wishes for your exceeding joy and gladness, and also my prayers for the health of our beloved President.

* * * *

I have been very pleased during this year to see my work extend among the poorly-paid curates of the Church of England, and I trust a great blessing will follow the introduction into their libraries of such books as "The Treasury," the "Sermons," and "Lectures to my Students." These gifts are sought with avidity, and welcomed with eager joy; and of all the pleasant letters which I receive, none are more courteous in spirit, or graceful in language, than those penned by clergymen of the Established Church.

Two years ago, writes one, you presented me with "The Treasury of David," expressing a wish that it might prove a "treasure" indeed. Your wish has been more than gratified, and now I have an acute appetite for the *whole* of your respected husband's works. I have the privilege of preaching the gospel five times every week, and if this is to continue to be a pleasure to me, I must keep my soul and mind well fed. Being still "a poor curate" I have to supply my wants on the lowest terms, so I write to ask whether in gratifying my ardent desire, any assistance may be obtained from that source of benevolence which formerly supplied "The Treasury of David."

My readers will be rejoiced to learn that with some little help from the Book Fund, this clergyman has now on his shelves a complete set of the "Metropolitan Tabernacle Pulpit," in addition to "The Treasury of David," and some smaller works of Mr. Spurgeon's.

* * * *

August 26.—Here is a sad tale of woe from a Wesleyan minister in Ireland :—

There is no book I am more anxious to secure than "The Treasury of David," yet I am not able to purchase it. Trade is so bad here that our town is an exception in the north of Ireland for poverty. We cannot clear many pounds a year towards a minister's support. *Many hand-loom weavers are working twelve hours a day for less than five shillings a-week!* We have help on this station from our Missionary Society in England; but notwithstanding this, we can only move on in these depressing times by the self-sacrifice of the minister; and buying books is out of the question. I have no private means, and I am neither able, on the one hand, to get my salary, nor yet am I disposed on the other to leave these poor people. I feel just in a position which would enable me to appreciate the possession of "The Treasury of David."

* * * *

I have been able to send a fair share of help to Pastors in Ireland. We have not many Baptists there, but our Wesleyan brethren bear the full brunt of hard work and poverty. That they know how to appreciate a gift of books the following letter from one of their number will amply prove :—

I have been wondering how it might be possible for me to express what I feel of gratitude. I cannot imagine. But I am confident that no thanks could convey to yourself or Mr. Spurgeon a tithe of the sweetness contained in the reflection that the loaves and fishes, blessed and broken by our Lord Himself, by Him handed to His disciples, and by them to the multitude, are being made the bread of life in very deed and truth to thousands who otherwise would faint and perish by the way, but who by means of this distribution are enabled to reach and feed upon that bread "whereof if a man eat he shall never die."

Oct. 2.—Committed to the faithful keeping of his father's God, our precious son sails to-day for his second visit to Australia. The cold and damp of our English winter made us fear for his somewhat delicate constitution, and if it be the Lord's will, the more genial climate of the colonies may develop strength and power to prosecute that which, we trust, will be his life-work—to preach to poor sinners the "unsearchable riches of Christ." Give the winds and the waves charge concerning him, O Lord! Let them waft him safely to his desired haven, and then do Thou guide him all his journey through, till both he and all who hold him dear shall meet to part no more!

I am glad to say that the Book Fund is not altogether unrepresented in the cargo which the good ship carries, though if I had possessed the means it should have been much heavier; for in Australia, as in other distant lands, books are vastly more expensive than in England, and more difficult to procure. The book-hunger of our most needy ministers at home may be as keen and absorbing as the appetite of a colonial pastor; but the former has many more chances of ultimately appeasing it, while hope gives him strength to endure and to wait. In the bush, or in outlying districts, where there may be little intellectual life, a man must depend very largely on his bookshelves for friendship and communion, and when these fail him, or prove uncongenial, he is very sincerely to be pitied, and ought to be helped. I should often send books to the colonies if the Fund could bear the heavy expense of freightage; but awaiting the kind services of friends to take charge of the parcels is so slow a method of transit, that practically my grants are few and far between. To the abundant affection which the generous people on the other side of the world showed our dear son on his first visit they added this kindness, that they have once and again helped, not only his father's many "works of faith and labours of love," but his mother's Book Fund; and now that he goes to seek once more health in their beautiful country, she would like him to carry a great blessing back to them. Father and mother both fervently pray that his life there may be a devoted and consecrated one, and that "power from on high" may be given him to win many jewels for the Master's crown.

Oct. 4.—Truly, this has been a "red-letter day" in Book Fund experience. My heart praises and extols the goodness of the Lord, and my hand shall at once record the mercy which, like a blessed rain on a thirsty land, has so sweetly refreshed my spirit. This afternoon a constant and generous friend brought £100 for the Book Fund. This was cause for devout thankfulness and great joy; for lately an unusually large number of books has been going out week by week, though funds have flowed in less freely. But it was not till a few hours after receiving this noble donation that I saw fully the Lord's tender care and pitying love in sending me this help *just when* he knew I should most sorely need it. By the late post that night came my quarterly account for books, and so heavy was it, that in fear and haste I turned to my ledger to see the available balance, and with an emotion I shall not easily forget, I found that, but for the gift of £100 a few hours previously, I should have been £60 in debt!

Did not the Father's care thus keep the sparrow from falling to the ground? A sleepless night, and much distress of spirit, would have resulted from my discovery of so serious a deficit in my funds; but the Lord's watchful love prevented this. "Before I called He answered," and though trouble was not very distant, He had said, "It shall not come nigh thee." O my soul, bless thou the Lord, and forget not this His loving "benefit"! A tumult of joy and delight arose within me as I saw in this incident, not a mere chance, or a happy combination of circumstances, but the guiding and sustaining hand of the loving Lord, who had most certainly arranged and ordered for me this pleasant way of comfort and relief. "I am poor and needy; yet the Lord thinketh upon me." A fresh revelation of His wonderful love seemed to be vouchsafed to my soul by this opportune blessing, and a cheque became "an outward and visible sign of an inward and spiritual grace." I hastened to my dear husband that he might share my joy, and I found in him a willing listener to the sweet "old story" of his Master's grace and power. Then, after a word or two of fervent praise to God on my behalf, he wrote the following letter to the friend by whose liberal hand our gracious God had sent this notable deliverance :—

> Dear Friend,—I should like you to know why you were sent here this afternoon, and what an angel of mercy you were to my dear wife, and so to me. The Lord bless you. Soon after you were gone, my wife's quarter's bill for books came in for £340, and she had only £280 apart from your cheque. Poor soul! she has never spent more than her income before; and if you had not come, I fear it would have crushed her to be £60 in debt. How good of the Lord to send you in the nick of time! We joined our praises together, and we do also very gratefully join our prayers for you. God bless you, and make up to you your generous gifts above all your own desires. I could not refrain from telling you this; it is one of the sparkling facts which will make happy memories to help to stay our faith in future trials, if they come. Again, God bless you.
>
> Yours heartily, C. H. SPURGEON.

* * * *

October 11.—£20 from a *new* friend to-day! My heart keeps whispering—

"Indulgent God, how kind!"

At the beginning of this week I had hesitated about sending my usual order for books, having less in hand than would justify a large increase of stock; but I ventured, and lo! the Lord has sent me all I need for present wants, and with it a firm assurance to my soul that "those who trust in Him shall never be ashamed." That £100 a week ago has brought blessings in its train; it has strengthened both heart and hands, and made the work go on with sacred mirth and joyful song. Truly, it is blessed to "wait upon the Lord," and gracious is the condescension with which He listens to our feeblest cry. I was greatly cheered the other day by a few words I read in the late James Hamilton's "Lectures on Prayer." He says:—

> Learn to ask God's blessing on little things as well as great. There is nothing which it is right for us to do, but what it is also right to ask that God would bless it; and, indeed, there is nothing so little but the frown of God can convert it into the most sad calamity, or His smile exalt it into a most memorable mercy; and there is nothing we can do, but its complexion for weal or woe depends entirely on what the Lord will make it.

* * * *

October 15.—Loving, grateful letters have been my daily "Morning Portion" lately, and only my own heart knows how I feast on the encouragement which they give. I so deeply rejoice in the joy of my poor Pastors, that I am sure my happiness must outweigh theirs! Yet sometimes they tell me they have hesitated for months before asking! Verily, they need not; for to place a few valuable works on their empty shelves is a source of inexpressible gladness. What a surprise, too, some of them get! "I thought," writes a good brother this morning, "that I might count upon one, or perhaps two, volumes of 'The Treasury,' and possibly a volume of "Sermons"; but when I opened the parcel and found five volumes of 'The Treasury,' besides the three others, my heart was too full to let me speak." "When the parcel came," says another, "I was in bed, suffering from severe pain in the head; I expected only the fifth volume of 'The Treasury,' but when I saw the many books, and read your kind note, I forgot my pains, and your kindness did what they had failed to do—it brought tears to my eyes. May our heavenly Father answer your prayers as you have replied to my request, by giving you more than you ask, or even think."

* * * *

These are truly "handfuls of purpose" for the dear friends who have given their help to this good work, and it will be hard to stay my hand from giving them :—

My dear Mrs. Spurgeon,—I cannot describe the grateful joy I felt on receiving the post-card yesterday morning, informing me that a parcel of books would be forwarded to my address; and on receipt of the precious parcel itself to-day, I was obliged to shed many grateful tears, "though not to weeping given." I beg, from the very bottom of my heart, to thank you, dear lady, for your great kindness, and shall not forget to pray that the great Head of the church may abundantly reward you for all you have lovingly done, and are doing, to encourage and help so nobly His humble, toiling, and, in some cases, almost broken-hearted servants.

Thus writes another grateful heart :—

Madam, and I must also say, dear Mrs. Spurgeon, and I don't know what to say next! This is far more than ever I hoped for. I received it as coming from my Master and your Master. He has made you the honoured instrument of "refreshing the bowels of the saints." May the

Lord return into your bosom sevenfold, nay, seventy times seven. I think I can say, "there is not another vessel" now,—I am full and abound. As to my wife, why, she is singing, and sweetly too—at least, I think so! We shall never forget this great favour: let the right hand forget its cunning first. We may be favoured to help God's cause some day; if not, God is right, and His ways are just, and His paths drop fatness.

And here I must close for to-day at least, or my gleaners will be weary.

* * * *

Oct. 28.—As part of the proceeds of his last lecture in London, I have the pleasure of receiving to-day £25 as the generous and graceful gift of *Mr. John B. Gough* to the Book Fund. Such a gift from such a man is precious and noteworthy, but not unusual, as I believe it is the constant habit of Mr. Gough to bestow blessings as well as to recommend them. Long as his name has been honoured in our household, and his special work admired and appreciated, it was not till his recent visit to England that we had the happiness of his personal acquaintance. Now he has been twice to see us, and a friendship has been contracted between us which, though interrupted by absence from each other on earth, will find its true fruition and best enjoyment in heaven. The hours we spent in his company have left frequent memories not only of pleasant mirth at the droll tales so inimitably told, but also of sacred joy in sweet and goodly words which "ministered grace unto the hearers." Cannot my friends imagine that it was a rare treat to listen to the converse of *John Ploughman* and *John Gough?*

No "pen of a ready writer" was there to record the good things they said, or to immortalize the brilliant "table talk" which graced each repast; but the sweet communion which knit our hearts together will never be forgotten by us, and so deep a flood of enjoyment came in upon my usually quiet life that day, that it will for ever ripple pleasantly upon the shores of memory. To our very dear friends, Mr. and Mrs. Gough in their far-away home in the West, I send loving greeting; and for this £25, which means so much joy and comfort for the Lord's poor servants, I give the warmest thanks of a grateful heart.

Nov. 1.—Two dear ladies brought me £50 to use in the Lord's work as I please. What bountiful kindness, its preciousness enhanced by my necessity! I divided it between the Book Fund and the Pastors' Aid; for in these times of universal pressure I can scarcely confine my gifts to *books* in those cases where I know that, though the daily bread is sure, it is often unaccompanied by more substantial nourishment. It was only the other day I heard of a minister whose last Christmas dinner was to have consisted of a loaf and steak because he could not afford better fare; and I know many whose most creditable fear of debt compels them not only to keep their book-shelves empty, but the cupboard very bare. One ceases to wonder at the oft-recurring sickness of many ministers' wives, and the extreme delicacy of their children, when one remembers their many privations, their lack of nourishing food, and their need of suitable clothing. " My income barely enables me to find plain food and scanty clothing for my wife and three children," writes a country Independent pastor. " Frequently I have saved a few shillings with the view of purchasing a volume of 'The Treasury,' but a pair of shoes or a little dress put the book aside." In this last matter of clothing for Pastors' families there is very much now being done by kind friends for their relief. I have elsewhere mentioned the many presents I received for them, and to-day (mercies never come singly) a large chest arrived from Scotland containing the wardrobes of two deceased gentlemen, sent by the desolate wife and mother. It has been a somewhat sad work to allot this valuable gift to seven needy Pastors; but their joy in receiving the good warm clothes will not be damped by any sorrowful remembrances of departed friends, and I rejoice beforehand in their joy.

* * * *

Nov. 20.—News comes from Africa of the death of Mrs. Johnson, one of the dear souls who sang so sweetly to us before leaving for missionary work there, and who joined in sending the message to me—" keep inching along." She is now singing the new song, and has full realization of the blessedness of being "for ever with the Lord." Stricken by the fatal fever, she has laid down her life in the land of her fathers, without having had time to tell the "sweet story of old" to those for whose sake she bravely dared danger and death. We weep not for her; Jesus has come and taken her to Himself, and her bliss is perfect; but the desolate heart of her husband claims our sympathy and fervent prayers. Encompassed by danger, exposed to scorching heat by day and deadly damps by night, weakened by fever and sorely cast down by the loss of his dearest earthly companion, our poor brother surely needs that we should "speak for him to the King" now in the time of his need and overwhelming distress. One feels that a return message of sympathy to him could scarcely bear a fitter termination than the words which came over the sea to me :—

> "Keep inching along, keep inching along,
> Jesus Christ 'll come by-and-by."

* * * *

December 1.—"Keeping watch at home alone." So says my dear husband in this month's *Sword and Trowel* tenderly referring to the loneliness which our enforced separation entails upon me. The pitying words set me thinking, and praying that I might be enabled bravely to fulfil the duty assigned to me. A "watcher" should be vigorous, vigilant, fearless, and faithful. May the Lord confer these virtues on me, strengthening me for the work which devolves on me now the Captain is away, and teaching me, in my weakness, to lean more heavily than ever on the arm of the Beloved. My little Book does not gather much material for record just now, for the days are so filled up with work that no time seems left to jot down quietly any notes of it.

The Pastor's usual mass of correspondence dwindles most remarkably as soon as his absence from home is fully recognized, but there still remains enough to employ all my time and energy when added to the regular and constant work of the Book Fund. The latter has greatly increased during the past week or two, so that I have had to redouble my efforts to keep pace with the demands on my time and attention, and the close of the day has found me too tired to tell of its varied experiences and duties.

Some days later.—"Keeping watch" now for news from a suffering husband, whose pleasant rest in the sunny south is turned into the sorrowful weariness of a sick bed. All the sweet, gladsome letters which told such charming news of lovely weather, blooming roses, "sea-birds sitting on the waters, forming rings, as if they were 'knights of the round table,' and, as the waves gently ripple, rising and falling like little boats"; and of happy work, done amidst such glorious surroundings that "it seemed like play,"—all this, and oh! so much more that was beautiful, exchanged for brief, sad telegrams, which seem to crush one's heart with fear lest the short, unsatisfying message should conceal more sorrow than it dare reveal. Now, "patience must have her perfect work," and comfort comes with the certainty that the Great Physician is there, and will sustain and sanctify, and in due time heal His suffering servant. From hundreds of hearts the cry has already gone up, "Lord, he whom Thou lovest is sick!" May we soon have an answer of peace!

Still later.—Blessed be God! Better news comes now! The telegrams have ceased, and letters written with unsteady pen by poor pained hands, yet inexpressibly precious, have arrived. In this trying time hard work has been a benefactor to me, for the urgency of the daily correspondence admits of no comfortable nursing of grief, and Book Fund management knows no cessation while the Lord sends so many needy applicants. Many sweet letters of sympathy come also and comfort my heart, and the one I here transcribe reached me at so opportune a moment that it was truly like "an apple of gold in a basket of silver":—

My dear Mrs. Spurgeon,—On three occasions you have sent me a fine parcel of books, and I have written some poor thanks as they have arrived. Now I write again, just to testify to the help they are to me every day. I am almost afraid to write to you, lest you should offer me some more ; *but please do not* do so just now, for I should be afraid to write you again if you did. My dear Mrs. Spurgeon, I so often thank God for the books and for you, and sincerely do I pray that you may be daily helped and strengthened. I have been thinking of you so much "*all alone*," now that the beloved President is away, and especially since last week's sermon arrived, with the sad news of his illness. God help him and comfort you too. I trust you will still be blessed and strengthened in this good work of yours, and at least that it will encourage you to hear that your books are a daily blessing in my study.

✢ ✢ ✢ ✢

The Pastors' Aid Fund

is a branch of the main business, which has naturally developed itself as the work prospered, and some dear friends keep a very warm corner of their hearts, and a very liberal allowance in their purse for it. For this I thank God, and thank them; for sometimes there are cases in which the gift of books would be but a cruel mockery if unaccompanied by other help, rarely asked; but how sorely needed, God and themselves only know. So much has been said on this matter, incidentally, in these pages, that I need dwell no longer on the painful fact of the minister's poverty, but simply tell how far I have been able to relieve it. This year £324 2s. has been distributed in *money* to Pastors in urgent need of pecuniary assistance; and I rejoice to know that these gifts have often blessed the givers as well as the recipients. Nearly all the friends who entrust me with funds for this special purpose receive private information of the allotment of their gifts, and into the suffering life of one dear donor this blessed work of mercy often brings a ray of sacred gladness and joy. In all cases I earnestly seek wisdom to use rightly the great privilege thus accorded to me, and I by no means underrate the responsibility which it entails. Full details of this part of my work are withheld from these pages from motives of tender consideration for the feelings of the recipients; but I must again express my unbounded gratitude to all who during this and previous years have placed so tender a trust in my hands, enabling me to cheer so many hearts, and gladden so many homes. The simple but eloquent words of a letter now lying before me describe the usual happy effect of a gift from this secret store: "You have sent a wave of joy into my house to-day, which will carry me over many desponding moments in the days to come."

✢ ✢ ✢ ✢

Coming now to the conclusion of these sadly irregular chronicles, I should like to promise—if the Lord spare my life, and prosper the Book Fund—to do better next year. The "happy thought," if it be a *happy* one, of reporting this little service in "diary-fashion" ought to be more satisfactorily carried out, and I hope to gather more discreetly and carefully the material to be used at the close of the year 1880. Experience has taught me that there is sure to be a fulness of goodness and mercy to supply the record; but the same teacher sadly proves to me that the "recorder" fails, and is at fault in not keeping her "book of remembrance" well posted up. But what memory can keep pace with God's mercies? or what uninspired pen can tell the thousandth part of His loving-kindnesses? "If I should count them, they are more in number than the sand." Could I cull the choicest flowers of language, and bind them in one delightful bundle of thankfulness, it might be an acceptable offering of gratitude to the dear friends who have helped me; but how can I worthily praise and extol the bounty of my gracious, loving God? "Thou hast dealt well with Thy servant, O Lord, according to Thy word." Blessed be Thy name, Thou hast daily loaded me with benefits; Thy hand has supplied all my need; Thy strength has been made perfect in my weakness. Thy loving care has watched over my work, and "there hath not failed one word of all Thy good promise" "upon which Thou hast caused me to hope." And what can I say more unto Thee? "Is this the manner of man, O Lord God?" Oh! poor dumb lips, that cannot speak His praise aright! Oh, faltering tongue, that as yet cannot "frame to pronounce" the syllables of heaven's own language!

> "How shall I praise Him? Seraphs, when they bring
> The homage of their lyre,
> Veil their bright face beneath their wing,
> And tremble and retire.
>
> Lost in thy love, yet full of humble trust,
> I close my worthless lay,
> Bow down the reverent forehead in the dust,
> And in meek silence pray."

Truly there are times when silence is more eloquent than speech, and we are constrained to worship "afar off," from very awe of His goodness. Such a season comes to me now as I sit pondering over all the Lord's marvellous loving-kindness. Looking back on the great and manifold mercies of the fast closing year, my spirit is overwhelmed within me, the weight of blessing seems almost too much for me; and I lay aside my poor, useless pen to bow the knee before Him in silent adoration and thanksgiving.

"I am not worthy of the least of all the mercies, and of all the truth which Thou hast showed unto Thy servant."

SUMMARY OF WORK.

Books Distributed during the Year 1879 :—8,045 Volumes.

Also 6,941 single Sermons for giving away. The recipients comprised 286 Baptists, 180 Independents, 358 Methodists, 88 Church of England clergymen, 49 Missionaries, 71 Evangelists, and 12 Presbyterians.

The Book Fund Diary

For 1880.

By Mrs. C. H. Spurgeon.

BEFORE the proof-sheets of the Report for 1879 are finally corrected and sent to press, I commence the record of the Lord's mercy in the New Year, 1880, and tune my lips to praise Him for "all the grace I have not tasted yet." May He help me to make this a faithful memorial of His goodness and guidance during the year,—if He spare me so long,—teaching me to reflect His love as the dewdrop does the sunshine, or as the mote which turns to diamond dust in the glory of a sunbeam.

The retrospect of His lovingkindness which engaged my thoughts as the old year died, filled my heart with admiring love and gratitude, and the consideration of the future is assuredly not less calculated to draw forth the tenderest feelings of confidence and loving trust. The God who has dealt so graciously with me in the past will not fail me in the time to come.

> "Man's plea to man is, that he never more
> Will beg, and that he never begged before ;
> Man's plea to God is, that he did obtain
> A former suit, and therefore sues again.
> How good a God we serve, that, when we sue,
> Makes His old gifts the examples of His new !"

✻　　✻　　✻　　✻

January 5.—It is to be hoped that for many the New Year will open with pleasant prospects of increased prosperity and comfort; but, alas! to some of my poor Pastors no bow of promise is visible; for dark clouds of distressful providences shut out any hopeful vision of a brighter horizon. I had a letter to-day from a country Pastor which greatly engaged my sympathy, and would have saddened my heart, only that the Lord enabled me to lighten his burden. Needing a certain book to complete a set, he says: "I would not ask you, only that I am utterly unable to purchase,—the prevailing agricultural distress makes itself felt in the minister's house. At midsummer I had to receive £5 less than last year, in the autumn the same thing was repeated, and £10 makes a big hole in the salary of a village pastor; the Christmas quarter I have not yet received, and I fear it is so little that the deacon does not like to give it to me; just add to this that another little mouth has been sent for us to feed, so that we have now five children, and you will see that we have plenty of room for faith and patience, but little to spare for books."

I do not find that, as a rule, these poor churches lack *spiritual* blessing. Where real poverty exists among the members, and the utmost they can give is yet insufficient for their Pastor's proper maintenance, there the Lord often makes the riches of His spiritual kingdom to abound and increase, and only to those who "withhold that which is meet" does He send the soul-famine which saps the life of many a seemingly prosperous "Zion." The Pastor, whose letter I have just quoted, adds to his sad story of need these significant words, "The word is blessed of the Lord to the saving of sinners, and the comforting of His saints." Only just lately I heard of a church, where the services are well attended, the work of conversion is going on, and everything is prospering spiritually, where yet the cause is brought to so low an ebb from the universal financial distress, that they have to dismiss their minister from sheer inability to provide him with the bare necessities of life! Oh! for a "Sustentation Fund," like that so splendidly worked by the Free Church of Scotland! Would to God that my poor little Pastors' Aid Society might one day grow to be such a "goodly cedar," and send forth equally glorious branches of comfort and protection for our ministers.

* * * *

January 12.—Last year I wrote rather doubtfully about the monthly distribution of *The Sword and the Trowel* magazine to poor Pastors. I felt disinclined to give much attention to this branch of the work, lest the more important part of book-giving should suffer, and I think I was also physically unable to undertake even the smallest additional enterprise. At the close of the year, however, the letters of acknowledgment bore such abundant testimony to the value set upon the gift, and the blessing it brought to the homes thus visited, that I am encouraged to persevere in the work, and, beginning the year with thirty-seven names, I hope soon to raise the number to fifty. Should it please the Lord to grant me the blessing of improved health, I may see possibilities of service for Him, which till now have been hidden from my eyes by the thick mists of pain and suffering. It makes all the difference to the charm and distinctness of a prospect, whether you look at it through a window-pane blurred with rain-drops, or see it by the cloudless sunshine of a summer's day!

In giving a few extracts from the letters of recipients of this monthly gift, I hope especially to interest those kind friends who first proposed the scheme, and have constantly enabled me to carry it out. A Baptist brother writes from the "Black Country":—

It has pleased God to give me many a blessing during the past year, but amongst those I have been able to turn to the largest account are the twelve magazines you have so kindly placed in my hands. Many of the articles have been read at our Monday-evening prayer-meetings, and after having been well perused at home, they are circulated among the "Black Country" men, and have done much good.

And another poor pastor thus expresses himself :—

I write to thank you for sending me *The Sword and the Trowel* during the past two years, and to ask you to continue to do so; for only those who, like myself, are in isolated spheres of labour, and receiving small stipends, can fully understand what a boon it is to have such an excellent magazine supplied gratuitously, especially when one's stock of books is small, and there are no means of adding to it. I assure you I look forward with the greatest delight to the first of the month, and if the magazine has not arrived, there is an extra prayer sent up for you, lest the delay has been occasioned by your more serious illness.

I have quite a nice bundle of these thanksgiving letters this time, the two I have chosen being fair specimens of the rest. All the dear brethren say the same thing, only in different words; the "melody" of true gratitude runs through all the "variations" of sincere acknowledgment. One says the contents of the magazine have been a "source of comfort" to him, another gladly confesses that he has been much "encouraged, cheered, and helped" by its perusal, a third has found it very "refreshing" to his soul, while a fourth "cannot tell me fully what joy and gladness" it has brought to his heart. This ought surely to be sufficient to rekindle our interest in the work, and I shall take these many letters as a sign from the Lord that I am to "go forward" in this special department of His service.

When I provide standard works of Divinity for the Pastors' shelves, I feel I introduce to him life-long friends who will never leave him, friends to whom he can turn for counsel, comfort, and encouragement at all times, and whose sweet companionship will only cease at heaven's gate; but a magazine is a "wayfaring man that turneth aside to tarry for a night," a very pleasant and acceptable visitor, bringing with him the healthful breezes of fresh religious information, giving impulse and quickening to the spiritual life of his entertainers, and leaving an unmistakable blessing behind him in return for the welcome so warmly accorded.

* * * *

January 15.—With a delicacy and tender grace which have deeply touched my heart, some of my dear friends have to-day sent "birthday gifts" FOR MY BOOK FUND. Nothing could have pleased me half so well; each token of loving remembrance is more precious to me than rubies, and skilful fingers have struck so loud a note of grateful praise in my soul, that for many months to come the pleasant melody will ring joyfully through my daily life. Many beautiful birthday cards have come bearing good and kind wishes; but the loveliest of them all was a Bank of England note so cunningly enclosed in the most transparent of tissues that the charming device of a large £5 in the accustomed corner was made the veiled emblem of the donor's loving congratulations to me, and his deep interest in my beloved work! To all those dear friends whose sympathy and help have been so tenderly blended to-day, I give the warmest thanks of my heart, and I know they will like to remember that their sweet gifts, after having so richly blessed my own soul, shall continue to spread gladness and joy in homes and hearts less favoured and less abundantly filled than mine.

* * * *

February 1.—Very grateful acknowledgments have been received from the Pastors in Jamaica, to many of whom I sent books last year. They call them "*precious treasures*," "*priceless boons*," and then delightedly assure me that the Lord's blessing has accompanied them, and will make them fruitful to His glory.

Taking up *The Baptist Magazine* to-day, I came quite unexpectedly upon a letter written by one of our missionaries, to whom, when a pastor in England, I had more than once sent a gift of books. It was like meeting and saluting an old friend, and, reading on with much interest his account of the joy and delight with which books, illustrated papers, magazines, etc., are received by the churches and schools over which he presides, I was greatly affected to find myself referred to as the donor of some volumes to native converts in the Bahamas! I had forgotten the circumstance; but this good missionary says—"A book sent from England is of the very highest service to me in my work here, more particularly if it has the name of the donor in it. It is a sight to see, and a joy to hear one of the brethren say, '*De lady ob de great Massa Spurgem gib me dis book tro' de Siety!*'" Poor fellows! How glad I am to have rejoiced their hearts, and how much I wish I had sent them more! For one can never tell how great a blessing may be enfolded in a sheet or two of printed paper, or what possibilities of spiritual conviction or comfort may lie in the pages of a single tract. I feel both humbled and encouraged by this "finding after many days" of the bread which I had long ago cast upon the waters,—humbled, because if all the opportunities of service which have presented themselves had been seized and used, the reward would have been infinitely greater,—but encouraged, by God's tender mercy in accepting and blessing the very little effort which yet was made in His name, and for His sake!

Oh that this year the Lord would "enlarge my coasts," not only in extending my work, and strengthening me for its labour, but by expanding my sympathies and teaching me the heavenly art of tender and successful ministry, so that the gifts of the Book Fund, scattered far and wide, may be "swift messengers, hastened by the King's commandment, to carry light and gladness, and joy and thanksgiving" into the hearts and homes of His anxious, weary servants.

* * * *

February 4.—Without unduly lifting the veil of kindly privacy which usually overhangs the loving gifts of the Pastors' Aid Fund, I shall now and then give my readers a glimpse into the inner sanctuary of a poor pastor's home, and let them ponder over some scenes which can scarcely fail to move their hearts to pity, and their hands to help. This morning a letter came to hand which tells its story of thankfulness very simply and sweetly, and so much has it refreshed and cheered my spirit, that I put it on record for future incentive and encouragement. Money, books, and clothing were sent to the good brother, for *all these* were most urgently needed, and I had received due acknowledgment of the gift when, to my surprise, this second letter came, and I take it as evidently the irrepressible overflow of a heart full of abundant satisfaction and joy. He says :—

A sense of gratitude compels me to send you these few more lines, to tell you not only of the good I have myself derived, but of the marked beneficial effect your great kindness has had upon my wife. The books you sent me have already greatly blessed me, and I assure you I have worked hard at them, and feel all the stronger for the work. Your dear husband's sermons, and the works of Hodge and De Pressensé, are gifts which, by God's blessing, cannot fail to benefit both myself and my people. But I wish more particularly to tell you how your kindness has affected my wife. Feeling a little anxious about the expected addition to our family, she is at times inclined to be sad ; but ever since your loving gifts came she has brightened up, and we have enjoyed the happiest, sunniest hours that we have known for a long time. Her feelings of delight on opening the parcel, and seeing the books and the garments, I will not venture to describe ; but when we found all this kindness crowned by the contents of the envelope, we could only ask the Lord to bless you very richly. After my day's work I feel constrained to tell you again of our joy, and you will please regard this note as an effort at expression by a heart overwhelmed with gratitude.

Dear souls! I know they feel far more than they can put into words, and that sometimes the very depth of their thankfulness restrains the overflow of speech. I bless God that there is an unwritten language of bowed knees, and happy tears, and glad sighs of relief from a burdened heart, which He well understands, and loves to listen to! How often have I found it far easier to thank Him, the Great Giver, than the dear human friends who are the dispensers of His gifts! one has to search out "goodly words" for their ears, and mould and modulate the sentences which convey our acknowledgments to them; but an upward glancing of the eye, or a tightening of the clasped hands, tells the whole tale to our tender Lord as fitly and as truly as though we poured forth torrents of eloquent thanksgivings.

* * * *

February 27.—Most of my readers and friends know that the first volume of "Lectures to my Students" was the seed-germ from which the Book Fund sprang into existence. I well remember with what entranced delight I read it, and entered more fully than ever, through its perusal, into all the joys and sorrows, the trials and triumphs, the inward sighings and the outward rejoicings, of a minister's life. I thought every man must be a better man, and ever preacher a better preacher, if he read it, and that thought grew till it developed into a scheme for supplying all the poor ministers in the land with books. Now, I wish to record the fact, that though the Book Fund has grandly outgrown its first proportions, and blessedly outstripped even my sanguine expectations in its extended prosperity, it still retains its loving allegiance to the little book which fostered it, and gives it always a deservedly prominent place in all its distributions.

Some thousands of "Lectures to my Students," both first and second series, have been scattered over the land; but there seems to be an ever fresh demand for them, and they never leave me without a prayer that God's blessing may rest upon them. Nor is this prayer presented in vain. "The reading of these books," says a young curate, "has been a profitable pleasure. I have been made aware of the rocks which lie in the course of successful preaching, some of which I can see I have sailed very near to, but which in the future I shall try to steer clear away from!" The benefit which young clergymen of the Church of England must derive from the perusal of such addresses is incalculable, and I never lose an opportunity of introducing the "Lectures" to their notice and favour. On every hand, and by all sects, the wise advice and sterling counsels they contain are appreciated, and the wholesome denunciation of errors and evils of every sort is not only endured but applauded. "How Mr. Spurgeon does show up our bad habits!" wrote a newly-ordained curate the other day, "he makes them seem so ludicrous, that I, for one, mean to try and abandon them." Nor less does the sweet persuasive earnestness of the writer fail to draw men's hearts to a solemn consideration of the sacred duties and responsibilities of the ministry. "I have just read Lecture No. 3, on the 'Preacher's Private Prayer,'" says a Wesleyan minister, "with much interest, and, I trust, with profit to my soul; indeed, I have been so *rebuked* yet *refreshed*, that I anticipate lasting benefit as the result of perusing the two volumes so kindly sent."

* * * *

March 8.—These last few days my sympathies have been vigorously stirred by the discovery of some very distressing cases of privation and poverty among our Baptist village Pastors. I select three of these to lay before my readers, and while I put the pitiful facts in due order, I would ask them to note the ascending degrees in the measure of misery.

No. I. is a hard-working, painstaking pastor, preaching five times a week, holding large Bible-classes, visiting, itinerating, and in every way doing his best for the people of his charge; he is married, has three children, and accepts and manages to exist upon a meagre pittance of £65 per annum, supplemented by a New Year's gift, which usually comes to about £10 or £12. He writes quite jubilantly, because this year this said gift reached the magnificent sum of £14! while he knows all too well, poor fellow! that insurance dues and doctors' bills will much more than consume this little offering. How is this good brother to obey the divine injunction, "Owe no man anything"? "He has no right to get into debt." No, certainly not; but should *we* be able to steer clear of such an evil, if £79 had to pay for everything we needed for ourselves and families for the next twelve months?

No. II. is in still sadder plight. For twenty years his salary as a village pastor has never exceeded £60 per annum, and, to use his own words, "*it has often been ten and sometimes fifteen pounds below that sum;*" this, with a wife afflicted for thirty years with complicated internal maladies, seeking aid from many physicians, and being "nothing bettered, but rather the worse," added to other domestic trials, and many deaths in the family, is enough, one would think, to crush all the preaching out of a man! "Few," he says, "save our heavenly Father, know the privations and struggles which we have endured these twenty years!" To a man so burdened with crosses and cares, the assistance of books seems indispensable; yet, till the Fund supplied his necessities, such precious helps were as far out of his reach as are the stars, and though they would have brought him light in darkness, food in famine, and almost life in death, he had to long and languish for them in vain. How could *books* be purchased when daily *bread*, though "sure," had to be sorely striven for?

No. III. stands apart upon a pinnacle of special and exceptional sadness. It is a *climax* of distressing circumstances, and, *I hope*, a unique instance of unusual need, combined with most painful indigence, among those whose names are enrolled as Baptist Pastors in our land. From a letter written at my request by the wife of the poor brother referred to, I glean the following particulars. The husband is weak and ill from the lingering effects of a bronchial attack which prostrated him two years since, a young child is in a delicate and critical condition, the wife, though in fast-failing health, has just become the mother of their *twelfth* child, all living save one, and *the last five are under five years of age!* Their income, from all sources—salary, small business, and gifts from friends included, never exceeds—will my friends believe it when I write it?—the pitiful, paltry sum of FIFTY-FIVE *pounds* a year! Can respectable poverty know a deeper depth than this? When I persuaded the poor patient wife to unburden her sorrows to me, she concluded her account with these words, "My poor heart is surcharged with grief; while I write these lines I can scarcely see for tears, yet the Lord knows what is best for us, and will lead us in the right way."

I confess I should have been ashamed to record this case, ashamed of my own comfortable and delightful surroundings, if I had not dried those tears, and lifted, at least, some part of the heavy burden which crushed this poor weary woman's heart! Blessed be the Lord, who so graciously entrusts me with means to this end, and constantly replenishes the treasury from whence I draw help and succour for His needy ones.

* * * *

March 14.—He gives this replenishing sometimes in a very remarkable and marvellous manner, and sets our souls a-wondering at the condescension which leads Him to such distinct detail of fatherly love and care. A notable instance has just occurred, and I ask my friends to listen to this sweet story of a "new" mercy, fresh from His tender hand. One of "our own" men, who has long been ailing, has at last been obliged to resign his charge, not alone on account of feeble health, but also because his people are utterly unable to keep their pastor in the common necessaries of life. "You must go to Australia," said one doctor after another; "it is your only chance for life!" But what was to be done with the dear but very sickly wife and the three mites of children?

Long they pondered ways and means, and the conclusion they arrived at was a hard one for loving human hearts, and cost them many a struggle—the poor wife consented to remain in England, working at her needle for a subsistence for herself and babes, while her husband sought in a far-off land the strength to labour for means which should reunite them.

At this juncture she wrote to me, acquainting me with the above arrangements, and there were certain facts in her communication which led me to desire intensely to overturn these present plans of theirs, and secure the emigration of the entire family. But how was this to be accomplished? The expense is great to convey so many to the Utopia of feeble folk, and the funds of the " Pastors' Aid " could not be made available for such heavy and unusual charges. I wrote again, suggesting and enquiring, and, meanwhile, the Lord sent me quite unexpectedly a sum of money which I could do no less than consecrate to Him for this matter. With even this, however, there was still a deficit of some sixteen pounds in the amount needed, and now it was that the wonderfully tender dealing of our God became so manifest. *The very morning* on which I received a rapturous agreement to my proposal that the whole family should go out, and the good news that the passage could be effected under exceptionally cheap rates, my dear husband came joyfully into my room, exclaiming, " Here's the rest of the money to take your protégés to Australia!" and to my amazed delight he explained that, on opening his morning's letters he found £15 as a personal gift to himself from an unknown correspondent, and forthwith felt that it was sent from the Lord for this very purpose about which our minds had been so exercised and anxious. Those notes seemed to come straight from heaven's mint into our uplifted hands, and the morning's hours were hallowed by a sweet sense of the nearness of an invisible and watchful love.

Nor did the Lord's thought for these poor exiles exhaust itself in this sole benefit ; for I afterwards received a parcel of new clothing from a gentleman, *a stranger*, containing the *very articles* which were needed to complete the outfit of the husband, and I was enabled to obtain all that was requisite for the comfort of mother and children. What joy to see the hand of the Lord sustaining, directing, and providing in so blessed and unmistakable a manner! Can eyes which have seen so clearly the goodness and lovingkindness of our God ever be obscured by the wicked mists of distrust and doubt?

* * * *

March 26.—This sweet Easter season has brought fresh blessings to my beloved work. Funds have flowed in freely to the Lord's treasury, and a spring-tide of gladness has filled my heart; for loving gifts and welcome offerings, like the buds and flowers, are appearing on every side. My Scotch friend has again sent the soft woollen shawls which are so prized as winter comforts; and a large quantity of *very good*, scarcely worn, garments have been forwarded from donors who, I presume, wish to be unknown, seeing that they entrust me only with the knowledge that their welcome present comes from "Meg and Singapore." But *the* "Easter gift," *par excellence*, must be more minutely described, though, even then, I shall fail to do justice to the pleasant fact. A generous friend, who has lovingly helped the Book Fund since its commencement, wrote thus the other day:—"I intend to send you an Easter offering *in kind*, of paper and envelopes for your work; for well I know the blessed use to which it will be applied." And to-day I have received the splendid and appropriate present, which almost overwhelms me by its magnitude. *Six reams* of pretty note paper, two sizes, with their proper complement of envelopes to match, and all charmingly stamped with initials and address! Is not this a gift to be pleased with and thankful for? There was no little excitement in my small sanctum when this grand present was unpacked. It was so magnificent in its proportions that, when released from its packing-case, it covered table, chairs, and sofa in the tiny room, and the question, "Where shall I put it all?" became a serious consideration to the happy possessor. Loving hands were busily engaged in opening the precious parcels, and delighted eyes were admiring the dainty quires as they lay so cosily in their boxes, when the sweetest voice in all the world—to me—said tenderly, "May you live to use it all, dear wife!" The owner of said voice has been as diligent and interested as the other folks in the room, inspecting, commending, and arranging; and very heartily did he join us all in praising the generous donor's thoughtfulness and liberality. I wish my kind friend could have been present to see the joy he had given, and the great delight his gift had conferred; but the Lord will find for him a better reward than that, and will return to him blessing for blessing, a hundredfold harvest of recompense for his many kindnesses to needy Pastors, and the consecration of his substance to many a sacred service.

* * * *

April 6.—A letter from Canada recently received must find permanent record here, as a sweet and touching expression of the love which the "old students" bear to their dear President, a love which, in the majority of cases, is "faithful unto death." This brother has been for many years a pastor in Canada, and in acknowledging a gift from the Book Fund, he thus declares the attachment which time and distance have not lessened:—

My dear Mrs. Spurgeon,—Brother A— arrived in due time, but not for some weeks did I receive the parcel of books you sent by him. . . . But now that they are here, and revelled in—put into their place in the bookcase, only to be taken down and admired afresh, and put back again—what can I say to *you*? If I did not feel and appreciate your generosity as I do, I could spin out words to any length by way of formal thanks; but as it stands I cannot. Down deep in one of the warmest corners of my heart, I have enshrined you, and in that sanctuary you will ever remain. May the love which prompted the gift, and took such pains in forwarding it, be rewarded by Him whose richest benediction I entreat for you. I need not say how the volumes will be prized and valued for their intrinsic merit, the inspiration they will supply, the food they will give to mind and heart, and also for the sake of the author, whose dear and beloved form I see outlined before my mind's eye every day, and whose ringing voice I fancy I can hear across the three thousand miles of ocean! God grant that I may be able to catch more and more of that high-souled, consecrated enthusiasm which breathes through his writings like the fresh breeze of morning! *You* will pardon the pride I feel in showing my friends the row of works by my dear President which I now possess; for with "The Treasury of David," "The Lectures to Students," and an *almost* complete set of "Sermons," I have an exhibition sufficient to make an old student clap his hands with delight. The single Sermons have been put into wrappers, and are now being circulated through the town. May they bear fruit abundantly! Please catch the ear of your beloved husband, *my* President, just for a moment, to whisper into it the unabated, the *increasing* love of one who can never repay him for his kindness. And now may the good Lord sustain and comfort you in your affliction and retirement, and in your chamber of pain, in the "dark and cloudy day," may "one like unto the Son of man" ever be near you. So prays your deeply grateful

———.

* * * *

April 24.—Yesterday saw the close of the Sixteenth Annual Conference of the Pastors' College, and the verdict of all who have taken part in its services is unanimous that it has exceeded in glory and blessing all former occasions of happy congress. Every day brought fresh token of heavenly favour, and "power from on high" rested on all the holy engagements and deliberations; but at the farewell communion the zenith of joy was attained, and one then present told me it was as if "Jesus himself stood in the midst of them, and said, Peace be unto you." Rapture unspeakable filled all hearts, while they "held him by the feet and worshipped Him."

My hand cannot record the sacred solemnities of this blessed season, for only in spirit could I join their assembly, or unite my heart and voice with theirs; yet many crumbs of the holy banquet have been brought to my table, and the echoes of their triumphant songs have reached my listening ears. Nay, more than this has been granted to me; for after watching all the week long for stray flowers or fruits from their abundance, I feasted last evening to the full on some of the same heavenly food, and even gathered up the fragments that remained in a basket of my very own. And thus it happened. At the conclusion of yesterday's services, some fifteen or sixteen of the brethren came to our dear home to spend the evening with us, and I felt as though I were entertaining the "wedding guests" who had been to the "supper of the great King." A gracious anointing still rested on them, the Lord had been "the light of their countenance" whilst they waited on Him, and the "afterglow" from the "Sun of Righteousness" still shone on every feature. Passing in review the sayings and doings of the last five eventful days, they magnified the name of the Lord for His goodness, and then they sang such heavenly music that I almost thought the angels would care to listen. Our souls were carried to the very gates of heaven, on the wings of these celestial songs, and a foretaste of the joy therein awaiting us was vouchsafed as we joined in the glorious chorus of praise to our dear Lord and Saviour. How precious these "drinks of the brook by the way" are to *me* no tongue can tell; but the Lord's tender love in providing such spiritual refreshment must not pass without grateful acknowledgment and blessing.

The Book Fund's memorial present this year to the assembled Pastors is a little volume entitled "The Glories of Christ," rich in suggestion, and teeming with hints, "which," says the reviewer in *The Sword and the Trowel*, "will many of them be of great value to preachers who need to be started on a train of thought." May God bless the little gift, and make it all the help I mean it to be to the dear brethren who will use it; and when it sheds a new light on some difficult passage of Scripture, or brings out some long-forgotten accord and harmony of texts, then may it also sweetly bring to remembrance the holy and happy days of the Conference of 1880.

* * * *

April 26.—I find that many poor ministers have long hesitated to apply to me for a grant of books, presuming that the gifts must certainly be limited to brethren of the Baptist denomination, and almost refusing to believe the good news that all needy Pastors of churches—in actual charge—are welcome to the proffered help and comfort. None are excluded who preach the gospel of Christ in truth and sincerity. This unsectarian character of my work affords me constant satisfaction and pleasure, and the delight I feel while furnishing the bare bookshelves in a poor Baptist pastor's little room is increased rather than lessened when I am permitted to place "The Treasury of David" or some volumes of "Sermons" on the study table of an ill-paid curate of the Church of England.

A day or two since, the good Earl of Shaftesbury paid us a visit, and on leaving he said to me, "Well, how does the Baptist book-giving prosper?" "Thank you, my lord," I replied, "the Book Fund prospers grandly, all the more that it is *not a Baptist* book-giving, but is free to all the Lord's ministering servants." If the venerable Earl could have seen my "day-book" he would have found full confirmation of this assertion, for, glancing down the long columns of recipients' names, one cannot but be struck with the constant repetition of the distinguishing titles of "Church," "Congregational," "Presbyterian," "Methodist," etc., and the comparatively infrequent recurrence of the word "Baptist" in the list. Thus, in these first four months of the year, I have already on my books the names of nearly four hundred ministers, who during that period have received grants from my Fund, and of this number just *one-fourth* are "mine own people." I am delighted to see that the longer record bears the names of fifty Church of England clergymen, and I believe I am justified in anticipating glorious results from the distribution among them of sound and scriptural doctrine. And if in some cases appreciation should lead to *appropriation*, and from many a stately pulpit in the land the gospel should sound forth full and free through the sermons first delivered in the Metropolitan Tabernacle, shall aught but joy and thankfulness fill our hearts? "I confess," wrote a vicar to me, "that though I do not preach your husband's sermons '*bodily*,' I yet so assimilate them into my own discourses that they are of the utmost value and blessing to me."

A growing desire is manifested by ministers of all sections of the church of Christ to acquaint themselves with the utterances of one whose words have been so greatly blessed to the conversion of sinners and the comforting of saints; and I have constantly found that a gift of *one* volume of "Sermons" has created such a *relish* for the "savoury meat," that in a short time I have been solicited to help in procuring more, even though the slenderly filled purse could ill afford any outlay. In such instances the Book Fund glories in its blessed service, and triumphantly spreading the rich feast before the longing soul, is inexpressibly thankful to be thus used of God in accomplishing His loving purpose of "filling the hungry with good things."

* * * *

May 3.—A legacy of £200 left to the Book Fund by an old and much-loved friend becomes null and void in consequence of legal inaccuracies in the will; and thus, though the dear deceased's tender remembrance of me is inalienable, I lose the splendid help to my beloved work which she intended should partly alleviate my grief at her departure, and in some measure compensate for the cessation of her constant loving aid.

I try to bear my disappointment bravely, and sink my own sorrow in sympathy with the President in the far heavier loss sustained in like manner by the Pastors' College; and though I felt at first to some extent "bowed down" by the unexpected failure of my promised good fortune, I am since upholden and comforted exceedingly; for I know that "the Lord is able to give me much more than this," and this puts all thought of murmuring from me, and enables me to look up again from human help to that infinitely more certain portion with which the Lord supplies all my need as it arises. Perhaps I needed such a lesson, and shall do well to learn it off "by heart." It is quite possible that I felt too elated on hearing of the generous bequest, and counted up my riches with somewhat of carnal pride mingling with the gratification which was allowable; certain it is that I once reckoned upon a grand total at the end of the year quite eclipsing all former amounts, and it may be that the Lord saw this was not good for me, and that the reception of too much "treasure laid up on earth" would have disturbed and imperilled that lowly posture of constant dependence on my God which He has taught me to delight in, and has so graciously honoured and rewarded. I think, also, I may learn from this untoward event to bless and praise Him more humbly and heartily for His grand and immutable "Will"! and that "His ways are not our ways"!

Such a painful experience of the instability of earth's fairest promises intensifies our joy and confidence in that covenant which is "ordered in all things and sure." No flaw, no legal error, no misplaced or missing word shall invalidate that glorious testament by which we are made "heirs of God, and joint-heirs with Jesus Christ." Never can our interest in that solemn "Will" be debated or denied —our legacy of pardon and peace here, our estate of perfect and eternal blessedness hereafter, being as assured and unalterable as the throne of God Himself.

* * * *

May 6.—There are in this pleasant world of ours many kind and tender-hearted people who, after perusing the Report of my Book Fund, straightway rush off to their bookcases, and in an enthusiasm of good-will pull down a pile of old books, and pack them off to me for my poor Pastors, in the full belief that they have thus rendered the best possible service to the Fund, and the Fund's Manager, and the Fund's Manager's needy folk. I should be very sorry to damp any kindly ardour, or seem ungrateful for proofs of willing sympathy; but I feel constrained to point out as tenderly as possible to my well-meaning but mistaken friends, that such presents are worse than useless to me. I am often puzzled how to get rid of the encumbrances which were meant to be blessings! Usually, when good people thus disturb the dusty solitudes of their bookshelves, the result is as follows:—A large number of volumes of *The Evangelical Magazine* and *The Baptist Record*, musty, perhaps, and always incomplete; some ancient "Sermons" by the venerable pastor they "sat under" half a century ago; a book or two of "Poems" by "nobody knows who;" a few old works on some abstruse notions; a "French Grammar and Exercises;" Mangnall's "Questions;" "Advice to a newly-married pair," and—I was going to say—a "Cookery Book," but I think that might be an exaggeration where all else is simple, earnest fact. Now, what could my poor Pastors care for rubbish such as this? The books might fill their shelves, but they could never feed their minds, and my work would fall fearfully short of its grand and solemn aim were I to mock their eager hunger with the mere semblance of a feast.

I would lovingly impress upon all my readers that the

Book Fund seeks to convey the richest and most substantial mental sustenance it can procure, to those who, by reason of well-worked yet ill-fed brains, find themselves in much the same condition as an impoverished field when the farmer has forced crop after crop from the soil, and neglected to supply the nourishment which such exhaustive measures demand.

John Ploughman's wife knows that poor pasture needs rich fattening, and she once heard John say that "sensible persons do not expect a garden to yield them herbs from year to year unless they enrich the soil; they do not expect a locomotive to work without fuel, or even an ox or an ass to labour without food; let them, therefore, give over expecting to receive instructive sermons from men who are shut out of the storehouse of knowledge by their inability to purchase books."

If dear friends have in their possession any of the Puritan Divines, or any standard works of sound theology, which they *know* would help to "thoroughly furnish" some man of God, I will thankfully accept and distribute them; for I want to bring about, by God's blessing, a better state of things in our ministers' libraries, and furnish their study tables with a fair abundance of sacred lore; but from a miscellaneous collection of valueless volumes I pray to be delivered.

* * * *

May 22.—When the Lord Jesus "dwelt among men," His teachings were constantly enforced by a reference to His own handiworks in nature; he drew illustrations from tree, and flower, and bird, and "without a parable spake He not unto them"; He "used similitudes" to impress and deepen the lessons of love and mercy which fell from His gracious lips.

I think the same tender teaching is still continued, though He has passed away to heaven, and our poor, dim human eyes cannot see His "matchless form," nor our dull mortal ears catch the heavenly harmonies of His divine voice: "He left not Himself without witness" in this matter, but still often condescends to convey counsel and comfort to His perplexed and weary children under the shadow of a metaphor, or through the significance of a parable.

Nor are these precious "object lessons" of the Great Master far to seek. In the common surroundings of daily life, no less than in the boundless stores of Nature's treasure-house, the observant eye, the listening ear, or the consecrated hand may find them, tenderly placed in the learner's way, fully prepared for use, and abundantly rewarding his diligent attention.

I often stumble on a message to my soul in unlikely and quaint places; and this morning I found in the columns of a daily paper a revelation of one of Nature's secrets, from whence I drew and took to my heart a most precious suggestion touching the "sweet uses of adversity." The writer of the article in question tells in graceful and forcible language the facts—long disputed, but now fully assured, bearing upon the production and formation of *pearls;* and though perhaps such a result of his labour never presented itself to the mind of the journalist, yet from his words one soul, at least, discovered a new way of treating troubles, and thanked God for thus revealing "under what ugly conditions the most exquisite results may be obtained."

In some unlucky moment (says the writer alluded to) the oyster has admitted into its shell a grain of sand, and the sharp-edged atom irritates the tender creature—so tender, indeed, that it will only live within walls of mother-of-pearl; and to defend itself against the obnoxious intruder, which it can neither eat nor expel, it covers the grain with the substance we call "pearl." The eccentric magician who thus, returning good for evil, endows with priceless value the vagabond atom, so incomparably worthless before, does not, however, remain content with having rendered its annoyer harmless, but continues to heap coals of fire on its head—continues, that is, to lay on film after film, smothering the wretched grit deeper and deeper in the precious substance, until the speck, once only a grain of sand upon the seashore, grows into the fascinating gem, against which divers stake their lives, and which the east and the west compete to buy.

They say that fable is full of morals drawn from "the fair pearl in the foul oyster"; but I think we may wrest yet another secret from the laboratory of the humble mollusc, and learn by its example to turn our troubles into treasures.

Have we a "thorn in the flesh," a fretting, wearing ailment, either mental or physical? By God's grace let us seek to cover and overlay it with the radiant loveliness of patience, meekness, and cheerful resignation! Our tender Lord will teach us the wondrous alchemy whereby our pains may be transmuted into the pearls of sweet obedience, our sufferings into the sapphires of love, our tears into the diamonds of sacred joy! Think of this, tried and afflicted child of God! Every pain borne meekly for His sake;—sorrow and suffering endured without murmuring;—bitter words restrained from love to Him;—wicked tempers checked and bridled lest His Spirit should be grieved;—all these efforts are, by His potent grace, gradually covering and concealing the distressing cause of your pain, and developing treasures fairer and more priceless than the "pearl full white and orient" which might worthily prove a "king's ransom."

The patient travail of the poor suffering oyster will perchance erewhile command the admiration of a world, and the result of its costly labour may adorn the diadem of an empress; but the hidden jewels of which we speak will win the commendation of the Lord of heaven and earth, and the possessor of the "ornament of a meek and quiet spirit" wears a pearl within his breast of peerless value, a treasure which, "*in the sight of God, is of great price.*"

Oh, my soul, see that thou set to work at once diligently to fashion gems which may be laid at thy Saviour's feet as trophies of His power! And when the Heavenly Merchantman comes, "seeking goodly pearls," offer thou to Him with humble joy the jewels with which His own love and grace have decked thee!

* * * *

June 1.—This morning I have received fresh and delightful evidence of the truth of my assertion that, "the gift of one volume of sermons creates a relish for more." Mental appetite increases by indulgence, and is rather strengthened than satiated by a rich and abundant provision.

If my friends will read the following extract from a letter received to-day from a clergyman of the Church of England, in connection with my remarks on aforesaid page, they will see what an excellent commentary it affords on my text, and how perfectly it establishes my theory, that to spread a feast of the richest and most substantial dainties of sacred literature is a sure way to *develop* mental hunger as well as to assuage it. Thus the letter runs :—

> I cannot thank you sufficiently for your munificent donation of books; I had no idea they were so excellent and suitable. What extraordinary toil and trouble must have been expended in their compilation and production! I thank you from the bottom of my heart, and bless God that He has disposed you to send these books to me. *I shall not fail to send you some money for some more sermons as soon as I can afford it. I should like all of them. I feel like a wild animal: my mind having, as it were, tasted—not of blood, but of such excellent wisdom—has an insatiable appetite for more.*

This needs no comment on my part, but I look up from transcribing this note to "thank God and take courage"!

* * * *

June 16.—The following communication deeply affected my heart to-day. It was addressed to my dear husband, and contained only these few words :—

> Rev. and dear Sir,—Please find enclosed a P.O. order for £2 1s. 6d., and a small slip of paper which will explain the use to which the money is to be put. It was directed to be sent to you by a Christian friend of mine, Mrs. D—, of Greenock, and was found in a drawer after her death. I may state that she had a struggle to support herself by her needle, and selling small furnishings, and was long in poor health, but her heart was in her Master's work, and she now receives her reward.

The little slip of soiled and torn paper bears the following inscription, written in a weak and cramped hand :—

> Silver threepenny pieces coming in in the way of business, and taken during this year. Dedicated to the Lord's work, under the hand of Mrs. Spurgeon, London.

Here is a veritable "widow's mite," which the Lord has noted as being cast with an unsparingly loving hand into His treasury! How sacred that morsel of paper becomes in my eyes! Such a gift as this is an endowment of blessing to the Book Fund. It is a true "sacrifice," a consecrated "offering," acceptable to the Lord, and well-pleasing in His sight; and I feel that such a legacy of love cannot fail to enrich my work in a far deeper sense than its mere money value would signify.

As I look at the few words traced by her trembling fingers, I wonder when the poor, lone woman heard of the Book Fund, and what induced her to interest herself in the welfare of my poor Pastors! I can imagine her unselfish joy when, one by one, the devoted coins came into her hands "in the way of business"; her delight at their steady increase, her reverent care to lay them by with prayer and thanksgiving, her humble satisfaction at thus storing up her substance for the Lord, whose "work" she must have loved so sincerely.

Now she treads the golden streets, and casts her bright crown at her Saviour's feet; pain and poverty, toil and trouble, all passed away for ever; but the story of the little silver coins so faithfully dedicated to His service will, I think, touch many a heart with its simple pathos, and "this thing that she hath done" shall be spoken of amongst us with well-merited tenderness, and teach us a sweet lesson of holy consecration and self-denying love.

* * * *

June 22.—My dear little book, you must faithfully bear the record of the Lord's great mercy to me and mine this day! With the loving shouts of the people still ringing in my ears—the warm grip of many fingers yet pressing on my hands—and my heart still throbbing with the unwonted excitement of appearing in the midst of a crowded gathering —I turn to you now in the quietude and rest of home to entrust to your pages a grateful memorial of a happy day!

The "Girls' Orphanage" has been inaugurated amidst great rejoicing, the Lord inclining His people's hearts to give liberally to the work, so that its "stones were laid in fair colours" of faith and hope, and my beloved sees this new "labour of love" abundantly prospering in his hands. Blessed be the Lord who thus giveth to His servant the "desire of his heart," fulfilling "all his petitions." The people gathered round with glad hearts and beaming faces, and many a prayer ascended from loving lips that the dear children, who should be housed and taught and cared for in the new homes, might all grow up there in the fear and love of God, and be a blessing in their day and generation.

The band of thirty little girls marching along in front of the boys ("place aux dames"!) attracted much attention, and touched all hearts; some of them are such wee mites, and they look very pretty and tender, when compared with the hosts of sturdy boys, who come tramping by in such overwhelming numbers that one wonders if there be any end to them! Few can look unmoved on such masses of orphan children; for in spite of their merry faces, their bright ways, and their happy laughter, the painful fact will force itself upon the mind of the observer, that every one of these little ones is taken from a desolate home, where the saddest of all earth's bereavements has been suffered; for the children are "fatherless," and the wife is a "widow." There was "April weather" on many a face to-day; I saw the tears stealing down cheeks on which approving smiles were struggling for the mastery; but the sunshine gained the victory, and the pitying drops were quickly wiped away, for the happy condition and appearance of the children led all to forget the sorrow which brought them there, in intense thankfulness for their present joy and future prospects.

If ever the strange title of "Godfather" were permissible, I think it would be in the case of Mr. Spurgeon towards his boys and girls at Stockwell; for God has made him, as it were, in His stead, a "father of the fatherless, and a judge of the widow"! The Lord bless him on his birthday, and on every other day, and give him many more years in which to be a blessing to the church, the College, the Orphanage, and the world!

* * * *

July 5.—The morning letters make their appearance with the breakfast-tray, and very often they bring such gratifying assurance of good accomplished and comfort bestowed, that the simple meal is either transformed into a love-feast, or blessedly interrupted by thanksgiving and praise. A day dawning with such brightness should yield a constant sunshine of holy joy and peace; but, alas! this world's clouds soon gather round the spirit, and too often the fair promise of the morning sky is dimmed and blotted by the mists of earthly care. Yet it is good to have seen the glory of a sunrise, even though the day prove dark; faith's glance pierces the clouds, rejoices in the light still there, and looks forward to a renewal of the blessing on the morrow.

The two following letters will be fair specimens of the "good things" with which my table is constantly spread, and by which the Lord graciously refreshes my spirit, and incites me to renewed effort in the work. The first is from a Congregational minister:—

Dear Madam,—When I wrote for the fifth volume of Mr. Spurgeon's "Treasury of David" I felt that you would place me under an obligation of lively gratitude by acceding to my request; but when, instead of one volume, I am the fortunate recipient of seven, and all of them of great interest and utility—to congratulate myself, and express my thanks to you, in a measure proportioned to your bounty, is a task more easily undertaken than adequately performed. Happily, where the will is present your kindness will esteem it to be more than the deed; my words, which are poor and imperfect in themselves, have yet this no inconsiderable merit, that they are the stammering utterances of the heart.

I am not a stranger to Mr. Spurgeon's "Sermons," having now and again treated myself to their perusal in numbers, and few presents could have been more acceptable to me than these four beautiful volumes, containing his weekly discourses to his congregation. I shall read them regularly, endeavour to drink deeply into the spirit of them, seek to get at the secret of their wonderful power, and, as far as possible, reproduce the advantage so obtained in my own poor ministry. The "Homiletic Encyclopædia" cannot fail to be of great service to me, and from the perusal of the other volumes I believe I shall derive stimulus and refreshment in my work. I join my prayers with yours that the gift may also be made the means of the conversion of many souls.

Dear Madam—I cannot exactly give you the blessing of "one who is ready to perish," but the blessing of a hungry intellect and heart, for which you have furnished such an ample repast, I do most sincerely and feelingly ask you to accept; and, above all, in the blessing of the Father, Son, and Holy Ghost may you have your reward.

The second letter is from a Church clergyman:—

My dear Madam—The books have arrived safely, and I must thank you very much for the kind additions you have made to those I mentioned. The "Lectures" I have long wished to possess; but I never for one moment imagined that the author's wife would be the giver. Need I say how heartily I reciprocate the prayerful wish that by their assistance, and through the power of the Holy Spirit, I may more clearly, more earnestly, and more humbly be enabled to preach the truth as it is in Jesus, and win for Him more glory than ever I have done before.

Your generosity and kindness is unparalleled in my personal experience, and it strikes me perhaps more because we are of a different creed and persuasion. I can but once more thank you deeply and truly; and earnestly pray that God's blessing may for ever rest on you and yours, and that you may be richly repaid out of His treasury for your kind and unselfish thought of others.

※　　　※　　　※　　　※

July 23.—There is an "exceeding great reward" in seeing the work of the Lord prospering in one's own hands; but when such prosperity overflows and engages other hearts, and hands also, we look up with adoring gratitude to Him who gives us such wonderful wages for such poor and feeble service.

I accept, as a gracious token of my Lord's favour, the fact that He has given my little Report for last year grace in the sight of so many of His people, and that in several instances its perusal has kindled the desire to help on the work it advocates, not only by donations to the Book Fund, but by special personal participation and interest. Friends have been led to think seriously of the needs of poor Pastors, many hearts have been roused to a consideration of the sad condition of a vast number of ministers, and to some the conviction has come with startling suddenness, that *their own* pastor, beloved for his work's sake, and honoured as a spiritual guide and counsellor, was, nevertheless, fainting under a pressure of temporal discomfort, from which the commonest measure of love and gratitude should have saved him. Happily, to those who are right-minded, such an awakening is efficient and permanent. From henceforth he who communicates to them of spiritual things, is "ministered unto" in earthly matters, and this being the way of the Lord's own ordaining, both are blessed, and mutual satisfaction and abundant provision proclaim peace in Zion's borders.

A very pleasing effort for the benefit and refreshment of Christ's poorer servants is recorded in a note received to-day, a portion of which I here transcribe. My friend says:—

I think you will be interested to know that I lent your "Report" to some friends here, and they were so struck by it that they found out six poor ministers in S——, and sent them twelve books on loan. The books are to go the round for a year, each pastor keeping them a month, and then fresh ones are to be sent out of their library, other friends helping by lending new books, and paying carriage. These good people have once invited the six poor ministers to B—— for the day, giving them a substantial dinner and tea, and asking ministers of the town to meet them in the evening for social intercourse and prayer. I tell you this, knowing you must feel interested, because it all arose from reading your "Report."

Interested! Yes, indeed! and intensely thankful to God that He has allowed the silent pleading of the little book to arouse Christian sympathy for His worn and wearied soldiers.

* * * *

August 1 to 18.—Amidst the confusion and inconveniences attendant upon a speedy removal to a new residence, the dear work of the Book Fund must suffer a temporary suspension. Correspondence may be continued, and promises of future bounty may make glad the hearts of longing Pastors; but for some few weeks there can be no regular preparation and despatch of parcels. Every Thursday of every week for these four years past has hitherto been devoted to this pleasant business, the labour of many willing hands being impressed for the service, and punctually every Friday morning the "Globe Express" van has come to receive and transmit the loving gifts. But alas for all order and rule in such times as these! Rooms are dismantled, shelves displaced, the books themselves are consigned to vast cases, and discomfort reigns paramount. What a stirring up of one's quiet nest this removal is! and how tenderly one learns to look on familiar objects from which we are to be parted for ever! The heart yearns over a place endeared by an intimate acquaintance of twenty-three years, and full of happy or solemn associations. Every nook and corner, both of house and garden, abounds with sweet or sorrowful memories, and the remembrance of manifold mercies clings like a rich tapestry to the walls of the desolate rooms. On this spot nearly a quarter of a century of blissful wedded life has been passed, and though both husband and wife have been called to suffer severe physical pain and months of weakness within its boundary, our house has been far oftener a "Bethel" to us than a "Bochim."

The very walls might cry out against us as ungrateful did we not silence them by our ceaseless thanksgiving; for the Lord has here loaded us with benefits, and consecrated every inch of space with tokens of His great lovingkindness. The sun of His goodness has photographed every portion of our dear home upon our hearts, and though other lights and shadows must be reflected there in coming days, they can never obliterate the sweet images which grateful memory will jealously preserve. Tender remembrances will render indelible the pictures of the sick chamber—which so many times had almost been "the gate of heaven" to our spirit; the little room, tenderly fitted up by a husband's careful love, and so often the scene of a scarcely hoped-for convalescence; the study—sacred to the Pastor's earnest work, and silent witness of wrestlings and communings known only to God and his own soul;* the library—where the shelves gladly suffered a constant spoliation and renewal for the blessed work of the Book Fund.

It is hard to leave all these sympathetic surroundings and dwell in the house of a stranger; but we believe we have seen the cloudy pillar move, and heard our Leader's voice bidding us "Go forward"; so in trustful obedience we strike our tent, and prepare to depart to the "place of which he has told us." And our new home may be to us a "Tabor," if our Lord will but dwell with us there! On our first view of it we were strongly reminded of Bunyan's description of the "Delectable Mountains," and every subsequent visit deepens that impression. "*A pleasant prospect on every side,*" said he, "*these mountains are Emanuel's land, they are within sight of His city, the sheep also are His, and He laid down His life for them.*"

The shepherds show the pilgrims the gates of the Celestial City, "*if they had the skill to look through their perspective glass*"; it may be that the Lord our Shepherd has called us

---

* In this room, by desire of the incoming tenants, has been placed the following inscription, written by Mr. Spurgeon:—

"Farewell, fair room, I leave thee to a friend:
Peace dwell with him and all his kin.
May angels evermore the house defend,
Their Lord hath often been within."

to the top of this hill to show us "*something like the gate, and some of the glory of the place*" beforehand, that our hearts may be set a-longing for the bliss of our eternal home. "Oh, Lord, if thy Spirit go not with us, carry us not up hence!"

* * * *

Westwood, Beulah Hill.

August 18 *to* 30.—In spite of the turmoil and trouble caused by the painful process of removal, our first fortnight on Beulah's Hill has been a time of great and unaccustomed joy. Blest for this period with a singular accession of health and strength, the new owners together visited the various spots of interest in their little kingdom, making pleasant discoveries every day; now tracing a winding garden-path to some unexpected opening, now looking with growing admiration upon the glorious views of earth and sky, ever breathing the bright clear air with a lively sense of exhilaration and refreshment, and constantly pausing to marvel at the goodness of God in "choosing such an inheritance for them." It seems almost like living a new life, and as if pain and sickness were left behind in the valley for ever! Unclouded sunshine rests on home and heart, the dear work of the Book Fund happily mingles its responsibilities with the new delights, and our unwonted surroundings are quickly endeared by this gracious and peaceful inauguration. "In the country of Beulah," says John Bunyan, "the air is very sweet and pleasant, and their way lying directly through it, they solaced themselves there for a season. Yea, here they heard continually the singing of birds, and saw every day the flowers appear in the earth, and heard the voice of the turtle in the land." These bright days and golden hours may not last long, but they are very precious in present possession, and will leave blissful memories behind them. "Here they were within sight of the city they were going to," says he, again, and sometimes we have seen so glorious a vision of splendour in the distant horizon that we should scarcely have wondered if across the smiling, sunlit plain, the turrets of the New Jerusalem had suddenly become visible, or if "one of the inhabitants thereof" had accosted us with a message from the King. Is it any wonder that we ask, as did Bunyan's pilgrims, " Whose goodly vineyards and gardens are these ? " or that the reply gives infinite peace and rest to our hearts—" They are the King's, and are planted here for His own delights, *and also for the solace of pilgrims.*"

* * * *

September 8.—Very soon after the sunshine and singing recorded in last month's pages, it seemed good to the Lord to take away our joy, and bring darkness and mourning into our pleasant places, by laying his dear servant on the bed of pain and languishing. "Shall we receive good at the hand of the Lord, and shall we not receive evil?" It may be He is thus testing our love and obedience, and to His glory and honour it shall be, if we are enabled to bless Him as truly when painful dispensations overtake us, as when great deliverances or gracious providences are vouchsafed to us.

Israel journeyed *from* Marah's turbid waters *to* Elim's wells and palms; in our case the way has led *backward*, and we have left the sweet resting-place to find our next halt must be by the side of the bitter pool. The Lord grant we may not even *think a murmur*, but gladly let Him " prove us there," praising Him in tribulation as cheerfully as in prosperity, and waiting meekly till His loving power is shown in turning the trial into a triumph. Our Father knows what is best for His children, and often mixes with our greatest earthly blessings some unpalatable sorrow,—some cup of " bitter water," which acts as a tonic to our spiritual appetite, and strengthens our relish for nobler and higher enjoyment.

* * * *

September 30.—The intervening days of this month are regretfully passed over without record of Book Fund experiences or correspondence, because affliction, both personal and relative, has prevented my usual entry of events. I am thankful, however, to say that the beloved work has not suffered through our suffering, nor have its loving gifts failed on account of my weakness. *Somehow*, I have managed to write the necessary letters, and keep all the machinery in motion, and now at the end of the month I am pleased to see there is but small diminution in the number of volumes despatched.

If I were to tell of "all the goodness and mercy" which has followed hard upon the footsteps of death and danger during the past month, I should most likely be able to interest my readers; but as it would be inexpedient to turn the "Book Fund Diary" altogether into an autobiography, I must forbear, and leave unrecorded, except in my heart, the special subjects of gratitude which fill my soul with joyful remembrance of the Lord's loving and tender care.

* * * *

October 3.—It would seem to be a matter of the very least importance as to which day of the week was chosen for the despatch of Book Fund parcels; but I have lately noticed so many expressions of grateful joy at receiving them on a *Saturday*, that I am delighted to find that even in this minor detail the work has been well and wisely ordered.

A Congregational minister thus writes:—

Accept my warmest thanks for the books, and also for the kind thoughtfulness which arranged for their reception on *Saturday*. Having been worried and worked over-much this week, and feeling very far from well, I was in a state of physical exhaustion and mental depression, which by no means augured well for to-morrow, when your parcel arrived. The very sight of it did me good, and when I opened it and discovered its precious contents I cannot tell you how many degrees better I felt at once.

"You have well-timed your present, dear Madam," writes a London pastor, "coming on a Saturday evening it has rejoiced my heart, and given my soul an impetus which I trust will remain with me all day to-morrow."

These are but two instances out of scores I have by me; but they suffice to show the silent yet blessed influence which this book-giving exerts on the minds of weary and overworked Pastors.

* * * *

October 19.—The two following letters, both from clergymen of the Church of England, will, I am sure, be read with interest; the first is written by a vicar in an eastern county, and he says:—

As we came up to the station, the porter said he had a parcel for me, which, to my joy, I found to be the valuable present I applied for, and something in addition. My dear Madam, your abounding benevolence has overwhelmed me, and I cannot find words to express my gratitude for such a treasury of spiritual knowledge and grace as I now possess in this marvellous work. I thankfully recognize the good hand of the Lord in it, and I trust He will give me the spirit of love and diligence to search into His rich storehouse of gospel light and consolation for my own good, and that I may be able to draw it out plentifully from time to time for the needs of my dear people, many of whom are now hungering and thirsting for it. There has been a great awakening here during the first mission week, and now I have to nourish the young plants in the garden of the Lord. Although I cannot repay the kindness you have extended to me, I pray God may still more visibly bless you and your talented husband even than in the past. If ever the Lord raises me in my circumstances, I trust I shall remember how much I owe you, and repay to the full. May the love of Christ be more abundantly with us, in our own souls, and be visible to us in increasing measure in our respective fields of labour. Last night I read nearly half of first volume of "Lectures to Students" with immense delight and instruction. The close study of the Psalms I shall begin with directly, D.V.

Then comes the testimony of a curate in the north of England:—

Your kindness has completely overwhelmed me! I felt, on the arrival of your parcel, as if I must be so unministerial as to jump for joy! I thank you from the depths of my heart for the truly magnificent gift you have so generously bestowed upon me. May the Lord reward you a hundredfold for your great goodness! As soon as I had read your very kind letter which came with the books, I knelt down and prayed, as you suggested, that "the gift might bring glory to God, as well as comfort and quickening to my own spirit." As the volumes lie before me on my table, my heart is full, and words can but feebly express with what pleasure I subscribe myself,

Yours ever gratefully,

Are not these and similar letters precious evidences of the real *helpfulness* of the beloved Book Fund work? A gift which sends a man to his knees, and is likely to lead him often there, must of necessity exercise a blessed and holy suasion over his daily life and solemn calling; and from him the mercy extends and widens, embracing others in its sweet ministry; for whether he be a preacher to tens, or hundreds, or thousands, all who come within reach of his influence will assuredly in some measure share the blessing.

* * * *

October 31.—Some weeks since the generous friend, whose munificent gift of writing-paper and envelopes for use in my work I chronicled on page 108, laid the Book Fund and myself under still greater obligations by sending a similar present for distribution to poor Pastors. It was almost, if not quite, as *wholesale* in quantity, nicely done up in packets, and ready for enclosure in my book parcels. This kindly considerate gift has already been much appreciated by my friends, all who have received it sending warm thanks to the thoughtful donor. Ministers usually have a somewhat extensive correspondence, and need, beside, a good store of writing-paper for extracts, notes of sermons, etc.; and the price of a few dozen quires with suitable envelopes is, in their straitened circumstances, always a matter of consideration. Those who receive this unexpected addition to my usual grants, will be well supplied with material for the labour of the pen for many days to come, and I cannot help earnestly hoping that my friend's loving gift may be used to such gracious purpose by each recipient, that all the words they trace upon the now spotless pages may be fitly spoken as "apples of gold in baskets of silver."

* * * *

November 30.—If funds were constantly flowing in, and a perennial spring supplied the golden streams which feed the Book Fund exchequer, no supplicating cry to heaven would be needful, no occasion given for uplifting of the hands in earnest prayer that God would "remember for good" the works of His poor servants, and fulfil to them His precious promise of unfailing help. I have been much "heartened up" under the present gloomy falling off of loving gifts to my Fund by referring to a short article in *The Sword and the Trowel* for 1876,* which the dear Editor wrote when

---

* "Watching the Ebb."—*The Sword and the Trowel.* 1876.

passing through a similar, but naturally much more serious, strait. He says:—

> The trial of faith by the decrease of supplies is meant to make us *give all the glory to God*. Continuance without change breeds carnal security, and that is the mother of self-conceit. It is a very beneficial thing to be made to see how dependent we are every moment, how readily we may be emptied out, and how impossible it would be for us to continue in prosperity if the Lord's hand were withdrawn. The best established work for the Master has no more endurance in it than a bubble unless He daily smiles upon it. To be laid absolutely at the Lord's feet, and to be made to stay there, is a most needful thing for us. We see that the Lord alone is our all-sufficient helper, and we give Him the more hearty and undivided praise. If such results come to us they will be "comfortable fruits of righteousness."

Many a time has the gift of money to my work been so directly from the hand of God that its reception has proved a veritable "means of grace" to my soul; but, on the other hand, I can also testify that a season of drought, like the present, has its own special spiritual blessing. Have we not often drawn a little child to our side by the irresistible attraction of some pleasant thing in our possession, ever and again apparently withholding it, that the timid little one may approach more closely, while its very craving lends it courage? Even thus does our loving Father sometimes deal with His little children. With a *detained* mercy in His hand He tenderly beckons us to draw nigh to Him, and when we can with full assurance of faith "come boldly" even to His feet, does He not give us the "desire of our heart," and add thereto blessings "above what we ask or even think"? Such a time of love more than repays for the patient waiting which precedes it, and the boon is all the more valued and precious since we have been taught to covet earnestly its possession. I take as a "token for good," and as a very blessed answer to prayer, a gift which I received this morning, and which has greatly impressed me. How easily the Lord can incline any heart to help! Never was a £5 note more welcome—never did one come from so unexpected a quarter! My readers can judge of my surprise and pleasure, if they read the following words which accompanied the money:—

> Dear Madam,—Some time ago you sent me "The Treasury of David," and another book, when I was at .... I now have pleasure in

sending you five pounds in aid of your Book Fund. Please accept this small contribution from a *Wesleyan Minister*, who admires your large-hearted efforts to do good.

I pray the Lord abundantly to reward this dear brother for so gracious and graceful a gift, and I look with divinely renewed faith and hope "to the hills from whence cometh my help," to Him who made and owns all the silver and the gold, and who can as easily send me £500 or £5,000, if my work required it, as this £5 for which I am so thankful.

* * * *

December 2.—Those dear friends who have been interested in my work from the commencement will not think the record of the year is complete without a word about the lemon tree. From the time when in a little pot, in my sick chamber, two tiny leaves, no bigger than a pin's head, emerged from the black earth and were tenderly covered by a *medicine glass*—to the present day when it stands in fair proportions, and boasts a height of seven feet or more—it has been closely identified with the Book Fund, and in some mysterious manner believed to be an emblem of my work. Friends used to cherish the pretty fancy, and send their gifts as "a few drops of water for the lemon plant," or "another leaf for your tree"; but though that pleasant fashion has fallen into disuse, there are many who constantly remember my favourite, and will be delighted to hear that its removal to "Westwood" has greatly contributed to its health and beauty. I do not, however, intend now to enlarge upon its charms, but rather to use an unpleasant peculiarity it has, in order to "point a moral and adorn a tale" I have to tell.

Attentively considering it the other day, I saw with some surprise that it bore a few very sharp thorns. "Ah!" I said, "dear emblem tree, are you so true to your mystical character as all that?" For, dear friends, Book Fund work is not *all* composed of pleasant fruit and flowers, there are some thorns concealed here and there which wound the hand which inadvertently touches them. Sometimes I receive an answer to the necessary enquiries I have to make, which hurts me sorely, and makes me wince. "Permit me to say I have no wish to be considered a *pauper*," wrote an angry man a day or two since, because I asked him kindly whether he came within the limits of my work, and possessed an income under £150 per annum!

Ever since the "Master" gave me this charge to keep, *He* knows I have tried to minister in gentle, kindly fashion to His servants; but occasionally the spirit of my service is overlooked by them, and my gifts are either claimed as a right or disdained as a charity. "Few and far between" are these ugly thorns on my flourishing, beautiful tree; tender and loving acknowledgments of my work are the rule, and when an exception comes I can well afford to forgive and forget it. Were it not that a chronicler is required to be faithful, and give fairly both sides of the history he is writing, I should have left unrecorded this painful part of a most pleasant and blessed service. The flowers of Paradise will doubtless be thornless, but here on earth one cannot gather many roses without pricking one's fingers, nor have a splendid lemon tree without seeing and bewailing its sharp spikes, nor possess any unmingled good but God's love.

* * * *

December 6.—Another large chest full of writing paper and envelopes has arrived from the friend who gives in so princely a manner! His first present came as an "Easter Offering," the second I must call a "Michaelmas Gift," and this certainly will be a "Christmas Greeting" to the Pastors who will receive it; for, in order that they may thus welcome it, I have had the allotted portions of paper and envelopes neatly packed in small parcels, and Christmas cards enclosed in each.

I think this is a fitting opportunity of stating that the absence of all items of stationery, etc., on the expenditure side of my balance-sheet, is due to the extraordinary generosity of this dear friend, who so liberally supplies me with the necessary materials for my large correspondence, that I "have all things and abound": indeed, I am not sure but that I could, upon the strength of his bountiful gifts, set up a small stationer's shop on my own account. If any friends having a talent for economy, and believing in the " I-can-do-without-it " principle, should receive a note from me, and be shocked at my using extravagantly good and ornamental paper, will they kindly remember that it is all *given* to me, in " royal portions," in an utter lavishment of liberality, with every device, and monogram, and stamped address, which could possibly please the most fastidious taste? And to his loving deeds my friend adds the adornment of kind and gracious words, for he concludes the letter which preceded this wonderful present to-day, by saying, " I need not assure you how much pleasure I have in sending these papers and envelopes to one who takes so much pains to aid and bless others, and whom I feel it a great privilege to help in this way."

* * * *

Here, too, I may becomingly record, though with a deeper sense of indebtedness than I know how to give expression to, the long-continued kindness of Messrs. Passmore and Alabaster, who annually print these "Reports" of mine without charge of any sort; and of Messrs. Straker and Son, who, on similarly generous terms, always bind them. This being the case, no exception can be taken on the score of expense to the pretty and tasteful form in which these good friends introduce my little book to subscribers; for it is all done by them from love to the cause, and no pains are spared to render the gift attractive and acceptable. Most gratefully do I, therefore, acknowledge my deep obligation to these large-hearted friends for so long and liberally helping forward my work. God bless and reward them! May they live, and continue the kindness for many years to come.

* * * *

December 13.—Laus Deo! Not long did my gracious God keep His child begging at the door of His mercy for needful supplies for her work! He has opened His hand, and satisfied my desire, and once more proved Himself to be "a very present help in trouble."

Last week I received a letter which was the forerunner of

the expected mercy. It was written by one who "serves the Lord with gladness" on a bed of suffering, where she lies waiting for the "consolation of Israel," with some of heaven's own peace and brightness already on her brow. She said:—

> I wish I could send you a cheque filled in for a large amount, and set your mind at rest about the Book Fund; but "silver and gold have I none"; however, I have found something *better than gold*, and I give you this grand promise, dear friend, with which I began the day, and which shall be performed to you, "I will fill their treasures" (Prov. viii. 21).

My faith was strengthened by her loving confidence, and two days afterwards the blessing came; for I received enough money to liberate me from all bondage of anxious thought, and set me on my way rejoicing.

I am telling an "old, old story"; but to reverent ears it will be as charming and fresh as ever: the story of the infinite grace and tenderness of God in Christ, and the *reality* of His watchful care over all who put their trust in Him. Is it not wonderful that God deals so lovingly with us in the smallest details and needs of our daily life? Yet it is the same in nature as in grace, "His tender mercies are over all His works." He "holds the waters in the hollow of His hand," but He also nourishes the tiny streamlets of the valley; He rules amidst the armies of heaven, yet He guides the dewdrop to the lip of a thirsty flower, and, blessed be His name, He stoops from the throne of the universe to the help and succour of one of the least of His children, and turns from the hallelujahs of angels to listen to a sinner's cry. I would I could praise Him for the "marvellous help" He has again given me! He has "put a new song in my mouth" for this fresh deliverance; but I cannot sing it half loudly enough! Did not the Psalmist say, "Praise waiteth for thee, O Lord, in Zion?" which some read "praise is silent to thee," as if it were impossible even for Heman and Asaph, and Etham, and all the harps, and all the voices of the multitude to utter his praise, and so they kept silence, waiting till He Himself inspired them. "God only knows the love of God," and only his Spirit can express it. What can I do but lay down the harp, and, like David, go in and sit before the Lord, and say, "Whence is this to me? and is this the manner of man, O Lord God?"

* * * *

December 17.—Almost as soon as my Christmas parcels had left the house this morning, there came a very delightful surprise-gift to me from the "Religious Tract Society," consisting of 120 nice books, and a large quantity of Christmas cards. These latter have been despatched this evening, their distribution (in packets) to about seventy poor country pastors, giving delightful employment to willing hearts and hands. I regret not being able to give away the books at once; but my arrangements for the despatch of parcels for the month having been completed, they must remain in stock till the new year.

This is the second bountiful present I have received from this excellent Society; for in May last they generously made me a very valuable grant of five hundred books, which have rendered me splendid service in enriching and enlarging my parcels. Very gratefully I tender my heartiest thanks to the dear friends with whom this generous thought originated, and to all those who kindly concurred in carrying it out; it has helped in a most pleasant and loving way many servants of the Lord in their arduous work, and it has been no small encouragement to me to receive so delightful a recognition of the importance and need of my efforts on their behalf.

* * * *

December 19.—This year of grace 1880 has been a very trying time for my poor Pastors, and I constantly wonder how some of them have managed to stem the torrent of trial which poverty, illness, and increasing needs have let loose upon them. Their griefs are indeed heavy, and their sorrows manifold; and no way seems opened to permanent alleviation of their terrible poverty and distress. Never before have I had so many sad tales of sorrow and suffering told to me. Never have I felt so painfully the burden such knowledge necessarily imposes, and never have I so sorrowfully realized the utter inadequacy of my efforts to relieve them. The sum of money (£313 6s.) which the PASTORS' AID FUND has distributed is an honour to the dear and liberal donors, and the Lord will accept it at their hands, giving them back blessing for blessing; but what is this among so many? When a £5 or £10 note is sent to some poor struggling brother, I am apt to say, "There, now, his trouble is over; his heart is made glad; the wolf has fled from the door, and in peace and comfort he can once more serve the Lord." But for how long, dear reader? Ah! here lies the sad shadow which constantly broods over this otherwise fair prospect of loving usefulness, and which, alas! needs a far higher power than mine to lift and disperse. There is such terrible and constant need in hundreds of our ministers' families, that though a gift of money does for a time help them, and tide them over their difficulties, the sad ebb soon sets in again and leaves them high and dry on the pitiless sands of poverty, reduced to a state of humiliation and despondency which is fatal alike to their position and power. Oh! that we had a reservoir of generous treasure which might be made to overflow on these desert places, causing them to "rejoice and blossom as the rose," or, to put it more plainly, and repeat a wish which I have before most devoutly expressed, would to God we had a "Sustentation Fund," after the manner of our sensible Scotch friends, so that *all* our Pastors might be raised above the fear of actual want, and set free to follow their sacred calling, unfettered by the chains of carking, worldly care, with which our present system binds them hard and fast.

I am told there are many difficulties in the way of such a scheme in England, but I can scarcely believe them to be insurmountable, and I would hail with vehement delight the day when this battle should be fought and won—when all our churches should be constrained, either by force of argument, or eloquence of speech, or power of organization, or all these combined, to put an end for ever to this grievous discredit to our name, and give to our poor Baptist Pastors throughout the land the precious boon of comparative freedom from anxiety concerning their daily bread!

Reading Numbers (chap. xviii.) this morning, I could not

fail to notice the splendid temporal provision made for the priests and Levites by the express command of Jehovah, and to contrast such rich and abounding supplies with the narrow means and straitened circumstances of so many of the ministers of Christ in these days. "All the *best* of the oil, and all the *best* of the wine, and of the wheat, and the first fruits," besides "all the best thereof" of other offerings—this was the priests' "reward of service" in those days, and when once set apart to the office all anxious thought or care about his maintenance in it was entirely removed! If the mind of the Lord has not changed concerning the way in which His servants should be treated, how grieved He must be to look upon the dire and dreadful poverty which crushes so many of them in these later times!

"I have given your priest's office unto you as a service of gift," the Lord says, and what a magnificent provision it was, dealt out with an unsparing hand! How earnestly I wish that some of the plenty enjoyed by God's priests under the Mosaic dispensation could be furnished to the tables of poor Gentile Pastors, some of whom, to my knowledge, go for days without tasting meat, and who would consider the luxuries set forth by the "firstfruits" an altogether unattainable gratification. See how God cared for the families of His servants also, and gave commandment concerning "thy sons and thy daughters with thee" (Numb. xviii. 11), who were to eat "of the most holy things reserved from the fire." He filled them with the finest of the wheat, and "satiated the soul of His priests with fatness," and again and again in this chapter is the promise repeated, as if with loving persistence He would press upon them the abundance of His goodness (see verse 19). Now turn to the facts of the present day, and say, "Alas for the minister's children!" Meagrely fed, and scantily clothed, they have a hard life during their childhood, and often grow up to despise the people whose niggardly and selfish treatment has ruined their father's prospects, or perchance broken his heart. Then, as time goes on, how can the boys be apprenticed, when every penny of the father's pitiful stipend goes for food and other necessaries? And what becomes of the girls? These and similar questions can be answered only by thankfully recognizing the kindness of friends whom the Lord raises up to succour His poor servants, and so I am brought by a very roundabout way to the end I had in view when commencing this paragraph, namely, to give my warmest thanks to those who, during this and many past years, have generously set apart a certain sum for the help of poor Pastors, and have honoured me by putting it in my charge to be distributed as occasion offered. And though I have been indulging in a somewhat sorrowful lament over the sad cases of poverty and need which distress my heart, I cannot fail to be inexpressibly thankful to those loving friends who have enabled me to do something to alleviate the need I have made known to them. God bless these generous hearts; what should I do without them? No trumpet proclaims their good deeds; the very recipients of their bounty are ignorant of their names; yet "their record is in heaven," and they shall be recompensed at the "resurrection of the just."

* * * *

December 26.—The days of the old year are fast passing away, and the pages of my little "Diary" are getting fewer and fewer: very soon its record of Book Fund experiences will be submitted to my friends for their kind approval, and its simple testimony to the unfailing love and goodness of the Lord will claim their earnest attention. I am very anxious that the business part of my Report should be satisfactory to my good helpers, and that the amount of work accomplished by means of their generosity should be accounted worthy of their increased interest and aid; but above and beyond this, my earnest prayer is that the Lord will use so feeble a work for His glory, and will bless the little messengers thus sent forth, to the comfort and strengthening of some weak ones, by leading them to more entire dependence and unwavering trust in a God who has dealt so gently, yet so bountifully, with me. Throughout the year I have tried to tell of His mercy and grace so tenderly that the sweet story might find instant response in every heart; but the words will fall coldly, and without force, unless He gives power to them, and makes them glow and burn, because written for His sake.

Friends will here see something of the way by which He hath led me, though the half is not told them of the goodness and mercy which have followed me; nor can they discern, as I can, where the rough places were made plain, the deeps forded, the deliverances wrought, or the loving guidance and "marvellous help" vouchsafed.

The year has been filled with His goodness, and all through its changeful scenes and varied experiences the golden thread of God's tender love has run, and the hand of faith has found it an unfailing clue to lead through the perplexities of mysterious providences, to the safe and happy walking of the King's highway. Resting for a moment, like weary pilgrims, at this milestone of the year, we pour upon it the "oil and wine" of our gratitude and love, and before we pursue our journey, we thus consecrate it for ever as an altar of praise to our God and King. Gather round, dear friends and fellow-helpers, and let us worship Him together at this boundary line of our lives. Surely we all have some special offering of thanksgiving to bring before Him, or some sweet song of deliverance to sing, and while we unitedly bless Him for the great things He hath done for us, let us clasp hands in sacred communion around this stone of Ebenezer which we have raised, and pledge ourselves to more steadfast service and fuller consecration in the days of our pilgrimage yet remaining.

VALE! Old Year! Thank God thy sins are blotted out, thy sorrows shall be no more remembered; thy tears are wiped away; thy weariness and pain are forgotten; all thy memories are gilded with the glory of unnumbered mercies.

SALVE! New Year! We welcome thee with gladness as an angel of light, though as yet thy face is veiled, and thy wings are folded. Thy closed hands are full of blessing for God's redeemed ones, and thy covering wings do but conceal "the lovingkindnesses" and "tender mercies" which are to be the portion of His children. Thou art our glorious King's messenger, bearing His sealed orders for the days to come, and whether thou bringest joy or sorrow, sickness or health, life or death, we welcome thee; for "we are persuaded that neither death, nor life, nor angels, nor principalities, nor powers, nor things present, nor things to come, nor height, nor depth, nor any other creature, shall be able to separate us from the love of God, which is in Christ Jesus our Lord."

In this confidence, and with this hope, I wish all my friends

"A HAPPY NEW YEAR" RIGHT THROUGH;

and if they reciprocate the sincere desire thus expressed, they can do much to fulfil it, both for themselves and for me, by remembering the needs of my poor Pastors, and helping on by their kind gifts that sweet service for their sakes—

THE BOOK FUND.

"For the administration of this service
not only supplieth the want of the saints, but is
abundant also by many thanksgivings unto God."

SUMMARY OF WORK.

Books Distributed during the Year 1880:—7,144 Volumes.

Also 6,262 single Sermons for giving away. The recipients comprised 258 Baptists, 154 Independents, 317 Methodists, 130 Church of England clergymen, 112 Evangelists, 29 Missionaries, and 22 Presbyterians.

The Book Fund Diary

For 1881.

By Mrs. C. H. Spurgeon.

Imprisoned Music: or, the Singing Log.

THOSE who delight in the sweet flow of softly-rhymed verse above the heavier diction of solid prose will gladly welcome a new version of the allegory of the "Singing Log," which appeared in the Report for 1879. A friend kindly took the trouble to put the little legend into verse, and my dear husband thought the stanzas so good that they ought to be better. With no small labour and pains he fashioned the poem anew, writing several fresh verses, and in general recasting the whole. The "new version," as he calls it, was sent home from Mentone, with the title of "Mrs. Spurgeon's 'Gem' reset," and I am very proud of my husband's commendation. Since "gems" are rare things with me, I naturally desire to make the most of this solitary specimen, and therefore I have great pleasure in reproducing the allegory under this more attractive form.

Thus polished and sparkling, I hope it may find even greater grace in the sight of my friends than on its former appearance; but beyond this hope there shines out a better and brighter confidence; for I think I may tell, without the shadow of a boast, how graciously the Lord has honoured the little parable by making it the messenger of comfort or content to so many of His people, that I have been amazed at His condescension in thus using it, and am encouraged therefrom to believe that its mission of love is not yet fully accomplished.

 AT the close of a dark and cloudy day,
  As the deeper night grew on,
 On my languishing couch I wearily lay,
  My joy for the moment gone.

 Within my room all was cozy and bright,
  Yet a shadow of night had crept
 Over my soul, and had hid from my sight
  The hand in which mine was kept.

 Depressed and saddened, I laboured in vain
  To gaze on my loving Lord.
 Oh, when will His presence return again,
  And light on my spirit be poured !

 Whence comes it my Lord so bitterly chides,
  And sends me such grievous pain?
 The sun, and the moon, and the stars He hides,
  And clouds return after the rain.

 HE HEARD : and an answer was strangely given,
  A still small voice from the throne ;
 No seraphim brought the message from heaven,
  Yet it came from the Lord alone.

 A while in my room reigns a silence deep ;
  The only sounds in mine ear
 Arise from the flames which crackle and leap,
  And flash forth a flickering cheer.

 When we suddenly heard a strange, sweet song,
  Like the robin's tender trill,
 A whisper, a sonnet, the flames among ;
  It caused our hearts to thrill.

 " Can a bird be singing this gloomy night ?"
  In startled surprise, we say.
 " Whence comes such an anthem of calm delight
  As from harps that are far away ?"

 In silent wonder we listen again,
  Till my friend in a whisper said,
 " 'Tis yon old oak log sings that soft, weird strain
  From amidst its fiery bed."

'Twas so; and, as once the Lord spoke out
  From the bush which burned with flame,
So now to our spirits, beyond a doubt,
  His voice from the oak log came.

From the heart of the oak fire had loosed the bands
  Of music imprisoned of yore,
When the trees of the field had clapp'd their hands
  And cried out the Lord before.

When its branches waved 'neath the heaven's blue
  Through the livelong summer day,
Full many a bird to their shadow flew
  With its carol glad and gay.

The song of the thrush and the hum of the bee,
  And the music of evening bells,
All sank in the soul of the old oak-tree;
  And now the sweet tale it tells.

The hardened growth of full many a ring
  Fettered fast the imprisoned lays,
Till these flames of fire their freedom bring,
  And they dance in the joyous blaze.

The fire which consumes has lent it a tongue,
  And the oak log sings as it dies:
It yieldeth its all while its heart is wrung—
  'Tis a song and a sacrifice.

*   *   *   *

And thus was a message most sweetly brought
  By the old oak log to me;
It raised me aloft from each gloomy thought,
  And from sorrow it set me free.

If trial and pain be as flames to my heart,
  To fetch forth its latent praise,
With joy I accept the sufferer's part,
  And would choose it all my days.

Preamble.

DEAR FRIENDS,—An accomplished writer once laid claim to the gratitude of his readers for having voyaged to fetch a metaphor all the way to the Guinea Coast and back; but I, whose lagging pen toils painfully across the white acres, must entreat your patience rather than your praise, while I try to tell you of a pretty parable which presented itself to me not a stone's-throw from my own doorstep.

Come with me into the garden, and you shall stand, in imagination, where I stood one morning and saw an unusual scene enacted. Here, just at the corner by the holly-tree, I was talking to the gardener, when I suddenly became aware of a sharp, tapping sound, like the stroke of a small hammer on some unyielding substance. Turning my eyes quickly in the direction from whence the noise proceeded, I saw a splendid thrush standing boldly in the centre of the garden-path, and, what do you think he was doing?—he was steadily and vigorously beating a snail on a large stone, and the loud taps I had heard were the blows which destroyed the poor victim's shelter, and laid his soft, succulent body at the mercy of his foe! Stroke upon stroke he gave, lifting the creature with his beak, and dashing it on the well-selected stone, till only a conveniently mangled mass remained, which he instantly devoured, and thus completed his victory!

I had read of such doings in books, but to see the manœuvre practised before my eyes, and a dinner procured in so unique a manner, filled me with wonder and delight. I am afraid all sympathy for the snail was lost in admiration of the ingenuity of the beautiful spoiler, and I would fain have applauded his clever trick, had I not feared to frighten him from his juicy repast. The saucy bird flew away when his meal was concluded, and left me still gazing at the spot where a very pleasant page in natural history had been unfolded. The incident had a fascination for me, and I pondered over it, thinking there might be a simile there as surely as a snail, if I only knew how to extract it successfully. I went to my husband for help and enlightenment, and after hearing my little story, he laughingly said, "Ah! I have a fellow-feeling with your thrush; for I find texts very difficult to crack sometimes, and many hard knocks I have to give before I get to the marrow of the word!" I found, then, I was to learn a lesson of perseverance in overcoming difficulties, and take the pretty bird's example as a constant persuasive to energy and earnestness in my work. One would have assumed that hard, round shell to be a very doubtful blessing to a hungry thrush; but former experience and a divinely implanted instinct had taught him to make light of the trouble which would ensure him so choice a delicacy, and, likely enough, in his bird-lore he had learned the secret that all things are the sweeter for costing us some pains.

To the impression which this garden scene made on my mind I owe some comfort and courage in my constant task of writing. I have seemed to hear again those decisive tappings whenever a new entry has been made in my journal; and a vision of the lovely bird—his speckled breast swelling with triumphant satisfaction over his performance—has always lured me to look beyond the labour entailed by this difficult part of my service, to the blessed reward which, by God's grace and favour, has so many times followed the effort.

Now, am I not indebted to my thrush for furnishing me with a preface as deftly and curiously as he helped himself to a repast, and may I not present my little book to you with the confident assertion that

"Prayer and Pains will do anything"?

The New Year opens with bright and cheering prospects for the Book Fund, seeing that Christmas and New Year's Gifts from kind friends have plentifully enriched its treasury, and placed ample means at my command for the furtherance of the blessed object I have at heart. A lady, writing to me

the other day, said she " supposed the ministers were nearly all supplied now"! Never was surmise more unwarranted and incorrect. The work is as urgent and important as ever, and the necessity for it as great and pressing. Did anybody ever hear of a preacher possessing as many books as his heart craved for? I never did; and I think such a state of contentment must be well-nigh impossible; for the more a man studies and enlarges his mind, the more he hungers and thirsts for knowledge, and seeks to add to his stores; and the intense delight he takes in his few precious volumes is a constant incentive to add to their number. I am daily receiving letters from Pastors to whom I made grants three or four years ago, whose mental craving, more stimulated than satisfied by the books previously given, is now urging them to seek further appliances for the development of thought and intellect. These good men might truly say—

"My hunger brings a plenteous store,
My plenty makes me hunger more."

They tell me with pleasing emphasis of the exceeding value and blessing of my former gifts, and they draw thence a plea for a renewed consideration of their needs. It would be, indeed, a hard heart which would refuse them, and with the coveted treasures at command send them empty away. Help in pulpit preparation, refreshment of spirit in times of deep depression, stimulus to private devotion, assistance in pastoral duties,—all these blessings, and many more, are enfolded in the precious pages bestowed by the Book Fund, which as truly blesses a minister's soul as it enriches his library. But although so many of God's poor servants have had reason to thank Him for the help afforded them in this important matter through the agency of the Fund, my ambition is by no means satisfied with the present attainments of my work. There are still hundreds of men in the ministry whose stock of books is totally inadequate to their needs, and who, though painfully conscious of their famishing condition, are unable to procure the aliment which would nourish their souls, and promote their spiritual and mental growth. If the Book Fund only ministered to the necessities of these long-settled Pastors, its work would be useful and important; but there is the fact to be considered, that our colleges of all denominations are constantly sending forth their young recruits to the battle of the Lord; and these are seldom, if ever, "thoroughly furnished" for the warfare which they seek to accomplish. To aid *all* these needy ones, to supply *all* these longing souls, would, without doubt, require both more means and more management than this quiet little service and its happy servant can ever hope to command; but with this high aim in view, according as God prospers us, so do we deal forth our treasures lovingly and gladly till they be exhausted.

The number and urgency of the applications for books steadily flowing on in almost uninterrupted course from one year's end to another, is a sufficiently strong proof that a deep and widespread scarcity exists, and the many loving acknowledgments which grace the pages of my Annual Diary are precious and delightful evidences that its supply is hailed with devout thankfulness and joy.

It is pleasant to feel impelled to continue one's work by a growing conviction of its importance and value; more happy still to be constrained to go on by dear love of the service itself; but, best of all, to be so blessedly certain of the Lord's will and help in the matter that one *dare not* give it up! Something of the sweetness of each of these conditions mingles with the emotion with which I write the first daily record of the new year. I therefore recommence my beloved work with renewed and hopeful energy, happily conscious of the blessing it will bring to hundreds of weary hearts, rejoicing beyond measure in my own share of its mercies and privileges, and leaning with absolute and entire dependence for strength, support, and success upon God, and God alone!

* * * *

January 8th.—Our "Silver Wedding Day" was to have been the occasion of great rejoicing, and of united praise to the loving Lord who hath led us by a right way, and shown us such abundant goodness all our journey through life. Kind friends had prepared congratulations and festivities, and all were looking forward to a good and pleasant time;

when, lo! a hindering hand is laid upon our schemes of joy, our rehearsal notes of song are hushed, and a "cloudy and dark day" overhangs the house where the dear master lies sorely sick. Yet, blessed be God! it is not all darkness; the eye of faith can see the "silver lining" to the cloud, betokening the brightness beyond, and promising fair weather and future sunshine for those who with prayer and patience wait for them. I look out from the window of the sick-chamber over the broad landscape which is the joy and glory of Beulah's hill, and I see across rolling fogs and billowy mists, far away on the plain, or upon the side of the distant hills, some favoured spots where the sun is still "lighting his beacon fire," and where warmth, and light, and beauty, like the angels in Jacob's vision, are ascending and descending a ladder of sunbeams set from earth to heaven.

From my vantage ground on the hill I see the lights as well as the shadows in this great picture before me; my eye o'erleaps the clouds and darkness, and rests rejoicingly on the distant splendour, and my heart finds comfort in reading the sweet lesson thus set before me. "Take courage, my beloved," I say to the dear sick one, "the sun has not ceased to shine, nor has our God forgotten to be gracious. Though we are enwrapped in gloom, over there some are even now rejoicing in present brightness, and by-and-by the clouds will pass away, and the time of the singing of birds will return again for us."

"After the storm, a calm;
After the bruise, a balm;
For the ill brings good in the Lord's own time,
And the sigh becomes a psalm."

Very consoling also, and precious, have been the many kind words which have reached us by letter as well as by word of mouth to-day; our eyes have filled with happy tears, and our hearts have been comforted by the sweetest of sweet messages from hundreds of loving hearts, who hold the dear Pastor in tenderest remembrance, and who, for his sake, unite my name with his when offering either sympathy or congratulation. One such precious missive, taken without choice from the mass of letters, will show something of the kindly feeling which has cheered us to-day, and seemed to fill the sick-room with "comforting creatures as well as creature comforts."—" Dear Mrs. Spurgeon," says this friend, writing the day previous, " to-morrow you will celebrate your 'Silver wedding,' and we should not like the day to pass without saying how devoutly we thank God that you and your beloved husband are spared to one another, and how earnestly we desire that the future may bring you the choicest blessings that our Father in heaven has in store. Unknown to you personally, yet your name, with that of dear Mr. Spurgeon, is enshrined in our hearts. Next to our blessed Saviour and each other, the love of our souls gathers around you and yours. . . . You will have a host of letters, so I will not detain you by writing much; but among those who shall utter their fervent congratulations, none will do so more lovingly than "Yours faithfully,

"————."

This is very sweet and pleasant; but a little note which succeeded it charmed me even more, and I put it on record here with the firm belief that its touching, childish plea for "poor ministers," and the pretty, unconscious grace with which the little maiden's precious coin is offered for their comfort, will induce many others who are quite "grown up" to follow her tender example. She writes: "Dear Mrs. Spurgeon, I shall be eleven years old to-morrow, and papa says it will be your 'Silver wedding day.' I have not a present worth sending you, but I should like to send you a half-crown towards a book for some poor minister who cannot buy books for himself. My papa is a minister, and I know how pleased he is if we make him a present of a book; but mamma says there are scores of ministers who have no one to make them presents of books except you. I wish I could send you ever so much more. Papa and mamma hope you and Mr. Spurgeon will live to see your golden wedding. I shall be grown up by that time, and perhaps have more money; then I can give you what will send more than one book. Yours affectionately, NELLIE." God bless the dear child, and grant that so fair a bud of promise may unfold under every happy influence into the fairer flower of consecrated womanhood.

Each year there has been occasion to record in my little book the quaint, yet tender utterances of some Quaker friend, either with reference to my work in general, or to a desired gift of books. These notes are always cherished with special veneration and pleasure, and though the epistle which follows has little to do with the Book Fund, yet its sweet sympathy with my now suffering husband endears it to my heart, and seems to claim for it a place among many other treasured remembrances. "Dear friend,—May I call thee such, though we are strangers as to the outward? In a time of late severe and protracted illness with my own dear husband, I have felt ofttimes such near sympathy with thee, that I trust the expression of it will not be an intrusion; I think not, because it has seemed something like an intimation of our heavenly Father's will that I should tell thee so; and also that we, in common with many others of the Lord's children, do bear you on our heart's best remembrance before Him. Much should we like our dear unknown, yet well-known friend, C. H. Spurgeon, to hear that 'morning by morning,' and 'evening by evening,' his portions have not only refreshed and instructed us, but brought him to remembrance, with desires that he may be comforted of God with the comfort wherewith he himself has comforted others. It is in my heart to say much more, but I will only add that I am—Thy sincere friend, ———."

* * * *

February.—There is quite a "run" of applications upon the Book Fund at this present time from clergymen of the Established Church, and I may as well confess that I have a special liking for their courteous letters and their frank appeal for books. I take it that there is commonly a real felt need of sound theological teaching, and a deep love of pure gospel truth, in the hearts of these young divines, when they solicit the gift of the works of the once despised Baptist Pastor from the willing hands of his wife; and next to bestowing books on "our own people," it pleases me most to place "The Treasury," the "Lectures," or the "Sermons" within reach of their hands and hearts. In some cases it may be quite possible that the volumes are sought for the scarcely admitted purpose of wholesale appropriation, but what then? notwithstanding every way, whether in pretence or in truth, Christ is preached, and we therein do rejoice, yea, and will rejoice. How many a young curate with small ability, but gracious spirit, might serve his Master well, and "feed the flock of God" with more convenient food, were he to cast aside his own "manuscript," and preach boldly and bodily a sermon from the "Tabernacle Pulpit"! I am told this is very often done, and I can but say, "May God bless the doing of it!" It is no secret that sermons (so called) are bought and sold at so much per dozen, and constantly read in the churches of our land. Would it not be a grand change to substitute for those formal, lifeless essays, the utterances of one whose earnest, living words, the Spirit of the Lord most constantly and signally blesses? Often when I am sending these volumes to clergymen, I feel a delightful anticipation of the blessed harvest that may spring from such seed, and I have the satisfaction of earnestly praying that God may "give the desired increase." "I am very glad," wrote a vicar to me lately, "that you have been able to help my fellow-labourer with the gift of sound evangelical books. I cannot but think such a work will have a very important bearing upon the spiritual well-being of many souls, and therefore I hail it with great pleasure." This is graceful testimony to the value of the Book Fund service; but still more encouraging are the grateful letters which record the thanks of those who have sought and obtained the boon of books they could not buy.

A young curate having been four years in training for missionary work, and waiting his appointment to foreign service, asked me for "The Treasury of David;" "for," said he, "I am desirous of having this most useful work constantly by me, to use both devotionally and as a help in the preparation of my sermons." My readers will see in what spirit he received the gift, when in acknowledging its safe arrival he wrote,—"After opening your parcel I could not help kneeling down and thanking first Him who is the Giver of every good and perfect gift, and asking Him to bless the books to my soul and future ministry."

Again, another curate writes, "I received on Saturday

evening a parcel containing nine volumes of Mr. Spurgeon's works; a present so munificent and valuable, that I am really at a loss how adequately to express my thanks. They are, indeed, most useful, earnest, and notable works, and have doubtless done, and will still do, an immense amount of good. Many thanks, also, for your kind wishes for my success in the ministerial career : I trust God will bless my poor efforts, and the perusal of the books you so generously sent, to the edification of His people, and to His own great glory."

An appropriate termination to to-day's entry will be the words of a postscript—brief, but full of blessed meaning—to one of this morning's letters:—" I know many a pulpit that is being better supplied through your gifts of books. The other week a brother minister wept as he told me that many souls would have to bless Mrs. Spurgeon's God-formed fund for better sermons preached by him."

Lord, I do praise Thy dear name for this sweet token of thy blessing and favour.

* * * *

If any proof be needed of the book hunger from which our poor Pastors suffer, it is here produced in the fact that one of them is willing to sacrifice his dearly-loved *pipe* in order to procure mental food, and has sent me the money which would otherwise have been spent in tobacco, that I may furnish him with an extra quantity of books. I do not know when I have had a letter which so much pleased me : not that I should ever grudge a good man his comfortable smoke, but that I so heartily admire the self-denial and determination which, after a hard battle, conquered the daily, and, as some might put it, the dirty habit of a lifetime. The good brother writes that he " has been trying to break off the long-acquired use of smoking, so as to devote the amount usually spent in tobacco to the purchase of Mr. Spurgeon's works;" and he goes on to describe how strong was the desire for the indulgence, and how many failures he experienced before arriving at the steadfast stage of complete indifference to his once absorbing solace. Doubtless the bodily discipline has strengthened his mental energies, and with Paul he has found it wise to "bring under his body, and keep it in subjection." It may be that the laying aside of this self-indulgence was necessary to his soul's health, and the untrammelling of his spirit, and that the Lord will give him "much more than this" in the refreshment of his mind and the increased power of his ministry. To do anything for Christ's sake "makes that and the action fine," and I gather from his own words that though "the struggle for the first four days was terrible," he is now rejoicing in his emancipation from a domineering and damaging habit; for he says, "I cannot express to you how thankful I feel that I have been enabled to overcome it." Five volumes of sermons will be purchased by this abstinence, and to these I shall add four more; and when they are safely lodged on his book-shelves, I know he will feel glad and grateful to see, in so substantial and precious a form, the hard-earned cash which otherwise would have been dissipated in smoke. And although the graceful blue wreaths no longer curl lazily up from beside the study fire, nor the long-accustomed lips any more press the slender, seductive pipe stem, the better incense of prayer and praise will not slacken; for the Lord will command that His servant's lips be "touched with a live coal from off the altar"; and such an inspiration will more than make up for it all.

* * * *

March.—Some days since, a great blessing came in the shape of a huge package of gentlemen's clothing, comprising a very extensive and valuable wardrobe, so large as to be capable of useful division among six or seven poor Pastors, and securing to each one a goodly portion. Herein I see again, as at other times, the goodness and gentleness of the Lord; for He sends these supplies opportunely, and with tender regard to the immediate needs of His servants. The parcel came from an unknown donor, and, at the time I received it, it was not only unexpected, but I had no applications on hand for such things as it contained. Almost immediately afterwards, however, there came letters from six Pastors, disclosing the saddest possible details of destitution and poverty, and we could but exclaim, "The Lord must have *meant* these coats and vests and beautiful undergarments for these special people!" I love to believe it was even so. Is He not at this very time preparing glorious array for the summer lilies, and weaving a tender green dress for the "grass of the field"? Are not the "eyes of the buds even now peeping through the black lattice of the boughs" in expectation of being "clothed upon" by the care of the great Creator, and is He likely to be unmindful of His *children's* needs? No, surely not; "for your heavenly Father knoweth that you have need of all these things," and if He so deck the lily and array the grass, "will He not much more clothe you, O ye of little faith?" So the pleasant task was given into my hands to distribute the raiment which His own love had provided for some of His servants, upon whose lips the doleful cry of "Wherewithal shall we be clothed?" was just beginning to tremble. "I had been asking God to send me a pair of new shoes and a pair of trousers," wrote one poor pastor, "and how to begin to thank Him I do not know. Our hearts were so filled with gratitude on seeing your kind gift that we saved our meal, for all appetite had fled in the excitement, the children skipped and clapped their hands for very glee, my wife got quite fidgety in thinking of her new dress, and the sense of God's goodness to us all completely overpowered me. The clothes fit me beautifully, and you will know I needed them when I tell you that those I am now wearing are in their fifth year." This pastor has three services every Lord's-day, and three week-night services; a wife and five children to maintain, and his income is £53 per annum! Yet hear what he says of his Master's service: "I am far from complaining so long as my God uses me, though in a very humble way, for His glory and the good of my fellow-men."

If God's birds and lilies seem sometimes to be better cared for than certain of His poor servants, is it not because *we*, as fellow-servants, are not anxious and eager enough to do the will of our Father in heaven? "If," says a well-known writer, "men are in a worse plight than the birds of the air and the flowers of the field, the blame lies at the door, not of divine, but of human providence." We might with delightful assurance be "labourers together with Him" in this matter of temporal provision for His dependent ones, for He would use us to feed and clothe them, even as He uses the sweet influences of sun and shower to beautify the grass of the field, or charges the willing earth with the commissariat of all the "fowls of the air." There is a deep and satisfying happiness to be found in ministering to the wants of God's servants, and every such opportunity missed is a loss of the sweetest and purest joy. Help some poor Pastors yourselves, dear friends, and you will find that the blessings you bestow upon them for the Master's sake will return to you like richly-freighted ships, bringing you a heavenly cargo of spiritual recompense.

* * * *

Continuing for a while the subject of the last entry, I will give a few more details from the letters of those ministers who received the gifts of clothing already mentioned. One says, "We are all very pleased with the share we have in the contents of the parcel. There is something for wife, children, and myself, and everything is so suitable and helpful. I scarcely know how I shall feel when I get on the nice warm clothes, and my wife says she will look as she once did, in her new dress. I must say I experience a certain amount of pride in the beautiful things, and the nice underclothes, and the wife says I shall look like a gentleman!" Certainly none could more deserve to wear the outward garb of "one of nature's noblemen" than this much-tried and much-enduring pastor. He has been battling this long time with no small tempest of adversity and sorrow,—all God's waves and billows seem to have gone over him, and he has been brought into the deepest of deep waters; but at the very moment of his saddest extremity the Lord wrought abundant deliverance for him, and through those dear friends who make me their happy servant in this matter he has been brought out of all his distresses, and a new song put into his mouth, of praise to our covenant-keeping God. He says, "I feel the load removed which has burdened me so long, I see my precious books saved from dispersion, I see the faces of my wife and children lit up with joy, I seem to hear the congratulations of those comrades in the conflict who have always stood by me,—what can I say to you, or to the friend who has so generously helped me, but that I thank you with tears and prayers, and bless the name of the Lord." "This poor man cried, and the Lord heard him, and saved him out of all his troubles." If I were to tell all I know of this pastor's sufferings, his pains, his privations, and his heroic patience, the revelation would bring tears of pity to my readers' eyes and murmurs of admiration to their lips; but I must forbear, lest my words should seem to intrude too far into the sanctuary of his inner life, and touch with undue familiarity on matters sacred to God and his own spirit.

But ah! as I turn over the pages of the letters which are so full of gratitude for help received, I note with aching heart the undertone of sadness which mingles with the surface song of praise. Even the present joy cannot quite blot out the dark lines of past anxieties and sorrows. "I have been so very unwell all the winter," writes one of the bravest little women I know, "that our expenses have been unusually heavy, and I had put nothing by for the little boy's advent, so when he came we had no money in the house, and having to take our salary little by little, times being so bad with the people, we hardly ever seem to possess any." "We never were so straightened as now," writes a pastor in Essex, "my income fell off last year more than twenty-five per cent., and I assure you we have wanted the common necessaries of life, and I have come to my last pair of trousers. When I put the 'note' into my wife's hand, she burst into tears, embraced me, and said, 'What a mercy God has raised up friends to be so kind and good to us!'" So the tears mingle with the smiles, and "the clouds return after the rain," and these poor, tried servants of God struggle on bravely through difficulties and anxieties which never ought to be allowed to oppress and burden them. "The people to whom we minister in holy things," wrote a pastor to me a short time since, "have but little conception, in fact, seem to have *none*, of the straits to which we are sometimes driven in order to pay our way and keep ourselves and our families respectable. I have had many a battle to fight with the devil on this ground, for he tempts one to give up the work which pays so badly; but, thank God, I could not live without preaching the gospel, though at the same time my heart often bleeds that I cannot provide myself with the books which would give me a greater fitness for the discharge of my sacred duties." I am afraid the charge of wilful ignorance brought by this minister against his people is only too well founded and universal. But what a thousand pities it should be so! Are there not generous hearts in every Christian congregation who will cast aside with shame this growing apathy to their minister's grave anxieties, and no longer bear the sin and blame of such an evil indifference to his cares and circumstances? There are hundreds of Christian ladies in England who sigh for some quiet, tender little service for their Lord, yet fail to see this, which waits even at their doors, and which would, if taken up heartily by them, not only introduce into their lives a definite, warm-hearted purpose, but would carry brightness and blessing, nay, a very revolution of joy, into ministerial homes all over the land.

* * * *

April.—Four crown pieces, labelled "Silver blossoms for the dear lemon tree," were sent to-day by a beloved friend to cheer my heart and help forward my work. She says, "I have had them a long time lying by; for my dear departed mother used to save them as a little present for me, and I never before could part with them; but when I read how you began your good work, I felt I must devote them to the Lord in the same way, and they come to you with love and prayer." This is a pleasant and unexpected result of my simple relation of the facts connected with the formation of the Book Fund; I thank God for it, and earnestly hope my friend's loving example may induce others to follow it, and consecrate their "hallowed things" to the Lord's service. I can testify that such an investment will well repay them; for the value of my pretty coins, which were a free-will offering to Him, has not only been restored tenfold, but a glorious "usury" of joy and satisfaction has been added, without which I should now deem myself poor and needy indeed.

There have been, also, other kind gifts placed (figuratively) at the foot of my beautiful lemon tree, for which I am very thankful. Let me say to all those tender, responsive hearts who choose this graceful manner of bestowal, that I greatly appreciate their sympathy, and that I earnestly wish for them a fulfilment in their own experience of George Herbert's quaint prayer :—

> "O that I were an orange-tree,
>   That busy plant !
> Then I should ever laden be,
>   And never want
> Some fruit for him that dresseth me."

*   *   *   *

Two letters this week, from dark and distant parts of the earth—one from Calcutta, the other from China, and both containing money for books—have brought good cheer with them, which must be shared with my dear friends. The Book Fund does not profess to do much for foreign missions ; but whenever an appeal presents itself it is responded to with loving haste, and many cheery little tokens of blessing have been received and treasured up as unexpected rewards for long-forgotten services.

Most of the staff of the "China Inland Mission" look to the Book Fund for a parting gift when preparing to leave home and friends for work in that land of idols, and it is delightful to know that the books thus given are a comfort to them in their exile, and a constant help in their spiritual life. The following letter from the wife of one of these missionaries will, I hope, lead many to pray for such devoted workers :—

Dear Mrs. Spurgeon,—My husband has for some time felt exceedingly desirous to possess the fifth volume of " The Treasury of David," and we have only been waiting for the Lord's goodness to enable us to send for it : now He has graciously given us a small sum, part of which we feel at liberty to devote to this purpose ; but instead of *purchasing* it, I write to ask you to give it to my husband, and accept the twenty shillings for your Book Fund. I cannot refrain from proposing this, because I know how greatly he values the *gift* you made him, when last in England, of the first four volumes. Oh ! they have proved to us a "treasure indeed"; we have half an hour daily at morning prayer over them, and never without profit, sometimes obtaining precious morsels as from the Lord's own hand, upon which our souls feed all the day long. We are here *alone*, His solitary workers in the midst of thousands of blind idolaters; but He is with us, and the sweet assurance of His presence sustains us in His glad and glorious service! Pray for us."

Is not this a lovely little letter? Its simple words fairly sparkle in my eyes like the jewels of the Kingdom. Here are love, joy, peace, long-suffering, gentleness, goodness, faith—and they drop like choice gems from the lips of this "King's daughter," while with sweet, unconscious grace she tells of her Lord's love and faithfulness. Need I say I sent her the fifth volume of "The Treasury," and other books to accompany it?

* * * *

The next letter is from a Wesleyan minister at Calcutta, and gives some hopeful tidings from that quarter; it shall speak for itself, and enlist your sympathies, as it did mine:—

Dear Mrs. Spurgeon,—You were good enough some time ago to present me with a most valuable parcel of books. They have furnished me with many sermons, and much incidental blessing and help. Here in India our work seems unusually laborious and discouraging, but there is one feature of it which is at least promising—I refer to the work among the Baboos, or educated natives, of this great city. . . . . They read greedily everything one gives them, and my purpose in writing you is to beg for a parcel of Mr. Spurgeon's little books to distribute gratuitously among them. They are the exact thing needed by these young men now, I believe. I hardly know if this comes within the range of your good work, but I hope it may, for it would contribute largely, I am sure, to the success of mine. I suppose my friends here would deem me an enthusiast if I were to say that I believe idolatry is on its last legs. But it is very certain that the great majority of the Hindoos in this neighbourhood do not believe in their religion; they have a profound contempt for their system, and despise themselves for submitting to it. They excuse themselves on the ground that their fathers did it: and in this unchanging East, what has been must be; and so for the present they show an outward respect to Shiva, and Douga, and Kali; but the days of these gods are numbered, and it only needs that the native mind be stirred up to a grand point of courage, and all this part of Bengal will come over to Christianity bodily. This is why I ask your help.

By the kindness of the Wesleyan Missionary Society, I sent out a good parcel of the books asked for by this good brother; and very earnestly do I pray that each little tractate and sermon may bear a blessing in its pages to the poor souls who have so long sat in darkness and the shadow of death.

* * * *

A friend just recovering from a long and painful illness, sends me £100 to-day for Book Fund and Pastors' Aid, as a thankoffering to the Great Physician and Healer. My heart is lifted up with joy at this great and good gift, yet at the same time it is overwhelmed with a sense of unworthiness of so much mercy and love. How gracious is the Lord to remember my work thus tenderly, and incline His servant to entrust this consecrated offering to my hands, making me the happy bearer of bounties and blessings to His necessitous ministers! Deep gratitude to my faithful friend, who has long helped me in this loving work, blends happily with sincere pleasure in his release from pain; and this sum of money, devoted and sacred, stands like an altar of gold before us, from whence the sweet incense of united praise and thanksgiving shall rise to the God who hath done such great things for both giver and receiver.

Now, with such a full purse, I shall be expecting fresh and frequent demands upon it; the Lord must have some prisoners languishing for the deliverance He has so mercifully provided, some fainting ones looking out wistfully for the succour now close at hand; and, oh, what a joy to be the messenger of His loving mercy, the distributor of His Kingly largess! I feel impatient to scatter this increase of goodness, and enrich at once all the destitute hearts and homes whose secrets have been revealed to me; but I must deal wisely with my wealth, tutoring my hand to obey the Lord's signal, and binding my desires to yield perfect obedience to His will. He knows whom to call to the feast His love has provided, and the guests when they come will be both willing and welcome. Often am I charmed by the sweet spirit of cheerful endurance and holy contentment, which is apparent in some of those servants of Christ who are most tried and burdened by earthly needs. Only this morning I had a letter which came to this blessed conclusion—"Many times when God has appeared for my help, I have truly felt I would rather be poor and straitened like this, and know so much of His goodness and faithfulness, than be above temporal care, and miss the sweetness of His timely help." Surely this is testimony which brings glory to His name; and to carry comfort to such witnesses for God is an enviable honour and privilege.

* * * *

May.—We have open-air concerts day and night now at "Westwood"; for the songs of a multitude of feathered choristers round about the house give us constant and delightful entertainment. During the day, blackbirds, thrushes, and a host of sweet-voiced finches, keep up a succession of chorales and concerted pieces with amazing zest and energy; but as night draws on, and the moon sheds her soft light over the landscape, our listening ears are charmed by the still more delicious music of the nightingales, who sing their lovely solos and duets from the covert of a bosky little coppice at the foot of the hill. What floods of liquid melody they pour forth from their tiny throats! One listens with almost bated breath to the marvellous notes, fearing lest any earthly discord should disturb with unseemly jar such heavenly strains, and wondering with vague solemnity whether the old philosophers were warranted in their assertion that "all sweet sounds moving by the mystic laws of number are an aspiration towards the music of the spheres, a reminiscence of the universal harmonies." Be this as it may, to hear the nightingale's lovesong is an experience which we who are near dwellers to a great city cannot expect often to enjoy, and the first time I threw open my window to admit the mysterious warblings I was enraptured, and felt quite prepared to endorse all that has ever been said or written in their praise. Then, when night after night the charming serenade grew louder and more fluent, alternately trembling with tenderness, and gushing forth with quick impulsive throbs of joy, I seemed to be listening to some stray notes of the unceasing symphony of praise which rises to God's throne from His glorious creation. My spirit was stirred within me, and I longed to swell the grand chorus, even though it might be but with *one* feeble note of unison. 'Tis true my offering of praise is but as a sparrow's homely chirp; but it may not be restrained; not a glad chirrup of deliverance, not a twitter of grateful thanksgiving must be lacking. The nightingale's song set my soul singing, and poor as the score is, it must be written down here, lest an occasion be missed of telling of the Lord's great goodness and mercy.

I look back on the past fourteen or fifteen years of my life, and all that time seem to have been passing through a narrow winding valley, where pain and weakness made the walking rough and difficult, and where sometimes the Shadow of Death fell across my very feet. Yet no terror reigned there, for it was a prosperous and fertile place, as valleys often are; the dew of heaven lingered in its depths, nourishing many sweet flowers of faith and patience, which perchance might have dropped in a sunnier spot, while now and again the weary traveller found "quiet resting places," provided with such abundant compensating delights, that in their enjoyment the toil and trial of the way were well-nigh forgotten. And now even this exceeding goodness is exceeded; for by the power and love of the Lord the "valley has been exalted," the season of constant suffering has given place to a brighter experience, and though health and vigour are very far from being perfect, there are times when so much of life's purest pleasures can be enjoyed, that one feels every song should be a psalm, and every breath should bear a burden of praise. Verily, God hath been very gracious to me; He hath brought me out into a "large place," and given me a "goodly heritage," where I can

"With the sunlight on my forehead
Stand upon the mountain's brow,"

and, gazing far below, see all the way by which He hath led me, and wonder at and admire the love and wisdom of His guiding hand. Oh, for the power to shout forth His praise!

"Lord, place me in Thy concert; give one strain
To my poor reed."

"*Bless the Lord, O my soul, and all that is within me, bless His holy name!*" And you, ye nightingales, sing your loveliest lays, and make the night-air vocal with your matchless music; bring the tribute of your minstrelsy to Him who gave you such ravishing voices; perchance ye shall lure other hearts, as ye did mine, to join in your celestial melodies; and the Lord will bend His ear to listen to the feeblest note of thanksgiving from the lips of His redeemed ones. So, "till the day break, and the shadows flee away," and the blessed time come when we shall "praise Him day and night in His temple," we will sing our "songs of deliverance," and comfort ourselves with His own assurance, that "whoso offereth praise glorifieth Me."

* * * *

A friend wrote the other day: "Are you getting on nicely with your 'Book Fund Diary?' I hope you will not forget to give us a bunch of May flowers in its pages." "How is this to be done?" I asked myself, somewhat puzzled by the friendly suggestion. Many days the question followed and perplexed me by its vexatious persistence; but to-day I find it unexpectedly and delightfully answered by reading "between the lines" of a letter received this morning containing only these few words:

£20 for dear Mrs. Spurgeon's Book Fund.
Altenberg, in Sachsen.

Who this generous donor is remains a mystery, for no clue is given to his or her identity; but I am quite sure the Lord inclined the heart and prompted the hand of the sender, and so I take the gift from *Him* with humble, thankful love. And these sweet surprises, these beautiful blessings which my gracious Lord so often sends me, shall be preserved in the pages of my little book as one presses a rose-leaf or a frond of fern.

"There is rosemary for remembrance,—
And there's pansies,—that's for thoughts."

And they shall be enshrined as memorials of His goodness to

encourage my soul in after days, or as precious evidences of His faithfulness, for others to look upon with admiring love.

* * * *

Worthy of a place among the sweetest flowers of remembrance which these pages have ever preserved is the following letter from a Church clergyman. No perfume of rose or lily can equal the fair fragrance of this grateful and gracious acknowledgment of blessing received ; no beauty of leaf or tender tendril can compare with the loveliness of this loving deed, and, though the words in which the tale is told are brief and simple, I lay them up before the Lord with great delight, and thank and bless Him for such a precious tribute to the value and importance of the work He has given me to do. After alluding to a painful bereavement which he had lately sustained, my friend says :—"When making application some time back for books from your Fund, I stated that my income was under £150 per annum. Since then it has been increased; for by the will of my father I became entitled to a legacy which I never anticipated, and I have now much pleasure in enclosing a cheque for £5 as a contribution to your Fund, and as a grateful acknowledgment of the great benefit I have derived from the perusal of 'The Treasury of David.'" To receive money in this way is one of the happiest experiences of my life. I do not think I should love the Book Fund half so well if it were supported in any other way than by those "voluntary contributions" which are so manifestly given because "the love of Christ constraineth us."

* * * *

I have constant testimony to the blessing which God graciously causes to rest upon the pages of the books sent out by the Fund. It is not to "The Treasury" and the "Sermons," and the larger works merely, that the honour is given of being as waters in a thirsty land, or as food to a hungry soul ; but the smaller messengers carry with them an influence and a life-quickening which can come only from the breath of the Spirit of God, which clothes the words with power, and makes them mighty to accomplish His good purpose in the hearts and minds of men. Dr. Fish's "Handbook of Revivals" has been signally owned of God as a means of rousing drooping energies, or as a timely help in seasons of blessed soul-awakening. "Thank dear Mrs. Spurgeon," wrote a pastor quite lately to my husband, "for the books she sent me some two or three years ago; amongst them was Dr. Fish's work, and I have often looked sorrowfully at it, taken it down from the shelf, read some portions, and put it up again with a deep sigh. Should I ever want it? Would God ever visit this town? *Now, it is invaluable,* and, acting on the hints there thrown out, I am earnestly endeavouring to harvest the fruit, and feed the lambs. 'Glory be to God!'"

A Primitive Methodist minister, to whom I gave this "Handbook," always carries it with him in his journeys round the circuit, and "finds it a great and blessed help" to him. Watson's "Body of Divinity," and the works of various authors which I have from time to time distributed, have all had their share of divine blessing; and my spirit is often refreshed by hearing how useful and precious the grants of the Book Fund have been. "You do not know how much good you have done me and my dear people," writes a country pastor. "I often feel sorely how needful it is to pour in knowledge if I am to pour it out; and you have given me an inspiration, which I hope will never cease."

Curiously enough, as I am writing the last words of this paragraph, there is put into my hand a guinea from a minister *not* rich in this world's goods, with these words, "Your Book Fund is doing such a good work, and is so great a blessing, that I wish I could give ten times the amount."

* * * *

June.—Taking advantage of my friend's suggestion to preserve a "bunch of May flowers" in the pages of my "Diary," I will this month give my readers some "leaves of June roses." They have fallen, fair and sweet-scented, from some charming letters just received; and will well repay me for gathering them up, and storing them safely, if their fragrance proves pleasant to the kind and generous helpers of my work.

With God's blessing, your husband's "Sermons" have made me what I am as a preacher; I always carry them about with me, and read them to those I visit.

In addition to "The Treasury," you have generously sent me some other valuable books, all of which are new to me, save by the catalogues sent from time to time by the publishers, which are generally as useful to me as the fabled grapes were to the fox.

You have filled my house with sunshine, and my heart with overflowing joy. The Lord bless you a thousandfold in return, and long spare you to be a comfort and help to His servants.

When I came home, my dear wife had all the books laid out on the study table. Our joy knew no bounds. I had been destitute of books so long, and now so rich a feast was spread before me, that we could only give vent to our feelings by pouring out our grateful thanks to Him for whose glory the gift itself was made.

Words cannot tell you how delighted I am with the books, nor how grateful I feel for them. "The Treasury" I had seen before; but I never expected to own the five beautiful volumes. I cannot hope to repay you either for them or the other books, or the letter you sent with them. I can, however, ask my Father to bless both you and your work, and I shall most earnestly do so.

I hope by-and-by to be able to purchase all Mr. Spurgeon's "Sermons," for I have met with no books where I got so much substantial food to feed on—so much fresh seed wherewith to grow my own poor harvest.

I am now in receipt of your most worthy and excellent gift of books, and acknowledge with heartiest thanks, and every expression of grateful appreciation, my lasting obligation to you and Mr. Spurgeon. His faithful and cheering words have often been wonderfully blest to me, and have filled my whole sky with heavenly light. It would be dishonest on my part not to acknowledge the spiritual benefit I have received, since I entered the ministry, from his precious "Sermons."

I am very, very pleased with the books, but find it impossible to convey on paper my deep sense of gratitude. It was my joy once before to receive a parcel which helped me exceedingly in my work. The volumes of Mr. Spurgeon's "Sermons" which it contained have been of immense assistance to me, and now this fresh cause for thankfulness almost overwhelms me. May God abundantly bless you in your great work of helping poor Pastors, for thus you very practically help the *churches.*

I received the books, and shall set apart an hour or two next week for special thanksgiving to God, and prayer for you and dear Mr. Spurgeon.

The "Sermons" are invaluable. An old lady told me lately that she always knows when the clergyman has been reading Mr. Spurgeon's "Sermons," as he preaches so much better afterwards.

I was perfectly astonished when I saw the large pile of precious treasures. In some books one finds a deep draught of thought here and there, but "The Treasury of David" is brimful and running over, and keeps running over like a spring of living, life-giving water. Your present will, through divine grace, prove a great blessing to my hearers as well as to myself.

These testimonies are a choice joy to me. They come daily, like the flowers, to cheer and refresh my spirit, and sometimes I wish my friends had not to wait twelve months for their share of the reward of service; but I try to *conserve* some of the sweetness for them—as the sugared rose leaves and violets of the sunny south are prepared—and hope I may not be wholly unsuccessful.

* * * *

A lady who manages a Working Meeting connected with one of our suburban churches writes thus:—"There has been a proposal made among a few of the friends who help us, that we should in future work for the poor of our own neighbourhood; but the majority of us are quite determined to do the little we can for those who are working for the Lord as ministers or missionaries. If you still think (as I am sure you will) that there is need for efforts like ours, will you kindly say so when you are writing to me?" The Society superintended by my friend has rendered gracious and important service to many needy ministers of Christ for several years, and I am sincerely thankful that most of the members mean to continue their work in the same direction. Not that I would for a moment ignore the claim of the poor dwellers in the courts and alleys to Christian charity and compassion—let their bitter poverty and their dense darkness plead for help and light with unanswerable pathos—but we must not on this account relax our efforts on behalf of poor ministers; not, at least, till an important change has taken place in their position and circumstances. Their needs are at present more urgent than ever they were; for the sad agricultural depression, which has for the last two years obtained throughout the land, has told heavily on the slender finances of country village Pastors. Constantly I am hearing of diminished stipends; and knowing, as I do, that at the best of times the salaries of so many of our ministers are pitifully meagre, I marvel at the patient endurance of these good men, and pity with all my heart the wives and children who suffer and share in the penalties of such enforced poverty. "Our income has fallen off by nearly one half," writes one of these distressed ones lately, "and, as a consequence, I have to get my salary *by dribbles*, as I best can. My people have never been able to give more than £50 per annum, but even this they cannot now provide. My last quarter's salary is not much more than half paid, and another quarter will soon be due, so you will see I am sorely tried, and know not what course to take." I am devoutly thankful to be able, by the Lord's goodness to help cases of this kind which come under my notice; but there are hundreds more who need timely succour, of whom I may never hear, or for whose wants my small store would be wholly inadequate. If our wealthy and well-to-do churches were to take up as a duty the care of some of the weak and feeble ones, what a lightening of burdens, what a curing of heartaches, would ensue! I bless God when I see signs of awakened attention to this important matter, and am delighted beyond measure when I find He has permitted my little book to stir up some pure minds to remembrance of the wants and woes of poor ministers. I had a letter lately which told a pleasant tale to my willing ears when the writer said, "Your Book Fund Report has led me to take great interest in a new Dorcas Society we have established in connection with our church; we work for needy ministers with large families, and send a box of new clothes about Christmas. I take your book to the meetings and read it aloud, and all are much interested."

* * * *

I should be intensely happy if my small service for the Master's servants were but the beginning of better things for them throughout England and elsewhere. What God graciously enables me to do might be very greatly extended and improved upon by others, and who can calculate the blessing and benefit which would result from united and considerate effort on the behalf of the many poor ministers of Christ who do truly "bear the burden and heat of the day"? Moreover, the work brings good wages. The gratitude of loving hearts is pure gold, and the blessedness of giving is never more graciously realized than in ministering to the necessities of the saints. "This day is one of good tidings," writes a country pastor, whose distress has been somewhat alleviated by the Pastors' Aid Fund, "if I should hold my peace the very stones would cry out against me. I felt the sweetness of communion with my God this morning, and could rejoice in Him as my portion; but scarcely had I risen from my knees when I received your kind letter, and the very precious gift it contained. My heart leaped for joy. It brought me again upon mp knees to thank my loving Father, and to invoke His richest benediction on you, who have been, and still are, as an angel of mercy, delivering me in the time of need. I had not been long in my study before the valuable parcel of books arrived, and now I find words but poor vehicles in which to convey the feelings of my heart. I tender you my warmest thanks, and join you in fervent prayer that these precious books may better fit me for my work, and help me to glorify my Master."

Is not such a letter as this a present and most pleasant recompense for a very small amount of care and trouble?

* * * *

July.—Two ladies were looking over the list of donations in the Book Fund Report for 1880, when the whispered enquiry passed between them, "Who can 'My Sea Gull' be?"

The curiosity modestly expressed by these friends may have provoked other minds; and though, as a rule, the names of my contributors are veiled by initials or private designations, I have no objection in this instance to reveal the identity of the owner of so singular a *nom de plume*. My dearly beloved son, Thomas, is "My Sea Gull,"—a bird of passage, truly; obliged to leave the dear home-nest, and cross the wide ocean with weary wing in search of health in a sunny land,—as yet finding no settled rest, and perhaps even now pluming his wings for another homeward flight. When his first voyage to Australia was decided on, he playfully announced himself as "Mother's Sea Gull," and ever since, the name has been a tender memory to me, and a home remembrance to him. Very pleasant to me is my dear son's love and care for my Book Fund work; in his very last letter came a gift to it, labelled, "A feather from Sea Gull's breast." Discerning eyes may note among the donations to its funds, not only his own love tokens, but many a gift from friends "over yonder," whose affection for him has translated itself in this graceful and delicate fashion. If those kind donors should ever read this little book, I should like it to express to them my tenderest thanks, my deepest gratitude, and say, as sweetly and persuasively as printed words can say, "For all your love and kindness to her son, his mother blesses you; for the help given to the Lord's work in her hands, may that gracious Lord reward you;" and if, as is probable, my wandering boy should see these pages before he once more gazes on his mother's face, let him read between these lines something of her gladness of heart for him, her great content in him, and her fervent thankfulness to God on his behalf.

* * * *

The following is from one of " our own " men, who pleads for a grant of books for a U.M.F.C. minister—with what result I need scarcely say. But a few sentences at the close of his loving epistle touch very tender spots in my heart, and I think friends will know how to make excuse for the little bit of maternal pride, and the larger share of exultation as the " President's " wife, with which I transcribe the following words :—" It is now nearly twelve months since dear 'Tom' preached in Ballarat. The people talk still about his discourse at the 'Academy of Music' to two thousand three hundred souls; also of his speech at the usual evening meeting on 'All for Jesus.' He stayed with me three or four days, and when he went away the house was quite dull. We keep ourselves posted up in these distant parts about home affairs, and very often on Wednesday evenings I read to my people something about dear Mr. Spurgeon and his work. I gave them, also, your Book Fund Report, which deeply interested them. Distance does not lessen our love for the dear place at Newington, nor for those whom God has so wonderfully honoured. If there is anything that will bring tears to my eyes, tears of love and gratitude, it is 'Auld Lang Syne.' There! they are in my eyes now, and I can scarcely see to write. The deepest love of my heart to you both."

* * * *

Those good friends who take pleasure in examining the details of my work may have noticed that every year there are some thousands of single "Sermons" sent away for distribution, and they may like to know that this is generally by request of some village pastor, who has at heart the spiritual needs of the people around him, and who seeks thus to reach some who cannot be induced to enter a place of worship. Not unfrequently, also, the request is made by a lonely worker who has to fight single-handed the giant evils of Ritualism and Rationalism, and he finds these "Sermons" like the "smooth stones from the brook," which in David's hand dealt death to the enemy, and wrought deliverance for Israel. Circulated as tracts among the people, they do their work silently yet surely, and many a heart receives its first awakening from the perusal of these little messengers, which were perhaps received carelessly, or admitted grudgingly to the home which they are destined, by God's grace, to brighten and sanctify. It is a pleasant thing to put such a sheaf of swift arrows into the hand of a poor pastor, that his bow may be "drawn at a venture" over and over again: at a "venture," did I say? Nay, rather with the blessed certainty that the Lord will direct these heavenly shafts to the joints of the harness, and cause wounds which He alone can heal. To-day I have a letter acknowledging the arrival of a parcel of these "weapons of war," which I sent to a small Yorkshire village, and the pastor tells me, with evident delight, of the joy and interest excited in anticipation of the opening campaign against the powers of evil. "We met together the other evening," he says, " to put the covers on the 'Sermons,' and do other work in the way of starting our Tract Society. It did my soul real good to see the unanimity and heartiness with which our friends undertook the work. May the good Lord help and bless them in its performance." I always feel very sanguine as to the result of such an undertaking, when it is done "heartily as unto the Lord"; for He, in His great goodness, seldom fails to command the blessing, even life for evermore, to attend the testimony of His servant by these "Sermons." I have endeavoured during this year to increase the number thus sent forth on their mission of mercy, and though I may never hear of the good which shall be accomplished by them, they shall surely bring " glory to God and goodwill to men."

* * * *

August.—A new source of pleasure in my work has opened up to me in the application of many *High Church* clergymen for gifts of Mr. Spurgeon's works. I regard this extraordinary circumstance with unlimited satisfaction, and while I attend to the demands of these longing souls, I experience a thankfulness which finds its best expression in a devout doxology. That the "Evangelical" party in the Church of England should desire and appreciate Mr. Spurgeon's writings is no marvel; for, as one of their chief men remarked in a recent letter to me, "they more accurately represent the theology of the Thirty-nine Articles and the Prayer-book than much of the rubbish which is foisted nowadays as Church of England doctrine upon the unhappy congregations"; but when men of decided *Ritualistic* views voluntarily seek the aid of the Book Fund in their eagerness to secure the "Sermons" and "Expositions" of the Baptist preacher, our first feeling of astonishment is rapidly merged into one of pleasurable expectation, and we cherish a hopeful, humble confidence that the Lord's hand is in the matter, and that He has His own purposes of love and mercy to perform by this instrumentality.

In one of the Midland counties the curate of a most "advanced" Ritualistic church wrote pleadingly for my gift of books; and his vicar, who has beforetime indulged in allusions to the Baptists of the town as "abominable dissenters," actually sent a very courteous letter of recommendation on his behalf. The books were forwarded, with earnest prayer that a blessing might rest on every page. In acknowledging the grant the recipient says, "I cannot thank you sufficiently for the trouble you have so kindly taken for one who is quite unknown to you. Tell Mr. Spurgeon I shall highly value his 'Treasury' and 'Sermons,' and hope to reap much benefit from his 'Lectures to Students.' I never write (I presume he refers to MS. sermons) without a prayer for God's guidance and blessing, and I shall study these books, looking for the divine enlightenment. I send you a view of my church—it holds about seven hundred people, and to-morrow I hope to assist in *five services*, and preach twice." Note from this experience, dear friends, how urgently the Book Fund needs your constant prayers, since such a responsible trust as this is vouchsafed to it. The volumes which you enable me to distribute are now continually passing into the hands of those who claim to be "priests" and the only authorized spiritual teachers of the people. I pray you, ask earnestly that our gracious God will give entrance and power to the faithful words so unexpectedly sought by them, and that He will show them, through these books, the beauty and purity and heavenly wisdom of a simple and unadorned gospel.

It is pleasant to see the rapid growth of kindly feeling among these gentlemen under the influence of the Book Fund's gifts. "I shall point to this present," says another High Church curate, "as an instance of kind Christian sympathy underlying considerable difference of religious opinion." When making application for a grant, this clergyman had conscientiously informed me that his views were widely divergent from those of Mr. Spurgeon on many important matters, and that, in fact, he was "what is called a Ritualist," though he did not admit the correctness of the appellation. "I rejoice, however," he says, "that there is much in common among all who really love our Master and work for Him, and I hope I need not assure you that your gift will be respected, treasured, and used, by the help of God."

* * * *

Singularly relevant to the above paragraph is the following letter, which came to hand a day or two after those remarks were penned. It speaks volumes for itself, and I insert it that its unusual statements may stir up our friends to constant use of "effectual fervent prayer" for God's blessing on the printed "Sermons"; seeing that He has thus wonderfully opened a way for them in unexpected places, and that issues so important and eternal depend upon their teaching. I give the letter almost in its entirety, suppressing only some few sentences which might undesirably lead to recognition of priest, people, or place :—

Madam,—Having heard that you kindly assist poor ministers with books, permit me to state that I am an ordained priest of the Church of England; and though prevented by age from holding any permanent curacy, I am engaged at a stipend of £30 per annum, in two villages, and have to go some distance on Sundays, in different directions, for morning and evening service. On the second Sunday in Lent this year I was needing a text, when suddenly I remembered the "Three Thens" (Isaiah vi. 1—8) by the Rev. C. H. Spurgeon, and gave it as a morning discourse at . . . I was afterwards asked by a district visitor what induced me to select so singular a text, and another hearer said she had never listened to anything like it before, while the majority of the people were so pleased, that during the nine Sundays I was there the church was full every afternoon. It seemed something new to them. When the Rector returned, though so many approved of my ministry, some of the better class complained that the sermons were too long, they *thought I was never coming out of the pulpit!* In country places fifteen minutes is the limit of time a curate is expected to take in reading his sermon. So now I have abridged many of the discourses in *The Sword and the Trowel*, and they have never failed to be acceptable. I met a carter driving his team the other evening, and he said to me on parting, "Ah, sir, the common people hear you gladly." Might I respectfully beg the favour of a few of the earlier volumes of Mr. Spurgeon's "Sermons"? I should deem the gift a great kindness ; for they would help me considerably for some time to come, and benefit the souls of many; for those I have already used have greatly instructed and built up in the faith those to whom I have delivered them.

Thus "Christ is preached," you see, dear friends, in most unlikely places, and, perhaps, sometimes in the very pulpits where, alas! "another gospel" has already obtained entrance.

Verily "God moves in a mysterious way His wonders to perform." What horror would have taken hold on the dignitaries assembled in the Church of St. . . . . on that memorable morning of their Rector's absence, had they known that they were listening to the utterances of the Pastor of the Metropolitan Tabernacle! But, doubtless, the Sermon they thought long and wearisome was a "savour of life unto life" to some of God's hidden ones there, and my heart sings with joy at the opportunity of helping this good man in his notable scheme of using those printed discourses to set forth "Christ, and Him crucified."

* * * *

September.—The mail from New Zealand this week brings me £41 3s., as the proceeds of collections made for the Book Fund on the occasion of my son's farewell sermons in Dunedin. The delight with which this grand sum is sent is rapturously expressed in the dear boy's letter, and the unselfish love which devised and accomplished so successful a surprise might well furnish a pleasant theme for a fond mother's pen. But although deeply grateful to my darling, and the generous friends at Dunedin, at the risk of most unwillingly damping the fervour of their joy, I have been obliged to confess my intense objection to a public *collection* for my work, and my regret that, even in this one instance, my rule of looking up to God *only* has been departed from. This is the first time the Book Fund has emerged from the quiet privacy which I covet for it, and it will, I hope, be the last occasion on which its modest services will be presented for the consideration and support of an assembly of people. All these years I have "made my boast in the Lord" that not a penny for its funds has, by my consent, been sought or solicited, but from *Him;* and I have gloried in the fact that my treasury has ever been entirely dependent upon His generous and bountiful hand. How right royally He has supplied me, let the records of my work tell forth to His honour and glory.

During the course of six years He has entrusted to me over nine thousand pounds for the supply of the mental and bodily needs of His servants, and during all this time there has been such a wonderful balancing of demand and supply, that I have been amazed at the condescension of the Lord in stooping to such details of careful love. Need I say that I am satisfied with His mercy? or that I prefer the sweet state of reliance on Him to any attempt to enlist earthly interest and favour? Even the very "trial of my faith," which comes sometimes from a low exchequer or the failure of some favourite spring, is too precious to be exchanged for anything less heavenly in experience than waiting till His voice is heard saying, "I will fill thy treasures." It is quite possible that many of my friends may fail to sympathize with me in these scruples, but none, I trust, will venture to think that in thus recording them I have forgotten the gratitude due to a very gracious act, or am insensible to the tender love which preferred the enrichment of "mother's work" above all considerations of self-interest. The entry which occurs on page 170, was written before I knew anything of this public subscription, and will so far prove to dear friends in the Antipodes that their loving gifts to my Book Fund are intensely valued by me; but, lest that should not be enough to convince them, I will again repeat in all sincerity that when the Lord inclines their hearts to remember my work for His servants, no offerings are more warmly welcomed or more affectionately appreciated than those which come to me from my son's loving friends, and bring with them, from the distant land of his exile, some pleasant tokens of his increasing Christian influence and power.

* * * *

It is often a matter of sincere regret to me that I have to confine my work within comparatively narrow boundaries, and limit my grants of books almost exclusively to poor Pastors of churches. There are hosts of local preachers and lay workers to whom the gift of a few books would be an incalculable boon; but, with the solitary exception of "Lectures to my Students," which I give to all who preach Christ—I am obliged to declare the Fund open only to ministers, to the exclusion of many earnest workers. The sole reason for this is that I have as much work to do as one pair of hands can manage, and any extension of the gratuitous benefits of the scheme to brethren not in "actual charge" would invite applications to which I might be unable to respond. So I keep plodding along in the old ways, only casting a wistful glance now and then on paths along which my feet would love to travel, were they but as vigorous as they are willing, and if my strength could keep pace with my spirit. Sometimes in a roundabout way, either as gifts from friends, or by small regular payments of their own, the worthy men of whom I speak do get some little help and comfort from my Fund; but there are so few who can either afford the reduced price I charge, or find a generous hand to aid them, that such cases are included in my usual routine of work without much additional labour. Let me relate an instance of the latter class, where Christian love worked her sweet will most winningly. One of "our own" Pastors, himself a very successful preacher, has for a deacon a good man who is a "local," whom God has greatly blessed in Bible-class work, and in bringing many souls to Christ by the spoken word. His very limited income, and the claims of a large family, prevented his expending money in books, and though he long hungered for "The Treasury of David," he could not spare the money to procure it. So his good pastor prepared a pleasant surprise for him, sent me the money for the volumes, and asked me to forward them, which I gladly did, adding the "Lectures to my Students" from the Fund. The good man's joy was great, and will be best told in his own words of acknowledgment. He says:—

I can but poorly express my thanks for the very generous present which I had the happiness of receiving by my loved pastor's kindness. To one who has to work for the bread which perisheth for wife, self, and seven little ones all day, and to do his best to perform not a few humble yet timetaking duties in connection with church, schools, and Band of Hope in the evening, such helps and hints as are contained in "The Treasury" and "Lectures" must be invaluable. I feel assured that the reading of these books will stimulate the brain, refresh the heart, and, above all, draw the soul into closer communion and fellowship with the Father and with His Son Jesus Christ. Already I am anxious for the Sabbath to return, that now, being better equipped for the Master's service, I may be the instrument of bringing many hearts under the influence of the thoughts and teaching of your dear husband, that so God's name may be abundantly glorified.

How fervently I wish that many who only *pray* that God's kingdom may come, would help those who are steadily working for it! The labourers are strong, and willing for service; but tools and appliances are sadly wanting. Who will come forward to supply them, and hasten on the time when men shall not need to say, "Know the Lord"; for all shall know Him, from the least unto the greatest?

* * * *

As the years roll on, I think I realize more thankfully than ever the great mercy and happiness with which God has filled my life, in permitting me to scatter abroad so abundantly the precious words He enables my dear husband to speak. It is a joyful task for a wife to dispense bread to the hungry, treasure to the needy, and cordials to fainting souls from her Lord's bountiful stores; but here is a better service, one of which an angel might be envious; for by this tender ministry saints are fed with heavenly food, the poor are made rich unto life eternal, sufferers are comforted with the comfort of God, and sinners are ransomed from everlasting death. How can I thank my Lord enough for giving me even a small share in the bestowal of such celestial alms and favours!

* * * *

The presentation of a useful and suggestive book to the three hundred ministers annually assembling in Conference is now an established institution, and it is only right that the kind friends whose contributions enable me to make the gift should possess some knowledge of its character and quality. My dear husband this year selected one of exceptional excellence, entitled, "In Prospect of Sunday,"* of which the reviewer in *The Sword and the Trowel* says, "We wish we could present a copy to every poor minister of the gospel in the three kingdoms. It is full of holy thought of a kind which begets thought, and has our warmest commendation."

Many grateful acknowledgments have been received from the Pastors accepting this book, all testifying to its great helpfulness.

---

* By Rev. G. S. Bowes.

October.—A few days ago, a search among drawers and boxes and little out-of-the-way corners resulted in the production of a miscellaneous collection of old chains, coins, brooches, rings, and trifling trinkets, which, being submitted to the valuation of a kind friend, were generously said to represent £6 10s. in cash, and the exchange of vanities for money was duly made to the great gratification of the vendor. With the six sovereigns and a half in one's hand, a private mental discussion ensued as to the final destination of the amount. "Should it go into the common treasury of the Book Fund, or the special purse of the Pastors' Aid, or—ugly, selfish thought!—might it not be used to purchase one pretty jewel for personal adornment?" Before the question was decisively answered, a letter was received which quickly settled the matter; for, thank God! the knowledge of His servants' needs soon dislodged all desire to use the money in any service save theirs. When I calculated how many blankets and yards of flannel my six pounds ten shillings would buy, I felt I could almost kiss the coins which by their potent magic could transform my useless trinkets into so many substantial winter comforts. I pictured to myself the joy and gratitude which would be felt by those to whom I sent such blessings, and tried to imagine the relief to heart and life which the possession of these needed comforts would bring. Yet I doubt whether I have not done a selfish thing after all; for the laying out the money for God's needy ones is a pleasure so exquisite that I feel sure their happiness in receiving must fall far short of the joy I have already experienced in planning the gifts.

I know there are hundreds of Christians who taste this blessedness more plentifully and constantly than I can ever hope to do; but are there not others, perhaps a large majority, who through thoughtlessness or forgetfulness "care for none of these things"? Surely it must be a reproach to many who profess to be followers of Christ that they stow away as useless in their houses, articles which would go far to increase comfort and brightness in a poor pastor's barely-furnished home; and that year by year on their wardrobe shelves lie garments which might have afforded warmth and solace to his shivering children. I know scores of ministers who do not have a new coat for the space of three or four years; yet some of their rich brethren, who claim to serve the same Master, have during that period spent on the *superfluity* of their dress a sum which would have comfortably clothed a whole family. "Do not think me troublesome, dear Mrs. Spurgeon," writes a much-tried wife, " but my poor little boys are in want of warm clothing now that the cold weather is coming on, and as we have a family of eight children entirely dependent on us, and our eldest daughter always ill, you will understand what a heavy burden my husband carries, and I am sure you will pity and help us." I did both, and put gladness into their sorrowful hearts; but this case is only one among so many, that I sometimes think all my efforts are unavailing, and I begin to feel the least bit discouraged. Oh, how thankful should I be to God if some who read these words of mine would straightway resolve to help me, and seeking out a weary, heavy-laden servant of God—I should not wonder if they discovered *their own minister* in such a condition—give themselves no rest till they had lifted his burden and comforted his heart!

✿   ✿   ✿   ✿

This year has been a notable one for valuable presents of books for my poor Pastors, and my earnest thanks are hereby given to the kind friends who have supplied me with volumes which I have been proud to distribute among those whose mental hunger has seldom opportunity of being satisfied except through the Book Fund. I am delighted to confess how deeply I am indebted to some of these loving donors, and with no small pleasure I quote the following sentence from the letter which accompanied a very choice addition to my store. "Dear Mrs. Spurgeon," said my friend, " I have given away a great many books in my day, but none with greater satisfaction than those I now send to you, for I feel that they will be speedily set to work, and go on duty at once."

Would that my record of "presents" ended with those

which call forth my gratitude and admiration. Alas ! I have to renew my yearly complaint that people in mistaken kindness *will* send me the rubbish they know not how else to get rid of. I remember saying in my last Annual Report that I had received almost every sort of inappropriate and unsuitable volume except a "Cookery Book," and I congratulated myself that such an indignity had not yet befallen my Fund. But I have now been brought to that "lowest depth;" for in one of the unwelcome parcels forwarded to me lately there are two musty old tomes which bear the title of

"The Complete Housewife,
and Accomplished Gentlewoman's Companion,
being a collection of upwards of seven hundred of
the most approved receipts for Cookery,
and above three hundred receipts of Medicine.
London: 1766."

After this I thought I might have borne anything ; but today has brought me a still sharper experience, and I feel constrained to exclaim against the cruel kindness of people who thus so thoughtlessly trouble and burden me. I had received an anonymous note bidding me expect the arrival of a case of books for my "*Clerical Library*, carriage paid as far as possible." With much anxiety I awaited the advent of the case, and when it made its appearance, its size was so imposing that I did not grudge the *nine shillings I had to pay for its transit*, confidently hoping to find many choice treasures in its contents. Judge, then, my annoyance and my indignation on seeing when it was opened that, with the exception of a few well-bound books of third-rate worth, the case was chiefly filled with old hymn-books, works by *Unitarians, and books against believers' Baptism !!*

Does it not seem cruel to mock my dear work thus, and give me a "stone" for my poor ministers who are asking "bread" at my hands? How to get rid of the rubbish was now the question. "Put the old lumber in the furnace," said an excited helper in the unpacking. "No," said another, whose manifest annoyance somewhat solaced me ; "no, it would only choke up the flues—it is not fit even for that use." The end of the matter was that the books were put out of my sight, and I was consoled by one proficient in the heavenly art of comforting; but even he could not quite charm away the grief of disappointed expectations. I had written to two or three ministers who needed standard Commentaries and other expensive theological works, telling them that doubtless such literature would be plentiful in this huge contribution to a "Clerical Library," and that they should be supplied *therefrom ;* instead of this, I had the mortification of confessing myself a poor deluded mortal, incapable of fulfilling the hopes I had raised. No remonstrance can reach an anonymous donor; but I can again plead very earnestly with all who read this little book, to refrain from sending *books* to my Fund unless they are standard works on theology, of real use and assistance to a pastor in his *preparation for the pulpit.*

* * * *

It is not my aim to fill as many shelves as I can in a minister's study with anything that comes to hand in the shape of a book. This would be an easily-accomplished task; but my work would lose its value, and God's blessing too, if such flimsy motives actuated me. I must have books well-chosen, appropriate, suggestive, sound, and spiritually-helpful, and with these I can carry on a work which, by God's grace, will have issues extending from time to eternity. What care I for the size or the binding, so long as there is "life" within? Hear what an "old student" says of the little brochure, "Glories of Christ," which was the Conference present last year. He writes thus — "It is the first book of 'living skeletons' I have seen. The Epistle to the Hebrews I have read more than any other part of the Testament; but this charming book has brought out a host of beauties which I had never before observed. I do not often get hold of a book that I can use as I have used this. Many, many thanks to Mrs. Spurgeon for it." This is the sort of thing that makes the Book Fund a blessing, dear friends, and I pray you, either send me the money to procure *such* books, or *such* books themselves, or leave me unencumbered by trash which a dealer in second-hand books would refuse to cart away.

Here, perhaps, may be the proper place to speak of the great kindness of all the publishers with whom I deal; for they seem in my case to put the idea of profit into a very secondary place, and to be almost as anxious as I am to help poor ministers. I think I have not met with a single exception to this rule, and I record the fact with much thankfulness.

* * * *

November.—A request came to-day for help of a kind which it is not in my power or province to afford. This does not often happen, and seldom have I the pain of refusing any such request. "But," said my counsellor, before whom I laid the matter, "you cannot take your funds for the purpose of *printing* books, however good they may be; and, wifey, you have quite as much work on hand now as you can get through." "Yes, indeed, that is true," I replied, and a moment's reflection showed me a very bright side of the fact, and drew from us both a grateful ascription of praise to our loving Father. "Do you notice, husband," I said, "how closely the Lord keeps the work within the bounds of my strength? Year by year, about the same sum of money comes from His hand. If one friend fails me, He raises up another, and, without advertisement, without offer or inducements of any sort, the stream of applications *from the right people* follows the course of the channel of supply. Six years now have witnessed this constant incoming and outgoing; a quiet, steady work, just fitted and moulded to the weak fingers which joyfully guide its machinery. Is not the Lord's tender care seen in this?" "Put that in your Report, wifey," said my "Head." So, I put it in.

* * * *

Can I give my readers too much of a good thing? So many fresh testimonies to the value of the "Sermons," and the constant use of them by ministers of all denominations, have reached me lately, that they seem to claim notice in my journal, and to be very meet and proper matter for its enrichment. A Wesleyan minister writes :—

You are doing a good work in this distribution of "Sermons." The world has never seen anything like the influence of that single pulpit, and I am one of those who pray for the continuation of its power. Very suggestive are these discourses to me. I do not preach them in whole or in part, but I get my sermons through their inspiration, *and from their texts, and as guided by their methods.* (The italics are mine, but are very significant). I am not unfamiliar with books, but nothing helps me to hit the centre like Mr. Spurgeon's "Sermons." These "leaves" are for the healing of the nations, as few other printed leaves can boast of being, and I find them an encyclopædia of evangelical truth and teaching.

Another preacher says :—

The weekly issue of Mr. Spurgeon's "Sermons" has, for many years, been highly prized by me. On Sunday afternoons, between my own services, I always set apart a special time for their earnest and prayerful perusal, and I can assure you I always receive much edification and refreshment from them.

* * * *

The following quotation is from the letter of a returned missionary, who, for the better prosecution of his ministerial work in England, solicited a grant from the Book Fund.

I am *very, very* thankful for your kindness, he says, the volumes will be a great help and comfort. The "Sermons" have been a treasure to me for the past fifteen years. Many a one have I put through my own little mill, and then given it to the people of the West Indies; and when they have said, "Oh massa, it be one berry good sarmont," I have thought to myself, " *Yes, it ought to be,* and I don't wonder you like it !'

Here is another extract to much the same purpose. A Scottish student missionary writes thus :—

Your dear husband's "Sermons" are always like marrow and fatness to my soul. I never fail to find in them food of the highest order. Not later than last week I read one on prayer, which I shall not soon forget. How it encouraged my heart ! How opportunely it came ! How it stimulated me to renewed effort in the work of soul-winning ! Time would fail me to tell you a tithe of the blessing I have received from Mr. Spurgeon's works, and I can assure you that the volumes you have sent will be a life-long treasure to me.

Precious testimonies! I bless God upon every repetition of them.

The following letters from an Independent minister and his wife will tell their own tale with simple eloquence. Some years ago I sent the good man some books, but I had reason to believe that a second grant would be as welcome and as well-used as the first; and with them, knowing his straitened circumstances, I enclosed a little present, which was thus gratefully acknowledged by the lady:—

My dear Mrs. Spurgeon,—When my husband unpacked the dress, and said you had sent it for me, I could scarcely believe him, for the gift was as unexpected as it was acceptable. I need not tell you that a salary of £90 per annum, with seven in family to provide for, does not leave much wherewith to buy dresses; and though my husband does not smoke, nor drink anything stronger than water, we have great difficulty in making both ends meet. But the Lord is very good, and always sends help in time of need. My very heartfelt thanks are due to you for such a suitable present, and will you also please accept my gratitude for your noble gift to my husband; he prizes the books more than jewels and gold.

This is evident from his own words:—

Dear Madam,—No language I can use can fully express my surprise and joy when I opened the parcel of books to hand this morning. How kind of you to send such a rich supply! Just the very books, too, on which, in many a bookseller's shop, I have cast a longing eye, and ardently desired their possession. For sometimes, having selected a text, and not seeing quite clearly how it should be treated, I would most thankfully have accepted Mr. Spurgeon's guidance and advice, and have thought myself happy to have followed in his footsteps; and now, through your generosity, I can consult him on many precious portions of God's Word. Your thoughtfulness in sending my wife so acceptable a present, and the abundant supply of note paper and envelopes you enclosed, show how truly you gauge a preacher's needs, and how liberally you supply them. When I first beheld the gifts my heart was full, and I could only say, "Bless the Lord"; but I really think if they had been personally presented, my tongue would have failed of speech from excess of feeling; however, I mean to show my gratitude by using the books constantly and prayerfully in the Master's service, and then I shall hand them down to my children as mementos of that honoured servant of God, whose "praise is in all the churches."

❉   ❉   ❉   ❉

The reference in the foregoing letter to a gift of "paper and envelopes" will be understood by those who read last year's Report, and there learned that I have a munificent friend, who not only keeps me supplied, for Book Fund work and private use, with all kinds of delightful stationery, but extends his liberality to my poor Pastors also; sending huge boxes crammed with packets of writing material, which are duly, and by degrees, distributed by enclosure in the parcels of books. I am under a covenant to apply to him whenever my stores are failing; but so lavishly does he stock my shelves that I have never yet had a chance of fulfilling my promise to "ask." All through this year his kindness has been constant and unvarying, and all the poorer Pastors applying for grants of books have had the satisfaction when opening their parcels of finding ten quires of good paper, with envelopes to correspond, provided by the thoughtful kindness of this dear friend, who seems never to tire of thinking, planning, and acting for the comfort and well-being of others. May the Lord Himself ever satisfy him with His favour, so that he may bear joyful witness to that faithful saying, "It is more blessed to give than to receive."

* * * *

A young clergyman wishes to bear witness to the benefit received from Mr. Spurgeon's "Lectures." I am only too happy to devote a paragraph to his letter. He tells me he has read my little book with interest, and till then had no idea of the hardships which many ministers had to suffer. He adds:—

I can well imagine what an immense assistance your Fund is to them. May it increase and grow as it deserves to do, and may God spare you many years to administer it in the same catholic, noble spirit! You have received many testimonies to the help afforded to young clergymen by your husband's "Lectures on Preaching;" let me add mine. Some time ago a friend lent me the book, and I there found *myself* portrayed in more pictures than one. It was not quite a pleasant discovery, and not at all complimentary to me; but it has enabled me to see myself as others see me; and I hope by God's help to benefit accordingly.

* * * *

Such a frank confession as the foregoing deserves commemoration in these pages; so also does the appreciative and kind note of another clergyman who, labouring in a large parish in the north of England, sought the boon of a gift of the books he longed for, yet could not afford to purchase. He acknowledges their arrival in these courteous terms:—

Dear Madam,—I am really very grateful to you for the liberality which has prompted you to act thus to me, a liberality, moreover, of Christian charity in its higher form; for you were aware that it was to a shepherd of a different flock to your own that you were sending your present. May God grant that the books may be useful in helping me to lead stray sheep, from whatever fold, back to the one great flock of those who love and follow the voice of the great Shepherd. I certainly did not know that I was asking for so very handsome a present as the five volumes of "The Treasury" make, and yet your kindness has added to it! I can but ask you to believe that my gratitude is real and heartfelt.

❈ ✻ ✻ ✻

December.—Yesterday, December 9th, deserves to be noted as a *dies non;* for that good gift of God, of which Solomon says, "Truly the light is sweet, and a pleasant thing it is for the eyes to behold the sun," was blotted out and obscured by an almost Egyptian darkness which fell upon us for long and wearisome hours. At 3.30 p.m. midnight had taken the place of "the perfect day," and spread her sable wings over the reluctant earth prematurely. From the high tower at "Westwood," nothing could be seen all around but black, lowering masses of dense darkness, which hung like funeral palls from the sky, and now and again lifted their fearful folds only to reveal a deeper and denser gloom beyond. Here and there the glimmer of a near gaslight could be discerned; but not a ray of Heaven's sweet beams pierced through the dreadful overshadowing, and a stillness more awesome than that of a real night hushed all familiar sounds. As hour after hour passed by, no enlightenment was vouchsafed us, nor could we tell when true night came to dispossess the rival darkness of the sceptre it had so strangely usurped.

Into all this dismal murkiness came two letters from

Mentone, telling of a placid sea, warm breezes, and clear bright skies—

> "Curtains of azure, and crystal wall,
> And dome of sunshine high over all"—

letters so full of joy, and good spirits, and glad delight, that for a moment the unbidden tears would gather, from the sheer longing I had to be in the sunshine too! But when the shutters were closed, the curtains drawn, and the dreary scene without excluded, I found I was in the land of Goshen still, and had "light in my dwelling"; for, like a star—better seen from the depths of a well than from higher ground—shone the conspicuous mercy that my beloved was spared this doleful experience. I knew the fearful darkness was not likely to stretch its hideous arms so far as the fair shores of the Riviera, and I blessed God for the comfortable certainty that "over there" the beauty and the splendour of an unclouded heaven were doing their sweet restful work on a tired heart and brain. So my gloom was dispelled by the light of my husband's happiness; for from the "South land" the sunbeams, imprisoned in his precious letters, travelled a thousand miles to cheer me, and by their gladsome message turned my night into day.

I wonder whether this is a faint picture of the comfort wherewith God sometimes consoles His bereaved children, by enabling them to realize the unspeakable blessedness of those who have "gone before." Temporary separations by distance are but the foreshadowings of a sterner parting, which, sooner or later, must divide us from those whose love seems to be our very life. Happy they who can look beyond the grim darkness of such a sorrow, to the unsullied light and bliss which the hope of eternal reunion affords.

* * * *

I have a letter to-day from a Baptist minister who has been twenty-one years a pastor, and during all that period his people have been too poor to give him more than £60 per annum. His life has been a weary round of privation and bitter need, yet he does not complain, but says, "I have much to encourage me in my work; my Father gives me that which more than compensates for poverty; for we have peace in the church, and He blesses His own word to the edification of believers, and the ingathering of sinners." *The Sword and the Trowel* has been sent to him all the year, and he pleads for the continuance of such a "boon," "having no money to purchase books." After telling me that the income of his little church is sadly lessened by the death and removal of some of his best friends, he goes on to say :—" If I look forward, the prospect somewhat resembles this December morning; there are no bright rays from the sun, for the clouds are full of drizzling rain, and gloom prevails all around; but God will send deliverance in His own time and way."

I think I know how to coax a sunbeam to break through the leaden sky and light up the sad heart of this servant of God with its glory; and long before the Christmas snows clothe the cold earth in regal ermine, he shall sing a cheerful carol of grateful thanksgiving to the loving Father in heaven, whose "tender mercies are over all His works."

※　　※　　※　　※

Very soon after making the foregoing entry, I was called upon to help another pastor, of whose adversities and embarrassments I have long been most painfully aware. His is a sorrowful story, and he would not like me to tell it all; but alas! it is only one among so many similar cases, that even if I gave the details, there would be no fear of betraying his special confidence. A small salary—a very large family—a weak and sickly wife—want of proper food—increasing expenses—constant debt and difficulty—consequent anxiety and depression of spirit—these are particulars which will as well apply to scores of Pastors in our land as to the one whose distress I have just had the happiness of relieving in some measure. What are these men to do? They struggle on for years, bearing their crushing burden as best they may, till at last the only resource open to them is an appeal to private Christian liberality. Emigration is out of the question with a tribe of children, and a removal to a larger sphere of labour is equally impossible, since no church cares to accept a pastor so heavily encumbered.

Both heart and head often ache with thinking over the woes of which I know so much; and were it not for the Fund, which is lovingly supplied by the liberality of some very dear friends, I should rarely be able to do aught but "weep with those that weep." But how often is my mourning turned into joy by the Lord's goodness, and His people's generosity! I sent off last week a large packing-case full of winter comforts to the house of a minister where the wolf has long been sitting on the door-step, eager to gain an entrance. Through the fraud of a false friend the little private income which cosily supplemented a modest salary was entirely lost, and troubles trod quickly on each others' heels, till quite a host of disasters invaded the once comfortable home, and shattered its peace and plenty. The little wife's pathetic appeal would have melted any heart. "Sickness upon sickness," she says, after telling me of the loss of the money, "has brought us heavy doctor's bills; none can know, and few could imagine, how we have suffered through straitening circumstances. I have a very poor supply of blankets and sheets, and our undergarments are all worn very thin, having been mended again and again; my husband also is sadly in want of clothes." To these deeply tried people the gift of a cheque, a goodly pile of garments, some material for making up, and two pairs of warm blankets, has been an opportune deliverance from evil, and, for a while at least, comfort and content will revisit the home, and songs of thanksgiving will arise from gracious and grateful hearts.

A good friend in Scotland has devised and carried out a novel plan of helping me to suitable books for poor ministers. He sends me thirty volumes of sound, useful, expository works selected with care and discrimination, all of them worthy to hold a place on a studious pastor's bookshelf.

He shall himself tell how curiously he obtained them. He says:—

Dear Madam,—I have this day despatched to you by goods train a small box containing the books enumerated in the enclosed list, which

I trust you will accept for the Pastors whom you aid by your "Book Fund." You may be interested to know the history of this little box. I am in the habit of frequently picking up books for my own use at the bookstalls, which are very numerous in this city. My wife suggested that I might, while thus engaged, look out for books likely to be useful to your friends (and ours too, I think I may venture to say), and buy them if in good order and cheap. The volumes now sent are the fruit of this suggestion, and I trust they may prove acceptable.

This is a capital idea, and might be carried out to great advantage by many Christian gentlemen, on behalf of *their own* ministers, with very great satisfaction to both parties. I should not be jealous, dear friends, if scores of you were to set up a private "Book Fund for Poor Ministers" on your own account; but I should rejoice with unmixed contentment at such gracious rivalry.

THE PASTORS' AID FUND.

The "Branch Business," as some of my friends love to call it, still rejoices in God's blessing, and prospers financially. I have this year received £425 6s., and given away £328 12s. 3d., purposely reserving so large a balance to carry forward to some months of the coming year, as one of my most faithful and generous contributors gave his donation so lately that it belongs rather to 1882 than to 1881. My correspondence with the principal donors to this little private "Sustentation Fund" is so constant throughout the year, that they will not look for the *printed* expression of my deep and heartfelt gratitude; they know that their goodness in entrusting money to me for this sacred purpose is one of the great mercies of my life, and that I daily bless God for the unusual privilege thus conferred upon me; but to those other friends who send now and again a loving little gift for my poor Pastors, with a tender word of sympathy with them in their sorrows, let me here give a warm and thankful greeting, and say, "The Lord remember your love and kindness to His poor servants—'in that day!'"

From what I have previously said, and the many sad cases referred to in this journal, my readers will know how terribly inadequate is the sum above mentioned to meet the needs of the *mass* of poor dissenting Pastors. This cup of cold water cannot refresh the hearts of *many* thirsty, fainting workers; yet I thank my God with all the fervour of which my soul is capable for what it can do, and that I am permitted to hold it to the lips of some, and watch the returning flush of strength and steadfast purpose light up their weary faces! The harvest of the Lord is great, and these labourers are truly bearing the burden and heat of the day: it is a blessed service to go to and fro in the field to carry to them the solace and relief which the "Master" Himself has put into our hands.

Praise be to God for every doubt of His faithfulness scattered to the wind, every murmur hushed, every fear quieted, every sob beguiled into a song, by the opportune gifts of His love through this Fund; for the year just closing has brought additional trials to many whose lot seemed already heavily weighted with sorrows, and the faith and patience of some have been tried as by fire; but who can tell whether the Lord is not even now rejoicing over the "much fine gold" which has come forth from the furnace to testify to His wondrous working, and to reflect gloriously the honour of His great name!

CONCLUSION.

Dear Friends,

The Diary of Book Fund work for another year will now soon be published, and presented to my readers; and, as usual, I ask for it a gracious and lenient reception. There is nothing new or startling in its pages, it tells the same old story of the needs of God's servants—how patiently they are borne, and how providentially they are oftentimes supplied. It goes over the same well-trodden ground of simple facts, urges the same pleas for poverty-stricken ministers, and gives thanks to God with at least the same abundant cause for gratitude that other years have gathered round them. The task of recording is always a difficult one to me, and it grows more serious as the years roll on, and the freshness of new and delightful experience tones down into the regularity of uniform, yet dearly loved, service. Still I have hope that, by the Lord's blessing upon it, this latest chronicle of His faithfulness and love will claim as warm an interest in your hearts as its predecessors. The truth of the proverb, quoted in my preface, that

"**Prayer and Pains will do Anything,**"

is proved by the very existence of this little book; and though I dare scarcely tell how much I believe I owe to my God in this matter, I may say there could have been no "pains" taken if He had not heard "prayer," and then turned both prayer and pains into "praise." He has allowed me to receive testimonies to the usefulness of my Annual Report, of which I never even dreamed, and He has sometimes invested it with so tender an influence over His people's hearts, that I have trembled at my responsibility when writing for another year. May I give just one quotation from a letter very precious to me, to show how the Lord can work by feeble means, and make them mighty to accomplish His loving purposes? The writer says:—

Dear Mrs. Spurgeon,—The reading of your Report of the Book Fund has been a means of grace to me. When I received it, I was feeling very ill, was much perplexed about ways and means, and I am afraid I was a little inclined to murmur at my somewhat hard lot. But as I read on, I became ashamed of myself, and I had to put the book down while I poured out my heart in supplication for those of my brethren whose case was so much worse than my own, and, as the Lord turned the captivity of Job when he prayed for his friends, so He gave me a song of gratitude when I pleaded for my brethren. I shall never forget the holy joy of my soul in that hour, and I trust that the peace of God which it left with me may never be recalled, or disturbed by a distrustful spirit, or an unthankful heart.

To have one such reward as this, is compensation most rich and precious for the expenditure of any thought and labour; but my Lord has multiplied these mercies to me, and recompensed me with kingly munificence. My fervent prayer is, that a like consecration may rest on this present booklet, though there is nothing in it that can bless without His blessing, nothing that can stir the heart unless His Spirit moves upon the face of the waters. But if its perusal may encourage faith, stimulate to action, lead to thankful song, or in any way bring an atom of praise to the glorious God who has "made all His goodness pass before me," I shall again most gratefully subscribe myself His very unworthy child, but

Your faithful servant,

SUSIE SPURGEON.

"Westwood," Upper Norwood,
Dec., 1881.

SUMMARY OF WORK.

Books Distributed during the Year 1881:—7,298 Volumes.

Also 10,517 single Sermons for giving away. The recipients comprised 241 Baptists, 138 Independents, 243 Methodists, 144 Church of England clergymen, 34 Presbyterians, 87 Evangelists, and 27 Missionaries.

The Book Fund Diary

For 1882.

By Mrs. C. H. Spurgeon.

A MESSAGE FROM MENTONE FROM MY DEAR HUSBAND.

SITTING in Dr. Bennet's garden, I saw, rising above a building, the top of a fine young pine, named *Araucaria excelsa*. Its highest point seemed a simple line, or straight shoot, the growth of the present year, not yet quite complete. Below were five little branches (I dare say that is not the right word, but I know no better), and these were succeeded by another length of stem, and then again a fivefold growth. Looking at it, it seemed to be like the Book Fund, with its annual periods of labour, and the consequent Report, which crowns the growth of each year. I know that a new Report is soon to be thrown out, and I remember the pain and labour of its development; but it will come as surely as the Araucaria will put forth its star. Each outgrowth is nearer heaven, and tends to the perfecting of the tree. To you, I dare say, each year's work has less in it whereof you might glory, even as the tree grows less as it climbs higher; but there is to the eye of an onlooker a beauty and symmetry about the whole of a work which is done for Jesus, and my love may rest assured that her service is beautiful to Him whose approbation is her chief reward. He marks the Book Fund tree, not as I do this pine, *in part;* but He sees it from the root upward, and notes each leaf of its evergreen foliage. You see, I have used my unaccustomed pencil to depict what I saw, and it is a feeble failure; but when all things done on earth shall have their photographs exhibited at the last day, your Book Fund will be " a thing of beauty and a joy for ever," and holy intelligences shall agree in the verdict of " Well done."

There, too, among the roses, oranges, geraniums, lemons, heliotropes, and olives, I thought of the time when this superb garden was little more than bare rock. Who made it what it is? Of course there was a master mind which arranged, and planned, and ordered all, and to him the garden belongs, and the honour of it. But I saw *a woman* toiling up from the shore, with a load of earth upon her head, as much as she could carry; she shot this down to form a terrace, and then she went down for more. How many times she laboured upward with her burdens I do not know; but I have rejoiced in the fertility which has come of all her many loads and labours. I wonder whether she has any idea of the exquisite odours, and dainty blossoms, and charming fruits, which are the result of her ascents and descents beneath a burning sun. I know another female burden-bearer, whose heaps of books and loads of volumes go to and fro in an endless fashion, borne, not upon her head, but in her brain and heart; and I know how she almost faints beneath the never-ceasing labour. But she, too, is carrying the essential ingredients of fruit-growing to places which greatly need it; pouring out fertile matter for thought upon shelves which else had been bare as the rock; helping the Lord's tillers to make gardens wherein shall grow choicer flowers than those which have enchanted me this day. Go on, dear bringer-up of blessed burdens: you may not, nay, you will not, see the full result of your continuous service; but He will see it who has set you to the work. "*Supposing Him to be the Gardener*," you will renew your strength, and your poor ministers will again and again see their libraries replenished, and their hands helped in their work of causing the wilderness to blossom as the rose.

NEW YEAR'S DAY, 1882.—It seems but as yesterday that we bade farewell to 1880, and greeted with solemn yet kindly welcome the year which expired last night; yet already some hours have passed away since our introduction to this new period of our existence, and without pause or hindrance the moments are silently and swiftly carrying us forward to meet the unknown joys and sorrows, the pleasures and the pains, of this year of grace 1882. Trite and commonplace as any remark on the quick flight of time may appear, there are seasons when the thought forces itself upon our consideration in an extraordinary way, and the fact assumes the importance of a new and startling discovery.

In the cathedral at Milan, a careful observer may note, at a certain hour of the day, a small round spot of light travelling steadily across the marble pavement. Nothing can divert its course, nothing can stop its progress. From some tiny and invisible opening in the vast roof, a sunbeam descends, and with its bright finger marks on the tesselated floor the silent yet certain passing of the moments. I shall never forget seeing this solemn portent amid the stately marvels of that matchless edifice, nor the awe with which one asked the question, "Is it possible that my life is hurrying to its end with such an awful persistency as this?"

> "Still on it creeps,
> Each little moment at another's heels,
> Till hours, days, years, and ages are made up
> Of such small parts as these, and men look back,
> Worn and bewilder'd, wondering how it is."

True, the same warning is given in the lengthening of the shadows, the movement of a minute-hand, or the wasting of sand in an hour-glass; but none of these ever spoke so impressively to my heart as did the fast and unfaltering pace of that small disc of light across the marble pavement of Milan Cathedral. Twenty years have passed away since I actually trod those "dim mysterious aisles" and gazed on the surrounding wonders; but to-night memory carries me back to stand once more beneath the fretted roof, amid the sculptured pillars, while at my feet the bright monitor still bears witness to the haste of Time's unwearied footsteps. In bygone years the glories of the silver shrines and splendid jewels of this vast treasure-house had each and all an irresistible attraction for the eager traveller; but now, when memory is set free to revisit the place, she hovers persistently around *this* solitary spot, and quietly folds her soft wings there in the restfulness of sacred contemplation. Here, then, I would linger a while, that I may *look back* through the vista of the years, and thankfully acknowledge the greatness of God's mercies, and the infinite number of His lovingkindnesses. They have been countless as the particles which compose these massive marbles, and far more precious than the costly gems which gleam with awful radiance on the dead and shrivelled brows of embalmed saints in the crypt beneath me. To the Lord I owe all the clustering blessings which enrich my life, and all the fair hopes of eternal bliss which transform even death itself into an angel of light. And what have I rendered to Him for all this grace and favour? What record have the fast-flying moments carried up to Him of my works and ways since I first gazed upon this strange register of their silent though rapid progress? Ah! there is no comfort to be gained by a *look within !* for faults and failures are ready to bear swift witness against me, and "unprofitable service" is inscribed on even my best performances; so the glance must be quickly raised from self to Christ, for "He is a sanctuary" where, with sin atoned for and forgiven, my soul can rest, and worship, and hide itself from all accusers. And may I not from here also *look forward*, and in such a place becomingly consecrate myself anew to His sweet service, resolving by His grace so to "redeem the time" in future days, if they be granted to me, that its quick feet may no more reproach my dull, loitering steps? for I realize with a profound solemnity that "the night cometh when no man can work," and that opportunities of service are now yielding themselves, which, if not immediately embraced, will be lost to me for ever.

But now the fair vision fades, and I am recalled to present surroundings by the sweet chiming of Sabbath bells, which ring out for evening worship. I listen to the distant music with sorrowful realization of my loss in being unable to join God's people in the services of His earthly courts, yet rejoicing that I can catch an echo in my heart of better and more heavenly melody; for the Lord's own gracious words are borne in upon my soul, like stray notes from the harps of angels, "I the Lord will hold thy right hand, saying unto thee, Fear not, I will help thee," and the power of this blessed promise strengthens and braces me for whatever work or suffering may be appointed by His love.

So, as I make this first entry in my journal for the New Year, and try to weave some tangled thoughts and floating threads of memories into a smooth and pleasant web of meditation, I sing at my work, and bless the Lord for all His grace and goodness, past, present, and to come, while from my inmost heart the prayer ascends, "Lord, make me more devoted and useful; let this seventh year of the Book Fund's existence be a holy and happy period, a very Sabbath of delight, more fruitful in blessing than any which have preceded it. May all the work be done as *unto Thee*, and for Thy glory, and may Thy poor ministers rejoice in plenteous increase from its stores, and in loving sympathy from its willing servant. Command Thy blessing upon it,

O my God, 'from the beginning of the year, even to the end of the year.' For Christ's sake. Amen."

* * * *

January 8.—A generous friend sends a very welcome wedding present, to commemorate the anniversary of the happy day which made me "Mrs. John Ploughman." A goodly cheque to my husband "for any work of the Lord most needing help," and to me a gift for my Book Fund of exceeding interest and value, as being another instance of hidden treasure brought out, and laid at the feet of Jesus through His love's constraining power.

Last year I was delighted when a dear friend felt impelled to give up her long-cherished crown pieces to the Master's use, and now I have the joy of receiving six splendid golden guineas of the third George's reign, with this touching inscription:—

"Hoards of many years at last given up to the Lord."

They have been heirlooms in the family for a generation or two, and are beautiful coins; but never so beautiful as now, when the glory of consecration rests upon them, and they are willingly and lovingly offered for the service of the work of the Lord. My friend knows she will never regret the dedication of these treasures to Him who says, "The silver is mine, and the gold is mine"; but I can promise her much more than a negative interest in the transaction; for her joy in giving has already outweighed the pleasure of possession, and the very act of self-denial for Christ brings its own sweet and satisfying reward.

* * * *

The eager enquiry by clergymen for Mr. Spurgeon's works, and their warm appreciation of them, as recorded in my last Report, has agreeably astonished many friends, and loud and hearty have been the congratulations offered to me on this most interesting and important phase of my dearly-loved work. I am very conscious of the gravity of the trust thus committed to me, and feel an increasing conviction that in this matter the Lord has laid a solemn charge upon the Book Fund, and I constantly seek His aid, that by a wise and discriminate distribution of the books, His gracious purposes of love and mercy may be furthered and unfolded. With the divine blessing on their pages, what may not the teachings of these volumes effect? "You will doubtless be interested in the fact," wrote a young curate the other day, "that your husband's works were the *chief* books I found on an episcopal table; they were lent for the use of men about to be ordained." I am sure my readers will agree with me that this is a remarkable "sign of the times," and one for which we should devoutly "thank God and take courage."

* * * *

February.—Taking down an ancient volume from my husband's book-shelves lately, I was greatly interested to find the following quaint story, which, with a rugged pathos of its own, serves to show that "history repeats itself" in the present low estate of many of God's ministering servants, while it carries with it an unspoken plea for those to whom a little display of careful love on our part would secure an exemption from much needless distress. Thus runs the curious tale:—

> There was one Phillipus, a priest among the heathen, so poor that he begged for his living, and yet he would go about and tell how happy he should be. "When," quoth one, "will that be?" "When I am dead," says he. "Then, poor fellow!" quoth the other, "thou art to blame that thou diest not quickly, that thou mayest be happy." And thus it is often with the poor, despised, distressed ministers of the gospel of Jesus Christ. "The Lord is our portion," say they, "and we shall be happy." "But when?" says the world. "When we die," say the ministers. "Why, then," says the world, "ye are to blame that ye die not quickly, to be happy in heaven, whom the world hath taken an order with never to be happy on earth." This is the voice of those who would rather put a church into their purse than any way empty their purses towards the church's maintenance.

* * * *

By the blessing of God we are trying to alter this sad state of things; and though our beginnings are small, we work on in patient hope of steady growth and progress, and even now see cheering signs of awakening sympathy among those whose co-operation will be the future life and power of our scheme.

I note with extreme pleasure a paragraph in a letter received to-day by my dear husband, and I look upon it as an earnest of brighter days for poor Pastors—the modest commencement of united and organized effort on their behalf, which I pray may extend and increase till these grievous woes are remedied, and these intolerable burdens removed. The writer of the letter in question is one of "our own" men; and, after giving his President some account of church matters and means, he says, "The Ministers' Aid Association, which aims at helping our brethren in this country, is doing good service in families where the pinch of want is most severely felt. This society is really an echo and reflex of a Book and Pastors' Aid Fund, of which you know much, and which has earned for one we need not name the loving title of 'The Ministers' Friend.'"

Here is the wherewithal of great rejoicing for me and all those friends who so generously help me; for if the Book Fund shall indeed become the mother of many such promising children, the Lord will have fulfilled our petition, and given us the desire of our hearts.

If only two or three strong churches in each county would look after and tenderly help the weak ones, there would be no more complaints of the bitter destitution of our village Pastors, and the work of the Lord would be manifestly revived throughout the land. May the Lord surely bring it to pass, and His name shall be glorified! Since making the preceding entry I have been in communication with the wife of another of "our own" Pastors, whose heart has been stirred with pity for the sorrows of her poorer ministerial neighbours. I gave her the name of one very needy, that she and the ladies of the church (by no means a wealthy one) might work with loving, skilful fingers for the necessities of the impoverished family. "We have begun to pray for them," she says, and I gather from her womanly, earnest words that her helpers expect the service thus rendered will bring them as much blessing as it will bestow benefit upon the poor recipients. Every stitch in the garments they make and send will enchain a gentle thought, every fold reveal a touch of sisterly sympathy, and the many loving prayers breathed over them will impart a sweeter fragrance than any earthly perfume can boast. Oh! that the happiness of so delightful a service were better known, and more ardently coveted—that gifts so good and gracious were less rare and capricious. If it be true that "the heart grows rich in giving," what millionaires might we not become by entering zealously into the brave trade of loving our neighbours as ourselves, and ministering constantly of our substance to the necessities of the saints! Such gains might be counted in the light of heaven, such riches amassed without fear of corruption or loss. But how many of us are thus "laying up treasure" in heaven? There are some on whom God has bestowed much of this world's wealth who grudge to give a coin of it to the poor and needy, and think themselves hardly used if any sort of etiquette compels the confiscation of one of their golden gods. What an awful sight must the poverty and emptiness of such a barren life present to the eyes of the angels! "He gave them the desire of their heart, but sent leanness into their souls." The Lord in His mercy deliver *us* from such a curse.

An aged minister of Christ, many years in his service, and still labouring in word and doctrine, received help lately from both Pastors' Aid and Book Fund, and writes most gratefully and tenderly of the cheer and comfort the opportune gifts brought to his anxious heart. It is pleasant to see how devoutly he is affected by the mercy, and how it has inspired in his heart a loving recognition of God's faithfulness and care. Says he—"We are both astounded at the goodness of the Lord to such unworthy servants, and cannot thank Him enough for inclining you to send us so needed a gift." This is just how I desire the help from the Fund should be received, straight out of the Lord's hand into that of His poor servant. He goes on to tell me how on the night previous to receiving the present he felt very much cast down and depressed in mind, and tried to sing, "In darkest shades if He appear"; but it was of no use, the notes died away on his quivering lip, and only sighs came forth from his oppressed heart. "The next morning," he touchingly says, "I had some liberty in prayer"—perhaps this was a foretaste of the coming deliverance; but after breakfast the sorrows gathered round his soul again—he began to count up the various items which must soon be paid—rent, grocer's and miller's bills, etc., and only £1 5s. in the house to meet them all; and Satan and a deceitful heart whispered that "the Lord had forgotten to be gracious, and His mercy was clean gone for ever."

Then came the parcel to him like a ministering angel, with both hands full of blessings, and he recounts again the delightful fact that its contents led him with a humble, thankful spirit to the mercy-seat, there to pour out his thanksgivings to his heavenly Father, who had sent such relief to his necessities.

* * * *

March.—This seventh year of happy and prosperous service brings me special gladness in the constantly multiplying testimonies which certify to the increasing value and usefulness of the Book Fund. Ministers who, five or six years ago, received a small grant of books, now write with pathetic earnestness for another parcel, their necessities having grown with their mental growth and strengthened with their intellectual strength. Moreover, their congregations largely share in the blessing; for the pastor's heart cannot be warmed with celestial fire, and his soul fed with heavenly manna, without his people feeling in a greater or lesser degree the precious influence of such a visitation. There are very few men like "Williams of Wern," of whom it is recorded that he remarked to a book-loving brother—" You read too much. My plan in preparing sermons is to examine the connection of a passage, extract its principle, and think it over in my own mind. I never look at a commentary except when completely beaten." This experience is rare and peculiar, and in the case of hundreds of Pastors positively unattainable; for the absorbing cares of poverty, the ceaseless demands of family emergencies, and the pressing burden of increasing liabilities,—these choke up the workings of the mind, paralyze the capacity for reflection, and render the poor servant of Christ doubly dependent on the written thoughts of others for assistance in the study of the Divine Word. Milton says, "A good book is the precious life-blood of a master-spirit, embalmed and treasured up on purpose to a life beyond life"; and we thank God that it is our joyous duty to supply this grand restorative to weary and over-worked minds.

To-day a pastor thus writes :—

How can I express to you the thankfulness of my heart for this repeated help you have given me! The books are polished shafts for the King's service, and the suitable selection you have made impresses me much. The stream of your kindness is strengthening and refreshing to the spirits of hundreds of humble workers for God. Your Book Fund is a "river that maketh glad the city of God."

In another letter this same good brother thus touchingly justifies his renewed application to the Fund :—

A heavy debt on my chapel, six in family, a very expensive place to live in, and a small salary, are my pleas for knocking again at the door of your Christian charity. No tongue can tell the extent of the cheer and help you render to the servants of God, and their churches and families, by the delightful ministrations of the Book Fund.

* * * *

The following letter is too good to be entombed among the mass of unrecorded correspondence. It also sets forth delightfully the glorious aim and object of my work; gives a bright glimpse of it from a poor preacher's own point of view, and enshrines a grateful and touching tribute to the kindness of those dear friends whose contributions enable me to carry it on :—

Dear Mrs. Spurgeon,—The parcel of books has arrived safely. No words of mine can express my gratitude to you for such a rich gift. It is the most valuable present I have received during my twenty years' ministry. I never felt at such a loss to know what to say by way of appreciation and gratitude for your kindness to one wholly unknown to you. May the Lord Jesus bless you more and more, and spare you many, many years—send you friends, and give you joy in seeing this noble work growing in your hands! If those who contribute of their wealth only knew the gladness awakened in our hearts—the stimulus and food supplied to weary, jaded minds—the instruction and precious truth which find their way into our sermons, and which in turn cheer and bless many other souls through these noble presents, they would feel themselves more than recompensed even in this world, and before the Master shall say, "Well done!" Surely you can never doubt that it was the Lord who put this work into your hands; it is as plainly so as if He had spoken audibly to you from the stormy cloud or the evening breeze. He knows how the poor minds of many of His servants are heavy and enfeebled in endeavouring to keep up the freshness of their ministry; constantly telling out, but receiving little in; isolated, and with few stimulating books; and He has honoured you to be an angel of mercy to bring refreshing and strength to them. We may never meet on earth; but your name and your work shall have an abiding place in my heart. I need scarcely say I had none of the books you have so kindly sent; and, strangely enough, they are *the very books I have long wished for!* How many delightful hours I shall have over them, if my life be spared! How many sermons they will suggest which I shall delight to preach! How they will refresh the work of divine grace in my own heart, and reveal the glories of Jesus Christ by me to others! My own dear pastor used in early life to impress on my mind the importance of earnest reading and studious habits, and I will promise you this, that, if I live, the books you have now given me shall be well and prayerfully used. With gratitude beyond expression,

Yours, ———

* * * *

Goodwin says, "Sermons preached are, for the most part, as showers of rain that water for the instant; such as may tickle the ear, and warm the affections, and put the soul into the posture of obedience. Hence it is that men are ofttimes sermon-sick, as some are sea-sick—very ill—much troubled for the present, but by-and-by all is well again. But *printed* sermons are as snow, that lies long on the earth, they are longer-lived, they preach when the author cannot, and—what is more—when he is not."

These words I read in my husband's study, and lifting up my eyes I looked with reverent love at the twenty-seven goodly volumes of printed "Sermons" which are the fruit of his lips in as many years, and my heart blessed God, not only for what He has done by them, but for all they shall yet accomplish by His grace TILL HE COME of whom they speak. I am never tired of imagining the possibilities of blessing garnered up in the pages which I am constantly sending forth, and when the precious testimonies to their soul-winning and edifying power come—as they do—in perpetual abundance,

I take them thankfully to my heart and confidently look out for more. Here is one which calls forth a song of praise :—

All last winter, in our little mission on the Labrador Coast, your honoured husband's "Sermons" were read in the Mission Church, Sunday by Sunday by the lady teachers, who were left by themselves for eight months, through the failing health of the devoted missionary, who had laboured there for many years. These simple services on the Sunday and week-day evenings, when Mr. Spurgeon's "Sermons" were the staple of the teaching given, were greatly blessed by God. Many sailors came from the ships anchored off the coast, and, with the resident fishermen, eagerly listened to the word of life, and not only were their hearts cheered and comforted, but some were brought to a knowledge of the truth as it is in Christ Jesus.

Blessed sowing of the seed! Who can tell what the harvest may be!

* * * *

Then here follows a more personal testimony, which gave me special delight in the perusal :—

Will you allow an old and worn-out local preacher among the Wesleyan Methodists to join your many correspondents in their acknowledgment of benefits received again and again from Mr. Spurgeon's sermons? Prevented by the infirmities of advanced years from attending the public services of the Lord's house on the Sabbath evenings, I am in the habit of having one of these "Sermons" then read to me, and the result has been a deep sense of personal obligation to the author, and an increasing conviction that it has pleased God to grant to the Christian church of our day, through the instrumentality of Mr. Spurgeon, a gospel light and power that, by the blessing of the divine Spirit, will tell not only on this generation, but on generations yet to come. Earnest and fervent are the prayers we offer that so useful a life may be spared; that the thousands who read the "Sermons" throughout the world may receive the truth as it is in Jesus, and that God may be more than ever glorified by the distribution of such precious books through your Fund. I intended a year ago, when I first saw the Book Fund Report, to send you a small gift; but I put it off, and did not think again about it until I saw the announcement on the "Sermons" that the "Diary" for 1881 was ready. On obtaining and reading it, I was sorry I had not carried out my former intention, and now I make the best amends I can for my neglect, by doubling the sum I meant to give before.

* * * *

April.—Blessed be the Lord for a grand flood-tide of

financial prosperity which has been rolling in these many months, and has borne me up on its glad waves far above all anxiety and carking care! The Lord hath "opened His good treasure," and bountifully provided for the charges of the work He has given me to do. In years gone by I have known what it was to be brought very low in money matters, and the trial of faith was painful and grievous; but deliverance, though it tarried a while, surely came; and, with it, such unmistakable interposition of divine faithfulness and love, that songs of triumph quickly succeeded the sighs of disquietude. Lately I have been spared this burden; but if ever the Lord sees fit to impose it again, I pray that the remembrance of former liberation and enlargement may so strengthen my faith in His mercy and power, that I may be unmoved except to closer waiting upon Him. Again I say, "Blessed be the Lord!" To Him first be ascribed all praise and grateful adoration; for "the silver and the gold are His," and of His own have we given Him; for "of Him, and from Him, and to Him, are all things"; and then to the dear friends whose love is a reflection of His own, and whose gifts are the choicer because given for His sake,—to them I offer the earnest thanks of many grateful hearts, all gathered up into a fervent benediction, which, though unheard on earth, is surely recorded in heaven.

* * * *

Some large sums of money have come to me this year, overwhelming me with thankful emotion; but the main strength of the Fund lies, I think, in the constant inflowing of smaller donations, which, like a tiny rill of living water, trickles on and on with unfailing regularity. Such a "continual dropping" makes sweet music in one's life, and again I praise the Lord for the blessed portion of both "upper and nether springs."

If my readers will bear with me a little longer on this subject, I will endeavour to catch some bright and sparkling drops from the rivulet, and present them for their refreshment and delight, confident that three such cups of cold water will be as acceptable to them as they were to me.

EXTRACT FROM THE LETTER OF A CHURCH OF ENGLAND CLERGYMAN.

Dear Madam,—You may remember my applying to you for some books last year, and the very kind response you made to my application ! It was indeed a kindness for which I shall ever feel most grateful. Since then, I am thankful to say, I am in a little better position, pecuniarily, and I feel it a duty, as well as a real pleasure, to send a subscription to your Book Fund, the Report of which I have just read. Please accept the enclosed guinea, with my warmest thanks for your generous help to me, and my earnest prayers for an increasing blessing upon your labours on behalf of the Lord's ministers. I already reckon you amongst my best friends, and only wish I could express my feelings in anything like adequate terms.

EXTRACT FROM A LETTER FROM ONE OF "OUR OWN" PASTORS.

Dear Mrs. Spurgeon,—Will you please accept the enclosed gift from our dear little girls, "Mercy" and "Grace," who would be glad to do much more for your Book Fund, were it in their power? We often remember you at the throne of grace, and ask that you may be made the means in the Lord's hand of helping and comforting as many of Christ's faithful, yet needy, servants in the future as you have in the past. Oh ! dear Mrs. Spurgeon, I have come across several cases in which you have stretched forth a helping hand, and spoken a cheering word to weak and struggling brethren, and it has been good to witness their evident joy and gratitude, and to hear from their lips expressions of the love they bear so true and real a friend. I pray that a spirit of liberality, and, above all, "the love of Christ," may constrain many of the Lord's own people to sustain you and your blessed work with all needed means, and to Him shall be all the praise, and honour, and glory.

ANONYMOUS NOTE ACCOMPANYING VARIOUS DRILLED COINS.

Will Mrs. Spurgeon accept this little store of "lucky money," that burned a hole in its box after its owner read the record of the Book Fund work? And will she also accept many hearty good wishes for its future prosperity, and the happiness of Mr. Spurgeon and herself?

* * * *

A pathetic little note received to-day has stirred my soul to renewed diligence in my happy work, and intensified my longing desire to try to satisfy the book hunger by which so many poor ministers are hopelessly consumed. I think when my friends read it they will, with me, feel afresh the joy of service in this matter, and while deploring the desperate need which urges on our efforts, yet rejoice that in so many instances it has been our privilege to confer the happiness of which my correspondent so touchingly speaks :—

Dear Mrs. Spurgeon,—This morning I have enjoyed the almost forgotten luxury of handling and inspecting a parcel of new books. In my early days, when I had no lack of friends, and no domestic responsibilities, the reward of each three months' hard toil was to collect my money and walk twelve miles to the neighbouring town, and spend an entire day in selecting books to take home with me. The next day I would spend in the delightful work of looking them over, and the pleasure I found in this occupation it is impossible to describe. The joy of these red-letter days in my youth has been almost effaced by the friction of the troubled years as they have passed painfully by. But as I sat with your books spread before me this morning, a gleam of the old happiness returned, and I was glad to find that my old love had not been quite starved, nor crushed to death. I thank you most fervently for your kind gift, and for the large number of books you sent "above what I asked or thought." I pray that I may be enabled so to use them that harvests of blessing may follow the sowing of such precious seed.

* * * *

May.—THE PASTOR'S RECOVERY FROM ILLNESS. "Shadow and sunshine is life," says Tennyson, in one of his poems ; and happy are we if, in the gloom of the one as well as in the glory of the other, we can recognize the loving leading of our Father in heaven.

Relative affliction is often a heavier burden and a greater grief than personal pain. We think it would be easier to bear any anguish ourselves than to see those whom we tenderly love fighting a fierce battle with a malignant foe, or lying prostrate and vanquished by a weakness no less terrible. Truly our days are overcast then, and not only is the sun obscured, but the night withholds its ordinary solace, for neither moon nor stars appear. When THAT sick chamber is occupied, there is no light in the sky, no sweetness in the flowers, no music in the songs of the birds, no delight in anything on earth. It is desert life for a while, and it doubtless brings to bear upon us an excellent discipline of patience and of humble waiting upon God ; we are taught to look more constantly and anxiously to the cloudy pillar for guidance, and while it tarries, and enjoins our tarrying also, we learn what good Bishop Taylor calls the " practice of the presence of God," and find how blessed a thing it is to "abide under the shadow of the Almighty."

Just emerging from the twilight of such an experience, and almost trembling with delight in the returning sunshine, let this page bear a grateful record of praise to Him who has again proved Himself "Jehovah-Rophi" by healing His dear servant after a long and painful sickness, and once more granting him strength to preach the word and resume his happy life-work. Ah! what thankful hearts we have when we see returning health smooth out the pain-wrinkles from the brow, give back the brightness to the kind eyes, the music to the voice, and the power to the dear hands which work so willingly and well when they write of "things touching the King"! Now the harps are taken down from the willows, and tuned to glad thanksgiving. The voices about the house, which a while ago were hushed to mournful minor notes, are ringing out joyously, with no fear or faltering. One footstep at least has grown lighter because the spirit of heaviness is removed, and with the sweet scent of the fresh May blossoms, and the awakening of life in tree, and flower, and bird, our hopes are renewed for our beloved, and our gratitude to God finds some expression in intense enjoyment of this great happiness. "Joy is the grace we say to God," and it is a comely fashion to be glad when He makes all His goodness pass before us.

> "From pain a keener bliss I borrow—
> How natural is joy, my heart!
> How easy after sorrow!"

* * * *

It is comforting to know that those who have wept with us during the afflictive time will now rejoice that the calamity is overpast. "Many loving hearts," writes a kind though anonymous correspondent, "even amongst those who are called 'church people,' have been anxiously watching and praying for your honoured husband's restoration to health. Our vicar is always delighted to communicate any good tidings of 'our friend,' as he delights to call Mr. Spurgeon, and we pray heartily for you both." Other friends write with earnest and tender congratulation, devoutly praising

God for the mercy He has shown us in withdrawing this sore trial of the dear Pastor's illness, and giving "pleasant words which are as an honeycomb, sweet to the soul, and health to the bones." In one loving, sympathetic letter I find the following lines quoted, and as they aptly set forth what I would fain hope has been our own heart-experience lately, I lay them as a morsel of pure frankincense on this my offering of thanksgiving to our kind and gracious God:—

> "And, day by day, whate'er betide me,
>   Herein I find my rest;
> Eternal mercy is beside me,
>   My Father's will is best.
>
> These passing moments make a ladder
>   That God, my God hath given;
> Some steps are shining, some are sadder,
>   But all lead up to heaven."

* * * *

A very pleasant and chatty letter from a minister in the Midland Counties gives an appreciative estimate of the contents of a Book Fund parcel, dwelling tenderly on each item, as if to assure me that all will be well loved and valued. I must confess to a decided fondness for such epistles, they are a delightful requital for the pains taken in the selection of suitable books, and an agreeable contrast to the short, but not necessarily sweet notes which are by some deemed a sufficient acknowledgment for the effort made on their behalf.

Dear Madam,—The new volumes are all in their places upon my bookshelves, and form a valuable addition to my little library. How much do I prize the five volumes of "The Treasury of David"! The three with bindings worn by frequent use look dull beside the gilded covers of the two you have kindly added; but all five have a sort of expectant look for the final volumes, which I hope one day to be able to obtain. I have no doubt but that hundreds are also waiting anxiously for the announcement of the sixth; for can you not understand that it is quite tantalizing to stop short of the glorious 119th Psalm? But we are confident that they will one day come from the pen of the gifted writer, and they will be hailed with universal delight. Who can estimate the labour of this great work? Yet this is but a small part of Mr. Spurgeon's doings; indeed, we have reason to "glorify God in him." The two handsome volumes of the "Sermons" I shall much prize. Already I have looked through all the subjects, and see that I shall find the nuggets as I need them. Rest assured that the "Sermons" shall be diligently read and honestly employed. The two volumes of "Lectures to Students" must be studied *at once*. I am very anxious to correct some suspected faults, and learn how they are to be removed. I was agreeably surprised at "Our Christian Classics," expecting to see only one volume, and lo! there are four. At present I have only scanned the contents, but hope to find in them some of the "old corn of the land.' The other books I have scarcely looked at yet, save the "Glories of Christ," which at your recommendation I have begun to study. On Sunday afternoon, while reading your Report for 1880, I was struck with the text quoted on page 37—"They came and held him by the feet, and worshipped him." This will be my subject for Sunday morning, and, as you intimated, I have found some thoughts ready to be appropriated in the choice little book. You have sent me an overflowing cup, and I hope to pass it round to many who will be refreshed by my public and private ministrations of the word. May the Lord bless, sustain, and prosper you more and more. Very gratefully yours, ———.

After reading such a letter as this, is it any wonder that I settle down to my work with renewed energy and satisfaction, blessing God for such comfortable encouragement?

* * * *

My "Conference gift" this year—or rather *your present*, dear generous helpers—was a very original and spiritual book bearing the odd title of "What Aileth Thee?" It has been much the fashion among authors lately to seek out curious designations for their mental offspring—whether appropriate or otherwise, does not seem to matter to them much; but in the case of the book in question the authoress in her preface disarms all criticism on the point by declaring that the title was chosen for her by one "who has spent her life for others, and by her own sharp experience knows the meaning of pain." One cannot even remonstrate after this, though we may be permitted to wish that so excellent and suggestive a volume had borne a more captivating title as a passport to our favour. "My business is with tears," says the writer, but she throws upon them so clear and holy a light from God's word that they turn into diamonds, and reflect the glory of the grace of God. Mr. Spurgeon says, "By whatever name this rose is called, its smell is sweet"; and he gives this testimony to the book's worth and helpfulness:—

"We have had quite a feast in reviewing this singular

volume; we found a sermon in it, and, what is far better, we were refreshed in heart, and were drawn away from the world into nearer communion with God." This will suffice to show that it was a fitting gift to the assembled pastors, and I hope that, as on other occasions, I may hear of its having admirably answered its purpose. The Conference has grown to be so large a gathering now, that I had to obtain 320 copies of the work at a cost of £40. Some few are left over, which during the year find their way to those ministers who were unable to be present at the annual reunion.

* * * *

In the garden there is a large and deep stone basin of water where some goldfish find a pleasant and congenial home. In the hot summer days their existence is somewhat slumberous; they bask in the sunshine, or hide from the heat in the miniature caverns formed by the rockwork, and comport themselves generally as very idle and sleepy little fish. If we watch them now, we shall see some lazily poising themselves in the water with scarcely visible motion of body or fin, while others are slowly swimming round, too indolent even to seize the prey which floats temptingly upon the surface of the water. But look! from the centre of the basin a *fountain* rises, and if we set this in motion a most notable difference is observable in their behaviour; their dulness is exchanged for transports of unmistakable joy. As soon as the secret spring is touched, and the mimic tempest commences, they are full of excitement, darting hither and thither like ruddy flames beneath the tiny wavelets, and now and again leaping up to catch with open mouth the refreshing drops as they patter down upon the surface of the pool. It is pleasant to stir up this happy tumult among the little shining creatures, and pretty to watch their delight in the gladdening showers; but one day as I sat looking on, pondering these things in my mind, I thought I could see in this simple circumstance a faint shadow of a grand and glorious reality. Might it not set forth the blessing which descends upon our hearts and lives when God graciously gives a revival of spiritual life and energy by the outpouring of His Holy Spirit? Have you not known times when guilty indifference to your best interests has stupefied your spiritual senses, and withheld you from holy activity? You have been listless and apathetic, just going the round of your daily duties, but with no heart, no enjoyment, no satisfaction in them; no looking up to God in loving dependence for the grace each moment of life requires. At such times you seem to make no progress in anything, but live like my fish, in a round basin, where the monotony of existence predisposes to sluggishness. Then, all at once—it may be in answer to an unconscious cry for help—there comes to you from above such a flood of joy, and revival, and refreshing, that you can scarcely believe yourself to be the same creature who but a moment before had been deep in the torpor of unconcern and carelessness. What a change has come over you! How your heart leaps to meet the blessed influence! What life there is in all your actions now! What "grace of supplication" rests upon your lips! What delight in all spiritual exercises! What sweet realization of the constant presence of the Lord Jesus! The fish in my fountain give forth no vocal praise for the refreshment they find in the descending drops of water; but you sing all the day long about "showers of blessing," and, under the gracious quickening which the Lord has vouchsafed, new life is infused into all your services, a holy activity chases away your self-indulgent langour, and the joy of the Lord becomes your strength. Happy souls, unto whom the Holy Spirit thus comes with power, and who are made to rejoice in "times of refreshing from the presence of the Lord"!

A smile at the quaintness of this conceit may yet cover a responsive thrill to the truth it is meant to illustrate. Let my musings by the fountain have the blessed result—at least upon myself—of instilling a dread of slothfulness in divine things, and of recommending the constant habit of looking up and longing for the gracious outpourings which God will not long withhold from His waiting and expectant children.

✳ ✳ ✳ ✳

June.—Letters both cheering and charming have been numerous lately, and I am anxious to give my dear friends some of the pleasure which has been so bountifully bestowed upon me. At this moment I have before me quite a pile of epistles, most of which bear words so grateful, loving, and tender, that their perusal is in itself a reward for the small service which called them into existence. But I am like an inexpert worker in mosaics, who has at his hand choice morsels of precious things, whose fingers are willing to labour lovingly under the influence of a deep and patient interest, yet who has many misgivings as to his dexterity in dealing with the materials provided, and anxious fears lest the picture which he is expected to produce should but feebly exhibit, as a whole, the intrinsic beauty of each gem-like fragment. Deep shadows, high lights, lovely colourings, tender neutral tints, all are here awaiting felicitous arrangement; but what if the eye should possess no artistic perception, the fingers lack "cunning," or in the very solicitude of disposal some clumsiness should mar the desired beauty, or some faulty filling-in should spoil the effect of the entire work? The glorious mosaics of St. Mark's, at Venice, have a groundwork of pure gold, the very perfection of completeness; these of mine are but roughly placed, irregularly formed, and they lack all sumptuous surrounding. Nevertheless, they are set in the cement of love, and I rely on their own intrinsic grace and beauty to cover all the deficiencies of my poor workmanship.

MOSAICS.

I have only a few things on earth, for my treasure is laid up on high; but I can assure you that the valuable present I have received from you shall, as long as I live, be numbered amongst my choicest blessings. Neither for the books nor for the kind wishes accompanying them can I recompense thee, "but thou shalt be recompensed at the resurrection of the just."

Since I received the post card intimating that you were going to send a parcel I have been full of anticipation. No boy could be more excited about a coming treat than I was in the expectation of your present —it even had a place in my dreams. You cannot imagine with what joy I fetched it from the station this morning, and now with all my heart I thank you, and pray the Lord may long spare you to labour in such a loving and useful way.

The parcel came duly to hand on Saturday night. Surely the time was opportune. My wife and I were both very very weary, she with household work, and I with sermonizing, and both with nursing two sick children. The books seemed to put new life into us.

Some eighteen months ago you kindly sent me "The Treasury of David," and other books. Words fail me to express the value they have been to me, or the gratitude I feel to you for placing such a store in my possession. As I then told you, my stipend as a Congregational pastor is only £80 per annum, and *this allows little or no margin for books*. [The italics are mine: I desire to draw my reader's serious attention to the sad fact so simply stated.] Therefore your kind gift has enabled me to work with far greater satisfaction than I could otherwise have done, and has been a cause of continual thankfulness.

Your very handsome present came safely to hand this morning, and I should be very glad if I could tell you how grateful I feel for this great kindness. But if you turn to one of the pages of your bright little Report for 1880 you will see how you have depicted my condition to-day. "Mists of pain and suffering" have been gathering around me for a week, but not too thick for the dear Master to shine through yesterday, for I was much helped in the services of the day; but now the "window pane is blurred with rain drops," and my spirit looks through silently and sorrowfully. I am sure you will let me defer writing in detail till the brain gets cloudless again. Meanwhile, please accept warmest thanks for so generously and promptly coming to my aid.

This is one of the *shadows* in my Mosaic—the picture could not truthfully be all bright.

* * * *

This has indeed been a day of gladness to me, for this morning I received your splendid present. For years my heart has coveted "The Treasury," but I had feared to ask, and hoped in vain for means to purchase. Since writing to you I have wondered at my own boldness, but you have so generously exceeded my request that now I am amazed at your kindness. I thank God for your Book Fund. I have spent a great part of the day in admiring, examining, and studying the precious volumes, and I hope to use them long for the glory of God.

The books you sent me were the most delightful gift of the kind that I have received during the ten years of my ministry. While unwrapping the volumes I was quite overpowered with a sense of God's goodness, knowing what a boon they would be to me in my work. Tears *would* come when I found " The Treasury of David." May our great Master bless you in this noble service ! *He* only knows what a struggle it is for some of us to keep up anything like a respectable appearance, and get a book very occasionally.

Now, dear friends, group together these variegated fragments of fact and feeling for yourselves, and see if the inlaying does not compensate for your love and liberality to the work which produced them. All the kind things that are said to me belong positively to you; I am but the hand which distributes your largess, and therefore receives on your behalf caresses of grateful acknowledgment. Let me try to repay them in these pages with compound interest!

* * * *

The late Miss F. R. Havergal used to keep what she called a " Daily Journal of Mercies," a record " partly spiritual, and partly material, in which the homeliest and most trivial occurrences were noted side by side with high religious blessings." May I quote the force of her fair example as an apology for presuming to transfer from my note-book to these pages a little home song which I have tried to sing "to the praise and glory of God." Debarred by various reasons from the joy of going up to the House of the Lord, and joining in the glad assemblies of His people, I feel constrained to confess here to a secret source of spiritual supply, and to acknowledge with deep gratitude of heart the blessed compensating privilege which I am permitted to enjoy on the evening of the ancient Sabbath. Many have found it true that God's house is where His presence is, and very sweetly has the comforting promise been fulfilled to His sick or disabled children, that "where *two* or three are gathered together in My name, there am I in the midst of them"; and I know that this record of His goodness to me will awaken echoes of grateful praise in hearts which have experienced somewhat similar blessings.

It is not in a desert that the Lord has rained down manna

for His hungry child, and opened a well of living water for her thirst; but here, in my own sweet home, and by my husband's side, and by that husband's hand, He has led me into green pastures, and beside the still waters, and restored my soul. Joyfully, therefore, let me tell of these streams from Lebanon, and glorify God for thus tenderly supplying all the needs of my soul. For some time past it has been the dear Pastor's custom, as soon as the texts for the Lord's-day services have been given by the "Master," to call me into the study and permit me to read the various commentaries on the subject-matter in hand. Never was occupation more delightful, instructive, and spiritually helpful; my heart has often burned within me, as the meaning of some passage of God's word has been opened up, and the hidden stores of wisdom and knowledge have been revealed; or when the marrow and fatness of a precious promise or doctrine has been spread like a dainty banquet before my admiring eyes. Shall I ever forget those solemn evenings when the sufferings of the Lord Jesus were the theme of tearful meditation; when, with "love and grief our hearts dividing," we followed Him throughout the night on which He was betrayed, weeping, like the daughters of Jerusalem, and saying, "There was never sorrow like unto this sorrow": or, the more rapturous time when "the exceeding riches of His grace" was to be the topic for the morrow, and we were fairly bewildered by the inexhaustible treasures of love and grace to be found in that fair "land of Havilah, where there is gold"?

Gracious hours are those thus spent, and unspeakably precious to my soul; for while the Lord's dear servant is reaping the corn of the kingdom for the longing multitude who expect to be fed by His hand, I can glean between the sheaves, and gather the "handfuls of purpose" which are let fall so lovingly.

Then come delightful pauses in my reading, when the book is laid down, and I listen to the dear voice of my beloved as he explains what I cannot understand, or unfolds meanings which I should fail to see, often condensing into a few clear, choice sentences whole pages of those discursive old divines in whom he delights, and pressing from the gathered thoughts all the richest nectar of their hidden sweetness. Thus a *poor prisoner* has the first sip of the "wines on the lees, well refined," the first morsel from the loaves with which the thousands are to be fed and refreshed on the morrow. How shall I sufficiently thank God for this drink of the brook by the way, this "holy place" within my home where I find the Lord deigns to meet with me, and draw out my heart in adoration and worship? Lord, I bless and praise Thee that thus Thou hast most blessedly fulfilled Thine own word, "I will not leave you comfortless, I will come to you."

"But what can this revelation have to do with the Book Fund work?" say some of my readers. Well, dear friends, just this—that my happy Saturday evenings show me more and more the value and helpfulness of good books in sermon-preparation, and make me feel how great is the privation of those to whom such gracious assistance is denied by their poverty. Even while I am enjoying the sacred pleasure I have tried to describe, and rejoicing that "at our gate are all manner of pleasant fruits," there stirs in my heart an intense pity for those poor bookless ministers, who sit sighing for thoughts in the face of their unfurnished shelves, and I long to lay at their door also the provision which is so stimulating and needful, so important to the minister, so refreshing to the people.

* * * *

A workman that needeth not to be ashamed should have tools of finest quality and adequate number, and though no amount of tempered and burnished steel will make a man a first-rate artisan, nor a multiplicity of theological expositions endue a preacher with divine unction and power, it is well understood that workers, both for God and man, have their labours lightened by the possession and use of choice implements of their craft. Seldom does the world produce a Quintin Matsys, who, with hammer and file alone, could persuade the rigid iron to assume forms of such grace and beauty that men have not yet ceased to count his labour a wonder; and in the kingdom of grace there is but one John Bunyan, whose immortal work was fashioned with no other aids than his Bible and Foxe's "Book of Martyrs."

A young missionary, writing lately for books, touches gracefully on this very point:—

> I know, he says, that there is no preparation for the work of God which can supersede the power which is acquired by patient waiting in His presence for His Holy Spirit; but next to this I earnestly seek the sanctified use of those "helps" I may be able to procure, that I may learn rightly to divide the word of truth.

Men must have helpful books if they are to preach good sermons. A constant reception of divine instruction enables the teacher to impart his knowledge to others. God's Spirit works by such means; for often on rising from his knees, where he has been seeking light on a shrouded text, the minister will find the needed illumination come through the printed pages of his well-beloved volumes.

Blessed seventh-day Sabbath evenings! Your sweet privileges shall incite me to still greater sympathy with poor Pastors, and shall awaken more earnest effort to supply their mental necessities.

* * * *

July.—The other day the sad position and prospects of some poor ministers were the subject of conversation between a very critical visitor and one of the home circle, and I heard a murmur against my poor friends, which much grieved and irritated me.

"An over-stocked market," said this unsympathetic grumbler, "is at the bottom of ministerial troubles. Most of them get as much as they are worth, and many of them have no business in the ministry at all."

Now, as a reproach always stings the sharper if there be just half a drop of truth on the extreme point of it, this sentence has rankled in my heart to sore purpose ever since it was uttered, and I feel constrained to deliver my soul on the subject, and testify what I do know, though I am neither called upon nor competent to argue out so intricate and important a question; moreover, I remember that I am a recorder, not a reformer.

That there are good men in the ministry who would do

God better service by coming out of it, I have no manner of doubt; they would make far better shoes than sermons, and more consistently occupy a pew than a pulpit; they are fitted to work with their hands rather than with their heads, and everybody but themselves can see that they have intruded into the sacred office, and lack the credentials with which a true ambassador of the King of kings is always furnished. Dwindling churches, empty baptisteries, lifeless prayer-meetings, fruitless services,—these all mark the course of such a man, and methinks he had better go and sweep a crossing, "doing it heartily, as unto the Lord," than seek to remain in a position for which his Master never designed him, and where, consequently, the dew of His blessing does not fall.

So much I must sorrowfully confess as regards some who have evidently mistaken their vocation, and there I leave them, for to their own Master they stand or fall.

But my reflections and my somewhat extensive experience in the matter both assure me that by far the majority of poor Pastors are true shepherds of the sheep, feeding the flock of God with loving care, bearing the burden and heat of the day with patient fortitude, enduring hardness for Christ's sake and the gospel's, doing good and faithful work which will have its reward in heaven. I do not believe that their poverty is the result of their unfitness for service, or is owing to repletion in their ranks, but that it is *partly* an outcome of the universal depression brooding over our land, partly a dishonour on the churches to whom they minister, and wholly a state of things to be ashamed of and remedied as soon as possible. I can with perfect truthfulness say that I know scores of men who toil on from year to year in the face of bitter privation, seeking not their own but their people's good, and in many cases hiding their sufferings, lest the work should be hindered. They are "heroes," some of them; and though the world never hears their name in song or story, it shall be proclaimed in that day when the Lord shall say, "Well done, good and faithful servant; thou hast been faithful over a few things, I will make thee ruler over many things; enter thou into the joy of thy Lord." I know one brother, with a wife and seven children, and barely £100 per annum to keep them on; yet he says, "Our need is very real, but the Lord knows it, and I would not for the world take the matter out of His hands!" And another, who writes, "With £80 a-year, a wife, and three children, I have but very little to spend in books; but it is God's work, and He will provide."

Are not these bright stars shining out of a dark night? Does not such sweet submission and cheerfulness under trial bring glory to God? This radiance of faith and trust would not have been visible in the daylight of prosperity, and so the very darkness is made the means of revealing the grace of God shining in the heart. "A few years ago," writes a very poor but successful preacher, "I was an untaught collier boy, yet from the depths God called me to labour in His vineyard, and by His grace I have been upheld till now. *My whole soul is in the work, and I would not exchange my pulpit for a throne.*" This is the manner of spirit God's ministers are of, and surely such men claim our hearty love and sympathy—men who, like Paul, are ready, not to be bound only, but also to die for the name of the Lord Jesus!

Those who are "called, chosen, and faithful" have necessity laid upon them, yea, woe is unto them if they preach not the gospel, and then it naturally follows that "even so hath the Lord ordained, that they which preach the gospel should live of the gospel."

I have said that some sensitive natures try to hide the fact of their poverty from the people, and it is often thus; but why do not their congregations open their eyes, their ears, their hearts, their purses? Is not the labourer worthy of his hire? If he has sown unto you spiritual things, is it a great thing if he shall reap your carnal things? Why, the rough men in yonder brickfield are far better paid than many a village pastor, and the wages of a head gardener, coachman, or valet would be comparative riches to some of our straitened brethren. There are people who act as if they thought their ministers were fashioned in a different mould to other mortals, not needing so much to eat or so many garments to put on; they deem them, in fact, so nearly celestial, that a little judicious starvation will transform them altogether into angels! (The experiment will succeed one day if they are allowed to persevere.) Ah! if they would but know it, this way of dealing with His servants is displeasing and dishonouring to the Great Master, and is likely to provoke His correction and rebuke. They do not, perhaps, go to quite such extremes as did the husbandmen in our Lord's parable, who, when the messenger came to them, "caught him, and beat him, and sent him away empty;" and yet—and yet I fear there have been cases in which it came to pretty much the same thing; and then is it any wonder that straightway that vineyard brought forth nothing but wild grapes? The minister's comfort should be the church's care, and then his care for them will be their constant comfort. An old writer says—"A minister's calling is not easy, but painful and laborious; as it is an honour, so it is a burden, and such an one, too, as requireth the strength of angels to bear it."

People of God, let your love for your Pastors flourish again; hold up the hands that hang down, and strengthen the feeble knees; help them with sympathy, prayer, and temporal blessings. "Bring ye all the tithes into the storehouse, that there may be meat in mine house, and prove me now *herewith*, saith the Lord of hosts, if I will not open you the windows of heaven, and pour you out a blessing, that there shall not be room enough to receive it."

* * * *

"*There is no present so useful to a minister as a parcel of books, except, perhaps,*—another *parcel of books.*"

So writes a longing pastor to-day, and his quaintly-put conclusion has a great deal of force and truth in it. If the first gift of these mental aids be received with enthusiasm and delight, the second is likely to be hailed with warmer demonstrations of welcome; for the worth and preciousness of such companionship have been tested and proved, and a great yearning takes possession of the man to gather around him a goodly company of authors whose friendly voices shall comfort, encourage, suggest, and stimulate when the work of the study presses hard upon heart and brain. Such fellowship is essential to a minister's happiness and success; and if his choice has been wisely directed, this intercourse will "do him good, and not evil, all the days of his life."

I have often remarked that the mental appetite is strengthened by indulgence, and constantly I find that those who can best use and appreciate exegetical works are the most eager for them : not because they have exhausted the stores already in their possession, but that their capacity for knowledge has been enlarged by the very process of reception.

A minister in a seaport town says :—

May I tell you that, having tasted of the good things Mr. Spurgeon sends forth, I shall not rest satisfied till I am the happy possessor of all he has published, or may publish? It is my privilege to own a few of his "Sermons." I have read them with delight and profit, and the result is that I pant for more. If I could have a few volumes by paying for them in monthly instalments I should be so glad.

And a London pastor writes :—

With all my heart do I—and with a hundred hearts, if I had them, would I—wish for heaven's richest blessing upon your noble work. With the exception of a few separate "Sermons" by Mr. Spurgeon, I did not possess any of his books. Your gift, however, has keenly sharpened my appetite, and as soon as I can afford it I hope to purchase some more volumes.

I should here remark that the volumes of Mr. Spurgeon's "Sermons" are sought after and studied as an encyclopædia of interpretation, exposition, and illustration, and the full indices brought out by the publishers render reference so easy that they are fast assuming the character of a homiletical commentary on the whole Bible. I know some ministers who even now carry out this idea ; for instead of purchasing the bound volumes, which consist of sermons preached from texts chosen from all parts of God's word, they prefer to gather single copies, and arrange them according as the texts are taken from each of the books of Holy Writ, and their testimony is that the plan is both pleasant and profitable. The disadvantage of loose copies is obviated by using lettered cases, and every week adds a choice contribution to some portion of the sacred store. May God in His tender mercy grant that the supply may not cease for many a year to come !

It would be a happy work only to distribute good and

helpful books by any writers. The welcome gifts of friends, and my own frequent purchases, prove that I am not insensible to the value and importance of works by other authors; but *there is* a very deep and tender joy in sending forth my husband's precious books, and I confess to a very real delight when, after giving a pastor his choice of other volumes, I receive such a reply as this, which came lately: " Thanks for your offer; but please send me ' The Treasury of David.' I can say of it what he said of Goliath's sword—there is none like it, give it me."

* * * *

August.—A letter from the far-off " land of Sinim " makes a pleasant interruption to the long line of home epistles which have lately claimed attention, and gives a welcome change to the current of our thoughts and sympathy. Friends will read it, I think, with tender interest, as I did; they will see that it is an application for books, to which I need scarcely say response has already been made, and if the acknowledgment should arrive before the end of the year, I hope to be able to insert it in these pages.

The writer, after telling me some particulars of his history previous to his settling in China, comes to the main object of his letter, thus:—

I know that in asking a donation of books from your Fund, my *need* is sufficient claim; but in order that you may be led to pray for us and our work, and that you may be encouraged in your own, I give you a few details of our life. My dear wife (who is also my fellow-worker), myself, and our two little sons, *are the only foreigners in this inland city.* [Think of this, dear readers, and realize their solemn position, if you can.] Month after month we see none but Chinese, and we are *alone*, as far as human sympathy is concerned; but, ah ! so satisfied and happy working here for Him who so wonderfully helps us in our trials, and paints a rainbow upon every cloud. We have a little Baptist church of thirty-one members. Don't smile at our tiny gathering—these souls are the fruit of hard labour, much sorrow, many prayers. They are all poor; but they give one-seventh of their income to observe the Lord's-day, and they bear the expense of a mission in a city seventy miles from this place, where until now the gospel had never been preached. I greatly feel the need of books; for preaching *daily* to the heathen, besides Bible-classes every evening, and the three services on Sunday, necessitates a serious amount of preparation. My little library has been well thumbed indeed, and if you can help me to feed others as well as myself, I shall be deeply thankful. You know that we inland missionaries have no regular income. As the Father sends it, so we are supplied. It is a life of perfect restfulness; but we have to practise strict economy—this is but right, the work needs every shilling we can spare for it.

I have waited *two years* before writing to you, in the hope of being able to purchase your husband's works; but I do not seem any nearer my object, and I at length decided to make the venture. Pardon me if I have taken too great a liberty, and, at least, pray for us, and for the heathen—the poor heathen—who daily perish while salvation is so near.

Is not this appeal irresistible? If I had ever closed my heart against the petitions of foreign missionaries, it must have yielded to this tender assault, and opened wide its door of sympathy to such a suppliant. But, happily, there are no bars of unfriendliness to break down, no entrenchments of formality to be forced, before the spoil of the Book Fund can be won; and only in the deep humility of the good man's mind could the necessity of an apology for his application be even dreamed of. With a very glad heart I sent forth the precious volumes which will carry comfort, refreshing, help, and light to that lonely worker in a land of darkness and the shadow of death.

* * * *

"Go abroad
Upon the paths of nature, and when all
Its voices whisper, and its silent things
Are breathing the deep beauty of the world,
Kneel at its simple altar."

Sometimes I wish very earnestly that I were an artist, and could with pencil or brush perpetuate some of the lovely little pictures which I come across when wandering within the enclosure of our Dulce Domum. There are everywhere sweet surprises of beauty to meet expectant eyes; and garden, fields, and orchard all yield their store of pretty sights to those who watch for them.

Let me tell of two occasions on which such observation was well rewarded, premising that the companion who shared my delight and discoveries was the dearest in all the world to me.

The grass was springing thick and fast for the hay

harvest, when one morning we went down to the field to admire the crop. Rain had fallen plenteously the night before; but this was one of the rare sunshiny days of the summer, and everything looked at its brightest and best, as we leaned on the fence rails and gazed down into the cool green depths of the dense verdure at our feet. Doubtless our thoughts took an imaginative flight, and measured the height of the forthcoming hay-stack before the scythe had laid low a single blade; but they were soon recalled, and our attention fixed upon an exquisite little picture which lay like a gem among the clover thickets of the rich undergrowth. On a streamer of one of the broad-leaved grasses a raindrop sparkled like a diamond, and by its side had settled a large and beautiful greenish-blue fly. The safety of the drop was secured by its position on the leaf, and from this crystal goblet so cunningly contrived and balanced the insect was drinking with full enjoyment and satisfaction. The most simple thing in the world, was it not? A drop of water and a fly! Yet, dear reader, my pen must fail to describe the attractiveness of these two common objects when thus brought together; the drop alone, or the fly by itself, would have passed unnoticed; but their association gave the charm, and the picture produced was one of nature's loveliest aquarelles. Looking long and lovingly, I think we learned this lesson:—

> "Teach Thou that not a leaf can grow,
> 'Till life from Thee within it flow;
> That not a drop of dew can be,
> O Fount of being! save by Thee."

Then, again, as lately as yesterday another simple combination of common things gave us much pleasure. I had plucked an over-ripe egg plum, to which the busy little gentlemen in black and yellow had been paying close and devouring attentions, and I was carrying it in my hand when we saw a very fine specimen of the "Red Admiral" butterfly resting on a flower. A desire seized me to obtain a closer view of its charms, and I very cautiously advanced the plum, gently offering the golden throne to the feet of the lovely queen; when to my surprise she lighted on it at once, and allowed me to carry her in triumph down the garden. But what a dainty picture was this! The exquisite contrast of colour was perfect, between the topaz-hued fruit and the regal robes of the quivering little beauty upon it, while her fairy-like poise on the plum, and the alternate opening and folding of her gorgeous wings were details which completed the fascination of the beholders. She even began to feed on the juices which the ravages of the wasps had set free, but after a while fluttered off to the flowers again, and the grace of the moment was gone.

In my poor fashion I have fellowship of feeling with Wordsworth when he writes,

> "To me the meanest flower that blows can give
> Thoughts that do often lie too deep for tears."

It seems a "Paradise Regained" to hear the story of God's love in every breeze, and recognize the wonderful touches of His hand on insect, leaf, and flower; and my intense delight in His creations of beauty must plead my excuse for permitting butterflies and dewdrops to intrude amid the serious business of the Book Fund chronicles.

The daily life and the dear book work have grown to be so indivisible, that now and again one is puzzled how to keep the former modestly in the background; but I may say in extenuation of this present outburst, that, being a little tired to-night of transcribing letters, I thought to refresh myself by thus recalling the simple incidents of some sweet strolls with my beloved. If any of my readers happen to share my passing weariness, they will the more readily forgive the insertion of such an impertinent paragraph.

* * * *

September.—The following sentences, taken from a letter addressed to the President of the College by one of his former students, will show that the Conference present of this year, mentioned previously, has not failed to accomplish some good work. This is a result I always earnestly anticipate, and any tidings of the usefulness of the gift to the Pastors is received with much satisfaction. This brother says:—" May I be allowed through you to thank dear Mrs. Spurgeon for 'What Aileth Thee?' It has so far given me six or seven sermons, and will, doubtless, suggest many more. Some of them have already been very richly blessed."

My absent son's last letter from Auckland also contains a reference to this book, and I transcribe it because I believe the dear friends through whose kindness the gift is annually made will be pleased to read his genial, loving words. "Let me thank you most lovingly," he writes, "for the kind present to the 'dearest son of the College.' The book is sweet, but the inscription is still sweeter. It came without any damage; and, though I have only had time as yet to read three or four chapters, I can speak only well of it. The style is unusual and eccentric, but the matter is very suggestive, and I like it much. I am happy indeed to be included in 'Conference presents,' though so far away. There's nothing like having a mother at head-quarters."

God bless the dear exiled boy, he is working well and faithfully for the Master, though separated from all his "kith and kin," and it would be strange indeed if his mother's heart did not feel very tenderly towards her long-absent one, and rejoice to cheer and encourage him in every possible way.

It will not be inappropriate in this place to record most hearty thanks to the many friends who have lately testified their regard for our dear son, by generous gifts of money and work to aid in the great undertaking of building a "Tabernacle" in Auckland. The father and mother of the young pastor feel very grateful for the help given and the kind interest manifested, and ask that the gifts may be followed by earnest prayer that the Lord will "send now prosperity," real, deep, and abiding to the church which has been the object of so much kindly thought and care.

* * * *

The arrival during this month of two huge cases of stationery for the use of poor ministers, and the Book Fund work generally, gives me a most pleasant opportunity of renewing my heartfelt acknowledgments to the generous friend who thus places at my disposal a most kindly and suitable present for poor Pastors. Since first I told, in the Diary for 1880, of his exceeding liberality in furnishing me with writing-material of all sorts, in quantity so large that, like the Lord's promised blessing to His people, " there was not room enough to receive it," there has been no cessation of his thoughtful kindness. Always planning some deed of love and charity, this good friend, about Christmas in that same year '80, began to send packages of paper and envelopes to be enclosed in my book parcels, and the kindly river of his benevolence has since then continuously flowed on, always full, and occasionally, as at its first rise, overflowing with a spring-tide of abundance; but never dwindling, as some streams do, into a dried-up watercourse which only mocks the thirsty wayfarer with the memory of bygone blessing.

My friend's bounty has cheered many hearts besides my own, and his gracious care for poor ministers has added much to the value and excellence of the parcels sent to them. I have put aside now and then a letter in which such an enclosure is mentioned in becomingly grateful terms; and when the dear donor reads the paragraphs, he will find conclusive testimony that his brotherly kindness has been esteemed, and his gifts, in most cases, truly consecrated to the service of the Lord. Thus, one good pastor says, "I will try to use to God's glory every sheet of the note-paper you have so thoughtfully enclosed"; and another writes, "I thank you much for the quantity of useful writing material, which is indeed appreciated by us, and shall be used in the service of the Master." "The thought of your considerate and practical kindness," says a poor Primitive Methodist minister, "in sending the writing paper and envelopes deeply affected me." Here, and in most other instances, I receive thanks altogether undeserved; for it is by my friend's thoughtful love alone that the paper is sent, and I am but his joyful almoner. The gratitude of those he thus aids comes to him only at second-hand; but I think and hope it gains both in volume and value by passing through the avenues of another grateful heart, and bearing thence an additional tribute of loving obligation.

The gift of writing paper and envelopes to a poor minister

is a boon which he well knows how to appreciate. "You can hardly think how welcome it was," writes one of the recipients. "It is one of the hardships of poverty to have to purchase paper and stamps, and we poor Pastors have much writing to do." Another assures me of the usefulness of the present, and of his delight at its fine quality, naïvely adding, "My frugal wife, when she saw it, said, 'My dear, you must be careful of this good paper, and not use it for ordinary purposes, it ought to last a long while for special correspondence." A country pastor, who is evidently accustomed to be on the look-out for mercies, and has learnt the happy art of finding the brightest side of everything, thus describes the feelings awakened in his heart by the gift he received:—

What a fine plan it is to have the books wrapped up separately in paper! As I unfolded each parcel it was like a fresh blessing, and impressed me more than if they had all been displayed at once. Then, too, what thoughtfulness of a minister's wants was manifested! A grand package of paper and envelopes, just the things we are constantly in need of; how much it will add to one's comfort to have them at hand, and without the expense of purchasing! Having opened all, for five minutes I think I might have been mistaken for a "Salvation Army Captain" leading in a Hallelujah chorus!

Of course it is only to the neediest of the Lord's servants that this gift is made; my chief business is with them and their sorrows, and to such my friend's thoughtfulness proves a very great boon. A hard-working pastor, not far from the city of London, writes:—

I untied the parcel, and had the pleasure of taking book after book from it, each one filling me with fresh delight; but when I came to the writing-paper and envelopes, I was indeed astonished. Surely, I thought, this is from one who understands a preacher's needs, for I have to write very frequently on the back of old circulars, and cut open old addressed envelopes, in order to save spending the cash of which I have so little. I most sincerely thank you for your wise kindness to one whose joy it is to preach Jesus, and for the kind provision you have made, enabling me not only to obtain thoughts, but to preserve them.

A poor country pastor, to whom a large parcel of books and garments and writing material had been sent, says:—

My heart is so full that I know not how to thank you. "The Treasury" has been indeed a treasure to me, and now this sixth volume promises equal if not greater riches. "Farm Sermons," "Feathers for Arrows," and all the other books are new to me, and will be of unspeakable benefit; and what a splendid present of note paper and envelopes, supplying a need which we poor ministers often feel when the purse is too empty to permit a visit to the stationer's shop! A thousand thanks for everything. You have lightened our hearts, and made our home glad, and we can only pray that the richest blessing of our ever-gracious God may rest on you and the friends who help you.

✻ ✻ ✻ ✻

October.—The applications for grants of books which have reached me lately have been so extremely numerous that once again I am compelled to lament my inability to enlarge the present bounds of the Book Fund, or extend its benefits to a wider class than is represented by "poor Pastors in actual charge, *depending wholly on the ministry.*" Lay workers, town missionaries, local preachers, Scripture readers,—all these are ineligible for grants, and the sheer necessity of keeping the work within the compass of my time and strength, compels strict compliance with the rules. Applications from brethren who are beyond the limits of my work are a grief and a burden to me. I *must* refuse them, though I long to bless them, and a letter of denial costs more time and thought than one of happy compliance, and, moreover, leaves a painful sense of imperfect service on the heart.

I should like it to be distinctly understood that these restrictions arise from no lack of sympathy on my part with Christian lay workers. On the contrary, I greatly honour those who, like the apostle Paul, "labour with their hands," that they may not be burdensome to the church of Christ, and preach the gospel of God freely, being chargeable to no man. I should rejoice to help them all, and gladden their hearts with gifts of books; for their need of aid in the preparation of discourses and addresses is increased by the fact that their opportunities for study are seriously diminished by the claims of business. But, alas! my inclinations outgrow my industry, my desires run far ahead of my diligence; I work to the utmost of my power, yet can accomplish no more than the small service of which this "Diary" gives partial record. If I could ply many pens together, during days that numbered four-and-twenty hours apiece, there might be reasonable hope of enlarging the range of operations; but while I remain sole manager, treasurer, secretary, and servant-of-all-work to the Book Fund, I see not the faintest prospect of an extension of its favours beyond the bounds already laid down.

* * * *

This fact grows to be one of the "shadows" on the bright picture of Book Fund work, toning down the glowing colours, and reminding one of the weakness and incompleteness of one's best endeavours. The *vast need* that exists is not met by my *greatest effort*, and I have the sorrow of seeing opportunities of usefulness vanish like a shoal of fish when the nets are not large enough to secure them. With almost the whole of my time given up to the dear service, I only manage to supply one class of hungry souls,—sending all others empty away, to their deep disappointment and my own sincere regret. If Christian people would but take the trouble to look into this matter they would be amazed to find what a serious book-famine prevails all over the land, and how eagerly all sections of workers for Christ stretch out their hands for the precious food, without which their mental powers flag and droop, and their service loses its vigour and freshness. For seven years now, without any break or interruption, the Lord has graciously enabled me to carry on the work He then gave me to do; but though I hope at the close of this year to record the fact, that at least *fifty thousand* volumes have been distributed by the Fund during this period of its existence, I am sorrowfully conscious that what has thus been accomplished is but as a drop in the ocean of want, or as dust in the balance of universal necessity.

Few people seem mindful of a minister's dependence on books; it does not enter into their thoughts that these are the good man's stock-in-trade, and that his business—sacred though it be—cannot be successfully and profitably carried on without "thoroughly furnished" shelves, and an abundant "reserve stock" of material from which he can constantly bring forth "things new and old." Because of this heedlessness on the part of the people, many a pastor fails in freshness and vigour of speech, and his discourses become dry and unattractive, while his congregation, lamenting this decline, and wondering at it, have not the sense to see that his empty bookcase reveals the sad secret, and silently reproves their neglect of their own and their minister's best interests.

I think the good time is coming in which the need of much book help to preachers will be more readily and universally recognized; and I shall indeed bless God if the work of the Book Fund has in any degree contributed to this happy result. A gentleman who, during the past year, has been the donor of some valuable volumes for distribution, seems to cherish some such hope for the future when he thus writes: "I pray earnestly for the success of your labours, and that you may be spared amongst us till your efforts will be no longer necessary. I do not mean that the desire for knowledge ever will or can be satisfied; but that a better spirit will take possession of my fellow-sinners, and lead them to think of making due provision for both the minds and bodies of their ministers. The chosen servants of our loving Saviour will then have ample means of furnishing a banquet for those who look to them for spiritual food."

* * * *

November.—A HOME CONFIDENCE. Other people may need blazing fires and noisy rockets to make them

"Remember, remember,
The fifth of November,"

but to me it is a marked day without any such demonstration, for my beloved said "Farewell" this morning, and is gone "over the hills and far away," and I am left alone to mourn my absent lord.

How quiet the house is after the bustle of departure! What a desolate feeling creeps into the heart when the last "Good-bye" has been said! it seems to seal a silence on all things till the same dear voice shall sound joyfully at the home-coming.

I wander into the deserted study, and think the very books and chairs look miserable, so I take pity on them, and bring in all the Book Fund paraphernalia, and the piano, and all the multitudinous belongings of a woman's sanctum; and here, in the master's own room, I establish myself, because it seems full of his presence, his work, and his love.

Poor dog Punchie comes to lay his head on my dress, and there is inexpressible sympathy in the droop of his uncurled tail, and the pitiful look of his eyes. Ah, Punchie, my dog! you will miss the tit-bits from that loving hand, and many a kind word and pat on the head; but your sorrow will not last long, nor your doggish brain realize the loss the master's presence is to all within and without the house. I expect we shall soon find out that there is more fact than fiction in the old Scotch song—

> "For there's nae luck about the house,
> There's nae luck at a';
> There's little pleasure in the house
> When our gudeman's awa'."

But we'll do our best, Punchie, to make all around us as happy as we can till "Johnny comes marching home."

Dear John! The "smock" is discarded, the old plough is turned on its side, the horses are unharnessed and led out to pasture, and the home which is so dear to him has to be left behind while he follows the swallows to seek softer breezes and sunnier skies. I mind me (John's wife may be allowed a country phrase now and then) just now of one of his pretty "talks" about "home." "Ah!" says he, "that word *home* always sounds like poetry to me. It sounds like a peal of bells at a wedding, only more soft and sweet, and it chimes deeper into my heart. The 'way home' to me is the best bit of road in the country. I like to see the smoke out of my own chimney better than the fire on another man's hearth: there is something so beautiful in the way in which it curls up among the trees."

But he has to go, the parting must be borne, for only in a genial clime, and in the seclusion of a foreign resting-place, can he find the perfect peace which by God's blessing restores his physical and mental strength. Away to the roses, and fuchsias, and olives, and palms, and oleanders, and bright southern skies; away from the bitter, biting winds which howl dismally over the hill-top, and tear wildly around the house; away from the fogs and frosts, to bask for a little while in constant sunshine, and breathe the sweet breath of countless flowers.

And does all go well with the watcher at home? What precious compensation from the Lord's nicely balanced providence comes to her at such a time? Well, much, many ways, though the enforced separation is a great grief. There are daily love-letters that are better than sunshine, when the "old, old story" is told again, and is all the sweeter for sounding over twenty-seven years of happy union! There are little things to do and have done for the absent one, which spring up like flowers by the pathway, and attract and interest the mind; there is the intense joy of sympathy in the enjoyment of the beloved, and a mental participation in all his pleasures which gives real happiness, and then there is the blessed anticipation of his return, when the days of absence will not be remembered in the bliss of seeing his dear face once more!

Meanwhile, Book Fund work claims and receives such increasing attention that there is scant time for pondering over troubles; the work keeps its worker always busy, and this daily labour is, doubtless, the best panacea for such a sorrow as this which annually befalls me.

> "Labour bringeth blessing,
> And time spent in doing hath a comfort in it."

* * * *

It was a rather singular coincidence that on the evening on which I fairly wrote out the preceding paragraph I received by the last post the delightful little paper which with joyful pride I have placed as a preface to my "Diary." It was accompanied by some sketches of the Araucaria, by the author's own hand, and a curious photograph of two women bearing heavy loads on their heads, and preparing, I presume, to commence their toilsome march up to the terraces. How happy the little packet made me, with its charming contents! I think its coming was a lovely illustration of the compensating comfort which cheers me in my solitude. Constant dear tokens of my absent husband's love and care for me are so exceeding precious that I rejoice over them as one that "divideth the spoil," and in their sweet company I am more than content to "abide by the stuff," joyfully waiting his return.

✻ ✻ ✻ ✻

Quite carelessly I took up to-day a volume of *The Sword and the Trowel* magazine for 1876, and was listlessly turning over the pages when I was startled into sudden interest by lighting on a "Letter from Mrs. Spurgeon to her Friends," describing the progress of Book Fund work at that early stage of its existence. Eagerly I read through the article, and I think I need not hesitate to confess that I was charmed with the sweet story of the Lord's loving dealings with me then. As I retraced the first steps taken in this pleasant path of service, and noted the gracious fulfilment of hopes then cherished, and the realization of expectations which seemed almost visionary, my heart glowed with loving gratitude to God, whose faithfulness has not suffered one good thing to fail, and whose lovingkindness has done " exceeding abundantly " for me, above all that I could ask or even think! Right royally have my petitions been answered, and as a King hath the Lord granted my requests! May I for a moment call my friends' attention to a paragraph from the old letter? It will surely glorify His gracious name to show what great things He taught me to expect, and then how grandly He surpassed them!

There was a pretty little sketch of the "lemon plant"* on the last page of the paper, and, after introducing it very lovingly to my readers, these words occur :—

> I have always cherished the fanciful idea that each leaf (of the little tree) must represent £100; so now you can count them yourselves, and smile at the magnificent future which I anticipate for my Book Fund. Twenty-one, are there not? That must mean £2,100, *and plenty of strength to grow more.* [The words are in italics in the original paper.] Well, it seems a great deal of money, certainly; but what a trifle it

---

* The lemon tree still flourishes vigorously, but has lost the symmetrical beauty of its earlier days. It is now a large tree, straggling and irregular, after the manner of its kind, and, as I will not allow it to be interfered with by grafting, it has as yet borne "nothing but leaves."—S. S.

must be to the God who *made* all the silver and the gold! Ah! I believe that some day—

"When grace has made me meet
His lovely face to see,"

the subscription list of the Book Fund will record its thousands of pounds, the once tiny plant will be a tree bearing fruit to perfection, and the dear old motto, " Spend and God will send," will be found true and unfailing to the end.

There, dear friends, when I read this I felt speechless with gratitude, overwhelmed with the perfectly marvellous goodness of God! Not only has He brought all this to pass, but He has exceeded the prosperity which then seemed to me so ambitious that others would have to realize it after I had "gone home." Not only has He given the "thousands" which I coveted for His poor servants; but into *these* hands, which I then thought would soon be cold in death, He has poured the riches, and has strengthened them to be His messengers of mercy and comfort to the many who were fainting and famishing for lack of mental food. "Come, magnify the Lord with me, and let us exalt His name together." Oh! that I had the power to praise Him as I would for the grace and graciousness of the last seven years! I need an angel's tongue to sing the song that vibrates in my heart, and "lips touched with a live coal from off the altar" to speak the words which burn within me when all His goodness passes before me. My pen should write music if it only knew how, and every word should be a sonnet to celebrate His love!

* * * *

In the light of all this mercy past and present, how ungrateful it seems to bewail an excess of work, and to murmur at the responsibilities which accumulate around so great a blessing! If the Book Fund grows and prospers, the labour attendant upon its management must increase also, and surely the same loving Lord who appointed the service when it was a "little one" will interest Himself in its accomplishment now that it has become a "thousand." I have always looked with longing eyes on the dormant possibilities of blessing which lie within the boundaries of my dear work, and I feel sure that in the Lord's good time He will awaken them, and speak the word which shall clothe them with power for service. In abler and stronger hands than mine the Book Fund could do marvels; but as yet no sign is given that the Lord means to transfer it. I hope, and wait, and gladly work; for the Lord makes my service a choice delight to me, and munificently repays my labour, and "I love my Master, and will not go free."

* * * *

December.—I should like to give a few more extracts from the very sweet letters which have come lately; I do not wish to weary my readers with them, but they are really the outward and visible signs of the inward and spiritual grace of the Book Fund work; the leaves which prove the tree to be in a sound and healthy condition. Moreover, dear friends, without this assistance I should have no Annual Diary to present to you; I should never trust my pen to write were it not that my scribblings are, so to speak, interlinear, and, thus enclosed and guarded, can "do their spiriting gently," and for the most part escape observation and criticism. Well, to begin my story, one recipient tells me I can scarcely conceive the pleasure which a poor country minister feels when he opens a Book Fund parcel, and finds himself the fortunate owner of volumes which he has vainly longed for, perhaps for years, and which, but for this Fund, would never have graced his bare shelves, or encouraged his sad heart. "Ah!" he says, "no one can tell how much you comfort those who toil in country places. You make them feel that some one cares for them, and sympathizes with their sorrows." Often the gratitude of those who receive grants seems well-nigh inexpressible, and their tongues refuse to lift the load of thankfulness which rests upon their hearts. It is sad to suggest that this feeling may be mainly due to the rarity of such a charity; the kindness is so exceptional that it makes a deeper impression. Is it not a pity that this should be so? We would not wish poor Pastors to be less grateful, but would give them greater and more frequent cause for the exercise of so lovely a grace. "If the rich only knew," writes another of my poor friends, "the joy a present of books carries with it, your fund would never suffer for lack of contributions." Just so; but the fact turned the other way is equally forcible, and the Book Fund manager says, "If the rich only knew the joy of *giving* such a parcel, they would not let her monopolize the gladness, but would seek to share more directly and largely in the profitable pleasure of such service."

It is touching to note how contagious is the happiness which the books bring into a pastor's home, and how rapidly it spreads throughout the household. The wife and little ones all come to gaze on "father's new treasures," and again and again I am told—"We all knelt around the table on which the precious books were spread, and thanked God for sending so great a blessing to our home." Sometimes, too, if a parcel happens to arrive during the pastor's absence, it makes a delightful opportunity for his wife to surprise and gladden him with the sight of the goodly volumes all laid out in grand array. Says one—"My dear wife opened the parcel before I returned home. I suppose she felt too much interest in it to leave it alone till I arrived. And what a splendid parcel it was! . . . I at once bowed my head in thanksgiving to the Lord, and asked His blessing upon her who had cheered my heart so much."

Constantly I am informed, with some astonishment, that the books sent were the very ones needed. Such sentences as the following occur almost daily:—"I do not think I could have had any books which I really required so much. It seems to me that you have been directed by God in your selection." And again:—"Surely God inclined you to put *that* book into the parcel, for I need it very much." These are seals to my little service which I think much of, and for which I thank my God very unfeignedly. Another pastor writes:—"I had been studying hard all day, and before they (the books) came, I had fallen into what Mr. Spurgeon very properly calls 'a fainting fit'; but the sight of so many valuable volumes, and the kind wishes expressed in your letter, quite revived me, and it was with reluctance that I laid aside one of the volumes at midnight, so full and fresh did it prove to be." Hear another speak:—"I found your splendid gift of books awaiting me, and though weary in body, and mentally depressed, the sight of them was so refreshing, that as I turned over my treasures one by one—although it was past midnight—I felt I could sing aloud for joy. So touched was I by your exceeding kindness that I at once went to my knees and thanked God for His great goodness to me through you." "I am delighted with the books," writes a young preacher, "and I thank the Lord and you very much. 'Jesus only' seems to me the very best sermon I ever read; it moved me as I have not been moved for a long while.

> 'Through my pulse the music stole,
> And held high converse with my soul.'

With these beautiful books I feel rich, and as if I should never be in want again."

Ah! dear brother, that is a very decided mistake of yours! Your appetite will be *increased* by such savoury food, and the more heartily it is received into the soul and digested there, the more certain and ravenous will be your hunger and yearning for more. It is always so; my long experience teaches me to know full well the signs of the famine-fever which my Fund so blessedly relieves, and I find that those who most eagerly grasp and assimilate the food with which I supply them, are liable to severe and repeated relapses. So be it; and may the Lord grant that the Book Fund may be always able to fill their "longing souls with gladness"! I could go on filling these pages with similarly delightful extracts, but must soon turn my attention to other matters which concern the history of my work. "One may quote till one compiles," says a clever writer; yet with that warning flowing from the point of my pen, I am about to disregard it just once more, and complete the preceding extracts with the grateful words of one who has been much blessed by Book Fund gifts. He says :—

> I am sure it will please you to know that the books you sent me some years ago have been of very great service in my work for the Master. My labours are continuous, and are sometimes a very severe strain both on physical and mental powers; and when I am feeling completely worn out, yet have to prepare a sermon, you can judge how thankfully I turn to the treasures you have so kindly given. Many

times while seeking something for my flock I have found strengthening and life-giving food for myself, and this makes me very grateful to God and to you for another addition to my scanty library. I desire to be a workman that needeth not to be ashamed, rightly dividing the word of truth. I long to feed the flock of God with the pure milk of the word, and to be instrumental in God's hands in leading poor sinners to the cross of Christ; and your precious gifts have helped me more than I can tell you, both in my pulpit ministrations and in my private devotions. I can never repay you for your kindness, but my Father will.

May these testimonies, so touchingly given and faithfully transcribed, induce many friends to interest themselves in a work which brings so much blessing to hearts sorely needing it!

* * * *

CONCLUSION.

The Book Fund has this year, I think, attained its zenith of prosperity, its meridian of usefulness, *under present management.* The Lord has given me more to do than in past years, and more to do it with, and I have done it to the very verge of my strength; but I do not think I shall ever again be able to record quite such another twelvemonths of uninterrupted sunshine and unremitting labour. As a gathering up or conclusion to my many little talks with my readers, I intend to glance at the most notable points of my work, and give a rapid summary of each, though I must necessarily repeat an oft-told tale.

First, as to the material of the work,—the books themselves. The item, "To Books," in my balance-sheet, will prove these precious things to be costly also, and will plainly show that the major part of the money with which I am entrusted is expended on *them*. I have given away more volumes than in any preceding year, and they have all been good, sound, theological helps, books that will teach men, and enable them to teach others. Kind friends have also sent again and again to replenish my shelves, and these contributions have largely aided to increase my distributions. I am not obliged to renew my complaint about having worthless and inappropriate books sent to me; for happily, I have received so few of that sort that I am only too glad to be silent over them. A noble list of gifts stands recorded on my ledgers, and for all these my very grateful thanks are sincerely tendered to the kind donors.

These gift books, I should like my friends to understand, are used to enlarge and swell my parcels—they are extra blessings; for with applicants the rule is to ask for "Mr. Spurgeon's works," and to get them, all others being accepted with grace, but with not so much favour. I had some difficulty in making this plain to a kind donor of books the other day. When she saw the Book Fund shelves stored with sets of "The Treasury," "Sermons," and "Lectures," and was told that most of these would be wanted for the next fortnightly despatch, and the shelves would then require re-furnishing, and that this process went on throughout the year, she looked at me with extreme astonishment; for till that moment she had imagined I only gave away the books which kind friends, like herself, had forwarded for this purpose, and that I depended upon such means for the working of my Fund. I am truly thankful that this is not the case; for much of the charm of my work lies in the delightful consciousness that I am daily spreading abroad the precious works of my dear husband; works which God has so signally blessed to the conversion of sinners and the comforting of the saints,—works, too, so full of holy instruction and spiritual suggestiveness, that no minister's library is complete without them.

Not once this year has my exchequer run low, and, to counterbalance that statement, notice this other—not for one day has the constant stream of applications failed to flow. But I must gratefully note the exceeding love and kindness of the Lord in sending supplies of money for my work with such amazing constancy and liberality. I have very much to bless Him for; but *this* mercy—of freedom from all anxiety concerning supplies—is a choice blessing, and He alone is to have all praise and glory for it. Dear friends, you know I never ask any of you for help; you send it because I ask HIM; but this year I have not had even to ask: before I called, He answered me, and the money has come in advance of my needs. You are pleased that I should give

Him all the glory, are you not? For you know that I am none the less grateful to you.

I turn over the pages of my day-book and see that during the past year a good many missionaries have been helped with books. India, Africa, British Honduras, Newfoundland, Nova Scotia, Jamaica, Australia, China, all these places and more are represented there by the names of some good men who have been furnished with the means of spreading the knowledge of Christ among the heathen. Little comparatively, however, of such work do I attempt, but confine my chief efforts to help for home workers. I find in England alone a sphere wide enough for my feeble operations; but a Cosmopolitan Book Fund is one of the future shining "possibilities."

In a very loving and tender way has the Lord made my Annual Report a joy and a blessing to others, and *therefore* a source of thankful rejoicing to myself. The last issued—that for 1881—found great favour, stirred much interest, and brought large increase to the Fund. I have treasured up many "good words" written to me upon the matter, and have been greatly encouraged by their sweetness and sympathy. "Accept the enclosed £2 for your Book Fund," says a lady, "you will only know in eternity the good you have been the means of doing through it"; and one who says she is "only a servant," sends 5s. with these kind words: "I look forward almost with impatience to the publishing of your charming Report, and wish on reading it that I had large means at my disposal wherewith to help so good a cause." A minister says, "I read the Report through before I laid it down. I found it a delightfully stimulating commentary on a text I am hoping to preach from to-morrow—'Serve the Lord with gladness.' I read extracts from it to my dear wife and daughter, and tears stood in their eyes, and joy and gladness glistened through the tears." "It surely ought to encourage you in your work of love," says another friend, "to *know* that you are making men more useful in their Master's cause."

There has been this year a large increase of *payments* for

books. In this matter I have diligently endeavoured to distinguish between those who *can* pay a little, and those whose poverty entitles them to a gift without question; yet, almost in self-defence, I have sometimes put forward this little barrier to the overwhelming flood of incessant applications. In other instances, ministers and clergymen have been only too glad to purchase essential books at a reduced price. Here, again, lies another " sleeping beauty " of a possibility. All the publishers with whom I have had transactions have been so kind and liberal, that untold treasures might enrich poor Pastors' shelves if only I had the time and strength to organize a scheme, by which, with some help from a Fund, the grand standard theological works might all be attainable by them. Will not somebody start a " Book Fund " which shall be a grand development of my little work, and magnificently supply all that is lacking in it? It would be a happy day for me were I to see this !

The monthly gift of *The Sword and the Trowel* magazine to about forty poor ministers still continues, but shows no increase. Here also the work points out a pleasant path of service where sweet flowers of encouragement would soon reward the search of a patient traveller. I am glad to know that some of my friends have already entered on it from previous suggestions, and are now regularly sending their monthly numbers both of "Sermons" and magazines to certain poor ministers, thereby conferring an inestimable benefit upon them and their households. A minister said to me the other day, " Your kindness has made too deep an impression ever to be forgotten. It brought gladness, the echoes of which are with us to this day; it strengthened faith, which has not ceased to grow; it produced an assurance of God's care and faithfulness, which calmed us in our deepest sorrows." Dear friends will you not seek more than ever to spread around you such blessing?

We come now to the last item in this simple summary of my work—THE PASTORS' AID FUND.

I think all my readers know that this effort grew out of the loving thought of one dear friend, who judged that *books* did not supply all the wants of a poor pastor, and that sometimes a gift of mental food might be a mockery, if not preceded or accompanied by the means of sustaining physical strength. To meet the demand which he was assured would come, and before the Book Fund was many months old, this good friend set apart a certain sum for my use as occasion required, so that when an exceptional case of need was brought to my knowledge, I was allowed to draw on my generous banker. His kind forethought has been abundantly justified and his liberality appreciated. Six years this wonderful kindness has been manifested, and it has attracted other gracious charities around it, and bound other friends of like noble large-heartedness to my poor clients' cause, so that each year lately my monetary gifts to poor ministers have somewhat exceeded £300.

I do not intend to say much about this part of my work, it is carried on quite privately, and the recipients are known only to me and their kind friends; but I may again mention the fact which has often been brought before you, that there are hundreds of poor dissenting ministers in England—rich England—who exist and bring up families on the bare pittance of £60 or £70 per annum. I *have* sometimes tried to plead the cause of these poor servants of the Master, whose empty larders, threadbare suits, and ill-clad children are a continual sorrow to me; but an occasional £5 has been the only result. I am thankful for even this, or for any little help; but I most devoutly desire to see the burden taken up by those to whom it rightly belongs—the churches themselves—so that by a united effort they would take up the load and remove it to the "land of forgetfulness." This dire poverty of our ministers is a stain on the banner of Nonconformity which might and should be washed away.

Only to-day I had a letter from a Scotch lady, now residing in England, in which great surprise is expressed at the state of things she finds here, and I grew hot with shame as I read it. She tells me of a good man, a "good preacher," too, she says, who is obliged to take to secular business, in order to support his family, because the stipend is so "miserably small." "Surely," says my friend, "there is a want of liberality among English Dissenters in the country!

The habit the people have in Scotland of giving something *every* Sabbath is a good one, the very poorest gives a penny or a half-penny, and almost all the working people give to the Sustentation Fund."

Ah well! they love and value their Pastors in Scotland, I suppose, more than we do, and so they take greater care of them; but, "brethren, these things ought not so to be." Even as I write, there comes sad and sorrowful confirmation of the pitiful facts before alluded to, in the case of two Pastors whose health has been shattered, and their hearts nearly broken, in the silent, constant, wearing struggle with extreme and bitter poverty. I cannot tell you about them—the tale is too dreadful for these pages; but I have wept over them, and helped them, and hope to relieve them still more, if the dear Lord sends the means. But, oh! that something great, and noble, and lasting might be done for these suffering servants of the Master! There *are* signs abroad of a more general awakening to their needs, and with all my heart I say, " God speed " to all and every scheme for their emancipation from such hard bondage—a bondage, moreover, which, methinks, is insulting to the King whose ambassadors they are. Meanwhile, as the " Book Fund " is " my little corner of the great Kingdom," I must work away there patiently and hopefully—" until the day break, and the shadows flee away."

* * * *

Dear friends, if, through the Lord's gracious favour, this little book, as in other years, speaks to your heart again, interests you in His sweet service, helps your faith and love, or comforts you in any way; above all, if it brings the least atom of glory to Him, I shall be well rewarded for writing it, and most likely encouraged to " try again."

Your grateful friend and servant for the Book Fund's sake,

SUSIE SPURGEON.

The Book Fund Diary

FOR 1883.

BY MRS. C. H. SPURGEON.

THE Lord's great love, and the constant kindness of friends, have enabled me to record another year of prosperity to my beloved work. How much I have been favoured, and how richly others have been blessed through the service which is thus supported, these pages will do their best to tell; but they can never reveal the infinite tenderness of God's dealings with me, nor recount the thousandth part of the mercy and grace which have made my cup to run over. The surface blessings of His love are visible, like the wavelets on a calm ocean's bosom; but they disclose nothing of the "depth which coucheth beneath," and is as unfathomable as eternity.

If it be a joy to comfort those who are cast down, and a happiness to have the power of making others happy, then must I be counted an enviable mortal; for in the Book Fund I possess a talisman of potent force, which works marvels of gladness in hundreds of homes, sets the joy-bells ringing in sad and weary hearts, and lights up many a poor pastor's dreary study with the golden rays of hope and encouragement.

Sidney Smith once wrote: "Mankind are always happier for having been made happy; so that if you make them happy now, you make them happy twenty years hence by the memory of it." If this be true of any sort of goodwill to man, it must be doubly applicable to the kindness which bestows books upon him—books which shall be life-long friends, cheerfully taking up their abode under his roof, and serving him faithfully and ungrudgingly till his death.

Langford, in his "Praise of Books," says so charmingly what I want to say, but fear to blunder over, that I shall proceed to embellish my little Preface with a few of his choice sentences, hoping thereby to inspire my readers with fresh interest in the treasures of which I have the charge.

Says he: "Books *are* friends, and what friends they are! Their love is deep and unchanging; their patience inexhaustible; their gentleness perennial; their forbearance unbounded; and their sympathy without selfishness. Strong as man, and tender as woman, they welcome you in every mood, and never turn from you in distress. As companions and acquaintances books are without rivals; and they are companions and acquaintances to be had at all times and under all circumstances. They are never out when you knock at the door; are never 'not at home' when you call. In the lightest as well as in the deepest moods they may be applied to, and will never be found wanting. The friendship of books never dies; it grows by use, it increases by distribution, and possesses an immortality of perpetual youth. It is the friendship, not of 'dead things,' but of ever-living souls; and books are friends who, under no circumstances, are ever applied to in vain. They can be relied on, whoever else or whatever else may fail. Books are also among man's truest consolers. In the hour of affliction, trouble, or sorrow, he can turn to them with confidence and trust. In the good sense of the phrase, they are all things to all men, and are faithful alike to all."

These encomiums fall sweetly on my ear, and awaken in my heart fresh zeal for my work. I long to introduce such friends to poor ministers by hundreds and thousands, and right sure am I that, when once they enter his door, they will be taken into his heart, and cherished as his most precious possession. It pleased me to go so far afield to seek golden opinions for my precious volumes, and I feel rewarded for the search; but I need only have turned to the letters which lie in fast-accumulating heaps on the Book Fund shelves, to glean from them many a graceful eulogy, many a grateful tribute to the worth of books, and to find that, on all hands, the vital necessity and value of these true helpmeets are most warmly recognized and acknowledged. Come with me, dear reader, and glance through the pages of the months; let us see what blessings the books have wrought, and how graciously the Lord has smiled upon the service and its willing servant.

ON this first day of 1883 my loving wishes hover round my living friends, and my heart says, with very tender emphasis, "God bless them all!" for, it may be that some who have loved my work dearly, may never see the record of this year's service,—or, it may be that the "servant" will be called to give an account of her stewardship to her Lord, before all the days in the "Diary" shall have been completed. Since I wrote my farewell to the Old Year, the Angel of Death has been busy on our right hand and on our left, calling dear ones home; and some have fled away to glory whom, with selfish love, we would fain have kept imprisoned here. But "the Master was not willing that they should be so far from Him any longer," and so they are gone to behold His face in brightness, and to know the bliss of being "for ever with the Lord." Very mournfully fell the Christmas greetings on our ears; and all the chimes we heard were muffled; for in the homes of our friends, dark shadows had gathered over hearts left desolate, and with sympathetic grief we could feel the chilling gloom of the fatal messenger's presence, though he but *passed our door*.

* * * *

We were expecting charming guests for all this festive season. We had invited health and joy, sweet content and holy merriment to meet around our board, and tarry for a while beneath our roof; the "garments of praise" were being prepared, and all the "daughters of music" were waiting to celebrate the coming festival. But it was not so to be. The Lord sent other visitors to our door; and when the time of rejoicing was fully come, behold, pain and grief, anxiety and dismay, presented themselves for admittance, and, at His bidding, silently took the vacant places of the guests whom we were hoping to entertain with so much joy and gladness. Sitting down with this sad company, we ate the bread of affliction, and drank the waters of Marah; our festal robes were put aside, and heaviness of heart covered us as with a garment; fast falling tears were our only music, and instead of making a joyful noise unto the Lord, there fell upon us the solemn and expectant silence of those who "fear evil tidings." The beloved of our soul was sick again, notwithstanding all the fair promise of renewed health and vigour which we thought secured by his lovely sojourn at Mentone; and while he thus lay prostrate, Death was taking away fond and faithful friends, dealing blow after blow at our hearts, till we seemed bewildered by calamity, and almost learned to dread the dawning of each day lest its light should reveal some fresh and dismal trial. How was it possible that our faces should wear any brightness in the midst of all this sorrow? How could we be made to realize that our terrible guests came not only as envoys from the King of kings, but were in very deed and truth, "angels unawares"?

* * * *

To the "praise of the glory of His grace" I now record our deliverance from this Valley of the Shadow of Death, and sing of the light at the end which shined into our hearts, and scattered the darkness with which unbelief and sorrow had well-nigh overwhelmed us. It pleased the Lord most marvellously to avert the long attack of sickness which threatened His servant, and when He had raised him up He comforted him so sweetly under the losses which had befallen him, that he was able to comfort others also with the comfort wherewith he himself was comforted of God. And it came about in this wise: Coming home one night sorrowful and weary, with the burden of bereavement pressing sorely on his heart, he was met with the question, "Do you remember how bravely Bunyan's 'pilgrims' passed the river, and what Greatheart said to Christiana, when she, as the first of his company, was called to come before the King?" "A word to the wise is enough"; very little more than that was said; but the book was taken down and the sweet allegory read with most blessed result; for, the next day, when another solemn visit to the tomb was paid, how sweetly and hopefully could God's servant speak! He had but tasted of the honey at the end of this rod, and lo! his eyes were enlightened, and his soul was no longer bowed down with bitterness. He could bid the mourners look from the grave to the golden gates of glory; he could say, "I hear the music of hope drowning the discord of fear; the songs of a joyous faith rising above the dirges of grief." He could point his people to the promised blessings of adversity, he could even stir them up to a joyful expectancy, and cry, "These clouds mean rich refreshing showers; these sharp frosts foretell heavy sheaves; blessings are on the way from heaven—their shadows fall upon us even now." Thus, blessed be God, we have "gladness for sadness," the night of our weeping is followed by the morning of joy; and though the experience has been a painful one, and has cost us many a tear, we know it has had a salutary effect upon our spirit, and has taught us the truth of the "Preacher's" words: "It is better to go to the house of mourning than to go to the house of feasting: for that is the end of all men: and the living will lay it to his heart."

If mourning friends, or fearful saints will turn to the last pages of the *second* part of Bunyan's "Pilgrim's Progress," they will there find solace for their grief, rebuke for their trembling, and stimulus for their courage. Every line glows with celestial light, every word seems to have caught the hues of the jewels in the City's foundation, every sweet thought comes like a "Shining One" to strengthen and comfort the soul. The wonderful "Dreamer" gives so entrancing a picture of the last days on earth of the King's chosen ones, that our natural shrinking from death is overcome, and we are ravished with delightful anticipations of the bliss awaiting us when "the trumpet shall sound for us on the other side." The glory that streams across the river dispels all mists of sorrow, doubt, and fear from the eyes; we can rejoice over our dear ones who have passed the flood and now stand in the King's presence; and in view of the time when our own feet shall touch the dark waters, we think we can say with Mr. Standfast, "The thoughts of what I am going to, and of the conduct that waits for me on the other side, do lie as a glowing coal at my heart. Lord, take me, for I come unto Thee!"

> "Spread thy wings, my soul, and fly,
> Straight to yonder world of joy!"

* * * *

Whether the sun shines, or the clouds gather, Book Fund work knows no pause or cessation. Its little stream may reflect the changes in the sky above it, but it still flows on and on, carrying, by God's blessing, gladness and fruitfulness wherever its waters find a channel.

Here is a letter bearing the date "CHRISTMAS MORNING, 1882," a date which will ever remain in our memories as one "writ in gloomy lines of sorrow"; but to this needy pastor the Book Fund had sent a loving present, and *he* sees the calendar letters sparkling with brightness, and rejoices to illuminate his note-paper with them. Let us listen to his grateful words, and comfort our hearts with some of his joy.

Your very generous gift arrived safely, and it proved to be so abundantly liberal that my dear wife and I could scarcely believe in our good fortune. Little did I think when I wrote about "The Treasury" that you would send so much more than I asked for. Our hearts are full, our gratitude is greater than I can express. All day yesterday, whenever I had a moment to spare, I was thinking about my new and precious possessions, and wondering what suitable words I could find with which to thank you; but now I feel that I cannot speak what my heart has to say. The value of the "Sermons" I will not venture to estimate. How often have I received stimulus in my work, and gathered holy suggestions from the volumes already in my possession! But these four, completing the set, have a peculiar interest to me, owing to circumstances of which I will tell you, for I am sure the knowledge will increase the pleasure you have in your loving service. Up to a short time since I had taken in the "Sermons" from 1877, and was keeping them for the purpose of having them bound; but, thinking that they might be a blessing to the men attending my Sunday Bible Class, I gave them up to be circulated among the members, and they were greatly delighted to have them to read during the week. Many testimonies have reached me of the comfort and help these single copies have afforded to the men and their wives, so that I had the joy of knowing that my sacrifice was not in vain. But now that word "sacrifice" is out of place! *The Lord has sent me back all my Sermons—clean, fresh, and bound!* . . . Altogether the parcel is a grand present, and will make this Christmas ever memorable to me.

* * * *

New Year's Day also brought a cheering word and gift from a pastor who has always been a faithful friend to the Book Fund. "I am glad," says he, "that the first time I write the date of the New Year, is in sending to you. May it be a very happy one to you and yours—not least to the dear boy who is far away. I enclose 30s. for the Fund, the result of our offering at the 'Watchnight Service.' It is not much, but it represents the first free gifts of some of the Lord's people to the Lord's work, and was given at five minutes after midnight."

Let me mention here, with very grateful joy, that I have lately heard of several instances in which my dear work has been remembered before the Lord in the *prayer-meetings* connected with various churches. This delightful intelligence has greatly refreshed me; for what blessings may I not expect when God's people unitedly bring my cause before Him in prayer? To *Him alone* I look for support, and sustenance, and success in this blessed service; but it is pleasant to think that many of the "King's Remembrancer's are constantly enquiring of Him concerning this matter, and lovingly pleading,

"Think upon it, ☩ Lord, for good."

* * * *

February.—What subtle charm works silently in the young, fresh months of the New Year, attracting to the Lord's treasury, at this season, those special and peculiar gifts which are so pleasant to jot down in my Diary? Have the "sweet influences of the Pleiades" a mystic power to draw forth the hidden treasures of silver and gold as well as to unlock the prison-house of the spring-flowers, and open the eyes of the buds upon every interlacing bough? I have again received presents of "hoarded coins" for the Book Fund, and as these always seem to me to bear unusual witness to the power of Christ's love in the heart, I hail them with joy, and appropriate them to his work with much thankfulness. A dear faithful friend, seeing the story of the "six golden guineas" in the Report for 1882, rejoices "that the lemon plant which before showed only silver blossoms, has now borne golden fruit," and she sends an old "spade guinea," the "gift of a dear one now in heaven," to increase the riches of the emblem tree. Very prettily she says, "I had forgotten that I possessed it till I read your dear book; but I fetched it at once, and I send it with the loving wish that God may bless it to the comfort and help of some poor pastor. It is only a trifle, but God can do great things with trifles, and I send this golden bit to Him *with a grateful heart for letting me know He wanted it.*" Enclosed with the guinea was a crown piece, which had hitherto been carefully treasured "in memory of dear departed parents." To-day a "valentine from Annie," when opened, discloses another crown-piece and some choice and tender words, proving that the special grace and beauty of consecration to Christ's service rests fully on this gift also.

I lay these and all similar moneys up before the Lord as very sacred things, and, till the time comes when the need of His servants necessitates their being changed into the ordinary currency, they are as a "memorial" in His sight. How much more satisfactory and delightful it is thus to put these talents out to usury, and glorify the Master and refresh His servants with the heavenly interest they bring in, than to wrap them up and hide them away in selfish and unlovely secrecy where they can give no pleasure to the Lord, nor be of any profit to our fellow-men!

* * * *

If any of my readers recollect my telling them, two years ago, of a clergyman who, for nine Sundays, preached Mr. Spurgeon's sermons in a church in the rector's absence, to the great delight and edification of the congregation, they will be interested to know that this same gentleman continues his most praiseworthy efforts in this direction, and constantly delivers the sermons in parish churches and elsewhere—condensed and epitomized, it is true, to suit the shorter service required in the Established Church, but none the less really and truly the gospel of the grace of God as preached by His servant, C. H. Spurgeon.

I have been quite charmed to hear from him again and again, and to find that so far from relinquishing the peculiar form of service to which he had devoted himself, he still holds on his course bravely, and is the means of bringing much blessing to the districts in which he labours. He writes, asking for more books; he wants material to "arrange and abridge," not being in the least desirous of concealing the fact that the discourses so shortened will be repeated *verbatim*, nay, admitting with a simplicity and frankness which almost provoke a smile that, "in fact, Mr. Spurgeon's sermons are the only ones which can be really understood either by myself or the congregation." The good man's naïve remark may cause us a moment's amusement, but does it not contain a very weighty and significant truth? If more sermons were preached from the heart to the heart, so as to be easily "understanded of the people," would not the Holy Spirit oftener set the seal of his blessing upon them? And do not many ministers lose the crown and glory of their sacred office by undervaluing the power of the simplicity of the gospel—the "*foolishness* of preaching"—while they insist on delivering erudite essays on abstruse theories, "darkening counsel by words without knowledge"?

Let us hear more of what our friend has to say on the subject "No address," he writes, "could have been more attentively listened to, or have given greater joy, than the one I delivered on Sunday evening, No. 1, in F. S., with very few omissions from the original. I feel that Mr. Spurgeon's words have a power in them, and leave an impression on the heart of the hearers, which other printed sermons fall short of: *people begin to enquire about the state of their souls after I have given them one of his discourses.*"

Although these proceedings are, doubtless, somewhat

irregular in the Church of England, I rejoice to be an accomplice in them; and I intend to do all in my power to forward a project which can only result in the glory of God and the salvation of immortal souls. I do not think my friend has a settled curacy; but it is a grand thing that he should go about proclaiming "all the words of this life," telling the "old, old story" in simple fashion, to those who perhaps have all their lives known only the cold, lifeless service of mere formalism; and occasionally, it may be, taking "duty" in churches where "another gospel, which is not another," is preached to unwary men. "Only a few Sundays ago," he says, "I delivered the sermon on . . . . (I must not disclose too many of his confidences), when every eye was fixed on the speaker, and hearts were evidently touched, and great delight was expressed by the people on leaving the church." Is it not sometimes true still, that "where ignorance is bliss, 'tis folly to be wise"? If these decorous parishioners, these loyal sons and daughters of old Mother Church, who, doubtless, would have thought it mortal sin to step across the threshold of a "*meeting-house,*" had but known that with attentive ears, and moistened eyes, and opening hearts, they had listened to the utterances of an unordained man, a dissenting preacher, it is quite within the bounds of possibility that prejudice might have hardened their hearts, and robbed them of the blessing which that day had brought to them. But they knew not, "the Lord being merciful unto them"; and so my friend, if he has not the gift of ministry himself, as I presume is the case, cannot, surely, do better than speak to the people the very words which have already been attested and sealed by the Holy Spirit with "power from on high." One thing is certain, this good man's heart is set on preaching Christ, and helping his fellow-men to heaven, and for this purpose he "sought to find out acceptable words," like the "preacher" of old, and God has given him his heart's desire. I should liken him to a wise master-builder, who, having on his own land no suitable or available quarry, goes cheerfully afar to find choice and costly stones, for the building he desires should be to the "praise and glory of God." I pray that his work may abide, as I believe it will, and that at last the "corner-stone" may be brought forth with shoutings of "Grace, grace unto it!" One more quotation from his letter, and then I must soon dismiss this very interesting subject. "For several Sunday evenings," he writes, "I have, with a friend's permission, invited to evening prayer a number of villagers, chiefly from ———, where the voice of the incumbent is scarcely audible, and on these occasions I read the greater part of one of Mr. Spurgeon's "Sermons," to the great delight of all who hear me. I write the sermon out, and this gives me greater facility in its delivery, making me fully at home with the subject." Then he goes on to tell me of a farmer, possibly the "friend" mentioned above, who first suggested the plan to him, and lent him single copies of sermons to practise upon, whispering that he had a large quantity of them in his house, but dared not lend them in the village, as he feared offending the vicar, from whom he held his farm. Perhaps this good farmer remembered that of old it was said, "He that withholdeth corn, the people shall curse him;" and so he cast about in his mind for a plan whereby his precious stores of spiritual food might be freely distributed to the famishing souls around him. But did any one ever hear of a more remarkable and unique method of compassing his desires, and "*catchin'* '*em with guile*," as "Dan'el Quorm" puts it? I think it must have been with some trembling of heart that he first made his startling proposition to the clergyman; but soon he would rejoice to see that the Lord had beforehand "prepared" the mind of His servant to discharge this singular office; and had, in His all-wise providence, arranged all the circumstances which led to so rare a result! All honour to the God-fearing farmer! May his barns overflow, his flocks and his herds increase, and the blessing of the Lord, "which maketh rich, and addeth no sorrow therewith," rest ever on his heart and home! Like Obed-edom, he has the Ark of the Lord in his house, and because of it the Lord will "bless all that pertaineth unto him."

* * * *

An almost unprecedented stress of work during the last eight weeks has left me scant time or strength to continue my talks with my friends in these pages. It is wonderful how they fill up *somehow*, with a line written now and then, and a great desire to do more and better; but if my excessive weariness is observable and patent to my readers in dull and prosy paragraphs, they must be pitiful and indulgent, for my days have been wholly spent in laborious correspondence, and the evening hours find me too jaded, both in mind and body, to be a genial or chatty chronicler.

There is a fatal break in the electric influence which should flash from head and heart to the hand ; no spark of thought, or light of fancy, comes to irradiate the darkness in which my pen gropes painfully.

I have received, during the twenty-eight days of this month of February, SIX HUNDRED AND FIFTY-SEVEN LETTERS; the figures are easily written, more easily read ; but they give faint notion of the amount of labour involved in the correspondence they represent.

The careful consideration of each application, the repeated enquiries rendered necessary by inexplicit writers, the anxious solicitude felt in selecting appropriate books for varying needs, the time and close attention required to keep up the constant, voluminous, and detailed entries which such a service demands : all these constitute the *work* of the Book Fund, and render it a very grave and pressing business,— one which its manager loves with all her heart, even while her hands can, sometimes, scarcely sustain the burden which it brings. Will you pray for her, dear friends ?

* * * *

March.—(AN ANGEL IN THE HOUSE.) Out of the terrible tempest of sorrow which lately swept over the homes of some of our friends, and brought death and desolation to their households, there came drifting to our shores a little storm-tossed barque, driven by the contrary winds of this great adversity, to seek shelter in our "haven under the hill." Such a charming little child ! A fair pearl of humanity washed from its bed by the troubled tides of life's ocean,— a tender white dovelet tossed from its nest by a rude blast of affliction,—a "little soul that stands expectant, listening at the gate of life,"—a sweet wee mitherless bairn, whose needs claim the shelter of warm hearts and the loving service of womanly hands. We give a fond welcome to the sweet stranger, taking him to our hearts to love, and to be loved, and have found a singular joy in renewing in some measure the experiences of days long past, but not forgotten.

It is twenty-seven years since "our own" babies' dimpled hands stroked our cheek, or their pretty voices made unaccustomed music in the house; but the cry of this little one awakens the long-sleeping echoes, and his tiny fingers stray among our heart-strings, touching again and again one of the old chords of purest and deepest melody. Watching his winsome ways, and noting the daily unfoldings of his exceedingly sweet and gentle disposition, I ask myself, "What shall this darling teach us, now that the Lord Christ hath set him in our midst?" I do not think we have been disputing who amongst us should be greatest in the kingdom of heaven, but the Master's words imply that humility is not the only grace illustrated in the daily example of His little ones. "Verily, I say unto you, whosoever shall not receive the kingdom of God as a little child, shall in no wise enter therein." So I set myself to know what special message to my soul lay hidden in that sunshiny face, or perchance, what well-merited rebuke to my unchildlike spirit might lurk amid the charms of his lovely and confiding nature. And I find that baby has been a "living epistle" of *faith* before my eyes, an unconscious exponent of the blessedness of simple dependence upon God, so that I think I understand more of its sweetness and power than I ever did before. For there is *perfect* faith and trust in baby's heart; absolute reliance upon those who love him; unquestioning confidence in their ability and tenderness. The tottering steps grow steady, and are ventured without fear, when his small hand is closely clasped in mine; he leans all his weight of babyhood on my arms, without the shadow of a suspicion that they could fail him: every promise that I give is echoed in sweet babblings from "lips that know no word of doubting"; and, oh, with what glee and rapture does he throw aside his toys and stretch out his pretty hands when I call him to my side! Thus am I taught not to fear or falter while my hand is held by a "stronger than I":—thus do I see the happiness of leaning hard on love which is omnipotent, and the wisdom of unhesitating faith in gracious words of peace and pardon ;—thus too, I think I can perceive, faintly shadowed forth, the joy with which I hope to obey the loving call to be "for ever with the Lord." The very caresses I give to baby are often strangely mingled with spiritual longings, and many a loving play with him ends in a prayer that I may "become like this little child." Is it any marvel, that with this sweet unwitting teacher on my knee, I see earthly things still made after heavenly patterns, and rejoice that "out of the mouth of babes and sucklings God hath perfected praise"?

Dear, bright-eyed, glad and trustful baby! Your little mission here has been a sacred one; your presence has brought a blessing with it! Your confidence in us has quickened our faith in God, and our love to you has given us fresh glimpses of our Father's infinite tenderness!

Ever through your future life, dear child, may these precious graces of faith and love adorn your soul; ever may it be true of you, as it is at this moment, that—

"𝔒𝔣 𝔰𝔲𝔠𝔥 𝔦𝔰 𝔱𝔥𝔢 𝔎𝔦𝔫𝔤𝔡𝔬𝔪 𝔬𝔣 ℌ𝔢𝔞𝔳𝔢𝔫."

* * * *

March 22nd.—The following letter, which I received to-day, is so amusing, as well as enthusiastic in its gratitude, that though lengthy I must transcribe it almost without curtailment, and certainly without comment, for it tells its own tale admirably :—

Dear Madam,—It is Monday evening; I have been away from home, and have just returned. On reaching our station, the first thing I did was to enquire if a parcel had come for me. The clerk answered, "Yes, it came this morning, and it weighs about two stone!" "Praise God for that!" was my mental response. But I do not think the porter who carried it up the hill felt quite so full of glee about it as I did; his looks as he entered the house rather suggested that he was glad to be rid of it. But now the parcel is laid open, and the books are examined, and what shall I speak? I have heard Christians say, when extolling the goodness of God, "I can never sufficiently praise Him!" and this is just how I feel, for I see the tender kindness of God to me in this gift of books from you. As surely as the manna came from God for Israel, so surely has this mental food been sent to me from Him. I asked Him to guide you in the *selection* of the books, and I know He hears prayer, so I believe what you have sent will be right for both head and heart.

Tears came into my eyes when I found your note, and there read: "This gift of books comes to you with many prayers and kindest wishes." How kind of you to say that! I feel I have a goodly heritage, "My cup runneth over!" I keep repeating the words of the Psalmist, "Thou hast put gladness into my heart, more than in the time that their wine and oil increased."

"Come along, cold winter," said a countryman when he got a new top-coat,—so, with regard to future work, so far as human helps are needed, I can almost say, "Come along, any quantity, I'm prepared for you!" What a thrill of pleasure went through me when I opened the parcel! Every volume, big or little, seemed to be laughing all over the face of it, and each one seemed anxious to speak first and tell all the news. 'Twas like a merry band of boys and girls bursting into my room and talking all together,—"We have come to live with you, Mr. ———, Mrs. Spurgeon has sent us; we have had a long ride, but we are none the worse for the shaking and the journey, for Mrs. Spurgeon took care to wrap us well up before we set off." "Well," I said, as I gazed upon them, "I am right glad to see you, but I did not expect so many of you; however, 'the more the merrier,' and I promise you all, you shall have the best place I can find for you in my house, and you shall be my constant and beloved companions." Dear Madam, —I feel so glad, that I believe I could write a letter a yard or two long! No child with a new toy was ever half so enraptured as I am with my precious possessions. "Bless the Lord, O my soul, and forget not all His benefits." Glory to His name! Praise Him for ever! GLORY!

[After enumerating all the smaller books in the parcel, and giving quaint welcomes to each one, which I am obliged to pass over for fear my readers should not be quite so much interested in all the details as I am, our "ready writer" comes to the more important works, and thus concludes his song of praise.]

Last of all, here are six precious volumes of "The Treasury of David." I have heard of them by the hearing of the ear, but never did I think that I should possess them as a free gift. O Lord, I thank thee! "Thou hast crowned me with lovingkindness and tender mercies." A beggar knocks at the door, and receives a slice of dry bread—this is kindness. But "little Johnny," gets a slice with *butter* on. Ah! my soul, this is *loving*kindness—*bread with butter on.* Dear Madam,— If you only knew how thankful I feel, you would never be discouraged, but rejoice in your work for evermore. May God's blessing rest upon you and Mr. Spurgeon! Please tell him I have long prayed for him, especially when he is preaching to the people.—Yours gratefully ———.

* * * *

Here is a loving little letter from a sweet Quaker friend. I place it in these pages to lie like a feather from a dove's wing beside the gayer plumage of ordinary epistles :—

Dear Mrs. Spurgeon,—Many thanks for thy report of thy interesting work; in acknowledging it, the opportunity is afforded me of telling thee that my warmest thanks are due to thee for thy deeply touching story concerning thy Saturday Sabbath. Each seventh-day evening since I received it has been brightened, solemnized, and blessed to me, as I have realized the scene passing in the "Westwood" study; and I have asked the Divine Master to supply to His highly-favoured minister the food meet for the strengthening and refreshing of his own soul and thine, while seeking to provide for the spiritual wants of both hearers and readers. I must own that the weekly " Sermons " have been received with extra love and blessing since I have thus held sweet communion with you in spirit on the last day of the week. I send the enclosed gift with my warmest sympathy with thy "labour of love," and with deep gratitude to the Lord for all the good things He dispenses to the world through His dear servant, thy husband.—I remain, thy friend ———.

* * * *

April.—Appropriately to the season of the year—in April, the "dripping month"—here follows a heavy shower of blessings, a perfect downpour of benedictions, a rain of recompenses, which has refreshed the thirsty ground of Book Fund service, and prepared it, I hope, for further fruitfulness :—

Accept my very grateful thanks for the large parcel of books which you have so kindly sent. The liberal gift is according to my Lord's usual dealings with His servant. I asked Him only for "The Treasury," but, as heretofore, He has given me "good measure, pressed down and running over." My heart is full of joy, but I cannot tell you about it, I can only pray, as I always have done since I knew Mr. Spurgeon's writings, that the Lord will bless and strengthen him more and more. I *do* envy those who have the privilege of hearing from his own lips the powerful words, which, when merely read, seem to send new life into my soul, and give quickening to all my spiritual forces.

I cannot say how very pleased I am with the volumes you have so kindly sent, nor how thankful I am for them. The sight of them has given me joy before I have read them, and I am expecting to spend many happy and profitable hours over them. That they will help me greatly in the study of God's word, and be a comfort and solace to my own soul, I have not the slightest doubt; and I thank you from my heart for your munificent gift.

Thank you very, very much, for the valuable parcel of books which I received yesterday. Oh, how the very sight of them rejoiced my heart, for I cannot tell you how long it is since I had a new book! A sort of inspiration seems to come with their very presence, and the load that often presses on my soul when seeking fresh material for future sermons is lifted off. I think my church ought to send you a unanimous vote of thanks, for they will reap largely of the benefit you have bestowed upon me. It is such a great pleasure to see one's sets of books nearing completion. You have made me feel quite a rich man, and perhaps the sweetest part of all is the knowledge that neither wife nor children have been robbed of necessaries to furnish me with these treasures.

I hasten to acknowledge the safe arrival of books. Good old "Matthew Henry" has been long reverenced, coveted, and sometimes consulted, but "Alas! master, for he was borrowed!" Now, here he is, all my own, clothed in leather like the old Puritans, and looking as solid and sober as becomes him. For volumes five and six of "The Treasury of David," thanks and thanks again. To-night I have a service, and I was trying, when your parcel came, to get at some of the "marrow and fatness" in Psalm cxix. 25, so the precious books were opened, and with a look into "The Treasury," and another look upward to the great Treasurer, I hope to be enriched and furnished beyond all expectation.

I can assure you, dear Mrs. Spurgeon, that it is a source of great comfort to those of us who are toiling in these dark and remote country districts to receive the assurance that we are not overlooked or forgotten by our friends. We are such creatures of circumstances, that a little human sympathy seems almost necessary to us, and gives a spur to our diligence even in the service of the Master. This expression of your kindness, in the form of a free gift of precious books, is most highly valued, my hitherto almost empty shelves welcome them warmly, and I know not how to tell you of all the gratitude that fills my heart.

You can hardly form an idea as to how these books will help me! Not directly *only*, by the intrinsic worth of their contents, but indirectly also. As I handle the volumes, they remind me that a loving heart has thought of me, labouring under heavy burdens. In seeking to serve Christ I have been called to relinquish home ties, and have cast myself entirely on His care. These books add to the many proofs I already possess that the Lord Jesus has not forgotten me, or the work which He has called me to do. I have been longing for "The Treasury" for more than three years, but it has been out of my reach. You will understand how highly I appreciate the gift when I tell you that I possess no helps on the Psalms whatever! Oh, how refreshed and comforted I shall be by these precious volumes!

Mr. Spurgeon's "Sermons" have often comforted my heart, strengthened my faith, enlightened my mind, stirred up my soul, and sent me on my way rejoicing. It is a most happy thought, this of your helping us to books, for we study them for others' benefit as well as our own; and in helping those who are seeking to help others the blessing so increasingly radiates, that who can tell where the good influence of your Book Fund will stop?

The books you have so kindly sent me have just come to hand, and I don't know what words to use by which I can best express my thanks. I do most heartily thank you for all your kindness; you have no idea how much you cheer the hearts of the Pastors of the churches. Yesterday afternoon I met Mr. ———, the Primitive Methodist minister here; his work is very heavy, and he looked tired and jaded, but he seemed to renew his strength and to look young again, as he told me with sparkling eye and beaming face, how good you had been to him; I can assure you that I shall preach with more joy and vigour on the morrow because of your kind present. It was good, indeed, to send the books at all; it was even better to send them on a Saturday.

I feel charmed with the Lord's love and kindness through you. My heart is full, and cannot express its delight and thankfulness. I was as impatient as any schoolboy for the arrival of the books; my hopes and expectations were very great, but when the volumes were unpacked and spread out before me, I found the reality surpassed my most sanguine dreams. On my knees I have blessed the Lord again and again, and now I ask Him to deal very lovingly with you, who have so greatly refreshed and cheered my heart.

Your valuable parcel of books is safely to hand, and here I am, up in my little sanctum, surrounded by the wealth thus kindly bestowed. I feel thankful that the mornings are light now, and not too cold, for I must be up an hour earlier every day to feast upon these choice dainties. Your kindness is very great, and your little note of tender sympathy cheered our hearts. My dear wife most sincerely joins me in loving, grateful thanks. Suffer me also to express the hope that God may reward you abundantly for this great service you render to so many of His poor servants in supplying them with helpful books. If our churches knew the value of such literature to their Pastors, I am sure they would not allow them to be so destitute as many of them are.

* * * *

Have my dear friends had enough for the present of these down-pouring blessings? I could keep them out in such pleasant showers while turning over many more pages of the "Diary;" but lest they be weary of the "rain which raineth every day," we will take shelter now, and turn our attention to other matters of interest connected with the work.

* * * *

The nineteenth annual Conference of the Pastors' College was this year looked forward to by us with much pleasurable anticipation. There had been no foreboding of the disappointment awaiting us, as the dear President had been enjoying fairly good health; but when all the preparations were complete, and hundreds of eager, joyful brethren were in attendance, then,—on the very first day of the gathering, the leader was laid low, and beyond conducting the preliminary meeting, took no part in the week's celebrations. Strange mystery of Providence—thus to fetter the hands which would have ministered to so many; thus to hinder the outpourings of the heart which yearned so tenderly over his "own sons in the faith"; thus to seal the lips which could speak so wisely and winningly of "the things which accompany salvation"! He was laid aside to suffer, instead of holding high the banner of the cross amidst a crowd of loyal soldiers; he was made a "prisoner of the Lord," instead of going up to the feast; and though his soul was full of zeal for the house of the Lord, and the "holy convocation" therein held, he had no choice but to humbly obey the mandate, "Be still, and know that I am God." And "patience had her perfect work," and God graciously gave His poor servant a calm and quiet mind, and carried the heaviest end of the cross for him; and day by day such cheering news was brought of blessing vouchsafed and sweet fellowship enjoyed, that we learned to thank the Lord as much for what he denies as for what he gives, and to know of a surety that "He doeth all things well."

Hitherto the Book Fund present on these auspicious occasions has been selected from the works of strangers; this time I decided to give the President's latest book, "Illustrations and Meditations: or, Flowers from a Puritan's Garden." I am now exceedingly glad that I was led to do this, for the gift will be invested with a special interest, and will prove a fitting memorial of the joys and sorrows of the Conference of 1883.

* * * *

Here is a little pen-and-ink sketch of a poor country pastor's position and prospects. I can vouch for the genuineness of all the details given; but the shadows around the home are even darker than I have drawn them, and there are accessories of privation and suffering which I have forborne to introduce. As it is, the outlines are sad and suggestive enough to excite sincerest pity, and as we gaze on them we wonder that such a state of things can be permitted in the Christian Church, and tremble at the verdict which the "Lord of the vineyard" will pronounce against those who have treated His messengers so roughly.

Behold, then, a minister of the gospel, a useful, earnest man, who has won the respect and confidence, not only of his colleagues, but of sundry High-church clergymen who are his near neighbours. He holds various positions of public usefulness in the place where he dwells, has the reputation of being a "clever" man, and is looked up to with esteem and affection by all classes; yet the salary given to him by the church over which he presides is so pitiably meagre, that poverty is a constant inmate of his house, and actual want, both of food and clothing, is no unusual experience in the household. He is pale and weak from recent illness, bowed down by anxious care, yet much domestic drudgery necessarily falls upon him, for he cannot afford to keep a servant, and his poor delicate wife is incapable of hard work, being subject to severe fits, brought about by a shock to the system through a fire. She sits and sews to the utmost of her strength, and when I first heard of her, she had just cut up all her own available clothing for the children. There are four little ones needing care and attention, the eldest aged seven (one child has fits), the baby nine weeks old; and for the wants of all these persons, and the solace of all this suffering, there is the fat portion of £61 per annum, and a free house! Well might an old writer on this subject exclaim, "God forbid that men should profit so little by their minister as their minister profits by them!" The painful facts of this case are communicated to me by a member of the Church of England, whose heart is stirred with pity for this much-tried man of God. "I feel deeply for him in the trials he has to bear," writes my correspondent, "but he has such a happy, trustful, thankful spirit, that he never complains, and he is so sweetly reliant on God, that when help comes, and prayer is answered, he seems lost in praise and thanksgiving."

Blessed be the Lord who strengthens and succours His faithful servant by secret supplies of both spiritual and temporal comforts; feeding him from afar by strange birds who fly on swift and joyful wing to do His bidding; and fulfilling the ancient promise, "Bread shall be given him, his waters shall be sure;"—but does this lessen the grave responsibility of those whose business it is to "provide meat for the King's household"?—I trow not. "It is most unjust and unreasonable," says the old author above quoted, "to keep ministers of the gospel poor. Men would have fire kept in the sanctuary, but allow no fuel; they would have the lamp burn, but provide no oil! How badly do they serve Christ and themselves in so serving their ministers! God will remove the candlestick if we love darkness rather than light; and take our faithful ministers away from us if we so ill-treat them, and unworthily reward them."

* * * *

In startling contrast to the sad picture just presented, I take from an American paper a glowing little sketch of a young pastor's experience, wishing, oh, how earnestly! that such tenderness and thoughtful care for God's servants as are here recorded could be manifested to the poor, struggling, poverty-stricken preachers of our own dear land. Dr. Talmage is said to tell his own story in the following words:—

A young man, a graduate of New Brunswick theological seminary, was called to a village church. He had not the means to furnish the parsonage. After three or four weeks of preaching, a committee of the officers of the church waited on him, and told him he looked tired, and thought he had better take a vacation of a few days. The young pastor took it as an intimation that his work was done, or was not acceptable. He took the vacation, and at the end of a few days came back, when an old elder said: "Here is the key of the parsonage. We have been cleaning it up. You had better go up and look at it." So the young pastor took the key, went to the parsonage, opened the door, and lo! the hall was carpeted, and there was the hat-rack all ready for the canes and the umbrellas and the overcoats; and on the left hand of the hall was the parlour, sofaed, chaired, pictured. He passed on to the other side of the hall, and there was the study-table in the centre of the floor, with stationery upon it, book-shelves built, long ranges of new volumes, far beyond the reach of the means of the young pastor, many of these volumes. The young pastor went upstairs, and found all the sleeping apartments furnished; came downstairs and entered the pantry, and there were the spices, and the coffees, and the sugars, and the groceries, for six months. He went down into the cellar, and there was the coal for the coming winter. He went into the dining-hall, and there was the table already set—the glass and the silverware. He went into the kitchen, and there were all the culinary implements and a great stove. The young pastor lifted one lid of the stove, and found the fuel all ready for ignition. Putting back the cover of the stove, he saw in another part of it a lucifer match, and all that young man had to do in starting to keep house was to strike that match. You tell me that is apocryphal. Oh, no! that was I. Oh, the kindness! Oh, the enlarged sympathies sometimes clustering around those who enter the gospel ministry!

* * * *

May.—" Is the day going to be fine?" said I, on awaking early one morning in the sweet month of May. "Well, I believe so," replied my companion, who was already stirring, "there are plenty of shadows about, and that is a good sign." *Plenty of shadows! How can shadows give the promise of ultimate brightness?* I mused a while, wondering at the apparently doubtful inference: then going to the window, I sought to solve the problem for myself, and stood gazing at the fair landscape which lay sparkling in the early freshness of sunlight and dew.

There I saw manifest prospect and presage of a glorious day, and sure enough the "shadows" foretold it; for "Westwood," as its name betokens, looks towards the west, and the sun, rising behind the house, throws the shadow of the structure across the lawn, like the gnomon of a huge sun-dial; while to every tree and bush and outbuilding it gives a "shady side" of very distinct proportions. Yes, there were "plenty of shadows" truly!—they abounded everywhere,—hiding in the deep recesses of the shrubberies, dancing on the surface of the water, creeping stealthily round every corner!

I watched them for some time, enjoying the delightful purity and peacefulness of the scene, reflecting happily on the many analogies between nature and grace, and trying to draw sweet spiritual parallels between the natural shadows and those dark dispensations which seem sometimes to eclipse the sunshine of our lives.

Some of the comfortable thoughts which since then have refreshed my heart in meditation, I would fain set down in these pages, hoping that they may comfort others; for though my words be weak and feeble, they will need but a mandate from the Lord to make them as an angel's breath, to blow away despair from some troubled spirit, even as the gentlest of summer breezes can lift and disperse the dense veil of mist that hangs lowering upon the mountain side.

Clearly then, I think, stands out the consoling fact that *there could be no shadows if the sun were not shining.* The obscurity is but the effect of the light beyond, the shadows are the promise of the substance which presently shall bring us blessing and brightness. A dark leaden sky—a heavy currentless atmosphere, can never develop these dusky forms:—when the cloud gathers thick in the heavens, and the showers water the earth, the shadows have all betaken themselves to a more congenial sphere, or have folded their dark wings in secret places to await the re-appearance of the glorious king whose faithful servitors they are.

Rutherford says, "Wants are my best riches, because I have them supplied by Christ." May we not borrow like heavenly rhetoric, and confess that shadows are our brightest blessings, since they are thrown across our path by the rising beams of the "Father of lights, with whom is no variableness, neither shadow of turning"?

So then, dear child of God, if thou seest shadows lying in the road which thou must take, conclude straightway that the sun of God's love is shining behind thee, fear not to "enter into the cloud," for by-and-by thou shalt lift up thine eyes and see "Jesus only," and shalt bless the grace which guided thee through the gloom to behold His glory. Hast thou not often prayed, with David, "Hide me under the shadow of Thy wings"? And how knowest thou but that thy loving Father is even now interposing His hand to shield thee from impending danger, or covering thee with His wing to soothe and comfort thee! It may be very dark beneath the feathers of the mother bird, but oh, how safe and warm are the nestling chickens! One of the grandest promise verses in the Bible has for its very centre of blessedness this assurance of safety and rest: "I have covered thee in the shadow of mine hand." Take heart, tried soul! If thou be one of Christ's purchased ones, thou canst trace all thy shadows to the shining of thy blessed Sun, and even while the darkness of some heavy sorrow rests upon thee, thou mayest sing low, trustful notes of praise to Him who

"Behind a frowning providence, still hides a smiling face."

But for a moment let us look beyond the darkness and

gather some comfort from the fact that *the shadows will vanish if we wait and watch patiently.*

The pretty sight I have spoken of is only visible from our windows before the sun gains his meridian ;—in a few hours the noontide splendour has transformed the dusky throngs of shadows which lay in ambush everywhere, and changed them into golden glories ;—they are transfigured,—they are "shadows" no longer; they are angels, white and glistering, rejoicing in the effulgence which first created and then glorified them.

Even thus, when our "Sun of righteousness shall arise with healing in His wings"—when, in the blessed noonday of our immortal life we dwell in the "city which hath no need of the sun, for the glory of God doth lighten it"—we shall look again on the dark providences, which in our pilgrimage we thought so mysterious and doleful, and find them, when illuminated by celestial radiance, to have been but Heaven's choicest blessings in disguise.

Yet another "comfortable thought" is, that *the shadows cannot really harm us.* How unreasonable are the fears which too often assail us when we are called to pass from the bright sunshine into one of the shady places! Are you afraid of that which has no power to hurt you? Do you tremble because the "great rock in a weary land" casts a shadow dark and deep? Or do you shrink from the cool shade of the thick cloud which comes between you and the sun? Nay, verily: then fear not these misty shapes; for though they may oftentimes look terrible, they are as evanescent and powerless as a vapour "that appeareth for a little time, and then vanisheth away." The "shadow" of a dog cannot bite; the "shadow" of a sword cannot kill; and even when we come to that sorrowful valley which is lying "darkly between, winding down into the night," it is but the "shadow" of death which we shall have to pass through; the king of terrors himself is conquered, chained, and unable to touch us.

In a recent edition of Bunyan's "Pilgrim's Progress," there is a very striking and suggestive picture which will illustrate my meaning. Christian is represented as having just reached the entrance of a deep ravine or valley through which lies the pathway to the Celestial City. High in the heavens the sun is shining gloriously, but none of his sweet beams fall on the pilgrim's road; for, hovering in mid-air, crowned and cruel, but restrained by Almighty power, is the dark form of the "Last Enemy," eclipsing all the light and brightness which would otherwise comfort and console the lonely traveller. Look closely and you will see that the "shadow" of this grim presence extends the whole length of the valley, and that Christian must walk on in the darkness, till the "shadow" is "passed through," and then, at the end of the way he will emerge from the gloom, and the welcome rays of the sun will once again surround him with their unobscured splendour.

In this picture we see the end from the beginning, and realize most vividly the pilgrim's present discouragement and approaching deliverance. We sympathize with him while he "walks in darkness, and sees no light"; but we know that the sun is still shining, and that soon he will again rejoice in its blessed beams. We may shrink for a moment from the awful form with outstretched wings and threatening gesture; but we are persuaded it has no power to approach the traveller, and we can almost hear him singing in the words of one of old: "Yea, though I walk through the valley of the shadow of death, I will fear no evil: for Thou art with me; Thy rod and Thy staff they comfort me."

So, again I say, "Courage, faint heart!" the "shadows" cannot hurt thee; nay more, they will turn into blessings while you watch them; nay, more still, they prove the existence of the fount of blessing itself, and, depend upon it, you will find very often, as I did, that "PLENTY OF SHADOWS" betoken the on-coming of a grand and glorious day! Lord, in shadow or in sunshine, grant to us, Thy children, the faith "which endures as seeing Him who is invisible."

* * * *

June.—It is a rare thing for me to discover any matter for merriment in an application to the Book Fund, or to find unintentional pleasantries wrapped up in an earnest petition for mental supplies; but a recent morning's post brought two letters, the contents of which at once provoked a hearty laugh, and have ever since served to excite a great deal of loving banter.

Since there is not the slightest chance of my correspondents being recognized, I will tell the little story, and let my readers enjoy the joke, which, all unwittingly, these writers have perpetrated. The first epistle was from a young man who evidently desired to possess Mr. Spurgeon's "Lectures to my Students;" but being either misinformed on the subject, or having evolved a whimsical conjecture out of his own brain, he asked me, deliberately and emphatically, to give him MY LECTURES! "*The lectures written by you,*" explained he, underlining the words lest there should be any mistake about such precious productions!

My husband made the richest fun of this blundering request. "Oh," he said, "*they're not published yet! That is a pity! They are first-rate, but they are only orally delivered.*" I let him go on in this style for ever so long, enjoying it to his heart's content, and then I triumphantly produced the second letter, saying, "Well, now we will hear the other side of the question, for the writer of *this* note asks me the price of "MY MASTER'S 'Treasury of David!'" Here was sweet revenge for me, and I duly exulted in it, "turning the tables" gleefully upon dear "John," who is very fond of calling me "the Missis"; and having a real merry time over the innocent insinuations, which, by a most curious coincidence, met in the same post. We laughed till we almost cried, and since then have made our friends laugh too; and now I seek to provoke a quiet smile on my reader's face by the repetition of the droll little story; but it strikes me very forcibly that if there had been any bitter truth in either of the two suggestions, no one would have had the chance of laughing at its disclosure. Ah! but there is, thank God, only love and peace in "Home, sweet home!" Of course "John Ploughman" is the master, as he ought to be, and *my master* too;—I am proud to confess his dominion and my sweet thraldom; but equally, of course, I am "the Missis," and if I do sometimes yearn to give a "lecture," I try so to fashion it that dear "John" shall think he is listening to a "lyric," and like it immensely.

And he does. But it couldn't be printed.

When you walk through a gallery of paintings, or, in your own cosy room, take up a charming book of travels, or a volume of "Picturesque Europe,"—or if you should be a delighted listener to the tales of a recent traveller,—do you not find yourselves drawn with special interest to those views or descriptions which recall personal memories, and of which you can say, "Ah, I, too, have been there! I remember that wonderful landscape, or that grand mountain, or that fine city; tell me more about *that*, let me gaze longer on the scene which carries my thoughts back to other times, and awakens a host of slumbering recollections!"

Even thus, a letter received to-day from an invalid friend evokes my tenderest sympathy, and claims my earnest attention, because, in some respects, the writer's experience recalls my own in days gone by, and his touching words are eloquent to my heart of those happy yet painful years when the dear work of the Book Fund was accomplished in a sick chamber, and all the necessary strength came as directly and daily from heaven as did the manna of old in the wilderness.

You shall hear what my friend says about himself and his service for the lighthouse-keepers; but I must first tell you that he has long been laid aside from active work for the Master, and that he suffers much both in "body and estate"; it may have been that in his own tossings to and fro at night the Lord first whispered in his heart the desire to help the lonely night-watchers on the sea-coasts,—this I do not know; but for a long time past he has found congenial and manageable work in sending forth pure literature to the dwellers in "solitary places." He is asking now for a repetition of a former grant of Mr. Spurgeon's "Sermons"; and, in his own words, you shall hear the details of his labour of love:—

Dear Mrs. Spurgeon,—You will be interested in knowing where your gift has been bestowed. Believing that the reading would be most appreciated by persons in isolated situations, out of reach of the ordinary means of grace, I have tried to avoid other men's line of things, and have sought those in the regions beyond. Lighthouses seemed to offer such a field. Those of the United Kingdom give me 600 addresses, ranging from the Shetlands to the Scillys; and from the lightships on the east coast to the coast-lights round Ireland. The dominion of Canada and the United States give 800 more, extending from Lake Superior to the Gulf of St. Lawrence; from Newfoundland to the borders of Mexico; and from California to British Columbia. To the keepers of most of these I have posted a small book-packet, containing, with other papers, one of the "Sermons." In that way Mr. Spurgeon's discourses have been placed within reach of 1,400 English-speaking families in both hemispheres, whose temporary abodes,—the storm-beaten tower, or the tossing lightship—quite isolate the occupants from the privileges of the sanctuary. In some fewer cases the "Sermons" have also been sent to station employés on the Canadian Pacific Railway; some of the Hudson's Bay Company's ports; Canadian Frontier Police, and new settlers in Manitoba.

Results are with God, I am content to leave them with Him who said, "My word shall not return unto Me void;" but I feel greatly privileged in being thus permitted to dispense somewhat and further the rich, gospel-laden discourses of dear Mr. Spurgeon. The work is just enough for my slender strength, and brings sunshine into this sick room all the year round. Through it, continuous blessings come to my own soul, while, best of all, it will be the means of bringing eternal salvation to the souls of others.

I have had the great pleasure of again sending a parcel of "Sermons" and suitable tracts for distribution by this dear afflicted servant of the Lord; and if any friend, on reading this paragraph, should feel his or her heart drawn to aid a work so unique and special, I will gladly take charge of, and forward, their contributions for this purpose. "The wilderness and the solitary place shall be glad for them;" they shall cause "The inhabitants of the rock to sing," while many at "the ends of the earth" shall thereby be led to look to Jesus and be saved.

*   *   *   *

"T. H. C." will, I know, be glad to hear that his beautiful spade-guinea brought me £1 6s., and that a very poor pastor was thereby speedily made richer by twenty-six shillings. The money came carrying the following encouraging message: "The enclosed coin is a memorial of a kind friend who died some years since. It has lain uselessly by until the owner read the very interesting Report of the Book Fund for 1882, when he resolved to give it to the Lord, and now sends it to Mrs. Spurgeon as a little help for her Pastors' Aid Fund, with earnest prayer for the continued and enlarged success of her loving work."

Many thanks to "T. H. C." I wish all friends who

possess such relics would "go and do likewise," consecrating them thus *wholly* to the Lord.

* * * *

July.—The kind friend who wrote the Report of my work for 1878, when I was too ill to compile it myself, had in it a paragraph to the following effect :—

> "The large proportion of Mr. Spurgeon's works shown in the list on a subsequent page is not to be attributed to the partiality of the almoner, but to the choice of the applicants, who express their desire to possess them. When we state that neither author nor publishers profit by the transactions, this fact should disarm the suspicion that the Book Fund, while benevolent in its intention, is commercial in its operation."

Five years ago this was written, but it still remains true ; and though the Fund's business has largely developed since those early days, the desire for my dear husband's writings keeps pace with the increased number and value of the grants. It is but seldom that I am asked for the works of other authors, and though I distribute a great many of them, they are unsolicited additions to my parcels, and rarely seem to give as much joy and satisfaction as the volumes which bear the name of "C. H. Spurgeon."

With regard to the last sentence in the passage above quoted, I am glad to be able to bear witness that the honourable fact therein stated is a fact still ; and, although I know of no "suspicion to disarm," I feel delighted to repeat that both author and publishers join so heartily with me in looking upon the Book Fund as a "work of faith and labour of love," that they joyfully relinquish the profits which are justly their due, thus enabling me to respond the more generously to the appeals of poor bookless ministers. All honour to them, and heartfelt thanks! May the Lord remember them for good!

* * * *

Looking through some of my letters to-day to see what I could glean of summer fruits for my dear reader's enjoyment, I thought it might be pleasant to make a "confection" of a few of the innumerable "good things" which are constantly dropping from amongst the leaves of my very large correspondence. There will be no novelty in this digest—can any new thing come out of a Report?—but it will at least convince any one who will take the trouble to read it, that, "partial" as I may be to my dear "Master's" books, I am by no means alone in my avowed enthusiasm.

Taking first "The Treasury of David" (it being seemly to give the place of honour to the *magnum opus*), I note the experience of a Congregational minister, who says concerning it:—"It has been most helpful to me in quickening and strengthening my spiritual life; it has enlarged my understanding, and added immeasurably to my store of knowledge. It has provided me with such savoury meat, and I have relished it so much, that now I seek diligently to obtain more. You could not have conceived of a truer or better way of helping a poor minister than by adding to the little stock of books which he fondly calls his library."

A pastor in the Midland Counties writes:—The cxixth Psalm has been a favourite portion with me for years, but I have found it difficult to commit to memory. Was this because 'its expanse was unbroken by a bluff or headland ... a great sea of holy teaching . . . . without an island of special and remarkable statement to break it up'? Be this as it may, henceforth I launch upon it with such a copious and accurate chart to guide me, that I long once more to explore the whole; and already it seems to lie before me like a vast lake, whose every creek, and bay, and island, promises some new scene of delight. It has been my custom for years to keep some work in reading as a sort of companion to the Bible; and when, on Saturday night, I saw the pains Mr. Spurgeon had taken to unfold the riches in this wonderful Psalm, I resolved at once to put it side by side with my Bible, and to study the whole comment which forms the bulk of the goodly volume. Thank you so much for sending me this Royal Banquet, and please thank Mr. Spurgeon for letting so many of us share in what he tells us has been a means of grace to his own heart.

"The Treasury of David" is so serviceable a work to men with small libraries that it is no wonder its appearance is hailed with joy and gladness when sent as a gift by the

Fund. "Many a hearty 'God bless him!'" says a country pastor, "escapes from our lips when the goodly volumes are unwrapped, and a glance into the pages reveals the treasures awaiting appropriation." "The Treasury" is a continuous stream of blessing, an unfailing storehouse of provision, a rich mine of sacred wealth; and, therefore, the poor Pastors, hungry and thirsty and needy, covet it earnestly as one of the "best gifts." A clergyman of the Church of England, in acknowledging the volumes which I had sent, writes :—" There is no work the possession of which could have given me greater pleasure than 'The Treasury of David.' A brother-clergyman of extensive reading said to me a short time ago, 'Whatever you do, get Mr. Spurgeon's 'Treasury of David'; it is by far the most valuable contribution to the literature of the Psalms.' Indeed, a glance at the volumes has convinced me that my friend was right, and that Mr. Spurgeon is a Christian philosopher of the Eclectic School. I only wish it were possible that he could do for the whole Bible what he is doing for this special portion."

As for the "Sermons," no words of mine can tell the blessing the Lord vouchsafes to *them*, not only in the conversion of sinners, but in quickening, arousing, and refreshing the preachers of the Word; they are prized and used largely as patterns and helps to pulpit preparation, and as constantly serve as aids to private devotion. A pastor in the far West of America says :—" I read a 'Sermon' for my own spiritual advancement every morning after the Bible, and this keeps me so full of good things that I am always fresh for my work. I use them as I use the water from my well—to refresh myself and regale my friends, serving them up in my own measure and manner." Again, a minister in England writes :—" Last week I was making a sermon on Col. iii. 2, 3; and, turning to Mr. Spurgeon's 'Sermons' for 1880, I found, on page 193, some thoughts which put my mind just into the right course; and, aided by the Holy Spirit, a difficult subject was made clear, and I was enabled to present it to my people; and this morning I was meditating on the Beauty of Christ as set forth in the words, 'Thou art fairer than the children of men,' and again I received much help from the same source. I just refer to these recent instances to show how great a boon you have conferred on me in putting these volumes on my shelves."

"I never allow my sitting-room to be without a few of Mr. Spurgeon's 'Sermons,'" says another friend, "so that those who come in may read, or take away a copy with them, and some very dear to me have thereby been greatly blessed."

May not this suggestion of quiet service for the Lord find a quick response in some timid heart? Those who cannot "speak a word for Jesus" might surely be able to place a few "Sermons" in the way of careless or seeking souls, and let Mr. Spurgeon speak to them, while they pray for the Word to be made fruitful.

"The amount of good I get from reading the 'Sermons' no tongue can tell," writes a grateful recipient; "they are full of savour and blessing! It is a marvel how Mr. Spurgeon can continue to pour forth such utterances as these sermons contain, and even to excel all previous efforts, as the last volumes abundantly testify. Of course, I say this looking at the human side of the matter; it is no marvel that the Lord, whom he serves, should thus show His divine power and sustaining grace in His servant."

* * * *

The first series of "Lectures to my Students" was the "first-born" of the Book Fund—the "beginning of its strength"—and it must not be passed over without loving notice, coupling with it now the two later volumes, of which some one has truly observed, "The very best of Mr. Spurgeon's work, and the very best things he says, are to be found in these Lectures." The joy with which I send out these volumes knows no qualification; I am as sure of my harvest with such precious seed as if the golden grain were already gathered within the garner. To young and old alike they bring wholesome instruction and weighty counsel—offered, too, with such genial grace that none can turn away offended. "I am delighted," "writes a minister of high standing, "with the sanctified common-sense which characterizes the two volumes of 'Lectures to my Students'; and though I have been some years in the ministry, I find valuable hints in them, and many echoes in my own answering experience of the need of friendly advice such as they offer."

"Thank you very much for the 'Lectures,'" says a young beginner; "from them I have gleaned many a wise suggestion, and in them I have met with many a hard, but not unprofitable blow. God bless Mr. Spurgeon for the loving, earnest, faithful words found in these volumes." In one case a very practical improvement in demeanour is induced by the perusal of these fervent addresses, and amusingly confessed thus:—"I have carefully read the 'Lectures,' and I believe they have done me good. *My wife says I have not so many silly ways as I used to have: I don't look at my watch so much when speaking, or use my handkerchief so vigorously!*" Then, again, comes testimony to higher influence:—"Mr. Spurgeon's lecture on 'Attention' benefited my delivery; but when I read the address on 'Earnestness,' my soul was led into the very presence of God; and, after a day spent in holy joy, I preached at night as I had never preached before, and two souls were brought to Jesus!" A learned doctor, who presides over a missionary college in Egypt, shall be the last witness on behalf of these precious books. He says, in a letter to me:—"I used the first volume of 'Lectures' last year with my students, reading it off in Arabic while they took notes. Mr. Spurgeon is easily translated even into Arabic—clear, logical, simple, solid. May his shadow never grow shorter!"

Surely all this is blessed encouragement to continue the distribution of books which are so powerful for good!

> "For every printed word becomes a seed
> That, planted, *must* spring up—
> A flower or weed;
> And he who writes—may write
> What millions read."

* * * *

I think, dear friends, you will know that my desire in transcribing these few testimonies out of the thousands at my command, is not unduly to boast of or triumph in my dear husband's works—to God be all the glory for all that has been done through them! But I want you to catch the tone of the bell which is always ringing at my door, and to see the quality of the provision which is being constantly handed out to eager applicants. These letters exhibit my work and its consequences far better than any amount of dry statistical information could do; and therefore I give them to you with a happy and grateful heart, and

"To the Praise of the Glory of His Grace."

* * * *

August.—There is a poor minister in one of our Midland counties to whom I have at divers times sent help in books, clothes, and money, and whose need of such assistance will not be questioned when I say that he has a wife and five children to keep on £60 per annum. Just lately one of his congregation has written to me concerning him, and her letter gives touching details of his joy in the welcome gifts. "I called to see him," she says, "the day after your last parcel arrived, and I had not been long in the house before all the books were brought for my inspection. *I wish you could have been there!* Both husband and wife were overjoyed, and shed tears of gratitude while telling me of all the kindness you have shown to them. The £5 note came at a time of great need, when they were passing through bitter trials, and you may imagine how thankfully they received it, as from the hand of the Lord, and what a comfort it was to them." This good man works hard for the scanty pittance above-mentioned; he has some meeting or service every night during the week, preaches three times on the Sunday, and visits much among the sick and the poor, to whom he can at least minister abundantly of the sympathy born of analogous experience, though of "silver and gold he has none" to bestow. "He has to go very, very short sometimes," writes his friend, "but I am quite sure no one has ever heard him complain, indeed he appears satisfied and grateful for the little his people can do for him. We often wish he had three times as much, for he is worthy of it; but the distress has been so great in the neighbourhood that we can raise no more, and he faithfully shares in the trials of his flock." I think this is one of the rare cases in which no blame is to be attached to the people for their minister's poverty. They are not living in comfort while he struggles with adversity, nor are they carelessly indifferent to his sorrows; but being all alike plunged in a sea of trouble, they gallantly breast the waves together, and he, like a heroic captain, leads them on, and cheers them with the hope of soon gaining calmer water. It has been a great pleasure to help such a man, and to receive the hearty thanks of his tried followers. "I am to express the gratitude of the whole church at ――― to you, dear Madam," observes my correspondent, "for all your kindness to our pastor; he has been wonderfully cheered and encouraged by it, and since receiving the last parcel of books, has preached some noble sermons, which have blessed and benefited us all; he had a miserably small stock of books before you began to contribute so handsomely to it, but now he is quite proud to show his library to his friends. All this we owe to our gracious God *through you*."

What a sacred joy to be allowed thus to strengthen the heart and the hands of a faithful toiler for Christ! It does me good to transcribe such a testimony as this, for it stirs up and reawakens my interest in my work, and incites me to further and fuller effort. Thanks be to God that the Book Fund has done *something* for scores of His poor servants; but oh for help to do more, and to do it better!

* * * *

Many and sorrowful have been the glimpses given to my readers in previous Reports of the pinching poverty borne by our dissenting Pastors, and I regret to say that I can chronicle no improvement in their circumstances or condition. Most of those to whom I have already given help, still need further aid, and scores of cases are constantly appearing where assistance of the tenderest and promptest kind is urgently needed. Our Lord's declaration, "The poor ye have always with you," is in no danger of being disputed while His own servants are kept at starvation point, and, like the Israelites of old, "made to serve with rigour."

I hear in roundabout ways of some poor ministers who would never tell of their own needs, but whose homes are miserably bare; they are lacking, not in comforts merely, but in the very necessaries of life, because the pastor's most earnest devotion to his Master's work and the church's welfare fails to secure more than the scantiest imaginable salary. In such homes, consequently, the anxious wife can know no rest from care; she is ceaselessly struggling to make one shilling do the work of ten or twenty; while the poor children have no chance of growing up strong, healthy, and happy, daily breathing, as they do, the depressing and stupefying atmosphere of this crushing and undeserved poverty!

We have all heard of a book which professes to tell us, "How to live on sixpence a day, and earn it," and very likely we have only smiled at the droll title, not desiring closer acquaintance with its contents; but I have to-day corresponded with a good brother who can bear witness that the task is not an impossible one, and that, undertaken *"for Christ's sake,"* it may even prove pleasant and satisfactory. He writes to say that his heart would be full of gratitude if I would send him a parcel of books, for he *depends wholly on the ministry, and that brings him in 3s. 6d. per week!!* He adds very naïvely, but pathetically, "So I am very destitute in every respect." I must confess that at first this tale seemed too terrible to be true, so I wrote to a gentleman of high standing in the locality where the young minister resides, and received from him an assurance that I had not been misinformed—"Truly sad is it," says this friend, "and yet most sadly true"; and then he proceeds to explain the circumstances under which such a pitiful state of things can be possible:—"The history of many a mining village is just this: when once coal is struck, the miners crowd to the place, and rows of cottages are built, and a humble chapel; a minister is invited to take charge of the little flock, and much good is done. But in ten or twelve years the mine is exhausted, the colliers are paid off, the people are scattered, and in most cases the pastor seeks another field of labour. Not so this good, faithful brother of whom I write! He might have 'left his few sheep in the wilderness,' and bettered himself in all respects full many a time; but so beloved is he by the 'little one' at —— and so dearly does he love her, that he will not leave her as long as it is possible for him to exist on the slender allowance which is all they have to offer."

Is not this devotion as beautiful as it is rare? The poverty, and self-denial, and suffering, are made sublime by the love to God and man which prompts and permits them. There is no grimness in this young man's penury, it is full of the glory of the grace of God; his scanty meals are daily sacraments, and his lowly lodging must be hard by the very gate of heaven. As he goes in and out amongst his poor flock, sharing their earthly troubles, and ministering to them of heavenly comforts, I can hear him whispering softly the words of the apostle Paul, with all humility making them his own: " But none of these things move me, neither count I my life dear unto myself, so that I might finish my course with joy, *and the ministry*, which I have received of the Lord Jesus, to testify the gospel of the grace of God!"

* * * *

But to what purpose do I tell these sad stories again and again, and every year find a fresh Miserere which must be played in a minor key? Will my readers be tired of these mournful cadences, and deem me unkindly importunate in bringing constantly to their ears such sorrowful songs? For eight years now I have sought to call attention to the wants and woes of poorly-paid servants of Christ, whose vocation entitles them to expect better treatment at the hands of Christian people; but how can I expect my faint protest to be heard amidst the din and turmoil of a thousand conflicting interests? Yet these poor Pastors so seldom obtrude their wrongs upon public notice, that though my voice can reach but a very little way, I am constrained to take up a lamentation for them; always hoping that, one of these times, it may penetrate to the ears and heart of some one who can speak loudly and forcibly on their behalf, and whose championship shall release them from the grievous bondage of unnecessary privation and suffering.

I fear me, however, that this is one of the wrongs which will need righting till the end of all things; for since the days of the apostle, who could touchingly complain of " lack of service" towards himself, this sin has lain at the church's door.

September.—A TALK IN THE TWILIGHT. My pleasant rambles in the Westwood gardens with my dear husband, about which I wrote last year, have this season come to an untimely end, by a severe fall and a fractured rib. The accident, which was very sudden and unexpected, might have had more serious consequences, so I bless the Lord that no worse thing befell me, and bear as patiently as may be the deprivation for a time of one of the chief pleasures of my life. In consequence of this mishap, dear reader, you must come and sit by my sofa, and we will talk in whispered words of the work which is so dear to both of us—dear to me as its founder and servitor, and to you as its benefactor and supporter for the Master's sake, whose servants are blessed by it. The first question you are sure to ask is, "*Does the Book Fund really get on as well as ever?*" How happy am I to be able to reply, "Yes, by the sweet grace and goodness of God, its prosperity and success are undiminished"! It has quietly developed into a great power for good, I trust; for the blessing of the Lord makes it rich, and thousands can now testify that its treasures have been poured into their hearts and minds, to their exceeding gain and benefit. There have been no startling episodes, no extraordinary events; all has gone on smoothly and gently, with almost the regularity and precision of clockwork. "*Does the money still come in plentifully?*" Yes: and it goes out with equal liberality. The business is brisk, the stock inviting, the customers are eager and numerous, and the credit at the Bank of Faith is unlimited. Is not this a state of things to be thankful for? The monetary affairs of the Fund seem to be always under the generous consideration of some dear friends; and the needs of the work are constantly met by a corresponding, or even exceeding, amount in hand. No anxiety on this score has befallen me for a long while; and most devoutly do I thank my great "Director" for so special a mercy as freedom from care in money matters. "*But there is always a large balance at the end of the year, and that leads some to withhold their contributions, under the impression that they are not needed.*" If that be so, I am sorry, but I cannot alter the fact: it recurs every year, and can be easily explained. When the balance-sheet is made up it is the Book

Fund's harvest-time and vintage, therefore the granaries are full, and the presses burst with new wine. Gifts come pouring in so fast about Christmas, that the exchequer rapidly overflows; and the joy is great, because such precious stores are laid up for the relief of famishing minds in months to come. Don't let a big balance frighten you, dear friend. It does not show negligence or idleness on my part, but points triumphantly to the exceeding riches and loving bounty of my Heavenly Banker and Provider. "*There is doubtless a large correspondence needful to keep up this work.*" Indeed, you are right; for the business of the Fund is conducted chiefly by the pen; and a vast amount of letter-writing is entailed in its management. Many hours each day are devoted to this duty; and, as I have about ten thousand names on the books, and these are constantly increasing, much time is taken up by the entries in ledgers, &c., some of which are so voluminous that they have to be entrusted to the patient care of a dear and faithful friend. Then all applications have to be much thought over, and suitable volumes mentally selected. Sometimes the cases need investigation, as to their genuineness; references must be made to former grants; questions have to be put concerning matters unexplained; and often a single application will necessitate two or three letters of enquiry before final acceptation. All this is the daily task and labour; but the daily delight, the daily wages, are found in the receipt of loving, grateful acknowledgments—letters so full of thankful joy and satisfaction, and of enthusiastic testimony to the value and usefulness of my work, that my reward is ever before me, and my cup is filled to the brim with the sweet wine of recompense. Other letters also often gladden me; many swift messengers of comfort, sympathy, and encouragement come and fold their wings at "Westwood;" and to-day, from over the sea, dated "Off Gibraltar," a missive reached me, which will ever be treasured as a precious souvenir of one whom "the King delighteth to honour." It is a letter from the hand of good George Müller, a kindly, graceful recognition of my little service for the Lord, and a generous offer of assistance in it. Such a distinction and favour I never expected to receive; but here it is—you may look at what he says, so lovingly, about "reading my last Report with great interest"! Can you imagine that? I thought at first my eyes must have deceived me, when I read it. And he offers to send me a quantity of his own books, to distribute to my poor Pastors, that he "may have fellowship with me in so good a work." I am charmed with his condescension and kindness; it is like a new version of the old story of the king and the beggar maid,—this prince of Faith's mighties stooping to notice such a "little one" among the thousands of Israel; this cedar of Lebanon bowing down to encourage the growth of a grain of mustard seed! There is little need to tell you that Mr. Müller's offer of books was gratefully accepted, or that, when the volumes reach me, I shall find it a real joy to enclose them in my parcels. The fragrance of faith must fill every page of such books; and the sweet incense of prayer surely lingers among all the leaves which bear such precious records of communion with God. Shall I not, therefore, be confident that, when the brethren open them, in the solitude of the study, these "beds of spices" may yield rest, refreshment, and invigoration to their souls? *"Have I been troubled lately by presents of unsuitable books?"* Ah! I see you smile as you remember my previous experiences in this direction, my disappointment and annoyance when worthless books come to hand, my difficulty (but for the garden furnace!) in ridding myself of the rubbish sent to quicken poor Pastors' brains, and inspire high and holy contemplations! But this year you may congratulate me on having received a splendid collection of gift-books, which have greatly enriched and enlarged the parcels it has been my joy to send out. When the noble list is printed, you will see what cause I have for sincere thankfulness to the wise and kind donors; for by these presents a greater *variety* of reading and information is placed at the disposal of those who are hungering after knowledge. *"You think the Book Fund has created a wide interest in the welfare of poor Pastors?"* Yes, it is wonderful to note the gracious manner in which the Lord inclines the hearts of friends to help me in my work in all sorts of ways, and I do bless Him for it! An instance, fresh in my mind, because it occurred to-day, will show you how tenderly all the details of the service are cared for. I wrote to a firm of merchants in London asking if they would take charge of a parcel of books for a poor lonely pastor in Australia, and forward it to him carriage free. "*Not a small favour to ask*," you say. No; but as the Book Fund could not pay the freight, upon their response to my request depended the minister's chances of having his bare book-shelf furnished; and the said shelf was one of the very barest that could be imagined! This morning's post brought the reply. "Yes, they would *always* willingly forward parcels to poor ministers in the colony without any charge," and this particular package should be conveyed direct to the remote inland station, where its advent would undoubtedly bring a store of gladness and blessing to the heart of the isolated minister. And—oh, most delightful climax of kindness!—a cheque for £10 was enclosed, with a graceful request that by its aid the intended gift might be made more excellent and valuable. When these tender providences touch me with such divine directness, my soul is filled with adoring gratitude and wonder, and my work ceases for a time to be an earthly business—it becomes a sacred channel of joy in the Lord, and of commerce with "things in heavenly places." "*Do I have all pleasure and no pain in my work?*" Well, I can almost answer "Yes" to that question, though occasionally a thorn is found among the roses. I am grieved when some trespassers overstep the limits of the Fund, and unlawfully take possession of its benefits; I feel disappointed when previous grants are ignored, and a second or third application is made *as if it were the first*, while my ledgers reveal a different story. But the sorrows are so few and small, and the joys so constant and great, that on the whole I may say I "rejoice evermore" in it, and have a most abundant reward for all the time and labour the dear service costs me." "*There are many more questions you would like to put to me, but you think I must be tired now.*" Well, dear friend, though I am somewhat weary in body, this little talk with you has refreshed my spirit, and the reiteration of all my mercies has awakened fervent desire to sing new songs of praise to the dear Lord from whom all blessings flow. You have been a patient listener to this rambling and imperfect account of my work, but I shall hope to anticipate your wishes for fuller details in the summing-up of the Report, and then give you all the information you desire to receive; so, for the present, good-bye, dear friend, and thank you for this little visit of sympathy. Be sure you remember my work in your prayers, beseeching a blessing on every book sent out, and asking for me grace that I may be found faithful in the "few things" over which the Lord hath set me.

* * * *

October.—A very touching letter has lately reached me from Auckland, New Zealand, the scene of my son's labours. The writer expresses so much loving sympathy with the work of the Book Fund, that I deem the letter entitled to insertion in these pages. Moreover, such tender little glimpses are therein given of "Son Tom" in his work as pastor and preacher, that I want those dear friends, who take an interest in his career, to rejoice with me in this sweet and simple testimony to the "grace which is given him of God."

Dear Mrs. Spurgeon,—It may be you will wonder that a stranger should address you, but you do not seem like a stranger to me; my heart goes out in warm love to you, for your dear son's sake, for your work's sake, but most of all for Jesus' sake. I have long wished to thank you for your precious little book. No words of mine can tell the good it has done me. Sick and lonely as I am, my heart truly sorrowed when I read of the sufferings of God's dear servants, for I think they should be the most tenderly cared for and loved of all people on earth; but the thought that *they* had to bear poverty, and sickness, and trial, drove away all rebellious murmurings concerning my own case, and now I am resting in quiet confidence in the Heavenly Father's hands. I cannot do much for Jesus, because of my weak, suffering body; but with a little self-denial I can help one of His poor servants, and I know it will be accepted.

And now I will tell you how the little book came to me. I had not been able to go out for many weeks, and I had often wished that Mr. Spurgeon would visit me; so one day I found courage to write to him, and he came at once—there was no need for fear—came the very day I wrote, and brought "Mother's book." "You will like to read it," he said, "it's my mother's book." I loved him for that! Ah! he does love his mother, and only the Lord knows what it costs him to be so far away from his dear home. But his heart is in his work, and I often wish you could hear his earnest pleading with sinners, and see the eager faces lifted to his while he speaks on his Master's behalf! We constantly bless the Lord for sending him here. He is doing a great and good work among us; he is so kind and sympathizing to all his people, and the sweet savour of his prayers will never be forgotten. I cannot repay him, I can only pray for him. It would grieve us very much to lose him; but still I should like him to come and see you, I think it would do him good, and I am sure it would rejoice your heart; but his work seems to require him here, and God knows best, does he not? Dear Mrs. Spurgeon, forgive my writing to you, but you have lightened so many heavy burdens, and brought joy to so many sorrowful hearts by the blessed work of your Book Fund, that I felt I must thank you, and tell you I pray for you very often.

* * * *

This same darling "Son Tom" of mine, who loves "Mother's work" very heartily, has sent me some extremely lively rhymes on the "Lemon Tree"; but most of the verses are so full of atrocious puns that I dare not admit them to the grave company of these records. I have, however, selected from among the merry host a few of the more sober-looking lines, and those old friends who like to remember the early connection of the little plant with the Book Fund, will understand the allusions made, and be glad to learn that the "tree" is still flourishing and beautiful.

I may add, that I never look upon its sturdy growth without a thrill of grateful memory and thankfulness for all the goodness and mercy which have followed my work since the time when the lemon-pip pushed its first wee green leaf through the black earth, under the shelter of a medicine glass!

> "Linked closely with the Book Fund, since
>   The Fund a fact became,
> Our lemon tree appeared in print
>   As emblem of the same.
>
> "No better crest the Fund could have
>   Than this same lemon tree;
> Twin plants they may, indeed, be termed
>   With common history.
>
> "From what a very tiny seed
>   The glorious Book Fund grew;
> To what proportions it would reach
>   Not e'en its planter knew.

"Some mocked the Fund, in fun, of course,
  'The money won't be found';
To her each lemon-leaf bespoke
  Another hundred pound.

"And now the Fund-tree firmly stands
  With shade, and sap, and scent;
A tree of knowledge;—all its leaves
  For Pastors' blessing meant.

"Live on, grow on, dear lemon tree,
  Be never moribund;
Fit emblem from the very first
  Of Mrs. Spurgeon's Fund!"

* * * *

I have always been exceedingly glad that the Lord put it into my heart to make the gifts of the Book Fund quite unsectarian. The work would have been crippled, and have had but a miserable existence if its sympathies had been confined within the narrow limits of a denomination. But now how widespread are its blessings! How grateful are the helped ones! How happy are the helpers! It delights me to think that if the Book Fund had a voice, it would be constantly whispering to onlookers, "See how these Christians love one another!" The parcels of books, as they go forth from my book-room to the studies of ministers of every section of the Church of Christ, are so many weighty evidences that Christian love and brotherly kindness are still believed in and cherished by those who stand fast by the "OLD-FASHIONED GOSPEL," though by this steadfastness we dare to differ from many of our *wiser* brethren; ay, and would even dare to *die* for that difference!

I will let you see this dear service of mine from a clergyman's point of view. "We thoroughly enjoyed," he says, "your little book, giving an account of your work. In these days of cold and shallow scepticism, of marked superstition, of controversies, often bigoted and bitter, within the pale of the Church of God; of godless living in many of its professed members,—such a book, recording, as it does, a real work, undertaken and carried out irrespective of party considerations, is a testimony to the world outside, that Christ and the members of His mystical body are really one, though the latter often affect an appearance of disunion. I am quite sure that nothing could more effectually break down our party-walls than work such as you have undertaken. Your little book is calculated to evoke the deepest sympathy from the hearts of God's people, and to incite them to a like desire, at least, for a large-heartedness to the cause of Christ, which is *one*, and to breathe a prayer that they, too, may know the joy which you feel in making others happy, and in giving to the 'Stars in the right hand of Christ' the power to become 'burning' as well as 'shining' lights."

A Congregational minister also writes thus encouragingly:—"Not a twentieth of the good your Book Fund is doing will you know until the day when the Master will give out to each his own reward. While very much of what is seen, in these days of business, will be burned up, surely some of the work done in cheering the hearts of the Lord's own servants will stand the fire, and remain as gold and silver and precious stones. I pray that more and more blessing may ever rest upon your most noble work."

* * * *

November.—A country minister, to whom I had some months ago sent a parcel of single "Sermons" for distribution, writes to say that they have been circulated amongst the people in six villages, have been read and re-read, and now he is longing for a fresh supply. But he felt he could not ask for more without trying to show that the poor people appreciated the spiritual food thus presented to them; so, "as a thank-offering and a token of true gratitude from some poor souls who have fed on the sincere milk of the word, and the strong meat contained in the 'Sermons,'" he sends fifteen shillings for the Book Fund! I think such thankfulness is lovely! But there is something equally cheering further on. He tells me of a young man, a hurdle-maker, who for some months has greatly enjoyed Mr. Spurgeon's "Sermons," and is so much in love with his writings that he always carries a "Spurgeon" book in his pocket, and now has begun to long intensely to call "The Treasury of David" his own. "You will think it a strange thing," says the minister, "that a man who works in the woods should desire to possess 'The Treasury,' but he has set his heart upon it; and, as he is very steady and saving, I think he cannot do better than spend that money on books which so many of our young men are wasting in strong drink and other evils."

I was delighted to offer "The Treasury" at a reduced price, and it was bought and paid for, a volume of "Sermons" being enclosed as a gift, with earnest prayer for a blessing; for "who knoweth whereunto this thing may grow?" A young man who fills his head with knowledge and his heart with grace, while others stand smoking at the streetcorners, or drinking in the ale-house, is worthy of all help and encouragement; and one may expect that he will make so brave a use of the books procured by his own industry and self-denial, that some day we may joyfully hear of his good and faithful service in the cause of Jesus Christ.

* * * *

A somewhat similar and equally gratifying case deserves to be placed on the same record. It was thus presented in a letter:—

Dear Mrs. Spurgeon,—Your little book tells of a minister who gave up his pipe in order to obtain your husband's books. I cannot do this, for I am only an apprentice to the shoemaking, and such luxuries are quite out of my reach; but I have begun to preach a little for Jesus, and I have long been hungering for some of the same precious volumes; so, to satisfy my appetite, I have sold a book which I possessed, and, with some extra help from a few friends, I have realized £1, which I now send to you, begging that you will lay it out for me to the best advantage; and if I could have part of "The Treasury of David"—oh, how thankful I should be! I crave eagerly for knowledge, and, by God's help, I shall obtain it; I am trying what prayer and perseverance and holy living will do to gain my end. Thank you very much for the motto in your book—"PRAYER AND PAINS CAN DO ANYTHING"; it has been a great help to me."

I exacted great things of that golden coin! I laid a heavy burden on each separate shilling! I expected them to do wonders, and they did not disappoint me! I made them bear the cost of books which would have gladdened any heart; but when that indefatigable young man heard what he might expect, his rapture made him still more ravenous, and he could not be content without Matthew

Henry's "Commentary"! So, again seeking the aid of a friend, he sent up the money for a second-hand copy, and almost went into a delirium of delight when the wonderful parcel reached him. "My treasures," he says, "my treasures have come, and I am lost in wonder, love, and praise! My greatest expectations are exceeded, and I don't know how to thank you! I joyfully recognize the hand of the Lord in the matter, and can only say, 'Bless the Lord, O my soul!' I could not feel happier if I had received a large fortune. To God be the praise!"

Not the least touching point in this little story is the fact that the friend from whom the money-help mainly came is himself a poor man, and that he trusts this eager young seeker after knowledge to repay him in due time the money thus advanced. What a debt of love and honour! May it be quickly paid, and bear the compound interest of gratitude and tender requital!

* * * *

The chief item of interest in this month's record is the commencement of another BRANCH BUSINESS, upon which I expect the dew of the Lord's blessing to fall—silently, copiously, constantly. I shall ask earnest prayer from my dear friends that my expectation may be realized; and if their hearts are drawn lovingly towards the new scheme by fervent prayer on its behalf, I know they will send me the means to carry it on to a successful issue.

I have undertaken to send out *monthly* four copies of Mr. Spurgeon's latest "Sermons" to all foreign missionaries who will gladly receive and use them, and the first consignment of 104 packets has been already despatched. The beginning is small, but the work has elements of mighty power in it; it will grow, and the Lord will give it increase.

Readers of *The Sword and the Trowel* will be familiar with the project; for long before this little book sees the light, they will have read of the formation of the new Fund, have perused with pleasure the letter of the "worker who longs for others to be helped as he has been," and will have seen, I hope, some delightful assurances of success and prosperity. But as my "Diary" is privileged sometimes to tell of what goes on "behind the scenes," I will now give it permission just to suggest the way in which I was "managed," and led to be the "manager" of this new business.

My readers are to imagine my morning-room, and the work of letter-writing going briskly forward, as usual, when—

Enter the dear Pastor—my "Tirshatha." *

"Look here, wifey; here's a capital proposition!"

His face is so beaming, and his smile so joyous, that I know there is some "glory to God and good-will to man" in the news he is bringing.

"Well, what is it?"

"A gentleman in Russia wants me to send out the 'Sermons' regularly to missionaries in foreign countries."

"Oh, that will be splendid! but how is it to be done?"

"He encloses £5 as the first instalment of a Fund for the purpose, and I can find another £5 to put to it, to begin with."

I say how pleased I am with the proposal, and we talk the matter over, calling to mind the abundant favour which the Lord always vouchsafes to his servant's earnest utterances. I know that the comfort and refreshment of such a monthly packet to lonely workers in strange lands would be incalculable, and I at once make up my mind that the pleasant little service shall be mine, for I see very plainly that this is the desire of my husband's heart; but I "bide a wee" before I make the offer.

"The money will be easily found," I say suggestively; "friends are sure to help a scheme so manifestly useful; but who will you get to do the work?"

"That's just what I want to talk to you about. Do you think Mrs. —— would undertake it, or Miss ——?"

Then follows a long consultation, in which we are agreed that certain ladies could well and easily do the secretarial part of the work, but that they could scarcely be expected to furnish or obtain the needful funds.

"I can be treasurer," says the dear Pastor; and he looks at me with such a winning, meaning smile, that I can conceal my determination no longer.

---

* For explanation of this title, see the Books of Ezra and Nehemiah.

"And I can combine it with the Book Fund!" I cry enthusiastically.

"Will you really? There! that's just what I wanted you to say, only I was afraid it might be too much for you; but if you *can* do it—why, it would be the very thing!"

I gravely assure him that the extra work demanded by this scheme will be cheerfully undertaken by willing hands in the household, and this assertion is subsequently verified by the glad and unanimous consent of all parties.

So, dear reader, with much joy and hopefulness, we made and sealed the compact, anticipating the blessing which, by the Lord's grace, shall accompany the monthly messengers to his servants at the far ends of the earth.

This new effort is to be strictly and entirely incorporated with the Book Fund, as a new graft on the old stock, and thus, though it will bear another kind of fruit, it will be nourished by the same sap, tended by the same loving hand, blessed with the same heavenly dew; and, if spared to write another Report, I hope to have some very pleasant news to tell concerning its growth, prosperity, and usefulness. Meanwhile, I earnestly beg all my friends to remember the work in their petitions before God, pleading for a blessing on the "Sermons" and the translations which will be given; for, "Thus saith the Lord, I will yet for this be inquired of by the house of Israel, to do it for them."

* * * *

THE PASTORS' AID FUND.

It gives me great pleasure to record the prosperity of this Fund, and to thank—with words that can never give expression enough to my gratitude—the dear friends whose princely generosity keeps this treasury always furnished with "enough and to spare." There are "three mighty men" whose hearts God has touched, who are the chief support of this "Branch Business"; but from many other contributors to the Book Fund I receive substantial help for the sorrowful needs of poverty-stricken Pastors. Quite a goodly sum came the other day from Russia for this purpose. Scotch friends also take a warm interest in it ; and throughout the year the Fund has been like an up-springing well, from which I have constantly taken " cups of cold water " to revive and refresh weary travellers across the arid desert of privation and distress. My private ledger shows that £340 8s. 3d. has been given to necessitous Pastors during the last twelve months ; this is about the usual average of the distribution by the Fund, and I can truly say that no worthy applicant has been denied. Blessed be the name of the Lord for entrusting so tender a charge to my care, and increasing my happiness by making me the bearer of so much comfort and relief to His servants :—

"𝕺, 𝕸𝖆𝖌𝖓𝖎𝖋𝖞 𝖙𝖍𝖊 𝕷𝖔𝖗𝖉 𝖜𝖎𝖙𝖍 𝖒𝖊, 𝖆𝖓𝖉 𝖑𝖊𝖙 𝖚𝖘 𝕰𝖝𝖆𝖑𝖙 𝕳𝖎𝖘 𝕹𝖆𝖒𝖊 𝖙𝖔𝖌𝖊𝖙𝖍𝖊𝖗 !"

* * * *

I am thankful also to say that more friends are personally interesting themselves in this urgent work, to my great delight and gratification, and are earnestly endeavouring to mitigate the sorrows of poor Pastors by quiet and generous assistance. I have in a previous page told how the wife of one of "our own" old students set herself and the ladies of the church to work to provide for the necessities of a neighbouring minister, whose long struggle with poverty had moved her heart to deepest sympathy. She has not grown weary of her loving mission ; but, with only slender means at her disposal, she has secured to the family very many comforts which they must otherwise have lacked. She has constantly supplied their most pressing needs, and been, from that time till now, a "ministering angel" to them. Similarly, a lady in a distant county—herself a late pastor's daughter—has most warmly taken up the cause of ill-paid ministers. She interests all her friends in the matter, solicits gifts of clothing and household stores, lays the needs of His servants before the Lord in prayer, and rejoices in abundant success and blessing. She has already helped some half-dozen poor families, and now writes for "more names."

These are only two examples of the many glimpses I get

of up-springing seed, of ripening fields, of fruitful vineyards; further on there will come a plenteous in-gathering of good things for poor Pastors, when the "shout of a King" shall be in their midst, and they shall "joy before Him according to the joy of harvest." I can sing even now, in anticipation of that blessed time—

"𝕺, 𝔐𝔞𝔤𝔫𝔦𝔣𝔶 𝔱𝔥𝔢 𝔏𝔬𝔯𝔡 𝔴𝔦𝔱𝔥 𝔪𝔢, 𝔞𝔫𝔡 𝔩𝔢𝔱 𝔲𝔰
𝔈𝔵𝔞𝔩𝔱 𝔥𝔦𝔰 𝔑𝔞𝔪𝔢 𝔱𝔬𝔤𝔢𝔱𝔥𝔢𝔯!"

* * * *

Passing now in review the chief points of interest in Book Fund work, a few words on each must bring my little Report to a conclusion. The number of

Books Distributed

is, I find, far larger this year than ever before. Friends will rejoice with me in this fact, and see in it a twofold significance; for, while it proves that serious need of mental provision still exists among ministers, it also shows that, by the blessing of the Lord, much has been done to supply their wants. Yes, a very busy day is every alternate Thursday at "Westwood," when the outgoing books crowd the vestibule, and the dear friend who packs them has need of all her strength and patience to accomplish the heavy task, even with the help of other willing workers, who are entrusted with minor details; and at night, when the "Master" comes home from his labours, he has to pass by a perfect wall of stacked-up parcels on his way to his study, and I know he breathes a prayer that the Lord will own and bless this little service done to His poor servants, and make every book a channel of grace to the recipient.

The monthly distribution of

"The Sword and the Trowel" Magazine

is still attempted, but only in a small way; for its price is so trifling that I think it should be accepted as a gift by none but the very poorest of the Lord's servants. To *them* I am more than willing to forward it, and any pastor who cannot afford the *threepence monthly* has only to write to me to secure it. I have this week had some grateful letters from those who have received the gift during 1883. An aged minister says that a late article by Mr. Spurgeon, entitled "We shall get Home, we shall get Home," was exceedingly sweet and precious to his soul, and that he always reads the magazine with pleasure and profit. "It is quite a boon every month," writes another, "and cheers the heart of a poor village pastor more than you can imagine"; while a third thus pleads: "Might I dare to ask that you will continue to me the monthly gift of *The Sword and the Trowel?* I do greatly appreciate it, but cannot afford to buy it."

The generous and faithful friend to whom I owe so many thanks for all sorts of kindnesses has again throughout the year kept me fully supplied with writing material for myself and for enclosure in the parcels. These

GIFTS OF STATIONERY

are very acceptable to poor pastors, and supply a want often overlooked, but none the less real and vexatious. They think *I* am very thoughtful for them, and they give me loving thanks; but the true care-taker is my considerate friend, who thinks no trouble too great to take to ensure the comfort of others, and finds his best reward in the joy of thus serving his Master. A few quotations from grateful recipients will illustrate their feeling on the subject better than any words from my pen. A country minister writes: "If you only knew how ill able we have sometimes been to spare the money for paper and envelopes, it would have given you even greater pleasure than it has done to send this wonderful supply." "I am very glad," writes another, "to receive a packet of stationery. The friend making this provision for poor ministers has been guided wisely, for very few know how much correspondence our work in country districts calls for. Many times have I wished that some one would be thoughtful enough to anticipate our wants in this respect, *yet never before have I had such a present*. It came, too, on my birthday." "The note-paper and envelopes," says a third pastor, "are as acceptable as they were unexpected. If I have been remiss in my correspondence hitherto, with such resources I shall be encouraged to mend my ways." There is no need to multiply examples of the grateful welcome accorded to this considerate addition to my gifts; it "goes without saying" that such kindness is valued by the poor Pastors; but it remains for me to express my sincere and affectionate thanks to the generous donor for this and many other proofs of his interest in my work; and this I do with all my heart.

There has been this year a notable and increased demand for copies of

SINGLE SERMONS FOR DISTRIBUTION,

and of little tracts and books, and extracts from the "Sermons." I have been constantly entreated to make grants of these to all kinds of Christian workers, whose experience has shown them the excellence of these spiritual tools, and the blessing which the Lord vouchsafes to their prayerful use. It was scarcely within the province of the Book Fund to comply with these requests, but I felt constrained to overstep the boundaries in such a matter; it would not have been wise to let slip such splendid opportunities of scattering the seed of life broadcast over the waiting furrows! Soldiers, sailors, railway porters, dockyard men, have all been supplied through their several missionaries, and I could tell of some very happy cases of impression and subsequent conversion through the reading of the "Sermons" and tracts by these toilers. As for the country Pastors and Evangelists, they can never have enough of the precious messengers; they use them in district and house-to-house visitation, and in loan societies; and they come to me so often for supplies, that I must break down the barriers altogether, and make up my mind to consider this sermon-distribution as another permanent and important "branch" of my main "business."

There remains now but to notice and assign its proper place to the new effort, lately inaugurated, of forwarding every month, per post, the

SERMONS TO MISSIONARIES IN FOREIGN LANDS.

Elsewhere I have explained the origin and purpose of this Fund; and, being yet in its extreme infancy, there is not much to be said for it, except that it bids fair to be a very robust and charming child. Two despatches of "Sermons" will have been made before Christmas, and I have already received answers from workers in Italy, Brittany, Germany, and Spain: these are all delighted with the prospect before them, rejoicing greatly in the refreshment and help to be obtained from the monthly feast. Sufficient time has not yet elapsed to bring replies from the distant heathen lands to which I have sent the little ambassadors of peace, but these will come in due course. As I expected and hoped, friends have warmly espoused the new cause, and my lists of contributions show that, so far, all the expenses of the scheme are most liberally met. Thank you a thousand times, dear friends, for all the generous love and kindness which, under the blessing of God, crown every effort of the Book Fund with continued and triumphant success.

Again I am constrained to say—

"O, Magnify the Lord with me, and let us Exalt His Name together!"

* * * *

At the manufactory of the "Gobelins Tapestries" in Paris, the weavers sit concealed *behind* the beautiful fabrics on which they are engaged, working from a pattern designed by some great artist, and perhaps only taking occasional peeps at the fair exterior and the marvellous effects which their patient labours are producing. Passing along the room in front of the brilliant pictures, the visitor's attention is concentrated on their loveliness. He knows that they are in process of manufacture by men whose persons are partially or wholly hidden behind the massive drapery; he may even see the work growing, thread by thread, under the weavers' busy fingers; but he gives scarce a thought to the workman, so ravished is he with the beauty of design, the richness of colouring, and the unique texture of these renowned productions. I have been thinking that, in a very humble fashion, I am like one of these weavers; for day by day I sit, carefully adding a few touches to my work, weaving in the bright threads of the Book Fund records, till a fair tapestry of its history for the past twelve months is completed, and then, in my "Diary," unveiling my work for my readers' inspection; displaying it, not as a triumph of *my* skill, but as a tiny part of a trophy of the Lord's great design of lovingkindness and tender mercy to His chosen ones. For truly the work is all *His*—in direction, in design, and in development. Its foundation lines were laid in His love and compassion, its pattern is traced in the golden threads of His faithfulness and favour, its embroidery is clustered with the precious stones of His mercies, and its beauty is great because of the "blessing of the Lord" upon it. Behind all this grandeur of grace the worker may well be concealed: it is enough that she should marvel at the condescension which placed her there, and taught her fingers to fashion this goodly work for the King and His servants. It is so great an honour to be allowed to put even one stitch into the tapestry of the wonderful providences which are being wrought all around us, that we might well crave to be employed upon the selvedges, or be happy only to ravel out the fringes of the great Master's designs, rather than bear no part in that solemn labour which promotes us to be "workers together with God."

I cannot tell why I have recalled a scene which must have lain long buried in the dark places of my memory; perhaps it is intended to comfort or reassure some timid, troubled worker who can see no beauty or utility in the service which yet he feels constrained to render, because of the love he bears his Lord and King. Courage, dear friend! You are to stand *behind* your work, whatever it may be. You are to labour diligently and faithfully at the wrong and knotty side of it, content to be unknown and unrewarded if the Lord so wills it; but restfully certain that, if you are doing what He tells you, the result may be safely left with Him. He will bring out all the harmony and beauty and glory of His own designs; and when they are perfected, and you are allowed to look upon the *right side* of the Lord's "marvellous work," you will wonder, not only at its splendour as a whole, but at the brilliance of the stitches which were woven in by you with so many sighs and tears, and you will never cease to sing to the praise of Him who "doeth all things well."

Dear friends, at this moment I gather up the last thread of my twelvemonth's task, and tie the finishing knot! Help me to thank the Lord for the happy completion of my little piece of broidered work! This is the *eighth* record of the Lord's love and faithfulness to me in the Book Fund; help me to pray that it may be approved and accepted by Him, and allowed to tell the story of His grace and goodness with irresistible power. If it may but show forth His honour and glory, I will thank Him for ever!

I lay the offering at His feet, asking Him to accept it for Jesus' sake; and then I turn to you—with empty hands, but a full and happy heart—and I say, once more—

> "O, Magnify the Lord with me, and let us
> Exalt His Name together!"

SUMMARY OF WORK.

Books Distributed during the Year 1883 :—11,351 Volumes.

The above books were apportioned to 332 Baptists, 216 Independents, 310 Methodists, 163 Church of England clergymen, 37 Presbyterians, 34 Missionaries, 61 Evangelists, and 2 Moravians.—Total, 1,155.

The Book Fund Diary

For 1884.

By Mrs. C. H. Spurgeon.

E are such old friends now, my dear readers and I—we have so long enjoyed familiar intercourse, and been for so many years delightfully associated in Book Fund work—that we need no formal introduction to each other. The commencement of this annual chronicle, which lovingly links our interests, and rivets our affections, requires no elaborate statement of the writer's aims and intentions, since these are well known, and most generously promoted; neither are fair words of promise for the future, of diligence and devotedness on her part, needful, seeing that the work is a well-spring of joy to her, and is so dearly loved, that its service is a perpetual delight. Our only ceremony is very simple, and soon concluded: we give (in intention) a cordial grasp of each other's hand; offer an affectionate New Year's greeting;—then a very tender acknowledgment of the past kindnesses of my dear friends is given and accepted, and I at once apply myself to the task of making the Book Fund, as far as lies in my power, as pleasant and beautiful a thing to read about as it is to direct and administer. Shakespeare says,—

"A honest tale speeds best being plainly told";

and I am going to test the truth of his assertion.

A winsome letter from a pastor, once a student, comes to cheer me at this special season, when the many meetings of friends, and the gathering together of loved and loving ones, suggest a somewhat painful contrast to my loneliness and separation from my beloved. I record it, not alone for its sympathetic sweetness, but to show how deeply the grace of gratitude is rooted in some hearts, and what fair blossoms of encouragement and blessing spring up unexpectedly in our pathway, when we have been enabled to " scatter seeds of kindness" as we passed along.

My dear Mrs. Spurgeon,—Among the many kind friends remembered by us at this joyous time—if not by letter, yet by loving and earnest prayer at the throne of grace—certainly the first must be your own kind self, and dear Mr. Spurgeon, to whom, under God, we owe so much. I have, therefore, the most sincere pleasure in sending you the enclosed card; and with all our hearts we wish you, and all your loved ones, a very happy and profitable season. Dear Mr. Spurgeon being away at Mentone, much of the joy and brightness of Westwood must have vanished with him; but this cloud has a silver lining, and, when we get above the cloud, we shall be able to see its shining side. We trust that the dear President is quietly resting after his many labours; and it is ever a glad impulse of love to pray that he may be sustained and strengthened, and brought back to us in renewed health, and with a fresh baptism of Divine power for the Master's service. Also I trust that your New Year may be cheered by the thought that there are thousands of loving hearts in which your name is enshrined, and whose prayers bear you up, like a sea of sustaining strength. Not least among these are the dear brethren in the College Conference, who have been privileged to receive your help, and who have known the power of your sympathy, and whose grateful affection is ever shining upon you and your work; never more truly and tenderly shining, than when your sun is behind a cloud. And, above all, there is the unfailing joy which beams upon us in the face of Jesus, who is " the same yesterday, and to-day, and for ever."

The writer of this letter could not possibly know that his assurance of prayerful remembrance was just the crumb of comfort my heart needed; yet so it was, and I thank him, and say, "A word spoken in due season, how good is it!"

* * * *

January 6th, 6.30 P.M.—I am sitting alone, in my husband's lonely study, the profound silence broken only by the ticking of the big clock; the volumes which line the walls look frowning and gloomy in the uncertain light of evening, and the precise orderliness of the whole room gives sad and significant sign of an absent owner. The first Sabbath of the New Year is drawing to a close, and the day, so fair, so bright, is going to die. All through the past twelve hours, the horizon has been glorified with light which seemed unearthly, and looking south, from these windows, across the many miles of country which stretch to the Surrey Hills, the vision has been so radiant that "thick coming fancies" could easily picture therefrom the jasper walls and pearly gates of the City which hath no need of the sun. The climax of this glory came with the sunset, when the western heavens were ablaze with fiery splendour, and the mingling and blending of colour were so wonderful and awe-inspiring that one could only exclaim in the words of the prophet of Patmos, "There was a rainbow round about the throne, in sight like unto an emerald"! But now the many-hued light is fading away, the crimson and green banners which were streaming in the golden haze have changed into murky brown clouds which straggle in great broken patches across the sky, hasting to go down to their lair, and I turn again from the window, cherishing the sweet thought that perhaps the dear one a thousand miles away has been gazing on the same glorious scene, and that, though so far separated, we have together been worshipping the great Creator of heaven and earth, blessing Him for the joy of being able to say, "This awful God is ours, our Father, and our Friend." Now, as I sit in the soft twilight, very tender thoughts steal into my heart, and delightful memories of sacred hours here spent with my beloved come crowding in upon me. The stillness constrains me to listen for the voice which has so often made music to my soul, and I look around upon the books which I have so many times taken down and read to him, as though they might almost sympathize with me in the loss we together suffer by his absence. But they are dumb, and make no sign; all their wisdom, and learning, and piety, are locked up within themselves; they are treasuries of which my absent lord has the key, they are like stones which only my Philosopher can turn into gold.

> "Dear absent love of mine, it did not need
> Thy absence to tell me that thou wert dear,
> And yet the absence maketh it more clear."

A little longer musing on this tender theme brings a painful sense of loneliness and discomfort to me. I almost begin to murmur against the circumstances which make the separation from my husband unavoidable, and I am fast falling into a fretful and peevish condition when—with a rush of joy no words can describe, I recognize the possibility of being no longer solitary and desolate; my soul is thrilled with the solemn and entrancing thought that in this very room the Master's Divine presence, so often felt, may again be realized by faith, and enjoyed by my longing, waiting soul. The Lord Jesus has been so wont to come to this spot to help and bless His ministering servant, that may-be —I thought it, and now I write it with all reverence—maybe *He will not have given up the blessed habit of such visits*, and I shall find Him, waiting here with His hands full of blessing, and His heart full of tenderness—even for me!

My spirit melted within me at this wonderful hope, and with bowed head and bended knee, by the Pastor's empty chair, I "sought Him whom my soul loveth"; I sought Him—and, blessed be His name, He would not let me seek in vain. My gracious Lord drew near, and strengthened and comforted His lonely child, and so filled my heart with joy and peace that presently I could sing, though in trembling tones—

> "This, this is rest, Lord Jesus,
> Alone with Thee to be;
> The desert is a gladsome place
> With Thy blest company.
> Amid the throng I might forget
> That I am all Thine own;
> I bless Thee for the desert place
> With Thee, dear Lord, alone!"

And now I tell of my weakness and need, and of His consoling presence and love; I record this tender episode of His grace, that He may be "admired in all them that believe," and that my sweet experience of His present help in time of trouble may be a "song to cheer some one behind me, whose courage is sinking low."

I intended this evening to write down some items of interest in Book Fund work during the past week; but this little story clamoured to be told, and has had its way—

God's way, I hope. May He bless the telling of its simple truth to the praise of His lovingkindness and condescending mercy!

* * * *

February.—The new work of sending the "Sermons" every month to missionaries in foreign lands is proceeding vigorously and successfully, and most delightful letters from all parts of the world testify to the joy with which the gifts are received. The devoted men who labour in China have a large share of the blessing; for, by the favour of Mr. Hudson Taylor, all the "Sermons" for missionaries at the stations of the China Inland Mission are taken out free of charge. The boon of fresh spiritual food to these isolated workers must be great indeed; some of them are so completely cut off from European society that for months together they see only the natives of the land, and, but for converse with each other, would hear only the discordant tones of a people of strange language. We who are dwellers at home can scarcely realize the thrill of gladness with which, under such circumstances, the arrival of a packet of "Sermons" from England must be hailed by those exiled hearts.

As these parcels to China do not go through the post, I send the monthly parts, thereby insuring five discourses for the four weeks, and the dear friend who so generously provides all my needful stationery, and supplies my poor Pastors also, has prepared famous strong envelopes in which to enclose the books, and has had them prettily stamped, and nicely printed with the sender's name in the corner! In these compact cases we expect the "Sermons" will travel safely into the interior of the Celestial Empire to their respective destinations, after reaching the general depôt on the coast.

For all other parts of the world the "Sermons" have to be entrusted to the post-office, and as I have not yet had responses from the remote stations to which I have directed them, I sometimes fear lest the little messengers should lose their way, or fall into evil hands. From India, Ceylon, China, Mexico, New Zealand, Texas, Jamaica, Newfoundland,

and Palestine, with all nearer stations, I have heard—but the workers on the Congo River, those at the Cameroons, and at other places difficult of access by post, have still to acknowledge the arrival of the packets.

At the present time we are sending to forty-four missionaries in China, and to one hundred and forty in other foreign lands; these numbers are augmented from time to time by new names, and we may thus consider the work established upon a very satisfactory basis, waiting the Lord's further pleasure as to its extension, and knowing that He can grant to us, if it be His will, unlimited power, both of resolve and resource.

A few extracts from letters are sure to be appreciated, and I therefore give the following:

From Palestine—

Just now, as I was starting on a missionary journey, your welcome letter, with Mr. Spurgeon's "Sermons," arrived safely. I need not say how glad I am to receive the helpful gift; but I feel very thankful that we, the natives of Palestine, have kind friends to sympathize with, and help us. I can assure you that these "Sermons" will be warmly welcomed whenever you send them. I shall not forget you in my prayers.

From Norway—

I wish to express my warmest thanks for your kindness in sending me your dear husband's "Sermons." They will be a very great treat to me; for I enjoy them more than I am able to tell you. Very few of our brethren in your highly-favoured country can know the loneliness we feel for lack of fellowship and communion with other workers. It is often many months, and sometimes a whole year, between the times we see each other's face; but these "Sermons," coming to us regularly, will cheer our weary hearts, and refresh our tired spirits.

From Trinidad—

Dear Mrs. Spurgeon,—The letter printed on the fly-leaf of your circular may have been the means of inducing you to undertake the work of sending "Sermons" to distant lands; but I am sure the Lord's hand is manifestly in the matter, for He certainly knows how acceptable Mr. Spurgeon's utterances will be to all missionaries, and how well adapted they are to comfort and refresh and inspire weary workers. The native preachers to whom you have sent them are delighted at the idea of receiving such treasures monthly, and beg me to thank you, on their behalf as well as on my own, for the great boon thus afforded us.

From Hayti—(a deeply interesting letter; I am tempted to give a lengthy extract from it)—

I beg you to accept my best thanks for the "Sermons," and I pray that the Lord may largely increase your usefulness, and abundantly bless this new effort. Just now I am besieged by the enemies of our town, and cut off from all communication with our churches in other places; my work as a medical missionary is largely extended amongst the wounded, in consequence of our unfortunate revolution. Every day some are missing, and others die from gangrened injuries. The doctors of the town will not go to treat the poor; they fear the shells that explode every now and then in the streets. Our town is in a beautiful valley, surrounded by three ranges of green hills, and on these our enemies' cannon are placed. The siege has now lasted four months, and no food can be obtained from the interior of the country; and, in addition to the famine, dysentery and fever are killing the people by dozens. Our Baptist Medical Dispensary will make a mark here never to be forgotten, and I believe the Lord will save some by this means amongst my ninety sick ones. I know there are some anxious to be saved. We have been visited by fourteen bombs and shells; our old Mission House is bored with holes; our chapel windows are broken, our benches spoiled, and our harmonium rendered entirely useless. But I do not mean to give up. (Is not this the language of a true hero?) I am about finishing at my own expense a little place, and a baptistery, in spite of all discouragements. The consuls have left the town, because they expect a general bombardment; but how can I leave my sick ones to die? They have no earthly friend to help them, they are penniless, and can have no medical care if I leave the place; and besides, our committee have asked me to stay till the revolution is over! Under my care I have some men who were wounded with rifle-shots in the spine; I have lent the "Sermons" to them, and they are delighted to read them.

What a scene of suffering, desolation, and woe is here pictured! Yet how calmly the Master's servant carries himself in the midst of the fast-accumulating horrors! How unquestioning is his obedience! how full of confidence in God are his determinations! how dignified and grand his self-surrender! There is a tempest of fire raging round the city, and a devouring sword is going through the land; famine and death wait at the street corners for fresh victims, and the cries of the wounded and dying mingle sorrowfully with the lamentations of bereaved and bleeding hearts; but the light of his holy courage and steadfast devotion shines steadily forth from his watch-tower, and the blood of souls will never be required at that watchman's hand.

When I read his touching letter, so brave, so resolute, so full of consecration to God and love to sinners, my heart said, " Lord, keep him as the apple of the eye ; hide him beneath the shadow of Thy wings."

How thankful I am that the " Sermons " reached him and his poor patients through the dreadful rain of the bombshells, and the menacing dangers of a cruel siege ! God must have given special charge concerning them, and doubtless He sent some sweet words of consolation or enlightenment by them to the souls of those sorely stricken men. I should feel richly rewarded for sending out the parcels if only this one instance of their acceptable work had come to my knowledge.

Let me beg of you, dear friends, to pray very earnestly and constantly that always, and in every place, the success of this new service may be assured by the gracious favour of the Lord upon it, and the attestation of His Spirit to the power of the printed gospel.

It is a great delight to drop such manna round about the tents in the wilderness, and to send such a flock of white doves with messages of peace to the regions beyond ; but the dew of the Lord's blessing must underlie the heavenly bread before its taste can be " as of wafers made with honey " ; and the olive-leaf in the dove's mouth must bear tokens that the " depths have covered it " ere it can fitly tell the story of abating waters, serene skies, and perfect safety.

Therefore, I pray you, for this let your requests be made known unto God.

* * * *

March.—" An excellent book," says Coleridge, " is like a well-chosen and well-tended fruit-tree. Its fruits are not of one season only. With the due and natural intervals, we may recur to it year after year, and it will supply the same nourishment and the same gratification, if only we ourselves return to it with the same healthful appetite."

This quotation, if I could but have had it ready on my lips, would have been a pertinent reply to the suggestion of a friend who was lately advocating a change, and—as he considered it—an *improvement* in my present system of managing the Book Fund. "Why do you not *loan* the books," he said, "and so keep the Pastors constantly supplied with fresh reading? The volumes you *give* them will lie idly on their shelves when once read through."

Unfortunately for me, my "happy thoughts" never make their appearance at the moment they are wanted—they are as shy as spoilt children, and quite as intractable; so, although I knew he was absolutely mistaken, my friend's opinion was but feebly combated, and very likely he retains the impression that to convert the Book Fund into a huge lending library would be a wise and desirable reform.

Lest any other friend should have indulged in a similar flight of fancy, I confide to my little "Diary," and thence to him, if he be one of my readers, my firm and deep conviction that to make the books the poor pastor's *very own*, either by gift or his own purchase, is the best, most beneficial, and only truly blessed way of carrying on the work. So far as I am concerned, it is the only *possible* way also. The notion of lending the volumes might commend itself to a well-managed society, with plenty of money and assistants at its command; but it would be an unreasonable undertaking for one person to attempt, and would soon end in an utter collapse of the whole affair. There are now on my books over TWELVE THOUSAND names of ministers who have received grants from the Fund: how impossible it would have been to have benefited such a multitude in any other way than by *giving* to the poorest, and allowing others to purchase at reduced prices!

A minister's library should be richly stored with commentaries and *works of reference;* these stand waiting their master's use and pleasure; they are not intended to be read through and done with, but are life-long friends, whose counsel and guidance are available at any moment, and whose presence in his study is a joy and refreshment to the pastor's heart. Just imagine loaning "The Treasury of David" to a man for a month, and then obliging him to pass it on to somebody else! I should call it a cruel kindness to set such a draught of nectar to his lips, and allow him to sip only once! I should be ashamed to put the golden treasure into his house, and then in effect say,

"Now, scramble for the thought-nuggets as quickly as you can, for the carrier's cart will call for the package to-morrow!"

No, my friends; not so would I deal with those whose searching of God's Word needs to be continually aided, directed, and stimulated. Theirs is the most solemn work that a mortal man can have committed to his charge, and my ambition is to place at their disposal such profoundly spiritual aids to its accomplishment that, by the blessing of God, they may be workmen needing not to be ashamed, rightly dividing the word of truth, making full proof of their ministry.

Books that *can* be read through at a sitting, and are either so ordinary or so feeble that the operation leaves no trace or effect upon the mind of the reader, are not the sort of literature that I covet for my poor Pastors, or that they would gratefully accept at my hands. I want commentaries on God's Word by the most devout and learned writers; I want books full of the marrow and fatness of the gospel, spread forth as a glorious feast for the satiating of their own souls; I want volumes that are storehouses of "things new and old," that God's ministers may draw therefrom abundant supplies for their work of feeding the flock of God. This deep longing of mine, to send forth only the best and choicest of theological works, makes me somewhat impatient of the obligation imposed upon me by the kindness of some well-meaning, but mistaken friends, who will most amiably persist in making my book-store the depository of all sorts of unsuitable volumes. Oh, if they would but send me the value of these *in money*, so that I could purchase books that would bless my poor friends, how much more grateful should I be! But they cannot quite see the matter as I do, they think *any* good book will serve a minister's turn; honey can surely be extracted by these bees, even from the dried leaves of a sapless old volume of ancient memoirs! So they send me parcels of books that might be useful for any purpose but mine, and at this moment the shelves of my book-room are crowded with gratifying but very inconvenient proofs of interest in my dear work. As this is not the first time I have indulged in a growl over such gifts, will intending donors lovingly take the oft-repeated *gentle hint*, and spare me further occasion of displaying a much-regretted discontent with their kindly-meant presents?

* * * *

In justice, however, to other friends who do the Fund good service by judicious contributions, and are therefore not included in the above criticism, I must say how thankfully I receive the gifts which are selected with reference to my known needs, and how pleased I am when a "Matthew Henry" makes his appearance at "Westwood," or a party of old Puritans come on a passing visit. I have several good and generous friends who are constantly on the lookout for such special books as they know I shall prize, and one gentleman regularly sends me the catalogue of a large bookseller's stock-in-trade, with permission to indicate the theological works I should like to possess. "*Mark them*," is about all he ever says to me; but this means a great deal, and I gladly take him at his word, and set "S. S., her mark," against all the *best and choicest* entries. Nor does he disappoint my faith; for many grand old works are thus consigned to my care, and duly passed into the hands of those who will search in them as for hid treasure. To him, and to all who, preferring to make their gifts in kind rather than in money, thus thoughtfully supply me with *really helpful* works, I give most hearty and unfeigned thanks.

* * * *

April.—As usual, I have copious extracts to give from the loving and grateful letters received from recipients of books. I believe these quotations are always read with very deep interest, and in selecting and arranging them, I feel I am giving glimpses into the very heart of my work; laying open, as it were, the secret springs which nourish its inner life, and make it prosperous and beautiful. Gratitude to God is the sweet fountain which supplies these constant streams of praise; the gifts are received *as from Him*, though my hand places them within reach; the sweet wine comes from the Land of promise, though my fingers press the blessing from the cluster. And if my poor

Pastors justly recognize the Father's love thus conveyed to them through earthly channels, how much more should I praise and thank Him, seeing that I am doubly blest in first receiving and then bestowing? To my Lord I owe the first conception of such a blessed service; from His tender compassion for a sick and suffering one came the choice delight of an occupation which soothed and refreshed my spirit; and as in past hours of pain and sorrow He helped me by teaching me to help others; so now, since He has restored health to me, He makes these ministrations to His servants a source of continual comfort and inexpressible joy. I think no one can read the following letters without rejoicing and blessing God for the happiness which the dear Book Fund work brings to poor ministers—*and to me*, even before it reaches them.

One of "our own men" writes as follows:—

Dear Mrs. Spurgeon,—The parcel of books you sent me has arrived safely. Your prayer that they might "bring gladness and blessing" was speedily answered. Like sunshine in April they came, when I was exceedingly weary in heart and mind, and my dear wife and I smiled through our tears as we saw the extent of your generous gift. Then the Lord heard our praises, as we went before Him with a new song for this renewed mercy. Inspired by these fresh helps to the study of God's Word, and for the ministry of Jesus, I pray that the dew of the Divine Spirit may so rest upon me that many jewels may be won for our King's own crown. And may you, dear Madam, be long spared to cheer the hearts of the Lord's poor labourers as you have cheered mine!

* * * *

The next is from an Irish pastor, warm, loving, enthusiastic, the sort of letter that, coming at breakfast-time, makes of that meal a love-feast, when we eat our meat with gladness and singleness of heart.

With deepest gratitude I acknowledge the safe arrival of your very valuable parcel. On seeing the numerous and handsome volumes, I could scarcely repress the feeling that you were *too kind* to me. Only that gracious Master who called me to His service could provide such a friend as you have proved to be. I think that the most acceptable gratitude I can show will be the constant repetition of my first act on opening the parcel: to fall on my knees and pray that the sweetest, richest, deepest realization of the Divine assurance, "It is more blessed to give than to receive," may be your present happiness and reward. My heart is stirred with emotion by your gift, and filled with gratitude for your practical kindness. Meanwhile, I do not forget for a moment the devout thankfulness due to Him who gives you grace to undertake, and friends to assist, means to accomplish, and supplies to continue, the hallowed toil which brings a blessing to so many souls. Unto His name be the abiding, increasing, and pre-eminent glory.

* * * *

From a clergyman, who is an intense admirer of Mr. Spurgeon and his works, I received the following encouraging testimony :—

Dear Mrs. Spurgeon,—I cannot find words to express my gratitude for the handsome present of books which arrived safely on Saturday. I was busy preparing my sermons, but I was obliged to leave off to look at the volumes which I prize so highly, and to thank God for His goodness to me through you. I was delighted to find the books by George Müller; little did I think when I read about his present in your Report that I should be one of the fortunate recipients. May the Lord bless you for so kindly remembering me!

What a blessing your Book Fund is to those of us who have but scanty stipends to depend upon! I have so many classes and services that I find the volumes of "Sermons" an immense help to me, and as soon as I have selected a text, I turn to the index in "The Treasury" to see if Mr. Spurgeon has preached from it, and generally, to my great delight, I find it; but too often, alas! it is in a volume which I do not possess. I have derived so much benefit to my own soul from these discourses that I earnestly crave for more of them, first, to feed on myself, and then by God's help to feed others. Your new work of sending the "Sermons" to missionaries in foreign lands is a grand one, and I shall be very glad if you will accept a mite for that Fund with my prayers and best wishes—I wish I could spare more . . . but you know my circumstances.

* * * *

Special interest is sometimes attached to the Book Fund grants by the fact of their chance delivery to the recipient on a day already made notable to him by a personal joy. Three or four years ago I mentioned the somewhat singular frequency with which my grants assumed the character of *birthday gifts*, and since that time I have constantly observed a recurrence of this same interesting feature in the work. The following letter will give a good idea of the way in which a parcel is welcomed under such circumstances :—

Dear Mrs. Spurgeon,—Please accept my best thanks for your generous gift, and your earnest prayers on behalf of my unworthy self. You will be glad to know that the Lord directed you to send me this gift on my birthday. A coincidence of this kind may be apparently accidental; but whether this be so or not, it will have for me an ever-abiding sweetness. You have made my twenty-seventh birthday both happy and memorable to me, and I register this gift of yours among the precious mercies of my life. Henceforth, upon so many anniversaries of my natal day as I shall be graciously spared to see, as surely as the light of the morning dawns upon my eyes, the remembrance of your kindness will revive in my heart. The books are just what I wanted, full of life and power. I look forward to sweet seasons of delightful intercourse with them. May you be long spared thus to encourage and aid the young servants of Christ! The consciousness of your earnest and loving sympathy moves my soul to its very depths, and I shall ever be, Yours very gratefully, ———.

* * * *

These letters are like the songs of larks, they are music on wings. Mark how the notes of thankful joy rise upward to the Lord, the Giver of all good things; the heart rests not with the earthly blessings, precious though they be, but soars heavenward to pour forth its gladness in jubilant thanksgiving and rapturous praise.

* * * *

But, apropos of sky-larks' songs, I must tell you, dear reader, what happened the other day, and how beautifully a sweet singer's confidence was rewarded, when fearlessly leaving her earthly treasures in our Father's keeping (Matt. vi. 26), she mounted upward to pay her full debt of daily orisons at "Heaven's Gate." You may find, perhaps, some "linked sweetness" between the little story and our present subject, or even, failing that desired end, may not be displeased with me for introducing the homely incident to your notice.

We were making a tour of the garden and pastures, admiring the beauty of the young year's fresh life—noting with tender interest all the charming details of newly-awakened responsibility in every living thing—marking the sweet, impatient growth of leaves still rumpled and creased from their recent unfoldings, and rejoicing in the whispered promise of golden days to come which trembled on every scented breath of the perfumed air.

Down in the Dale field we came across a skylark's nest,

built in the long grass, a lovely little soft-lined cup of cosiness, with three pretty brown eggs in it. The sweet songstress had flown at the approach of human footsteps, and thus revealed the secret place of her wee home to inquisitive but kindly eyes. We looked with profound admiration on her happy work, and then quietly retraced our steps, having loving sympathy for the poor little fluttering heart which might perchance fear the despoiling of its treasures. A day or two afterwards the visit was repeated; but imagine our consternation when, on opening the gate of the field, we saw that the *cows* had been let into that pasture! How would the great, clumsy, sweet-breath'd creatures treat the little home in the grass? Would it not be crushed and trampled by their unheeding feet? We had placed an upright stick near the nest to show its position, and very doubtfully we made our way across the field, fearing to find ruin and desolation where we had left peace and prosperity.

When we reached the spot, our surprise and delight were great to find the home intact, and the wee birds safely hatched; for *though the cows had munched the grass close down to the ground all round the nest*, not a hoof had touched the little inmates. So, there they were, three cunning mites, with stubby bodies, and big downy heads, cowering close together in instinctive fear of the human presence which overshadowed them. The cows grazed quietly by, and overhead the pretty mother trilled forth her delicious carol in the morning sunshine, pouring out her heart's gratitude and gladness in libations of song! And there, till the little birds were feathered and flown, the cows were every day pastured, yet never a hurt came to the wee nest in the grass! Who watched over the mother in her peril as she sat upon the eggs? Who guarded the nestlings in their hourly danger when the slight protection of her tender body was removed? Who shielded the tiny birds from the tread of the great beasts' feet? Did Daphne know that the nursery on the ground-floor must be cared for and respected? Or did Strawberry's mother-instinct tell her that little living hearts beat as truly in that wool-lined cup as in the sweet hay-crib where her own darling was lying? I cannot tell—

the matter is too deep for me; but the lark knew all about it, and it may be that, could our ears have been opened to understand the language of her hymn of praise, as she rose higher and higher in the calm blue sky, we might have caught, here and there amidst the joyous notes, some such words as these:—

>Not one,
>>Not one of them,
>>>Is forgotten
>>>>In the sight of God.*
>Not one,
>>Not one of them,
>>>Shall fall to the ground
>>>>Without your Father.†
>FEAR YE NOT THEREFORE.
>>Are not ye
>>>Of much more value
>>>>Than they?

Did she not do well thus to sing and trust? Oh, sighing and doubting reader, cast away your fears, and follow her fair example; you shall not only joyfully leave your earthly cares with your heavenly Father, but you shall get nearer to God's throne than you have ever been before!

* * * *

The "Conference-gift" this year was Dr. Hanna's "Life of Our Lord on Earth," a book pre-eminently useful, instructive, and delightful. Originally published in six volumes, the new edition, in a somewhat abridged form, which was chosen for our Pastors, was the last literary effort of this venerable servant of Christ, who cherished an earnest desire that it might be brought within the reach of the largest possible number of readers.

It claims and deserves patient and prayerful study, and I think both will be accorded to it by our dear brethren, who greatly value and delight in the present thus always happily associated with their yearly festival, and "Feast of Tabernacles."

---

* Luke xii. 6. (R.V.)   † Matthew x. 29.

May.—We will now return for a short time to our letters, even at the risk of a little monotony; for they give most delightful evidence of the blessing which the Lord in His tenderness causes to rest upon the Book Fund work, and they indicate in some degree the honour which He bestows on His dear servant's writings.

The next few extracts will be taken exclusively from the communications of clergymen of the Established Church, who are justly reckoned among the kindest and most courteous of my numerous correspondents. When my Book Fund was first established, I did not contemplate the possibility of its being serviceable beyond the circle of the poorer Dissenting Pastors; but the Lord has graciously " enlarged my coasts," and given me the joy of ministering to all sections of the Christian Church. I make poor clergymen as heartily welcome to the Book Fund gifts as "our own men" from the College, and I am often cheered by seeing how universal and keen is the desire to possess my dear husband's works, and to profit by the patient labour he has expended upon them. Again and again have newly-ordained curates told me that, at their examination, the Bishop has recommended the "Sermons" to them, or has said, "Get Mr. Spurgeon's work on the Psalms, there is none like it"; and many a cordial letter comes to "Westwood," from country vicars and rectors, begging that their young curates may participate in the Book Fund benefits. I think my friends will be very pleased to read such kind words as these which follow from five different clergymen.

> Dear Mrs. Spurgeon,—I desire to thank you sincerely for the valuable parcel of books which has just arrived. The least comforting part about it is that there's no more to follow! (This was the fourth grant.) However, I am very grateful for all your kindness, and if ever I should become a well-to-do rector, there is no fund that I know of that I should have more pleasure in helping than your Book Fund. I feel sure that thousands of poor ministers thank our covenant God that He put it in your heart to commence and carry on such a blessed service. It is a work which is more than twice blessed—I would rather say, ten thousand times ten thousand! My book-shelf is not so very slenderly furnished now—thanks to your liberality—but I shall not rest satisfied till Mr. Spurgeon's seventh volume of "The Treasury of David" finds a place there. My wife joins me in love and gratitude to Mr. Spurgeon and yourself.

Dear Madam,—I have this evening received your handsome present of books, and as they lie on the table before me, I can hardly realize that they are indeed *my own*. I thank you most sincerely for this grand and useful addition to my small stock of helpful literature. If God spare me for a long ministry, these books will adorn my library when your revered husband and yourself shall have entered upon your eternal rest, and they will remind me of one whose zeal in the Master's service I pray that I may ever strive to imitate, desiring earnestly to possess like earnestness, power, and love for perishing souls. I shall remember the Book Fund before the Throne of grace.

Dear Mrs. Spurgeon,—The books you have sent will be invaluable to me. I feel that in order to understand God's Word, and to sustain freshness and vigour in preaching, much reading is necessary, especially *such* reading as is contained in your husband's works. I have been a reader of Mr. Spurgeon's "Sermons" for many years, and if my means permitted, I would purchase all that he has published. If it be ever in my power to help on the work of your Book Fund, I shall gladly do so; and I now pray that God's blessing may richly rest upon it.

Dear Madam,—The long-looked-for parcel has this moment arrived, and the first thing that came into my hands on opening it was your kindly-worded letter, which gave me great pleasure. I hasten at once to tender to you my heartfelt thanks and gratitude for a gift of the highest worth and value I have ever received in my life. I trust, with the blessing of God, and the guidance of the Holy Spirit, to be enabled to glean and gather from these books precious truths that will be both helpful to myself and to my people. Now that I am possessed of a "fiddle"* of so good and sweet a tone, my earnest desire will be so to wield the "stick" that I may draw forth many a soul-winning tune. Allow me again to thank you from my heart for all your kindness.

My dear Mrs. Spurgeon,—The interval since I received your costly and unique parcel of books on Saturday has been to me one of the gladdest and happiest seasons of my life. Every spare moment since their arrival I have been digging into the wondrous mines of spiritual wealth which these precious volumes present, and feasting on the rich, soul-refreshing dainties which they provide, and my spirit has truly been quickened and comforted, and made joyous thereby. You could not have sent me a better selection; it is a storehouse to which I shall continually resort. I thank you from the very depths of my heart, and my dear wife joins most sincerely in this expression of gratitude. May your life, and the life of your beloved husband, be long spared for such kindly deeds as these!

* * * *

I have had the pleasure of helping a good brother in the Holy Land who is devoting his life to the service of the

---

* See "John Ploughman's Pictures."

people there, and amid great hardships is following the apostolic plan of making known the gospel by going everywhere preaching the Word. He has been through Palestine on foot, almost "from Dan to Beersheba," and, knowing something of Arabic, he is able to speak to the people "all the words of this life."

He tells mournful stories of the very slow progress made by missions in the country, and says he has long felt it to be a disgrace to Christians that these benighted people should be left to perish, no man caring for their souls. "Little as I and my wife can do," he writes, "we are at least disposed to try what simple Christian life and talk, and reading of the Scriptures, and (as far as may be possible) St. James's idea of 'pure and undefiled religion,' can by the blessing of God effect in this land."

Two months were spent among the "Lebanon savages," and then a journey on foot, and alone, through the country which once was "Thy land, O Emmanuel!" revealed so sad a state of things among the depraved and neglected inhabitants, that an intense desire was aroused in our friend's soul to carry the lamp of life into this gross darkness. The determination was soon taken, the consecration quickly made, and then, to render himself proficient in the difficult language which must be mastered, the first thing needed was an expensive lexicon and grammar. How were these to be obtained? Our friend is poor—as this world reckons riches—and it seemed as if the books were quite beyond his reach; but, one day writing home to England, he mentioned his need to a friend, a clergyman, and begged him to devise some method of supplying the indispensable treasure. There was the Lord's loving guidance in this; for the clergyman, who was himself unable to give such costly works, yet knew of my Book Fund, and at once wrote to me, hoping that the precious gift might be within my power and province. I had to overstep my rules a little; but the request, the special need which prompted it, and the singularity of its presentation, were sufficient excuse for the brief departure from ordinary regulations. I procured the books, and the good clergyman forwarded them, and thus, between us, we made the poor man very happy. "What a beautiful

Evangelical Alliance!" said he, when he received them—*"a Baptist minister's wife sending books to a Wesleyan preacher, through the intervention of a Church clergyman!"*

Since then I have regularly forwarded the weekly "Sermons" to this devoted man, and I know they bring great joy and comfort and blessing to his heart. Will my dear friends, as they read this paragraph, ask the Lord to help and strengthen the lonely worker in that desolate land—a land so cursed by the sin of its people that it is no longer holy ground and "delightsome" in God's sight, but it "perisheth, and is burned up like a wilderness, that none passeth through"?

* * * *

June.—From the breezy heights of Beulah Hill we command a lovely and uninterrupted view, not of the fair earth merely, but of the fairer firmament above it; our windows are observatories whence many a longing, loving glance is cast heavenwards, and one of the chief pleasures of restful or contemplative hours is found in silently watching the ever-changing aspect of the sky, and noting the manifold glories of that wonderful cloud-land which divides our earthly home from the promised inheritance on high. I never tire of gazing on the beautiful mysteries of the clouds. I love to watch the grand and solemn rolling of black and rugged masses, when storms are abroad, and the wind is marshalling them to a dread convention of brooding tempests; and equally well I love to see them when, in summer days, the cloudlets float like flakes of driven snow across the deep blue ether, and lose themselves at the feet of mountains that rival the Alpine peaks in beauty and sublimity. Sometimes the watcher will see a cloud of such celestial beauty that to his enamoured fancy it looks

"As though an angel, in his upward flight,
Had left his mantle floating in mid-air."

Or anon, with pensive pleasure, he may mark

" Clouds on the western side
Grow grey and greyer, hiding the warm sun."

But under all aspects they are enchanting and suggestive; their very movements are restful to my spirit, they always speak to me of the Lord's great power and love, and many a time have burdens of care been lifted from my heart, and carried away, by these celestial chariots, " as far as the east is from the west."

* * * *

This is rather a lengthy preface to the relation of an incident which was remarkable for its brevity ; but I have been betrayed into such rambling by the fascination of the subject, and the fact that it was whilst engaged in my favourite recreation that the following pleasant portent presented itself to my admiring eyes.

We were standing at the window, my dear husband and I, noting the splendid effects of the sunset upon a bank of fleecy clouds which skirted the horizon, when all at once we noticed an unusual object in the sky, and perceived that a winged creature of uncommon size was sailing slowly and wearily towards us from the south-west. As it drew nearer, we could see that it was a large *sea-bird* of some kind, and with the greatest possible interest we watched the stranger's flight, till, in passing over our house, he was hidden from view. The sight stirred my heart strangely. "That must be our darling's harbinger," I said, "bringing us a message from our home-coming boy." "Your 'Sea-gull' will be with you soon," its brief presence seemed to say ; "the waves are bearing him swiftly home, and the God who guided me here will bring him safely to your embrace." Surely it was a happy omen ; it comforted me to think that the Hand that

"Wings an angel, guides a sparrow,"

had directed this sea-bird's course, and bidden the beat of his heavy pinions speak a language of love to my longing heart. But, please God, my "Sea-gull," when he comes, will not pass away as quickly as did this herald from the ocean. He will fold his white wings for a little while, and nestle by his mother's side, and gladden her life with his sweet presence, and bless and be blessed in his own dear home.

Blow softly, O propitious gales,—and ye rolling billows,

bear securely on your mighty shoulders the good ship which carries this beloved son across the world of waters. Let there be no " sorrow on the sea " to this dear voyager, O Lord ; but do Thou give the winds and waves a charge concerning him, to bring him safely to his desired haven ; and may every ocean breeze waft the sweet message to Westwood, " I am coming—I am coming home ! "

* * * *

A letter to my dear husband to-day, enclosing 10s. for the Book Fund, contained also such sweet encouragement for me, that I feel my soul must make her boast in the Lord about it ; for I am sure He sent it as a cordial to revive my drooping spirits, and therefore " the humble shall hear thereof, and be glad." He knows what hard work I find it to write these Annual Reports, and so He often sends me cheering, and help, and comfort, as I labour—paying me extra wages, as it were, because the work is difficult ; sending me double portions of meat from His table because I am weak. How blessed it is to serve Him ! Oh that heart and hands and life might be more consecrated to that service ! The writer of the letter in question is an aged disciple, who has known and loved the Lord for many years, yet to him my little books have been made the channels of blessing, and I could clap my hands for joy, while I marvel at the wondrous grace which chooses to work by such insignificant means. The good old man tells his Pastor that while lying on a bed of sickness last year, he used to read my little " Diary for 1882"; and he says, " Her trust in the Lord for success in her labour of love was the means of reviving my faith, and helping me to put more confidence in my blessed Lord, whether for life or death. I love the motto she has chosen for this year : ' O magnify the Lord with me, and let us exalt His name together,' and I think that this last Report is the best of all, if that can be. These 'Lectures to *her* Students' are read with much profit, as well as pleasure. May the Lord long spare you both for the comfort of His chosen, the extension of His kingdom, and the advancement of His glory ! " This sweet morsel gave me strength and solace for many days.

Let me try to describe for you a scene in a minister's study on a certain Saturday evening; it is a picture on paper, but it was a fact in real life, and it will serve to show you how the Lord uses the Book Fund parcels to carry comfort and strengthening grace to His tried and troubled servants :—

The room is small, and very poorly furnished, a tiny fire burns in the grate, for it is mid-winter; but, beyond this, there is an absence of all the suitable surroundings of a minister's study, and you can count the *books* upon your fingers. The pastor sits there with bowed head, and weary body, after a day of heavy work, and, shall I tell it? of very scanty sustenance. A deep sense of responsibility is upon him, and he feels the weight of souls on his heart; but, in addition to this, special cares, just now, press upon him heavily: troubles of church and building matters, questions as to ways and means, fightings without, and fears within, which vex and grieve him sorely. He tries to cast his burden upon the Lord, and put the cares in the background; for he has to seek and plead for a text for to-morrow morning's service: but the troubles seem to roll in upon him like the waves of the sea; and though, one after another, precious promises and glorious truths present themselves as he turns the sacred pages, he can fix on no text which brings him deliverance, or comes to his heart with the power of the Spirit, as *the word* which shall first satisfy his own soul, and then refresh and bless his people.

Weary and faint—*he is very, very poor*—and almost overwhelmed by the difficulties of the way, he turns to the fire with his open Bible on his knee, and sighs. Oh! such a sigh! Will the angels hear it, I wonder, and come and minister to him, as they used to do to their sorrowful Lord? Perhaps so; but his heavenly Father has also prepared an earthly solace, and the answer to his cry is even now at the door. The bell rings, and a large parcel is left "For the Pastor," and is taken at once to his room. In a moment he feels that relief has come; he knows the superscription, and divines the contents; in his joy he almost caresses the package; then, with trembling fingers, he cuts the string, and spreads the treasures out before the Lord. Yes, literally "before the Lord;" for now you see him kneeling by the side of the open parcel, thanking and blessing God for such opportune mercy, for such streams in the desert, such blossoming roses in the wilderness. While prayer and praise mingle on his lips, his hand rests upon a small book of Mr. Geo. Müller's; this he takes up and opens, and the first words which meet his eye, standing out in bold relief, shining as it were with heaven's own light, are these:—

"OPEN THY MOUTH WIDE, AND I WILL FILL IT."

This is what he needs, this is God's message, this is "the word with power," and the command is obeyed, and the promise is fulfilled, in that first rapturous moment of enlightenment. He has broken down completely now, the tears are running down his cheeks, but they are rills from the fountains of joy, not of sorrow, and will refresh and heal his spirit. The Lord Himself has spoken to him, an angel has strengthened him, and after a season of adoring communion, he rises from his knêes, strong to labour or to suffer, as his gracious Master wills. That Saturday night will never be forgotten by him, so well-timed was the mercy to relieve his misery, so precious was the light which shone in upon his darkness.

If we could have gone with him to the house of God on the Sabbath morning following, we should have seen that the blessing so graciously given was resting on him still; nay, more, that it was so abundant in the plenitude of its life-giving power, that it overflowed from his heart into the souls of his people; for saints and sinners alike wept, some over sin, some over recovered joy, and both over the goodness and grace of God in the face of Jesus Christ. God's message to one heart repeated itself to many, and there was rejoicing in heaven and earth that day!

* * * *

July.—Thursday evening, July 10.—About 10 p.m. my darling son was in my arms, and the sweet and long-anticipated joy of seeing his dear face, and hearing his loving words, and rejoicing in his welcome presence, was granted to his waiting and expectant parents; and I really think that the pain of five years' absence was almost annihilated by the pleasure of the first fond kiss! "Mother's Sea-gull" has returned again, the Lord has brought home His banished, and while our mouths are filled with laughter, and our tongues with singing, every word we speak seems tender with gratitude, every blissful moment of reunion bears up to God a tribute of thanksgiving for so great and choice a mercy.

My "Diary" may not record all the details of this rapturous meeting, for a Book Fund Report should not be *altogether* an autobiography; but it cannot be quite silent on the subject which has brought me such exceeding gladness, nor can it refuse to score some notes of praise, while the joy-bells are ringing so merrily in my heart. Sixteen thousand miles to come home to see father and mother! Weary work these long journeys are, and "Sea-gull's" wings grow very tired; but goodness and mercy have followed him all the way, and the love, and light, and welcome of HOME more than make up for it all.

Many prayers were ascending to heaven from both sides of the world, that a safe and prosperous voyage might be vouchsafed to the beloved traveller; and I think my friends will be interested to hear of one special instance in which these petitions were answered in a very remarkable manner.

At my request he will himself tell the story of his singular adventure, and thus enrich "Mother's Book" with a precious testimony to the power and prevalence of prayer.

"It was a happy circumstance that the good ship 'Iberia' arrived at Adelaide on a Lord's-day morning, and remained till noon of Monday. I was thus enabled to spend some four-and-twenty hours ashore, in company with valued friends whom I had not seen for nearly six years. The Pastors of the several churches, being occupied with their forenoon services, had sent representatives to welcome me to South Australian shores, each in the hope that his evening meeting might be attended and conducted by the new arrival. The delegate of the one who had telegraphed his petition to Tasmania and Melbourne was the successful applicant. He who came first had to be first served. I cannot refrain from recording the glad fact that the hurriedly-arranged service was full of blessing; for quite a number had occasion to praise God that the word by the way was the means of their conversion. I could not regret a delay which gave me another opportunity of proclaiming the saving truth; and though delays are proverbially dangerous, this one certainly did not prove so to the precious souls that were born for heaven. Mine was but a flying visit; yet the good seed was dropped into hearts already prepared for its reception. Who can hesitate to sow beside all waters after such tokens for good?

"On the following morning it was my pleasure to breakfast in company with several ministers of the city and suburbs, and to converse and worship with them. Having left all details concerning time and train in the hands of mine host, I succeeded in catching, though very narrowly, the eleven o'clock train for the Semaphore, off which place the homeward-bound steamer was anchored, awaiting mails and passengers. It should be known that, at a certain junction, the railway branches for Largs Bay, where, as at the Semaphore, a long pier juts out into the shallow sea. These jetties, though two miles apart, are about equidistant from the moorings of the Orient steamers, the difficulty being to know for certain from which the start should be made, and at which boats can be obtained. At the aforesaid junction we alighted, by order of our *cicerone*, and crossed the platform to a train bound for Largs Bay. It soon after appeared that this step was fatal; for the guard informed us that he was not leaving for half-an-hour. Then it dawned on us that the carriage we had just vacated would soon reach the Semaphore, from whose pier, undoubtedly, the last steam-launch for the 'Iberia' would leave when the train arrived. Poor I was left in the lurch, with the faintest possible hope of securing my expected and paid-for passage. It having been decided that we must walk to Largs Bay, the whole party tramped along the rails, and arrived at the pier-head about ten minutes to noon—hot, dusty, and anxious. But what flickering flame of hope remained was quite extinguished when we discovered that *there was not a boat to be had.*

"A signal-staff and code were useless for want of a signal-man, and the telephone by which we hoped to communicate with the Semaphore was within a barred and bolted door. Looking towards the other pier, we saw a little launch steam off, and out came handkerchiefs and newspaper-signals of real distress; but on she steamed, heedless of our signs and shouts. It was useless to trudge off to the distant jetty; for all the boats were now alongside the big ship, waiting to bring the friends of passengers away. In this dilemma, one of the party—our conductor, indeed—volunteered to hasten to the Semaphore, to signal, if possible, to the departing steamer.

"Anxiously we traced him hurrying along the sandy shore, and saw him stop a horseman, to whom, as we supposed, he confided the story of our distress, that he might hasten it to the signal-station. Meanwhile, we could plainly see that the anchor was being weighed, and soon the white wave at the vessel's stern showed that she was off and away. Oh the misery of those moments! I had been praying earnestly, but feared at last that my desires were not to be fulfilled. The launches were now returning, one steering for the Semaphore, the other for Largs Bay. On the latter were some of my friends, who had kindly brought all my luggage with them. I was not to be dissuaded, however, from making yet another attempt to reach the ship. The master of the little boat offered to try, though it was not a bit of use, as he imagined; but he did not know that we had sent to the signal-station, and that we had been praying that the mission might succeed. Off we steamed on the apparently hopeless chase.

"Clearing the jetty, I noticed a most remarkable combination of flags fluttering from the Semaphore, which I could read (the code being written in my heart) to mean—'For every sake, stop! A son of the best parents in all the world wants to get home to them, and cannot wait an extra fortnight!'

"On we steamed! Another puffing launch hurried after us from the other landing-place, and overtook us. Our messenger was on board, so we transhipped, without stopping, into the swifter boat, and proceeded 'full speed ahead!'

"A man in the bows waved a great flag as a signal of distress; but alas! alas! the 'Iberia' grew small by degrees, and tantalizingly less. The chances (?) were against us, certainly; but we kept bravely on, though the skipper persisted in giving us such cheering intelligence as that, shortly before, an Orient liner refused to wait for fifteen passengers. He reminded us that it was a mail steamer we were chasing, and gave it as his decided opinion that '*it wouldn't stop for the Governor.*'

"But as GOD would have it, after about three quarters of an hour's steaming, I was able to shout out, 'She's heading round!' Her stern soon gave place to her bows, and the monster bore down upon us. 'You're saved! you're saved!' said one of my ministerial companions, and our grateful hearts were very glad, *how* glad cannot be told by pen and ink. My friends were pleased enough to get rid of me (under such circumstances), and right heartily did I shake hands with them just before getting alongside.

"Arrived on board, I found myself the hero of the hour. No one grudged the brief delay. Who could help rejoicing that perseverance had been rewarded? But I was a wonder unto many. What on earth (or on ocean) could have induced a vessel of 4,000 tons, carrying Her Majesty's mails, to put about for an insignificant-looking mortal of only 'nine stone weight'? Nothing, either on land or sea, accounted for the marvel, and only some of us knew that the Lord had put His hand on the steering-gear of the skipper's heart, and made him give the order 'Hard-a-port!' Humanly speaking, it was the signal that did the work. The fourth officer happened to notice it, though not supposed to be on the look-out for signals when quitting port. He kindly reported the fact to the captain, who, for the reason stated above, broke through rules and regulations to pick up the unpunctual passenger. Having climbed the bridge in spite of the warning to trespassers, and grasped the captain's hand in gratitude, I could only praise God from whom all blessings flow, and continue the voyage to 'Home, sweet Home' with a glad heart, assured, by such a Providence at the start, of safe conduct and a happy advent.

"So may it be with my fellow-voyagers on this sea of life. May their extremity prove God's opportunity; then the recollection of their difficulties will only help them abundantly to utter the memory of His great goodness! May it be ours to anchor at last in the desired haven!

> 'And when the shore is gained at last,
> Who will count the billows past?'"

* * * *

What a tender Providence does the above little story proclaim! Yet it is only one link in the chain of wreathenwork of mercies which has bound my darling a happy captive in his Father's loving care. "*The Lord had put His hand on the steering-gear of the skipper's heart.*" There's the key-note of the song, therein lies the sweet rhythm of the simple melody. Yes! Blessed be His name—

"𝕿𝖍𝖊 𝕷𝖔𝖗𝖉 𝖎𝖘 𝖓𝖎𝖌𝖍 𝖚𝖓𝖙𝖔 𝖆𝖑𝖑 𝖙𝖍𝖊𝖒 𝖙𝖍𝖆𝖙 𝖈𝖆𝖑𝖑 𝖚𝖕𝖔𝖓 𝕳𝖎𝖒."
"𝕿𝖍𝖊 𝕷𝖔𝖗𝖉 𝖕𝖗𝖊𝖘𝖊𝖗𝖛𝖊𝖙𝖍 𝖆𝖑𝖑 𝖙𝖍𝖊𝖒 𝖙𝖍𝖆𝖙 𝖑𝖔𝖛𝖊 𝕳𝖎𝖒."

I pray that this little record may strengthen our faith in prayer, in Providence, and in perseverance.

* * * *

There does not seem to be space in this month's pages for anything but the joy of this merciful home-coming. So much am I in love with "Son Tom," that, like David Copperfield, to whose enraptured senses "the sun shone Dora, and the birds sang Dora, the south wind blew Dora, and the wild flowers in the hedges were all Dora's to a bud"; the charm of this long-absent son's presence sheds a new and special brightness over life and its many blessings.

But Book Fund service is not neglected—is not even slackened. Poor Pastors shall not go sorrowing and bookless because a great gladness has come to our home and hearts. All the work goes on as usual; the routine of receiving and answering letters, the consideration of applications, the selection of books, the entries in ledgers and day-books. The only thing that can suffer loss is this Report; it may be that the *record* of my work will flag a little during the next few months; I may be brief in my notings through the very pressure of happiness; I may be so busy with my darling as to leave scant time for my "Diary"; and if this should happen, I must pray my friends to pardon me, and of their clemency so read "between the lines" as to make them fuller and more complete.

* * * *

August.—The dear friends in different parts of England, whose hearts have been stirred by the Book Fund Reports, to help the families of poor ministers, by personal or combined effort, are all finding that the work grows in their affections, and that difficulties and discouragements melt quickly away beneath the warmth of their tender and loving interest. They like to report progress to me, and I am charmed to hear of their industry and enthusiasm, blessing God that by their efforts many more of His needy ones than my hands can reach are helped, and comforted, and strengthened. "We sent off yesterday," writes a lady, "over one hundred articles of clothing to different families of poor ministers; and as we definitely prayed for guidance as to where they should be sent, we know they have gone to the right people, and will be a relief to the poor overburdened mothers. It is indeed sweet work, and brings its own reward. Thank you very much for all your loving sympathy with us. I do not think we should have ventured on the undertaking had you not so lovingly encouraged us to make a beginning."

The *need* of this kindness, on the part of Christian ladies, towards our poor country Pastors, is by no means lessened since I wrote last year; cases of extreme poverty are continually coming before me, and the Pastors' Aid Fund claims all the supplementary assistance that warm hearts and skilful fingers can devise.

* * * *

It has been one of my long-cherished desires, that those poor ministers who are judged needy enough to receive loving help, either from individuals or a society, should have that aid, not once merely, but periodically, as long as any deep poverty existed. Spasmodic effort on their behalf is better than total inaction, but it is not satisfactory or dependable, and is unworthy of those who really long to help the servant for the Master's sake. I would fain persuade a church, or a friend, or a family, to undertake one or two cases entirely, making themselves responsible for the poor pastor's comfort and well-being, constituting themselves his special benefactors and guardians, receiving the sacred charge from the Lord Himself, and expecting as reward to hear from His own gracious lips that sweetest sentence of approval, "Inasmuch as ye have done it unto one of the least of these My brethren, ye have done it unto Me." What a lifted burden it would be, were a score or so of the very neediest Pastors thus placed beyond the reach of Poverty's painful grip! A letter now lies before me, which, in a very few words, tells a tale of hardship and heroism not at all uncommon among our Pastors. The writer says: "I am not in a position to purchase books; my salary *reaches almost to a third* of £150, but our Master is good, and always makes things go right. We are out of debt, only we are mighty debtors to God, and ever shall be." To help this good man and his family once would be a kindness, certainly; but to *keep on* helping him, so as to assure him of something supplementary to that pitiful £50 per annum, would be more like the lovingkindness of our Great Exemplar. My Pastors' Aid Fund gives money in dire necessity and trying times of pressing want; but it is for the common wear and tear of everyday life in the poor minister's family that I beseech consideration and helpful sympathy. Sometimes a nice parcel of clothing is sent by kind-hearted folks to a poor pastor's house; there are suitable garments for father and mother, shoes and socks, and all sorts of indispensables for the children, and the reception of such a blessing marks a red-letter day in the household, and sets free a long pent-up flood of grateful thanksgiving: but the good donors are too apt to forget that all these things have an ugly habit of *wearing out*, especially under the pressure of the incessant service which is demanded of them by their needy possessors. The Lord does not in these days see fit to repeat the miracle of wilderness-life, when His people's clothes "waxed not old upon them, neither did their shoes wax old upon their feet." It is our business now to be miracle-workers *for Him ;* to replenish the scanty store, and supply the modest requirements of His servants, with a loving and considerate hand, *until they reach the rest which remaineth.*

"But to have only £50 a year must be exceptional poverty, even for a poor minister," says a reader. Well, I admit that the salaries of my poor friends generally reach to about £70 or £80 per annum; but I know a good many who receive only the smaller amount, and my wonder is how they live, and preach, and work upon such inadequate provision. My heart often aches for them when I hear of their patience, endurance of hardship, and privation; yet I notice that they are happy in their poverty, and content to be only "rich towards God" if He will have it so. "My stipend is £50, with use of house," writes one of these followers of Him, "who, though he was rich, yet for our sake became poor," "and I am married; but neither my dear wife nor I complain—far from it: to His praise be it spoken, that more happiness and blessing have been ours since we gave up all for Christ, than ever before. We are where the Master would have us be, and both of us are rejoicing in the work. God is blessing His cause here; so we find *His smile and low fare* agree admirably."

I have so often and so urgently pleaded the cause of poor ministers, that I am perplexed as to what fresh arguments should be brought forward, what new and potent advocacy should be used on their behalf. All the old pleas still hold good: their position as servants of the King of kings; their calling, as shepherds of His flock; their special need in such special work; their entire and scriptural dependence on the ministry; and the unmistakable will of God concerning their abundant maintenance while engaged in His service. All these substantial reasons for tender regard to their welfare are in as full force as ever, and their own brave endurance of privation and pain for Christ's sake, and His church's sake, should surely be an additional impulse to our kindly sympathy.

Somebody said to me once in a letter—"Three empty things often keep company: an empty bookshelf, an empty head, and an empty chapel; while as a consequence there follow—empty pockets, and empty cupboards, of poor ministers, who lack and suffer need." Now this is very true, but the statement is upside down, it wants reversing; for I could tell of scores of instances in which the empty pocket and the empty cupboard were actually responsible for the three former "empties," the *cause*, as well as the consequence, of inefficiency and feebleness. It is usually a lack of liberal ministration *from the people to the pastor* which results in the famishing of the whole community. "Put the whip in the manger," says John Ploughman. The homely proverb covers a wholesome truth. Keep your minister's table well provided, and you shall be fed with the finest of the wheat; see that his earthly cares do not press on him painfully, and your own hearts' burdens will be lifted by his heavenly teachings; supply him with this world's needful comforts, and he will not fail to bring you solace and consolation in the time of your extremity. If he has sown unto you spiritual things, is it a great thing if he shall reap your carnal things?

* * * *

Sometimes, however, the churches are so poor that the members are absolutely unable to give more than the scantiest pittance to him who is over them in the Lord. How can they spare money for his maintenance when every penny they can earn is needed for the common necessities of their own households? A church composed mainly of farm-labourers, miners, colliers, fishermen, or mill-hands— and God be thanked that such churches do exist—cannot, even by united effort, so care for their minister as to place him in a position of ease and comfort. They need help from outside, and this might be forthcoming if each large church would undertake the care of, at least, one small one; or if more of those who possess abundantly this world's goods would take to heart the poverty of these poor servants of the Lord, and by judicious aid relieve them of some of these crushing burdens; or if you, dear reader, whoever you may be, whose eyes now read these words, and whose heart, perchance, is touched by the sorrows of these men of God, if YOU will do all you can to help one such poor minister before the close of another year.

Here are some sentences, from the pen of an aged pastor, which bear a sadly seasonable testimony to the truth of the painful facts I have tried to bring before my dear friends. He says (the words read as if they had been wrung from a very sore heart): "I have served three churches, one of which I was instrumental in raising from the verge of extinction to strength and influence; the second was brought into existence by my own efforts; the third was certainly strengthened in every way. I have had much affliction and many trials during the forty years of my ministerial life; have brought up six children; and my salary *never reached £100 per annum;* indeed, has often been very much less. Mine is no solitary case; hundreds of Baptist ministers, of unblemished reputation and devoted zeal, could tell a similar tale."

What think you, my readers? Can the Lord feel anything but displeasure at such a state of things?

These men are His ambassadors, and He looks that they shall be treated with the respect and honour due to their position and credentials. When they send back reports to their King (and they cry day and night to Him in their grief and pain), when they tell Him of the manner of the country, and the ungenerous policy of its inhabitants, do you not think His righteous anger must be stirred against such a people? Should you wonder if He avenged His own elect, and that speedily?

* * * *

October 2.—In my contribution-list for September there stands the simple announcement, "Sale of coins, £1 2s. 6d." The few words and figures are commonplace enough, but they conceal a depth of loving meaning beneath their homely phraseology. This year, as at other seasons, I have been privileged to receive many love-tokens for the Master from tender souls, whose pity for His servants' needs, and whole-hearted consecration of themselves to Him, constrained them to lay their "hidden treasure" at His dear feet.

In the hope that others may be induced to follow so good an example, under the influence of a like spirit of unselfish love to Christ and His cause, I transcribe the inscriptions which accompanied the gifts:—

Coins given to me by my dear parents. I have had and treasured them as long as I can remember; now I give them to the good work, praying that they may take the Word of life to some hungry soul.

Coins found in a dear one's pocket after death. May the Lord bless the mite, and cause it to do some good to a living, longing heart! Sweet memories are awakened by these silver pieces, but they will be sweeter still when given to Jesus.

In remembrance of a dear child now at rest.

The enclosed coin has long been treasured in memory of an aged friend, but is now gladly offered up for use in the Master's service. Will Mrs. Spurgeon accept it as a tiny offering to her Book Fund, with the best wishes of the sender, and the prayer that it may carry a blessing to some waiting one? The idea of sending this was suggested by reading page 19 of "The Book Fund Diary for 1883," and the writer adds her testimony to those there recorded, that it is far better thus to consecrate our treasures, than to hide them selfishly away.

I have enclosed a few treasured trifles, and have been weak enough to shed tears over them in memory of past days. They have been very dear to me, so I trust they may do some good in the Lord's work. If I only gave Him what I did not want or care for, I could not ask Him to bless and accept the gift; but these have all been tokens of love to me, and so I give them back to Him with a loving, thankful heart

Those who can "read between the lines" will find something worthy of perusal in the above paragraphs. I think it is beautiful to see these small alabaster boxes broken at the feet of Jesus, and I have no manner of doubt but that the sweet odour of such loving deeds still "fills the house" where He is, and comes up before Him with acceptance. But how little, after all—even when we have brought a choice thing—have we done for Him who *died* for us! Oh for more love and less selfishness! Shall we not think now what we can give Him, what we can do for Him, what we can consecrate to Him?

This month I have somewhat more to say concerning the distribution of single "Sermons," which has become part and parcel of Book Fund work. So mighty a power for good is found in this simple and unobtrusive agency, that applications for grants are constantly on the increase. Pastors ask for two or three hundred copies of the weekly penny "Sermon," that they may give or loan them in the villages, country towns, and cities; for they find that a well-organized scheme of house-to-house distribution of these discourses proves a great blessing to a church and people, in bringing forth the hidden ones, and in reviving spiritual life in all. The Lord gives them entrance into the hearts, as well as into the hands of the people; they are read with eagerness by persons who would not look at a "tract"; they find their way into places where a so-called "pious book" would not be tolerated.

"Spurgeon's 'Sermon,'" say the rough men, "ay, let's see what he has got to say; we've heard tell of him these many years"; "Spurgeon's 'Sermon,'" answer the poor weary women, "yes, you may leave *that*, may be I'll look at it when I've time"; and when the "Floral Leaflets"* are in the distributor's hands, the little children crowd around and beg for the pretty bright pictures of birds, and leaves, and flowers, which cover the wonderful words of life within. Like the dear Master, whose messengers they are, it may be said of them that the common people hear them gladly, and many a hard and unassailable heart has received its first blessed wounding from the silent speech of the printed word, which the Holy Spirit makes quick, and powerful, and sharper than a two-edged sword.

All over England, Pastors write to me for more help in this direction, and speak most encouragingly of the results which have followed previous gifts; and I have had the joy of sending many hundreds of these soul-winners into the north and west of benighted Ireland. From Connaught there came a fervent appeal for a gift, and with many prayers I consigned a large package to the care of a

---

* "Welcome to Jesus," 32 Floral Tracts, by C. H. Spurgeon. Price 6d. Drummond's Tract Depôt, Stirling, N.B.

missionary who constantly travels into remote parishes where ignorance, superstition, and consequent darkness reign supreme. The "Sermons" are an immense boon," he writes; "there is so much food and real nourishment in them that none can read without being profited; I shall gladly make the use of them which you suggest, viz., to read them first, and then lend or give them. Such literature is much needed, for a great many neglected Protestants in these districts *never see anything of the kind*, and appear to be destitute of all religious and spiritual life."

Think, dear reader, of the possibilities of blessing which these "Sermons" have carried into such a region, and let a cry go up from your heart to God,—"Lord turn many souls from darkness to light by the reading of the precious words which we have helped to send to poor Ireland."

* * * *

A country pastor writes:—

I am very, very grateful to you for the parcel of Mr. Spurgeon's "Sermons," which has reached me safely. The grant will help me in carrying on my work of tract-distribution; and nothing could be more suitable for this purpose than your husband's "Sermons;" for we pray that they may counteract the ceremonialism which is being taught and preached in the parish-church here. I can promise you they shall be well applied.

Never, till we enter the home above, shall we know all that God hath wrought by these circulated "Sermons;" but almost daily so much blessed testimony to their value is received, that we are stimulated and encouraged to extend the work as far as possible. It is a "sowing beside all waters" which the Lord is sure to bless; the seed is precious, it is scattered broadcast in His name, and He will most certainly give the longed-for increase.

* * * *

There has been a sad falling off, during the last few months, of *special* gifts for "Sermon Distribution in Foreign Lands." This has greatly surprised and disappointed me, for I thought and hoped that the work would take fast hold of the affections of God's people, seeing that it promised to carry light, and life, and love to those who are labouring in dark lands, among dead souls, with very little communion to cheer and comfort them. I expected that this new phase of my work would have had for *all* my friends the charm and beauty which one dear lady finds in it : "You and your Book Fund," she says, " are on my heart day and night, *especially* the new branch for the dear foreign missionaries. I pray over the precious seed to be thus sown in all lands ! What sweet and blessed surprises you will have by-and-by; and not you only, but also the good friends who send means to carry on the wondrous work ! "

I should have rejoiced heartily in a generous and continued appreciation of this delightful scheme ; but happily the failure of special donations does not affect its prosperity ; for when I undertook the service, I fully incorporated it with the Book Fund, and till death do them part they are one and indivisible. The foreign " Sermons " go out regularly every month, and the parcels of the Book Fund are despatched every fortnight; not once during the past year has this arrangement been disturbed. It may be quite possible that dear friends have intended a portion of their gifts to be devoted to this purpose without saying so; for I have had most liberal help from them, and have been constantly supplied with abundant funds for all my little plans; and if this be so, I can only very gratefully thank them, and confess that "actions speak louder than words."

The Lord has given proof upon proof that the work is a comfort and refreshment to His exiled servants. If my readers could see the quantities of letters which have come from all parts of the world since I reported progress in February, and could read all the glad and grateful words therein contained, they would have no doubt about the importance and blessedness of this labour of love. Here is the witness of a worker for Christ far away in China. Can any one read it without rejoicing that he, and such as he, should have this crumb of comfort as regularly as the months come round. He says :—

> I wish I could tell you how our souls are refreshed, as, wearied in body and mind, my wife and I sit down at the close of the day, and I read one of the "Sermons" you send us. It seems to cheer us so! We

have no opportunity of hearing the Word preached in our own tongue; but the perusal of one of Mr. Spurgeon's "Sermons" *more than makes up for the loss of other privileges.* Of late there has been, to my mind, a greater richness and fulness in them than ever before; in former years I have been much helped and refreshed by them; but lately I find considerably increased power and blessing. When I am enjoying them, I long to reproduce them *verbatim* to the Chinese Christians here, with the same power with which they speak to my own soul, and very often I read them several times that I may catch their spirit, and copy their fervour. In this heathen land we sorely need something to strengthen and stimulate our weary souls; and next to God's own Word, Mr. Spurgeon's "Sermons" are the most helpful and precious.

There! if I had only received that single letter from abroad, and heard that one song of joy from a gladdened soul, I should feel inclined to believe that the Lord had given me sufficient warrant for continuing the work; but since He adds testimony to testimony, and sets so many seals to this loving little ministry, my hands and heart are strengthened in it, and I shall joyfully carry it on to the praise of His dear name, and the comfort of His banished ones.

* * * *

November.—The dear invalid friend, whose quiet service of love in the distribution of "Sermons" to lighthouse-keepers was mentioned in last year's "Diary," still labours on with increasing delight and success. Referring to my comparatively new work in sending the "Sermons" abroad, he says:—"I feel sure that your last 'Branch Business' has before it a fine field of great usefulness. To many a lonely and dispirited toiler in foreign lands the 'Sermons' will be as refreshing as was the angel's visit to Elijah in the desert. A writer in the February number of *The Congregational Magazine* refers to 'a man with a face as full of Christ as Spurgeon's 'Sermons'! Surely sermons with such a character deserve to be scattered the wide world over"!

I think so too, and it has given me great joy to make another grant of a thousand copies to this good brother, who is "the Lord's prisoner," and cherishes and rejoices over his little service as fondly and faithfully as the Count in the dear old story tended the pretty flower "Picciola," which sprang up between the stones in the court-yard of his prison-house, and brought innumerable blessings to the captive. "May I tell you," writes my friend, "what first led me to think of the lighthouse-keepers? It really originated in the Tabernacle, the birth-place of so many good works. Rallying from a dangerous illness, but with the prospect of being an invalid for life, I was reading the account of the dear President's pastoral silver-wedding, when a remark of Dr. Stanford's on the immense circulation of the 'Sermons,' suggested to me that I, too, could do something by distributing them through the post. Having a number of unbound copies, I began to send them to invalids, and to persons prevented by duty from attending God's house; but addresses soon failed me, and then, the case of the lighthouse-keepers, like a gleam from one of their own towers, flashed across my mind! Here lay my work; this to me was very clear, and soon all information about them, with a list of six hundred 'Coast Lights,' came to hand from 'Lighthouses and Lightships.' Thus I was able to reach the English keepers. After a while I obtained American and Canadian lists; and last summer, through your much-appreciated kindness, all other English-speaking countries were in the same way placed within my reach."

* * * *

How easily and happily could scores of people commence and carry on a similar work, even though it might be on a much smaller scale! Earnestly do I wish that some would be persuaded to try it! Blessing to themselves and others would most certainly be the "peaceable fruit" of such a loving and unobtrusive service. I know of one dear lady who has taken all the Fire Brigade Stations in London as her special sphere of usefulness, and to them she despatches the weekly "Sermons" as soon as published, breathing, I doubt not, earnest prayers over their pages as she folds and wraps them up, that their words may be the power of God unto salvation to those who read them. She is perfectly certain that the precious truths these "Sermons" contain will reach and change some hearts, though she may never know on earth how many souls God will give as a reward to her gentle ministry. Will there not be some more volunteers for this peaceful service?

The good friend in Russia, who first suggested to me the scheme of sending the "Sermons" to missionaries, and who, in fact, inaugurated the work by giving the first £5, has now doubled his liberal gift, and writes earnestly requesting that I will extend and increase this most useful and important agency. "Can you not prevail on the Mrs.—— and Miss ——, of whom you speak in your Report," he says, "to undertake the work with you, and thus enlarge it? I long to see it increase tenfold, and do not think I am wrong in believing that no greater blessing could come to our lonely brethren in their far-off homes than a monthly packet of your husband's 'Sermons.' Nay, I believe that, could they be sent to *every mission-station,* they would change, to a great extent, the result of missionary work." He thinks it should be only the *beginning* of good things to send out six hundred and ninety-two "Sermons" every month, as I now do—he wants to see the number of recipients doubled, or even trebled! I fear it is not possible for me to do more than I am doing at present; but I should indeed rejoice if there could be found some whose hearts the Lord will incline to undertake a work which promises such abundant fruitfulness.

* * * *

It is a great joy to know that in sending forth these "Sermons" we give the people real soul-food,—the true bread of life; no husks, no adulteration, no secret empoisonment, but the pure, simple corn of the Kingdom; words whereby they may be saved, which shall afterwards strengthen them as they grow in grace, and in the knowledge of our Lord and Saviour Jesus Christ.

Here is a testimony concerning them from one who has learned their value during many years of a somewhat stormy life, and as it seems just to fit into this place I am glad to transcribe it.

Mr. Spurgeon's "Sermons" have been, and still are, an unspeakable blessing to me. In sorrow, in trial, in difficulty, they have given me no small comfort and strength. They have brought a heavenly atmosphere around me, and have been to my poor dusty heart as the refreshing dew. They have laid hold of me as with hooks of steel, and have kept me from falling, and fastened me permanently to the grand old doctrines of the Puritans. They have made me gentle, hopeful, forgiving, patient. They have stirred me like a clarion-call, and rallied all my powers, and made me, like the war-horse, ready for the fight. They have opened up before me new beauty in the Word, made Christ more real and precious, filled my heart with an intense love to Him, and made me more anxious to do good to men, and glorify His holy name. When my home has been shadowed by sickness, and darkness, and death, I have taken down the volumes, and read until my heart has grown calm, and I could say, "Father, not my will, but Thine, be done." When troubles have sprung up in the church, and my mind has been worried and baffled, I have gone to the same volumes, and have found words of wisdom, guidance, and counsel. When my soul has been cast down, when gloomy fears and dismal doubts have whirled within me, I have found in the "Sermons" some experience very like my own, and been led therefrom to the only source of solace and succour. Truly, they are to my soul "green pastures" and "still waters," where I can always find food, comfort, quietness, and rest.

Dear friends, the Lord does constantly, and not in rare instances merely, graciously cause His Spirit's power to rest on the printed discourses of His servant. Are you not therefore glad and thankful that you, by your kind help to the Book Fund, have enabled me this year to send out nearly twelve thousand copies of these messengers of mercy?

* * * *

There has been this year a curious indication of the non-sectarian character of Book Fund work. I have received and granted applications from a Quaker, a Waldensian, an Irvingite, three Moravians, and a Unitarian! This latter says, "Shall I be taking the bread from the children if I ask for a grant?" I thought *not;* indeed I felt drawn to give him a good portion of savoury meat, fearing that his soul must be well-nigh famished upon "strange doctrine," and praying that beyond his own desire and intent the living water might filter into his soul. He sends me a declaration of the principles of Unitarians, a document which causes me much distress, because it shows that some people manage to leave out of religion that which seems to me to be the very life and joy of it; but as he is also so candid as to say that he reads Mr. Spurgeon's "Sermons" with pleasure, I cannot but hope that my husband's *declaration* may help to amend the present sentiments of this friendly correspondent. God grant it may be so!

✳ ✳ ✳ ✳

December.—"My Sea-bird" has flown. My son's bright visit is ended. Laden with loving gifts, satisfied with favour, crowned with success in his enterprise, and followed by the fervent prayers of all who know and love him, he has gone to the land of his adoption, and if the Lord will spare his life, we look forward to a grand future of usefulness for him in Auckland. I am "sorrowful, yet alway rejoicing." He is so precious that to lose him must needs be a bitterness, yet *because* he is so precious, the sorrow is almost turned into joy. "*Therefore* also I have lent him to the Lord; as long as he liveth he shall be lent to the Lord."

Happy mother! whose two beloved sons count it their highest honour to "spend and be spent" in the service of their father's God!

✳ ✳ ✳ ✳

This last month's record ought to be nothing less than a jubilant psalm of thanksgiving right through all its days. There is so much to be grateful for; so much more blessing than I can ever remember or recall, so much mercy past, present, and to come; such tender guidance, such plentiful provision, such daily loadings with benefits, such manifold lovingkindnesses, such gracious dealings of my God; that it would need a seraph's tongue to tell out the blessed story in all its charming detail. Would that I could write in these pages some golden words of grateful love, which should shine forth to the praise of Him who hath done marvellous things for me, whereof I am glad!

"Ah! that's very fine," says one, "it's easy enough to sing when all goes well with you; would you have been as ready to shout for joy if the Book Fund had been a failure?"

Dear friends, I do not know what I should have done if God had not blessed my work, or, after having blessed it, had withdrawn his favour from it. But such a calamity has not befallen me, and it surely is not worth while to contemplate troubles which the Lord never sent, or to speculate upon our behaviour under trials which He has not allowed to come near to us! Blessed be His name! I have to sing, not of "mercy *and* judgment," but of mercy absolute and regnant, of grace the sweetest and tenderest, of care and love the most faithful and Divine. And though the song be sung by feeble lips, it is a glad and willing service. Did you ever think how the instruments of music have to suffer violence while the harmony is forced out of them? See how that man's brawny arm belabours the big drum, while its notes roll like thunder through the air! Look, with what a strong, nervous hand the strings of that harp are crashed and twanged, before the liquid music is set free from its reluctant veins! Note how, even on the delicate viol, the bow seems sometimes to inflict a long-drawn agony, while it fetches forth a "concord of sweet sounds"! They have all more or less to be struck, and beaten, and buffeted, before they can yield up the imprisoned minstrelsy.

Not thus would I desire to utter the praises of my heart, though it is better that we should be made to sing by suffering than be left for ever silent. I would pray that my gratitude might be like the music of an Eolian harp among the trees of the garden in the soft summer-time, when every passing breeze kisses its tuneful strings into entrancing melody; and the softest sighing of the zephyr awakens answering echoes from within. I would have my waiting, thankful soul respond to every breath of God's daily favour with a tender song, and throb with instant recognition of all His gracious influences and dealings.

Thus would I have it, I have said; but alas! how often "to will is present with me, but how to perform that which is good I find not"; my insensible heart has sometimes to be *struck* by the rare magnitude of a mercy before it gives forth the sweet peal of soul-music which should be for ever ringing through my life. My thankfulness should flow out like the first red juice which quits the grape as soon as the clusters are touched by the foot of the treader; yet, I sometimes fear my praises are like the thick, clogged liquid which is tardily extracted with long and weary labour from the dregs of the wine-press.

But take courage, my heart! this time there may be some precious drops of choicest vintage to offer thy gracious Lord, some low soft notes of grateful love which shall reach His listening ear. "Hope thou in God; for I shall yet praise Him, who is the health of my countenance, and my God."

> "Not for the lip of praise alone,
> Nor even the praising heart,
> I ask, but for a life made up
> Of praise in every part."

*   *   *   *

If I did not try to bless the name of the Lord for all the goodness and mercy which have followed me throughout another year, I think the very ledgers, and day-books, and cash-books, which are in constant use in my work, would rise up from their places, and bear swift witness against me. What a tale they tell! What lists of love, what manifold mercies are here inscribed! Take up the day-book in which the names of the Pastors are entered as soon as their applications have been accepted. See how column follows column as regularly as the weeks come round, and bless God on my behalf, as you note that I have been enabled to carry on the work without a miss or a break. Reflect for a moment on the labour involved in the constant correspondence, the selection of books, the management of the work in detail, and the sending out of some thousands of books during the year. Shall I not praise my God for strength given in weakness, and for the grace which has kept me steadfast in purpose and practice? It is all of Him, from first to last, and I have been but the willing channel through which His benefits have flowed down to His servants.

Now look into the cash-books, and see in their well-filled pages another definite and delightful proof of the Lord's tender love and provident care. Has he not satisfied me with good things? Has he not fulfilled all my desire? Not once have I had an anxious thought concerning money, so abundantly has he supplied all my needs. My books praise Him on every page, they are written evidences of His faithfulness and grace, and methinks they would indeed cry out against me if I failed to confirm them with the better testimony of a living, loving heart and voice. Even so, I do, most kind and gracious Lord: "While I live will I praise the Lord: I will sing praises unto my God while I have any being."

The poor Pastors, who have been helped during the year, rejoice to join me in blessing God and thanking the dear friends for all the solace, comfort, and mental refreshment which the Book Fund brings to their hearts and homes. Their grateful letters are a constant joy to me, believing, as I do, that their abundant thanksgiving will redound to the glory of God.

❃ ❃ ❃ ❃

THE PASTORS' AID FUND

has shared in the general prosperity of the whole work, and its loving gifts have carried life and light into many dark places. Should I reveal the secrets of this part of my service, my readers would both weep and smile; for I could tell them of sorrows which would make rivers of water run down their eyes, and then I should quickly wipe them all away by recounting the happy sequel of wants relieved, and burdens removed, and heavy hearts made glad again, by the timely help this Fund has rendered.

May the Lord remember with His choicest mercy the dear friends who, year after year, give me this precious privilege of ministering to the necessities of the saints, and brightening the lives of hard-working Pastors, by a judicious gift in a time of need! Unfortunately, such times are the rule, and not the exception, in the history of too many of our village ministers; and to help these weary ones, and bring a song to lips that are accustomed to sighing, is a service in which an angel might ask to be employed.

I have this year distributed £330 17s. 6d. among poor Pastors, and I believe no money was ever more urgently needed, or more worthily bestowed.

❃ ❃ ❃ ❃

A great many parcels of clothing have also gone out from "Westwood" to needy households; for some friends prefer to send these gifts to me, though our noble society at the Tabernacle, with dear Mrs. Evans as its manager, can really attend to this matter far better than I can. Yet to those who *will* choose me as their almoner, I give hearty thanks for their kindness, and promise to distribute any future gifts with pleasure, provided only that the clothing sent be in good condition, and suitable for the persons for whom it is intended. I have very thankfully received several parcels of *gentlemen's* clothing this year; these are specially prized, as a suit for a poor pastor is a very heavy item of expense to him. If friends would remember this need when looking over drawers and wardrobes, and would send the spoils thereof to Mrs. Evans, Metropolitan Tabernacle, Newington, S.E., they would be bestowing a very great boon on my poor Pastors, and greatly increase my debt of gratitude.

* * * *

The supply of writing-paper and envelopes for poor ministers, so constantly furnished for many years by a dear and faithful friend, has been as abundant and liberal as heretofore. This means that not only have I had enough for the needs of my poor friends, but that I have been obliged sometimes to stay my benefactor's hand, having no more room in which to store his overflowing munificence. "Must I pull down my barns, and build greater?" is my cry when the huge cases of stationery come in, and one wonders how to dispose of the riches of liberality which seem ever on the increase. Still, vast as are the supplies, we manage happily to distribute them, and the gifts are always a great boon to the poorly-paid minister, who is compelled to use much writing material in his work, yet knows not how to spare the money to purchase it. Whenever I receive an application for books, written on paper that looks as if it had been made of water-gruel, I at once make the mystic endorsement in the corner of the sheet which instructs my "packer" to "put in this parcel a plentiful supply of stationery." Sometimes the surprise is great to a poor pastor when he finds himself thus unexpectedly stocked with supplies so useful and desirable, and it is with much astonishment that he lifts out the neatly-wrapped parcels of paper and envelopes which rest so snugly among the precious books. But lately there has been, I think, almost as much anticipation as amazement in the matter, for my friend's kindness is of so many years' continuance that the Pastors now often *ask* that a gift of writing-paper may accompany another grant of books, reporting so much comfort and help from the last bestowment that they feel emboldened to seek a repetition of the favour. My dear friend will, I hope, take this fact as a grateful acknowledgment of his liberality and a graceful compliment to his generosity, from those who thus joyfully accept it, while I can do no less than thank my God upon every remembrance of him.

* * * *

The monthly gift of *The Sword and the Trowel* magazine to some of the *very poorest* of the Lord's servants is still continued, and it never fails to meet with a cordial reception. "It is a monthly treasure," says one; "its variety and vitality increase with its years, and we all look forward to its coming, sure of some cheering news, or inspiring theme, or richly-suggestive article." "I need hardly say how warmly we welcome it," writes another country Pastor. "My dear wife and family rejoice in it as much as I do myself; and for the comfort and refreshment it has brought us for so long a time I desire most sincerely to thank you."

"I am very grateful to you for sending me the magazine for so many years," says one who has little earthly help and comfort; "I do hope you will try and send it again next year, for I need it quite as badly as ever I did, and I prize it very much." These poor ministers could ill afford even the very small amount this periodical costs, and therefore I am glad to give them the pleasure of receiving it freely; but I do not supply it gratis to others, who should, I think, be able to spare *threepence a month* to secure so helpful a paper.

CONCLUSION.

I have been urged by some friends to gather into one volume all the records of Book Fund work, beginning with the "Letters to my friends" which appeared in *The Sword and the Trowel* as early as 1876. A warm-hearted friend writes, "Your Reports are my yearly feasts. *Do reprint them from the commencement.* They ought to be brought out in one volume; for the account of the *beginning* of such a work is always very helpful and stimulating, and later readers lose that sweet early story. It ought to go over the world in a form that can be kept, and again I beg for a reprint."

There are also frequent applications for the earlier "Diaries" from persons who are able only to secure the latest published copy, yet long to see how the work gathered and grew in the days gone by; and one of these friends, kindly wishful to encourage me in my labour, tells how she sent a copy to a lady accustomed to read little else but novels, and how her heart rejoiced when she received the following message:—"When I took up the little book you gave me, I thought it would be as dry as Reports generally are; but I could not put it down until I had read it right through, I was so thoroughly interested, aroused, and surprised!"

I can truly say that I, too, am *surprised;* but it is with a great joy, when the Lord gives any power and blessing to this simple tale; and if it be His pleasure that I should publish the story of His great goodness during ten years of my life and the Book Fund's, I am delightedly willing to obey. I desire that this intimation of my friend's proposal should call forth an expression of opinion from all my dear readers on the subject; and this will, in great measure, help me to decide the question. "Vox populi vox Dei," is not always true; but in this case I think I may take the judgment of very many friends as an indication of what the will of the Lord is.

* * * *

Now go, little book, and do thy best to tell how good my gracious God has been to me during the past twelve months. Thou mayest freely make thy boast in the Lord; for thou hast nought to do but to praise and exalt and glorify His dear name. Yet thy sweetest words must fail to show forth His tenderness; thy loudest praises will but whisper of His grace; thy most glowing gratitude will never reach beyond a feeble recognition of His faithfulness;—but go, and God be with thee; for I send thee forth with earnest prayer that in some way or other, as aforetime, thou mayest be so blessed of Him as to refresh His saints, and strengthen the faith of His servants, and find grace in the eyes of His people, and then humbly lay thy loving tribute of praise and adoration at His feet.

* * * *

Yet once again let the heavenly wind sweep across the harp-strings, and stir the solemn music of my soul. "Awake, O north wind; and come, thou south; blow upon my garden, that the spices thereof may flow out."

* * * *

"The Lord is my strength and my shield; my heart trusted in Him, and I am helped: therefore my heart greatly rejoiceth; and with my song will I praise Him."

* * * *

What aileth thee, O my soul? The notes of thy thanksgiving are trembling on thy lips; thy psalm of praise is dying away in faintest cadences! Hath the Lord laid His hand upon thy heart-strings, and hushed their music by an overwhelming sense of His goodness? Doth the weight of His mercy so oppress thee that the sound of thy song is stilled to mortal ears, and is audible only to Him?

SUMMARY OF WORK.

Books Distributed during the Year 1884:—9,149 Volumes.

Also 11,981 single Sermons for giving away. The recipients comprised 243 Baptists, 158 Independents, 318 Methodists, 172 Church of England clergymen, 16 Presbyterians, 24 Missionaries, 73 Evangelists, 1 Quaker, 1 Unitarian, 1 Waldensian, 3 Moravians, and 1 Irvingite.—Total, 1,011.

The Book Fund Diary

For 1885.

By Mrs. C. H. Spurgeon.

New Year's Day at "Westwood."

MY dear Reader,—Will you pay me an early visit on this first morning of the New Year, and taking the most comfortable chair to be found in my cosy sitting-room, sit by the side of the blazing wood fire, while I proceed with the business of the day—opening and answering the goodly pile of letters which are awaiting my attention? It may interest all who love the Book Fund work to know exactly what I have to do, and how I do it; so on this auspicious morning I will take my friends into full confidence, and let them peep into every letter as I open it; sharing with me the pleasure or pain, the content or the anxiety, to which the correspondence may give rise. Before us lies a day's work we shall not get through till sundown; are you willing and able, dear friend, to spend such a busy day with me?

* * * *

A tiny square box, addressed to me in my son Charles's handwriting, first claims my notice. I wonder what it can contain, and on opening it, I find, to my great surprise and pleasure, a pretty little sovereign purse, with one of those satisfactory coins inside, and a morsel of paper with a memorandum to the following effect:—

𝕬 𝕹𝖊𝖜 𝖄𝖊𝖆𝖗'𝖘 𝕲𝖎𝖋𝖙 𝖙𝖔 𝖉𝖊𝖆𝖗 𝕲𝖗𝖆𝖓𝖉𝖒𝖆𝖒𝖆'𝖘 𝕭𝖔𝖔𝖐 𝕱𝖚𝖓𝖉
𝖋𝖗𝖔𝖒 𝕾𝖚𝖘𝖎𝖊 𝖆𝖓𝖉 𝕯𝖔𝖗𝖆.

It is a new and very amusing experience to have my son's little ones helping in my life-work! True, the wee mites do not know much about it at present; in the blissful ignorance of childhood, such tender, sheltered blossoms are all unaware that out in the world, cold winds are blowing, and biting frosts are reigning: let them enjoy the warmth, and gladness, and *couleur de rose*, as long as possible. But at least this New Year's Gift promises well for future training and bringing up in the way they should go, and,—who can tell?—in days to come they may take up "Grandma's" work when she is at rest, and carry it on more extensively, and not less lovingly, than she has done! "*Grandmama*"! Ah me! How the days are going by! It seems but as yesterday that the father of these two little maidens was my own bonnie baby, laughing, ay, and weeping too, in what I then thought a most wonderful and exceptional fashion; yet so many years have flown away, and he has travelled so far on life's journey, that now *his* babies crow and cry even as he once did, and make sweet childish music in his house, *and call me " Grandmama"!*

> "Growing older!
> With a sigh we say it,
> That the early freshness of the dawn,
> Rosy-tinted, rich in thoughts and fancies,
> Seemeth farther at each birthday morn.
>
> Growing older!
> Joyously we say it,
> Reaching onward to immortal youth,
> And the fount of bliss that never endeth,
> Promised us by Him who is the Truth."

It will not do, however, to grow prosy over my venerable position, as a *maternal ancestor*. I must "wear my honours meekly," I must persuade the rosebuds to lie lovingly by the side of the "sere and yellow leaf," and teach the dimpled fingers to smooth away the wrinkles and the coming crow's-feet, and be as wise and tender a *grandmother* as the Lord would have me be. So a letter is written to the dear son whose love for his mother is one of the joys of her life, thanking him for the sweet remembrance on behalf of his wee maidens, and invoking God's rich blessings on him and his;—and thus ends the examination and reply to our first New Year's missive.

* * * *

But there lies on my table, awaiting completion, a letter to that other darling son, who at this moment is on the mighty waters, sailing away from mother and from home, to go and serve his God and his people in the distant colonies. Before I open another epistle, *this* one must be finished; it is to meet him at Naples, where his ship touches, and must carry a word of comfort and of lingering farewell, and assure him once again of mother's fervent prayers for his safety. It is with a great yearning over him in my heart, and eyes that grow dim with tears as the pen runs on, that I fill up the last pages of my love-letter to my absent boy, and sealing it with a sigh, which is, in reality, a prayer, I drop it into the post-basket, and then turn to engage resolutely in the business of the day.

* * * *

The letter which comes now to hand is from an Evangelist who, not knowing that the work is for poor Pastors only, asks for a grant of books. He is trying to win souls to Christ; has a wife and four children, very little money, and very few books. I reply, informing him of my rules, which prevent full compliance with his request, but offering him a parcel of "Sermons," which he can first read, and then distribute to his people. This offer he will be sure to accept; and, having by me some good second-hand volumes, I shall put in a few of these also, and the poor man will rejoice as over great spoil. This is better than a total denial of his request; for the blessed truths contained in the "Sermons" will be certain to feed his soul, and then, when he scatters them, who can tell where the precious seed may fall, and flourish, and bring forth fruit?

* * * *

The next missive proves to be an acknowledgment of the safe arrival of a parcel for a minister in Wales. There has been a great deal of previous correspondence with this brother, a rather long delay in accepting his application, and so there may be an extraordinary depth of meaning in the few words by which he assures me that he received the parcel, and was "*very thankful*" for its contents.

* * * *

Then I open one which promises to give me great content. It is from a former student of the College, now a worthy and hard-working pastor in the vicinity of London. He says:—

Dear Mrs. Spurgeon,—My cup runneth over. The books have safely arrived. Dr. Gill's "Commentary," five volumes of the "Sermons" of the dearest friend I have in this world, the last volume of "The Treasury," and a nice lot of paper and envelopes. I feel perfectly unable to thank you for such a splendid gift, though the Lord knows how grateful I am to both Him and you for the help which the last hours of the Old Year have brought me. That God may pour down rich blessings in the New Year upon yourself and your beloved husband, and all the works of your hands, is the earnest prayer of the recipient of this noble and generous gift.

* * * *

Again I find the letter I take up is from one of "our own men." I have long sent the weekly "Sermon" to him, and he gratefully says that he cannot permit the year to close without thanking me for what has proved so helpful to himself and others. So his acknowledgment reaches me on New Year's morning, and his kind wishes make a chime of pleasant music in my heart. "May your noble work be a fount of unfailing delight, throughout the year!" he says; "may your opportunities be many of cheering the poor servants of God; and, with ample means and renewed health, may your service be a perpetual joy and comfort to yourself and to others!"

I sent a New Year's gift of 20s. each to about a dozen of the very poorest Pastors I knew, and the next letter from the pile on the table proves to be a thankful little note from one of these sorely-tried men. I cannot tell you how poor he is, I mean that I could scarcely make you believe the struggle he has to keep life in himself and family, and present even a commonly tidy appearance in public. Yet mark the sweet and chastened tone of his acknowledgment: "The Lord hath prepared of his goodness for me"—these are his words,—"my cup runneth over, may my gratitude keep pace with my mercies!"—and then note the tender grace with which, after blessing God for the unexpected gift, he asks for a benediction on the friend who was but the Lord's messenger: "May your soul be filled with all the fulness of God, and the New Year be to you and yours the brightest and best you have ever known, continually blest with the Divine presence and favour!"

My heart responds to this prayer, "Amen, Lord, so let it be to Thine unworthy servant, that the sweet work which Thou hast given her to do may be all the better done because of the lifting up of Thy countenance upon her!"

* * * *

A lay assistant in the Church of England next asks to be presented with Mr. Spurgeon's "Lectures to my Students." He sends the necessary testimonials as to his position as a worker for the Lord Jesus, and six stamps for the postage of the books; so I at once enter his name in my ledger as a recipient of the gift, and have the volumes wrapped up, addressed, and placed in the post-bag.

* * * *

Then I take up what proves to be a letter of earnest thanks for a parcel of mingled mercies—stores for the mind, clothing for the body, a little replenishing for the pocket—which I had sent to a poor minister last week. You shall look over my shoulder, and read what he says:—

My dear Mrs. Spurgeon,—Words fail me to express what my dear wife and I feel as we look on your valuable gifts. All I can say is that through your kindness I have another proof of my Heavenly Father's care for me and mine, and this fills my heart with deepest gratitude. When my wife saw the money enclosed, she exclaimed, "Oh, what a mercy!" And if the dear baby could speak, she would tell you of the comfort she enjoys in her warm clothing, but at present her happy looks are her warmest thanks. The books will be a great boon to me, and I pray I may use them aright; this new treasure increases my responsibility, for where much is given, much will be required; but the Lord will help me to profit by them, and teach my people to profit also. I thank you with all my heart.

* * * *

My hand next lights upon an envelope bearing a familiar and always welcome handwriting. The letter is from a dear friend whose face I have never seen, though her heart has been revealed to me in a beautiful and tender friendship. For many long years she has been confined to her couch by sore affliction; but from that sick-bed she stretches out loving hands of help and cheer to others, and manifests for all invalids a special concern and interest. Her love for me, and for my work, began, when I, too, was a constant sufferer, and it ceases not, though I have been led out of the rough road where her feet still linger, and where she waits with gentle patience for the Master's voice to call her home.

When the intervals of comparative freedom from pain will permit her to use her pen, she writes long and brilliant letters to a large circle of correspondents. A stranger, reading these charming epistles, could scarcely imagine that they came from an invalid's hand, so bright are they, so cheery, so vigorous, so free from all the conventional sentiments and subjects of sick-chamber experience.

If all sufferers could learn in the school of affliction such sweet lessons of sympathy and unselfishness as this dear friend has evidently "got by heart," the world would be the purer and the better for the presence in it of its many sons and daughters of weariness. Her own trials and sorrows—by no means few or small—are scarcely mentioned, or only lightly touched on, while all the sweet energy of her nature is expended in drawing waters of consolation from the Divine Source, which she finds unfailing, and pouring them forth for the refreshment of tried and fainting souls. She is like Rebecca, who, not content with saying, "Drink, my lord," fulfils the servant's petition, and testifies to her own election as the handmaid of the Lord, by adding, "I will draw water for thy camels also."

Dear L—— is one of God's angels upon earth, one of His holy band of night-watchers; her soul's light shines so brightly through the battered lantern of her frail physical life, that I verily believe the Lord keeps her here to lighten the dark places in other people's hearts, and to show how splendidly His grace can give power in weakness, strength in infirmity, gladness notwithstanding suffering, and visions of future glory through the black lattices of present pain! Thus, one of the sweetest missions of this lovely life is to comfort all who mourn, and send tender messages of cheer, or encouragement, or appreciation, to workers and waiters; and this she does with so much loving perception of their needs, and such rare sympathy of heart, that the comforted one wonders how she "knew all about it," and feels that the word in season—fitly spoken—was indeed given of God.

To-day, this is but a wee business note from the dear ministering hand, yet the concluding sentences are full of gracious power and meaning—" May the New Year bring new strength to you, and 'fresh springs' open for your comfort! Lovingly do I remember your needs in prayer, and ask that you may find grace sufficient for all. As the year ends, with its varied story, *a deep thankfulness is in my heart for the mercies so abundant*"—mark this, ye who have health and strength, and "all things richly to enjoy," yet never feel a throb of gratitude to the God who gives it all!

* * * *

(*Now we find it is time for* " *refreshments, and for the plates to pass round,*" *as* " *Son Tom* " *so saucily said in his lecture on* " *Brighter Britain.*" *We will adjourn to the dining-room, my visitor and I, and since we cannot invite you, dear reader, to join us there, and listen to the* " *table talk* " *of C. H. S., we will promise to be but a short while absent, resuming our work as quickly as possible.*)

* * * *

The first letter I open on our return contains a £10 note for the Book Fund, and thus " refreshment " is graciously given to both body and mind. Very grateful am I to the good friend who has sent this handsome New Year's gift, and I bless the name of the Lord for inclining His people to remember my work of love. May this offering be accepted by the Master, and while His servant sends thankful acknowledgments, and tries to express her gratitude, may He reward the kind donor with the smile of His love, and the light of His countenance!

* * * *

Two other letters of grateful acknowledgment must be more expeditiously dealt with; for time is flying, and the heap of epistles on the table still looks large and formidable. In the first, the dear good man says he is astonished at the munificence of the present he has received, it is far beyond anything that he hoped for or expected; and he prays that I may be enabled to give to many more needy ones just such a store of solid help and real joy as he is now blessing God for. The second pastor thanks me warmly for the January number of *The Sword and the Trowel*, which is an earnest to him of its free gift all through the year—a boon which he thoroughly appreciates; and, as the post brought him also a little New Year's gift of money, he exclaims, "So much mercy in one morning! It seems to overwhelm me!"

Ah! these very poor country ministers, dear souls! they have such close companionship with POVERTY, and look so constantly into her wan and haggard face, that if the smiling eyes of PLENTY do but peep inside their doorway, they are dazzled and breathless, and think they have seen an angel!

* * * *

What can I say concerning the communication which I now open and read? It is on a subject which is claiming some attention at the present time, and stirring up both interest and protest among all classes of religious people. It is, in fact, an earnest plea for "Faith-healing," an enthusiastic entreaty to me to induce my husband never to have any more pain! ("*O wad some power the giftie gie me*"!) And it comes from one who says she has herself been thus healed! "Dear Mr. Spurgeon's 'Sermons' have been so much blessed to me," writes my correspondent, "that I long for him to be quite well also; do, dear madam, *believe for him*, and ask him to accept healing from the Lord." This lady tells me she was an invalid for four years, consulting the first physicians in London, yet getting rapidly worse, till she was at last persuaded to go to the Faith-healing Home through the importunities of her little daughter, who, having heard of the wonderful cures wrought there, kept saying, in sweet childish fashion, "Do go to 'Beth-shan,' dear mamma; Jesus will make you well; do go, please"; and though scarcely able to totter from her door-step to the carriage, the mother went, to satisfy her child's longings, and returned—she believes—healed! This was two years ago; and she says she promised the Lord that, if he would heal her, she would write to Mr. Spurgeon, and beg him to "give his pain over to Jesus," and trust Him for the healing of the body as well as of the soul.

I must answer this dear lady; but I confess I know not what to say. I am not convinced of the truth of the dogmas advanced by these brethren, nor of the possibility of such marvellous deliverance from physical pain as they promise to obedient souls; and yet I fear even to seem to underrate the mighty power of faith in God, or to appear for a moment to misinterpret those words of our blessed Lord, "If thou canst believe, all things are possible to him that believeth."

In spiritual matters, it may be that many of us are too prone to linger in the shallows of faith, and to think, when we are wading only to the ankles in these "waters of the sanctuary," that we have felt all the power and force of the sacred stream. Why not measure a thousand cubits, and be brought knee-deep into the holy river? Nay, listen, and wonder at the possibilities before you! "Again he measured a thousand, and brought me through; the waters were to the loins. Afterwards he measured a thousand; and it was a river that I could not pass over: for the waters were risen, *waters to swim in*, a river that could not be passed over." Oh for a plunge into the depths of such a promise as this—

"According to your faith, be it unto you,"

and the joy of finding it unfathomable! Did you ever try it, dear reader? Or are you satisfied to

> "Linger shivering on the brink,
> Fearing to launch away"?

* * * *

The next communication contains a promise from a friend of boy's clothing for a poor minister's son, which I gratefully accept, and undertake to bestow on the right person; the only difficulty being, among so many needy ones, to choose the neediest.

After this I find a note of "sincerest thanks for the precious gift of books" from a poor minister in Wales, whose total income of £5 per month may presumably find him in bread and cheese, and a roof to shelter under, but can by no stretch of the imagination be deemed sufficient to procure him the luxury of much standard literature!

Yet another epistle encloses twenty shillings from a kind friend, for a "needy servant of Christ"; and at once I send a postal order off to one who is sorely pressed with anxieties, who will see in it a precious proof of his Heavenly Father's loving care, and will most probably receive it as a direct answer to a petition of which I knew nothing. What a joy and privilege it is to be a channel of blessing from the Lord to His servants! I pray that nothing in me may ever hinder or divert the glad stream of His bounty which is now flowing so freely and fully to His needy ones, and rejoicing my own heart as it goes.

* * * *

Commencing afresh upon the heap of letters still lying before me, my visitor is surprised by sudden glad and jubilant sounds which escape my lips as I examine the contents of the next letter. "What have you found now?" is asked with interest and curiosity. O joy and delight! I hold in my hand a Scotch draft for twenty pounds! All my own for my dear work, and enough to make thankful hearts by the score! Is it not a beautiful New Year's gift? And the kind donor has added such sweet words of cheerful encouragement and loving approval of my little book, that I seem verily to have received my "apples of gold in baskets of silver." My soul blesses and praises the Lord for this mercy, which will bless so many others; and then I try to express, as best my emotion will allow me, the deep gratitude I feel to the friend whose gift has brought such gladness.

* * * *

I am often greatly straitened when thus attempting to translate the fervid metre of my intense thankfulness into the plain prose of written language. Coldly and feebly do my choicest words seem to set forth my gratitude for a mercy which, though so constantly renewed, has as yet lost none of its wonder and marvel in my eyes. That for so many years, without a word of solicitation, dear friends should have sent me abundant means to carry on this work with ease and comfort, is plainly and positively the Lord's doing, and my loving amazement at His goodness increases with every repetition of His favour. But I find it easier to thank *Him* than to make my acknowledgments to His people, and so it comes to pass that often, when I long to lay some tender tribute of loving, grateful language in my dear friends' hands, I am conscious of a miserable failure, and can only turn to the Lord, and say, "Lord, undertake for me; make these dear friends know how precious their kindness is to me, and do Thou Thyself reward them by returning the blessing wherewith they have blessed me tenfold into their own souls!"

* * * *

Is it to be counted a strange thing, or may I not rather see God's sweet providence in the matter, that the very next epistle I take up, after receiving the £20, is an application for help?

A poor minister's wife writes, "with very great reluctance," to solicit aid in clothing, or in money; as her husband has been unwell for some months, doing his work with the utmost difficulty, and his illness has necessitated the expenditure of the little savings which they depended on to provide themselves with winter comforts. She says, pleadingly, "we have never asked for help in this way before"; and her reference to "savings" shows her to be a thrifty woman; but what will my readers think of these good people's struggles and endurance when I say that all the income they have to depend upon is less than £40 per annum, with a chapel-house! This is a magnificent provision for an ambassador of Christ, is it not? I have scarcely patience to tell the tale, only that, before telling it, I have with quick and joyful fingers divided my Scotch present, and sent off the fourth part to bless and comfort the hearts of these patient servants of the Lord Jesus. And now I shall write to Mrs. Evans, to beg a parcel of nice warm garments for them from our POOR MINISTERS' CLOTHING SOCIETY, and in this way, for a time at least, their sorrow will be turned into joy.

Blessed be God, I have not to mourn over an empty treasury when His poor pensioners come knocking at the door! He puts the money into my hand ere yet they have entered within my gates, and thus sweetly He forbids me to send them empty away. O good and generous Lord, how liberally dost Thou deal with Thy poor dependents! Before we call Thou dost answer, and while we are yet speaking Thou dost hear: how is it that we ever dare to doubt Thee, with such constant and overwhelming proofs of Thy love and care before our eyes?

* * * *

I pass rapidly over the two epistles which next present themselves—one is an application for books from a clergyman, which I immediately decide to grant, and thereupon enter the details in my ledger; the other contains a donation to the Fund, which I at once acknowledge with many thanks; but I pause a minute or two at the third letter, as it promises to yield matter for a paragraph of special interest. I must explain. About a week ago I received a note from a Congregational minister, enclosing a post-office order for a nice little sum of money, and asking me to lay it out in the purchase of books, making it "go" as far as possible. The volumes were to be for presentation, as a testimonial of esteem and gratitude, to a young man, who, as secretary to the Sunday-school, and organist to the chapel, had rendered loving and important service to the cause of which the writer was pastor.

I should have been delighted to do this for any one; but when, reading further on in the letter, I found that the person thus to be honoured was one of the "old boys" of the Stockwell Orphanage, I was conscious of an excess of interest in the matter, and of a thrill of gratitude to God for this accidental and unexpected proof of the success and value of the training given in that Institution, so dear to its founder's heart. "I assure you," wrote the minister, "that he is worthy for whom we do this, and he would prize your husband's works more than any others, for he regards Mr. Spurgeon as *better* than a father to him."

The books were chosen and sent, and the letter now in my hand is the acknowledgment of the safe arrival of the parcel, and a brief notice of the presentation, which took place last evening. "Many very kind things were said," writes the pastor, "about the recipient of the present, and also concerning the 'Father' of the boys and girls of the Stockwell Orphanage; but though Mr. ——— was so overcome with emotion that he could not speak much, what he did say showed how highly he valued the gift."

This is a pleasing little episode in my work. To help strangers is a great joy, since it is always more blessed to give than to receive; but to be asked to assist in aiding and honouring one of the young men brought up from childhood in our own Orphanage, is to have the happiness doubled, because it comes nearer the home and the heart. Even in this roundabout way there comes a fulfilment of the Psalmist's declaration, "Blessed is he that considereth the poor." Storms move in circles, so the scientific men tell us; the glittering spear of the lightning-flash rests not till it reaches again the cloud from which it issued; and the wise man of old wrote that "all the rivers run into the sea, and into the place from whence the rivers came, they return again." Does it not seem that in the spiritual world there must be a principle identical with this wonderful law of Nature? That gruesome old proverb, "Curses, like chickens, come home to roost," may be true enough; but far more incontestably certain is it that blessings encircle those who bless, they return like clouds after the rain,—they come back to the hands which freely scatter them; and there is ever a joyful incoming to the soul that has learnt the sweet art of constant outpouring of itself in love and blessing for others.

* * * *

We have now almost reached the end of the work for New Year's Day; there remains but one more letter, and a quantity of pretty cards, bringing kind wishes and congratulations for the season, which must await inspection at greater leisure. My patient visitor must be getting quite tired, and though still interested in the many phases of the work which have presented themselves during the day, will be glad to say, "Good-bye, and God bless you!" It can scarcely be said of me, as it was of the governor of the wedding-feast at Cana, "Thou hast kept the good wine until now"; for there was no sorting or arrangement of my letters—I took them as they came, and they have all been enjoyable; but it is pleasant to me that I finish up my day's work with a draught of pure gladness, a sacred refreshment and cup of joy which comes to me without fail, as surely as the first day of the New Year presents itself.

At a WATCH-NIGHT service, in a chapel not far from London, the pastor has for some years been in the habit of bringing to his people's remembrance my little service for the Lord's poor servants, and asking their prayers and praise on its behalf. At midnight, while the year is dying, their thanksgivings to God for past mercies carry with them a song for the Book Fund; and, as the New Year is entered on, their prayers for help and blessing on the untried path lovingly enfold a petition that God will make me strong to work for those who so sorely need my ministrations. Then follows a free-will offering to the Lord for this work; and in the letter now before me the pastor sends £3 for my acceptance, as the result of the first collection taken in the year 1885. Is not this a choice and beautiful thing to do? May the Lord very graciously accept this early "first-fruit" from the hand of each loving giver! I find my heart always very tenderly touched by the love thus manifested; and I am glad that to-day this letter has lain so long concealed beneath all the others; for it comes forth at the last as a bright crown and climax to the labours of the day, a topstone to the work, which gracefully and fittingly closes and completes it.

I give the pastor's note word for word, and as I transcribe its sentences, I thank God for praying friends, and ask that, in return, the Lord will make all grace abound towards them :—

My dear Mrs. Spurgeon,—It is always a special joy to me that the first offering we present to the Lord in the New Year should be sent to the Book Fund. Of course I should be glad if the amount were larger, but such as it is, it is freely given. It is given, too, with much prayer, for your work was tenderly remembered at the Throne of grace, and the first public prayer in our sanctuary, in 1885, was for you, and for the dear President, that God's presence may go with him to give him true rest.

May this be to you a very happy year! The Lord send health to your home, and take the dear boy, who is upon the sea, safely to his desired haven, and give even larger blessing to the Book Fund than it has ever known before! Yours very sincerely, ———.

* * * *

So now the day's work is ended, and the pen may be laid aside, the ledgers shut up, the writing-table, with all its business paraphernalia, pushed into its own special corner; and the busy writer has time to fold her hands in happy idleness, reviewing the labour past with grateful complacency, and blessing God for all the help and strength given for so tender and sacred a service.

The day's doings, represented by the letters, have passed before you, my dear friends, like a series of pictures or dissolving-views, each different, many dark with shadows, yet all truthful, and every one presenting some glorious aspect of God's grace and goodness for your admiration and delight.

You can only say, on looking back over the hours we have spent together, "How tenderly loving and gracious are the Lord's dealings with both service and servant!" It is no wonder that the work is the joy of the worker's life, for

God gives such succour and support and satisfaction in it, that reward walks hand-in-hand with labour, and sowing and reaping are done in a day! Any one might crave to tend so delightful a vineyard, where the Lord's care is constant, and His wonderful promise of old is fulfilled—"I the Lord do keep it; I will water it every moment: lest any hurt it, I will keep it night and day."

* * * *

Good-bye, my dear visitor, you have seen to-day something of the Lord's abundant goodness to me in my daily life-work; could you not carry home some honey from this hive of sweetness? "O taste and see that the Lord is good, blessed is the man that trusteth in Him!" His loving power and grace have wrought all the work, and by means so feeble and unlikely that none can fail to see His hand in it! Herein is full proof that weakness and unworthiness need be no hindrance to service for Him! What matters it that the tool be rough and inefficient, so that it is held in the Master Workman's hand? Its incapacity but reveals and exalts the perfect skill and matchless force with which He wields it! Let Him but condescend to *use* us, and we shall find that our actual fitness lies in our own helplessness; we shall learn that in our greatest weakness His strength is most manifested, and shall understand the depth of meaning in the apostle Paul's words, "Most gladly therefore will I rather glory in my infirmities, that the power of Christ may rest upon me."

Once again, good-bye. Let us ask for the Book Fund and its friends, and for each other, that during all the days of this New Year, the portion of Naphtali may be granted to us, that we may be

"Satisfied with favour, and full of the blessing of the Lord."

* * * *

Feb. 28.—Dear friends will readily admit that there can be no reason to think the work of the Book Fund is decreasing, when I tell them that this month has seen a repetition of the extraordinary pressure of correspondence which was experienced about two years since, and which then, as now, occurred in the month of February. I remember recording the fact that in twenty-eight days I had received 657 letters—this time the number has reached SEVEN HUNDRED AND FIFTY-FIVE! Coming in the following detailed order, my readers may imagine how full of busy interest these weeks have been :—

Monday, Feb. 2, to Saturday, Feb. 7 ... 260	letters.
Monday, Feb. 9, to Saturday, Feb. 14 ... 154	,,
Monday, Feb. 16, to Saturday, Feb. 21 ... 177	,,
Monday, Feb. 23, to Saturday, Feb. 28 ... 164	,,
755	

It is a good thing for me that the pens of these ready writers are not in such a state of feverish impetuosity all the year round, else one of two events must come to pass—either the days must be stretched to twenty-four hours, as the dials of the clocks have been, or the Book Fund manager must run away, and find a "lodge in some vast wilderness," where postmen's knocks and letter-bags are all unknown.

* * * *

As a curious instance of the power of unconscious personal influence, there came to my notice just lately the following true little story. I tell it because I think it will help us to see how effectually—when He pleases—God can and does use the weakest and meanest things to bring glory to His name, and comfort to His servants : and it ought certainly to teach us the necessity and joy of being so entirely consecrated to Him that the habits of our daily life may prove our implicit obedience to the command—"Whether therefore ye eat, or drink, or *whatsoever ye do*, do all to the glory of God."

Some years ago, on a glorious summer's day, there was a gathering of ministers and friends at a house in the suburbs of London. They had met for religious conference and the enjoyment of friendly intercourse, and in the beautiful grounds of their host's residence they found ample opportunity for delighting themselves, not only in each other's society, but in the beauties of Nature and the wondrous works of God's hand, so lavishly spread around them. Time was pleasantly and profitably spent; many were the wise and kind words uttered, and the communion of saints was felt to be very sweet and precious by all assembled. Among the guests was a famous " singing pilgrim," and after the breaking up of the principal meeting his presence drew together a little band of those who loved to make melody in their hearts to the Lord, and song after song rose up from amidst the flowers, till the trees of the field did clap their hands, and the air was filled with such a concord of sweet sounds, that the birds in that beautiful garden must have wondered at the unexpected rivalry of praise. Presently a song was given which claimed special attention and interest. The words were rough and quaint, and wedded to a strangely weird melody caught from the lips of some pious Northern fisherfolk. One seemed to hear in its singular harmonies the deep bass of the noise of many waters, mingled with the glad cry of the sea-birds as they flew across the waves; and when, at the end of each verse, the ringing chorus of

"Oh! Jesus is a Rock in a weary land,
A Shelter in the time of storm"

was repeated again and again, the effect was very thrilling, and many eyes were dim with happy tears.

The hostess, who, just before, had joined the singers, and helped to swell the chorus, boasted but small musical talent, and possessed only a weak and untrained voice; yet, with all the power and fervency she had, she sang the lovely, quaint words, and made up what was lacking in the science of her song by her evident heartiness and sympathy.

I expect she was at the moment inwardly realizing, not so much that this is "a weary land," as that at all times, and in all places, Jesus is indeed a Rock and a Shelter to the trusting soul. When the song was ended, she mingled with the company, and entertained her guests, wholly unconscious that the Lord had wrought His purposes of mercy by her means, and spoken to a soul through her lips.

Two years after this little gathering, which I have thus briefly described, and when the circumstances had altogether faded from her memory, she received a letter from a foreign land, which the writer concluded thus:— "May I tell you how you were once the voice of Jesus Himself to me, in a season of very deep depression? It was two years ago when the London Pastors were invited to your home at ———. It was not anything you *said*, for I never spoke with you in my life, but your singing of the little lyric, "Jesus is a Rock in a weary land" went to the very depths of my heart. It stayed with me in its sweetness for a long, long time, and even now sometimes, when I glide into the strange, weird air on my violin, the joy of that happy gathering comes back to my soul, and I remember with thankfulness the power then given me to trust very confidently in the 'Rest for weary sinners made.'"

That lady was a very happy woman when such a delightful piece of news came to her. To think that God had used her poor little unmusical voice to carry comfort into His desponding servant's soul was enough to make her sing all her life long! "Oh!" she said, "I felt as if, for ever after this, every power of my being must be wholly consecrated to such a Master, and that I would do all to His glory who had thus condescended to make me so unconsciously His messenger of blessing! I would sing, and talk, and work, and write with this sweet hope before me, of being again allowed to honour Him, and, perchance, refresh His weary ones."

I cannot tell you whether the Lord has since then laid His hand on the same string in that woman's heart which gave forth such tender tones to His touch; but I do know that for all who believe on Him he has provided, and is ready to bestow, the needful grace for a life of holy consecration and obedience; and that He can so conform us to Christ's image that we may reflect on those around us somewhat of the light of His countenance, and thus be a blessing and a joy to all.

* * * *

Songs in the Night.

"*What time I am afraid, I will trust in Thee.*"
"*I will trust, and <u>not be afraid</u>.*"

When the master of the house—the "houseband"—is away, we lonely ones at "Westwood" realize in an especial manner our complete dependence on the Lord for safeguard and protection both night and day. We know that the tender committal of home and its inmates to the Father's care, when the farewells are said, is always renewed and repeated by our absent one; and at our own evening worship the prayer that He will "hide us in the shadow of His hand" while we sleep, and guard us from all evil, is never likely to be forgotten or omitted.

But, notwithstanding this actual appeal to the Preserver of men, and a conscious belief in His love and power, I had lately acquired a foolish habit of lying awake in the night-watches, with ear intent to catch the faintest sound, heart ready to beat wildly if but a window-sash shook in its frame, and every nerve on the alert to assert itself in throes of painful alarm at the least indication of any unusual movement.

What if Punchie's fierce bark were to ring through the house in the darkness, or the sharp peal of the alarum should give sudden warning of the approach of danger? What if evil men should try to "break through and steal," or a spark unwittingly dropped, and smouldering long, should at last burst into flame, and quickly enwrap us in a fiery and fatal embrace? To tolerate such imaginings was to be tortured by them, and I suffered greatly, till some nights ago the dear Lord ended all this for me, and sent so blessed a ray of enlightenment into my "dark place," that at once I laid my head down on the pillow quite comforted. My painful care for the house and its inmates was all gone, because *He* cared for them; my watchings were over, because *He* watched; my fears were all allayed, because faith in *Him* was triumphant and complete!

And it came about somewhat on this wise: The two texts which I have placed at the head of this paragraph had been much on my mind during my wearisome nights; but they had evidently not then found entrance into my *heart*. I had thought of them without fully realizing their depth of blessed meaning; they had lain on the outside of my soul as fair lilies lie on the surface of a pool; but now I was to discover that they were fast anchored by strong roots in the exceeding great and precious promises of my God.

In a moment there dawned upon me the possibility and blessedness of being absolutely without fear *because I trusted in Him*. "*What time I am afraid.*" "Yes," said I, "that is just now, dear Lord, when the creaking of a piece of furniture startles me, and the very thought of the bark of a dog strikes terror into my heart." "*I will trust in Thee.*" As I said it, deliverance came. "Do I *really* trust in God?" I asked of myself; and I could steadfastly reply, "Yes, blessed be His Name! I do trust Him; and I know He can keep us in perfect safety; moreover, I am assured that He never fails those who put their trust in Him." There came a pause, the light had broken in, and I was wondering at the fast-fleeing shadows. "Now surely, my heart, thou canst go on with the other text, and boldly say, 'I will trust, AND NOT BE AFRAID.' What sort of trust dost thou call this that wakens, and listens, and imagines all sorts of evil instead of calmly sleeping and resting in the sheltering arms of the Blessed One? If thou dost honestly trust Him, thou shouldest certainly not be *afraid;* for thy faith should deal a death-blow to all thy fears." And it did, dear reader; then and there I gave up all my nervous apprehensions. I surrendered myself and all my belongings to the Father's keeping, and I have had no more gloomy fancies, or midnight watchings. I have laid me down in peace and slept, because He only has made me to dwell in safety; or if any wakeful hours have come, my mouth has praised Him with joyful lips, while I remembered Him on my bed, and meditated on Him in the night-watches.

Why do I tell such a simple little tale of personal and private experience? Well, just because it was a real and blessed fact to me, and I think that the relation of such instances of God's tender care and love, in even the minor matters of daily life, not only helps some of His timid and distressed ones to cast their burden on the Lord; but it is also graciously accepted by Him as a grain of sweet incense laid on the golden altar to His praise and glory by His grateful child.

If any courageous and lion-hearted people fail to understand my terrors, there are others who, having groaned under the pressure of like irrational disquietude, will sympathize with me in my past bondage, rejoice in my emancipation, and take heart of grace themselves to seek from the Lord by simple faith as complete and perfect a deliverance as His mercy has accorded to me.

There are many seasons in a Christian's life when he is "afraid" with much more need and reason than I could urge for my nervous alarms; but there never can be a day, or an hour, or a moment, when he may not "trust" his God absolutely, perfectly, totally; and, as surely as he does that, so surely will faith overcome fear—trust will lift him over the trial, confidence in God will end the conflict. Not to night-watchers only, but to those who, day and night, find fears and foes to fight with, do I lovingly commend my two "Songs in the Night," to be sung in any time, and to any tune—

"What time I am afraid, I will trust in Thee."

"I will trust, and not be afraid."

* * * *

May 10.—A most blessed and joyful Conference has ended with this week. It has truly been a season of refreshing from the presence of the Lord, a time of pleading and power in prayer, of spiritual satisfaction and enjoyment, which will not soon be forgotten by those who shared in its sacred delights. Every night, when the dear President returned home, he had tidings of new joys to tell, fresh wonders of grace to talk about; and, late as was the hour, he seemed reluctant to go to rest while yet such a mighty burden of unsung and unrecorded mercies lay upon his grateful heart. All the papers that were read were full of unction and sweetness, all the Pastors seemed endued with power from on high, and throughout the week the Spirit of God was manifestly poured out upon the solemn assembly.

Thus I heard from day to day of the "good times" which were going by, and I rejoiced with them that did rejoice; "For thou, Lord, hast made me glad through Thy work: I will triumph in the works of Thy hands"; but on Friday, the last day of the days of feasting and gladness, "she that tarried at home divided the spoil," and a portion of meat in due season was granted to the servant, from the well-provisioned table at which the guests had so richly fed.

Some eighteen or twenty of the ministers came to spend the last evening at "Westwood"; and they brought with them so much of the fragrance of the sweet spices and precious ointment which had been laid at their Lord's feet, that my soul was quickened and refreshed by sweet communion with them. They even *looked* like men who had been on the Mount with Jesus, beholding His glory; and their presence, their prayers, and their songs of triumph were to me a foretaste of heavenly rapture and delight.

The evening all too soon came to an end. I could have looked and listened all the night long; but I was reminded that we were still on Earth, and not yet in Paradise, by the fact that we had to say "good-bye," and part.

All the dear brethren were much pleased with the annual present. This time it was, Sir Richard Baker's "Meditations and Disquisitions upon Certain Psalms," a book of great excellence, as my readers will know when I give Mr. Spurgeon's opinion of it, as found in his "Commenting and Commentaries." "O rare Sir R. Baker! Knight of the flowing pen! His 'Meditations and Disquisitions' are altogether marrow and fatness. We have often tried to quote from him, and have found ourselves so embarrassed with riches, that we have been inclined to copy the whole book."

God ever bless the Pastors' College! Very tender memories linger round its name and work! When the dear President first had it laid upon his heart to train men for the ministry, or rather, to help those who were called of God to preach to prepare themselves for their life-work, he began with one young brother. We were but newly-married, and had great difficulty in meeting the expense of maintaining such a full-grown son; but the help the Lord sent was so direct and marvellous, that our faith was strengthened to ask and expect great things, and we had the joy of not only seeing our grown-up family still growing apace, but of receiving proportionate means for its maintenance. Many moving tales could we tell of anxious hearts, and an apparently failing purse, in those first days of trial; but *always*, yes, *always*, our God put our fears to flight, and sent the needed funds to us—sometimes from an utterly unexpected quarter. Since then, well may we say, "What hath God wrought!" From the first day until now more than seven hundred men have been sent forth to preach the gospel, and the dear President says of this his chosen life-work in the last Report: "It was commenced in faith, it has required faith to carry it on, and it has rewarded the faith exercised concerning it. To him who led the way in the work it has been a spiritual education, by which spiritual life has been tested and strengthened. In no one point has it disappointed our confidence in God concerning it, though it has brought upon us a thousand trials which else we might not have enjoyed. We have nothing to do in the review of it but to thank God and take courage."

Although the editorial "we" in the above paragraph is not at all intended to refer to the President's partner in life's joys and sorrows, she would nevertheless suggest her modest claim, being the nursing-mother of the Institution, to avail herself also of that mysterious plural phraseology, and to say with all her heart, "God bless *our* College, and *our* Pastors, and *our* Students, and—emphatically

OUR PRESIDENT."

Excursions from an Arm-chair.

By the aid of a large bundle of letters which lies before me, and with your cheerful concurrence, my dear reader, we will now take a few mental journeys, following some of my parcels to their destination, and witnessing, as far as is possible, their reception by the persons to whom they are addressed. As we travel in imagination only, we shall not need train, or boat, or carriage; we can pass quickly at our own sweet will from one country to another, and in a moment transport ourselves from a far distant city to some quiet country village in our own dear land. We shall have no fussiness of departure, no burden of baggage, no expenses of transit, no weariness of body, no discomforts of strange resting-places; from our arm-chair we shall flit across the seas and back again, and, without removing our feet from our comfortable footstool, we shall measure many leagues of land in our wanderings. Prepare yourselves, therefore, for this pleasant tour, which will have also this advantage, that we shall, Asmodeus-like, take a peep into many homes and hearts, and be privileged to see and hear many charming views and voices, without once interrupting or disturbing those whom we visit, or giving them—unless we so will it—even a suspicion of our invisible presence.

* * * *

Into the fair land of France we will take our first pilgrimage; a way not often trodden by the feet of those who bear Book Fund parcels, since but a few of the Pastors of the Protestant Church are sufficiently conversant with the English language to read its literature to edification. But here, far away in the region of the "Basses-Pyrénées," lives one who has solicited the boon of an English Commentary, and fully proved he can use and understand it by admirably expressing both his need and his gratitude in the language in which it is written. We shall hear what he says; and as we listen to him, we seem to see him standing at the door of his modest little cottage, with its vine-covered porch, lifting up his eyes to the "everlasting hills" which overshadow the sweet valley where his lot is cast, and blessing God for the English friends who have so kindly enriched his far too scanty library, and furnished him with companions who can cheer his loneliness, and comfort his heart.

Dear Madam,—It is impossible for me to express to you all my deep and heartfelt gratitude for the beautiful, or rather the magnificent, grant of books which has lately reached me from your hands. It is, indeed, quite a "Treasury" of deep thought and spiritual experience. I have been able, as yet, only to glance at these eight volumes; but I intend to make good use of them, and I feel sure the blessing of God will rest on my study of them, not only for myself, but also for the flock the Lord has given me to lead to Him. May He bring to pass all the kind wishes contained in the little note I found in one of the books!

French Protestant ministers are greatly in need of wise and loving help at this present time. In a former letter this brother said, "Now, more than ever, Protestant pastors have a great work to do in France. The people are tired of the clergy, while, on the other hand, infidels are trying to make way, and they boast of their science, comparing it with the too well-known ignorance of the Romish priests." Good helpful books must be of immense importance to one in such a responsible position; for the man of God needs to be armed at all points to repel these cruel and cunning adversaries.

* * * *

Passing quickly from the interior of "La Belle France" to the coast, we find ourselves in a thronged and fashionable seaport town, much frequented by English visitors, and teeming with seafaring men of all nationalities. Down one of the narrow and crowded streets we come to the door of a "Sailors' Institute," and entering, we find a young man busily employed in preparing a large quantity of Mr. Spurgeon's "Sermons," for distribution to the mariners who will congregate in these rooms in the evening. Our friend is the Secretary of the Institution, and also a very earnest Wesleyan minister, toiling early and late in the Master's service. We made his acquaintance some time ago, when he asked for "The Treasury of David," and added a special plea for these poor friends of his, who need so much a helping hand, and a kindly warning voice, when exposed to the temptations of shore-life. He told of his scanty library, and of the still scantier means which prevented any replenishing of it; he said that to supply his own people with good food four times a week, attend to his many duties at the rooms, and conduct a special religious service for the sailors weekly, was very hard work for a young man; and he hoped that, as Mr. Spurgeon's works would be more valuable and helpful to him than anything else, I would gratify his intense longing, and do the best I could for him. So the precious parcel of books was sent, and to-day, on our visit, we not only find him rejoicing over his newly-acquired possessions, but already joyfully dealing out the words of life to the seafaring men in whose welfare he takes so warm an interest.

God bless him and his work! He says the congregations have been trebled within the eighteen months of his residence. May the Lord add daily to their number of such as shall be saved!

* * * *

Crossing now the "silver streak," we land serenely, and with no qualms either of conscience or condition, at a town on English shores, where we quietly enter the modest little lodging of a newly-ordained curate, who lately sought from me a gift of books, that he might do his Master's work more thoroughly. And this is what he says of the gift now that it is his :—

Dear Mrs. Spurgeon,—The parcel of books has just arrived. How can I thank you enough for such a help to my heavy and responsible duties here? They are just the kind of books which will guide me aright in this the beginning of my ministerial career; and I feel to need such help, for the town is large, and the work great, and of myself I am so incapable of battling with the adverse influences at work that for any assistance I am most grateful, and do very gladly accept it for the furtherance of the Saviour's name and cause. Please receive my warmest thanks for the books.

As we leave this young servant of Christ in his lowly room, gratefully looking into his new treasury of helpful thoughts, can we do better than earnestly beseech the Lord to give His Holy Spirit's power with the books, that their teaching may sink deep into his heart, and bring forth precious fruit in his ministry?

* * * *

After this we take our places in a train on the London, Chatham, and Dover line, and for about an hour enjoy a pleasant ride through fertile fields, and rich pastures, and sweet sylvan scenery. Then we alight at the roadside station of a lovely village in Kent, which looks so smiling and picturesque and peaceful in the sunlight, that one would fain believe that sin, and sorrow, and sickness, might never enter within its borders. Alas! how different is the reality from the appearance! We have proof enough as we pass along the village street that evil is present here, and that, though living in an earthly paradise, man still flees from his Maker under a consciousness of sin, as he did in the original Eden. But we have come to seek the minister, and must be about our business. We call at a pretty little house, and entering without the ceremony of knocking (our invisibility gives us this privilege) we search out the wee room which is set apart as the pastor's "study," and we find him there amidst the "most admired disorder," surrounded by volumes new and old, and evidently enjoying what we housewives should call a "regular turn-out," or "spring-cleaning." "What can all this fuss mean?" you say. Well, only this, a Book Fund parcel arrived yesterday, and the good pastor is not only experiencing the delight of dusting, arranging, and placing these newly-acquired treasures on his shelves, but he has said to himself (and to me), "I intend to share with Mrs. Spurgeon in the blessedness of *giving*. I have some good local preachers working with me—poor men, but true and brave, and to them I shall give some of the old books which are displaced by these precious modern ones. Thus the seed Mrs. Spurgeon has sown shall at once bear good and unexpected fruit." Now we understand the reason of the disordered room, and the secret of his eager energy; and as we look around, and note the scanty furniture, and the few comforts (we know he has a family to bring up and educate on only £80 per annum), we admire his noble purpose and his cheerful piety, and rejoice to have had the double happiness of giving, and helping him to give!

The twelve new books are ranged on the shelf, and make a pretty show; but while we linger looking at them, and at him, we resolve that it shall not be long before some other volumes come to keep these company, and make glad the heart of this poor, good, generous man. God bless him, and all his local preachers, and all their work!

Behold, the scene changes, and we are trudging along a country lane in Cambridgeshire, and overtake a colporteur, on his rounds, earnestly engaged in reading a volume of "Lectures to my Students," which he had received from the Book Fund the day before. Presently a farmer comes by in his trap, and asks him up to ride. Our friend with the pack very cheerfully mounts the gig, and we mount also, only, like "Brownie in the churn," no one knows we're there. At the end of the journey, the following brief dialogue takes place:—

Colporteur: "How much am I in your debt, master?"

"Two words will pay it all," quoth the farmer.

"Thank you," says the man of books.

"That is it," answered his friend, "you are clear now."

So we are all landed on the road again, and the colporteur goes on his way to the village, bearing the gospel message, and speaking words of comfort and cheer to weary hearts. At home, in the evening, he has to write to the Book Fund manager, to acknowledge her gift, and as we look over his shoulder, we see that he partly reproduces the morning's conversation. "Thank you, very much, Mrs. Spurgeon," he writes, "and though I cannot hear you say it, I believe that I am 'clear,' at least if I make a good use of your gift." If we wait to read the ending of that letter, we must admire the tender sympathy which offers a sweet morsel of encouragement to his fellow-worker in these kind words: "While going from village to village I often call upon the good pastors, and many times it has been said, 'See what Mrs. Spurgeon sent for me; God bless her; her gifts have been a *great* blessing to me!'"

* * * *

From the green lanes and country villages frequented by our bookselling friend, we take a long and rapid flight to a large city in the North of Ireland. We do not stay to mark its public buildings, or watch the tide of its commerce, or note its parks and pleasant places; we go direct to the house of a clergyman, a curate of the Episcopal Church, and are shown into his study. I say "shown in" because, dear reader, it suits us at this time to manifest ourselves, seeing that the good man is going to tell us about the gift which has come to him from over the sea, and we cannot expect him to talk to imperceptible visitors. So, when he appears, and we introduce ourselves, a very courteous greeting is given, and conversation quickly turns to the desired subject.

"The parcel of books reached you safely?"

"Yes, indeed, and I should have written at once to thank you for them, but was prevented doing so fully by pressure of parochial duties. I did send a card to relieve your mind."

"Thank you, yes; but I am anxious to know how you like 'The Treasury of David.'"

"I really find it difficult, if not altogether impossible, to express how deeply sensible I am of the debt of gratitude I owe to you for presenting me with that most valuable work."

"You have already glanced at its plan and scope?"

"I have read a page or two in one of the volumes, and like it extremely. I feel sure that it will greatly assist me in obtaining a sound knowledge of that precious portion of God's Word."

"I enclosed a volume of Mr. Spurgeon's 'Sermons,' did I not?"

"Yes, and I shall also set a very high value upon that handsome volume. I shall pray that the discourses may be as much blessed to my soul as they have been to the souls of so many."

"What do you think of the 'Lectures to my Students,' and the volume on 'Commenting'?"

"I expect to profit much by them, I look forward with the greatest pleasure to reading them, and I can assure you they shall be carefully and prayerfully studied."

"Did I send you only these?"

"You kindly included others which, in addition to being deeply interesting, will, I am sure, prove instructive and helpful."

"It was a great joy to me to send them."

"It is simply one of the many instances of the love and power of the cross, and will continue to be a memorial of the real unity which exists in the hearts of Christ's faithful people; and if my study of those books redounds to the glory of God, and to the praise of our Lord Jesus (as I pray it may) you will feel more than rewarded."

"I do feel fully, amply repaid; sometimes 'my cup runneth over. The grateful appreciation of my gifts is always delightful, but above and beyond this is the joy of knowing that God's blessing rests on them in so large a measure."

"Very earnestly do I crave that blessing on these volumes. The high value and extent of the gift—far more than I expected or deserved—render it difficult for me to thank you at all adequately, or as I should like to do, for it; but I pray that every blessing may rest upon you, upon the author of the books, and upon all the work we do for the glorious Master."

"Amen, dear friend; thanks for your kind and grateful wishes! May the light of God shine upon every page of the books I have had the pleasure of giving you; and for many years to come may they be your choice companions, your reliable counsellors, your unfailing sources of cheer and comfort! Fare you well!"

* * * *

Our next call is at the house of a young Baptist Minister in a small village in the midland counties of England. He is in a very lonely and isolated sphere, cut off from the rest of the world, as he himself says, "almost as much as poor Gordon was at Khartoum," and needing reinforcements to his library to enable him to carry on the warfare against evil, and for the Lord Jesus Christ. He solicited and received a grant of books which I expect will have brought him intense joy. We will hear what he has to say about them, allowing him to tell the story straight on, and without interruption.

This morning I received your beautiful parcel of books. Being a little tired with the three services of yesterday, I thought I would rest and refresh my soul a little; so I have been carefully reading some extracts from each of the volumes you sent me, and if you care to listen to my brief experience of their value, I should like to tell what I found in them. The remarks on posture, etc., in the second series of "Lectures to my Students," afforded me huge amusement and instruction. I am sorry to say that I recognized *myself* as figuring in some of those ungainly postures. But the book has done me good, and made me resolve to cure these faults. It is indeed a pity that the Gospel Message should be hindered by the ridiculous attitudes of the "Gospeller." The lecture "to workers with slender apparatus," in the first volume, gave me much encouragement, and fired me with enthusiasm; while that on "Commenting" was read with deepest interest. "The Treasury" has already furnished me with matter for a comment next Sunday on my favourite Psalm (the eighth), and I hope and believe that God, by His Spirit, will bless the teaching. I feel as if it had placed a key in my hand to unlock the spiritual significance of the Psalm. Next, I read a paper on the books of the New Testament in Olshausen's works, which strengthened the muscles of my working faith, and deepened my love for the Master, who has given such ample convincing testimony to His own Word. Then I read through Mr. Spurgeon's "Sermon" on "Supposing Him to be the Gardener," and it had the same effect on my soul that a holiday ramble would have had on my body. I could almost see the tender, delicate hues of the flowers—could almost smell their sweet perfume. Lastly, a chapter in Valpy's "Greek Testament" supplied me with matter for a sermon on Matt. . . . But there, I must not inflict a sermon on *you*, though my heart is already "inditing a good matter," and I long to "speak of the things which I have made touching the King." Very speedily and happily the whole morning has passed away, and I am filled with deep gratitude to you, and to our Heavenly Father, who put the thought of this kindness into your heart, and who will bless and reward your work of faith and labour of love.

As we take leave of this pastor in his secluded corner of the vineyard, we rejoice to know how much the Book Fund present has stimulated and brightened his life, and we hope these good results will remain with him for many a day to come.

* * * *

Not a long journey this time. We go a few miles by rail, and are set down in a busy manufacturing town, where the din of machinery and

"The noise of moving wheels and multitudes astir"

are heard from morning's dawn to nightfall.

What a change from the quiet hamlet in "Sleepy Hollow," our last stopping-place, where the sweet songs and sounds of Nature alone broke the stillness, save when the creaking of the farm-waggons returning from the fields, or the occasional rumble of a wheelbarrow down the village street, added a not inharmonious chorus! Now we have come into the midst of busy human life, and the minister we seek must be a busy man, with the weight of the care of many souls on his heart, and the burden of the daily necessities of the toiling masses around him pressing heavily on his spirit. Such a one will surely hail the comfort and help which books can give as a precious and greatly-to-be-desired boon. Well, let us enter his room, and see whether we can gain an insight into the feelings with which he received the large parcel we sent to him yesterday! The books are lying on chairs and table, loosed from their wrappings, and looking already at home, albeit they are not yet installed in their places. Their present owner is writing fast and eagerly, glancing at them every now and then with loving, hungry eyes; and we, in virtue of our ghostly privilege, not only read what he is writing—which would indeed be an unwarrantable liberty were we not invisible—but we actually take notes of his letter for future use and good service. And this is what he is saying:—

The books have come, and your munificence has taken me by storm. Coming home late on Saturday, on my way I looked into a bookstall, where my heart yearned to take some of the inmates by the hand and lead them safely home. But lo! when I reached my house, I found quite a company of new friends awaiting me. While the voices of homeward-bound revellers sounded painfully outside my door, I poured out my heart to the Great King, and thanked Him for the right royal gift His daughter had bestowed on me. I read far into the night, and arose early this morning to greet again my lovely friends with their golden harps (the volumes of "The Treasury of David"), and now I sit down to give my thanks to you. I cannot express them, they will not dribble from the end of a pen; they want to come in a flood. Your gift has stirred feelings that had long lain dormant, and were, to all appearance, dead; emotions which only *mother's* kindness used to awaken, and which I had almost forgotten. It has been like "the touch of a vanished hand" to me, and the "sound of a voice that is still," and I thank you with my whole heart. I had not dared to hope you would send "The Treasury"; but you stayed not your hand even there, and I feel its lovingkindness very deeply as I look on the many volumes with which you have enriched me, and read the good wishes you have expressed. Again and again I thank you, and pray it may long be your joy to send smiles and holy laughter into many a heart and home.

There! was not this worth coming for, even into this noisy, dingy place? We cannot fail to be encouraged by such an appreciative reception of our loving service, and the young pastor himself will be all the brighter and better able to work for this tender little experience, which has evidently awakened hallowed memories, and will inspire high and holy resolves.

* * * *

We will now take a longer journey, and travel far away up north by land and water till we reach one of the wild and wind-swept islands which lie off the Scottish coast. The weird and solemn beauty of the place attracts many visitors, but just now, in the sunshine of a summer's sky, it looks so fair and peaceful that one can scarcely realize that here, in other seasons, storm and tempest wage their fiercest, wildest conflicts.

We land from the steamer in one of the beautiful bays which afford such convenient harbours for the fishing-boats; and passing quickly up the one principal street, we presently turn aside into a lane leading away from the noise and bustle of active, work-a-day life. Here, in a very small cottage, built roughly of stones and mud, we find two lone women living—mother and daughter—the former so grievously afflicted that all who know the details of her terrible sufferings wonder how she survives under the constant pressure of such dire physical infirmity and pain. We are not going to her bedside, she is unable to bear the presence of strangers, and very few could endure to witness her pitiful condition; our sympathy is sufficiently excited by the knowledge that she is very old—utterly helpless—blinded by disease—wasted almost to a skeleton—and suffering constant agonies of bodily pain. While we wait for the coming of the loving, dutiful daughter who has so patiently tended the poor sufferer through long years of fiery trial, we will sit in this tiny outer room from whence we can see the mighty Atlantic billows rolling into the bay, and we will comfort our hearts with the thought that the same God, who holds these great waters in the hollow of His hand, sustains, and cares for, and pities, and will perfect, the afflicted soul whose only hope is in Him.

"But are we following a Book Fund parcel into this strange place?" you say. Yes, even so; though this is not a minister's house, and "standard works of reference and divinity" might not be suitable presents to the inmates of this humble home. But I have twice had the happiness of giving great comfort to these burdened ones by gifts of "Sermons" and devotional reading, and we have come now on purpose to hear the long story of gratitude and joy which is certainly awaiting us. See! the door opens, and a woman of a sad countenance approaches. Listen! she is speaking now:—" Mrs. Spurgeon," she says, "likes to know of the good done by the books she sends out, and no one has more cause than I have to thank God for them. Yes, it was about eighteen months ago since she sent me the first parcel, and in it was that wonderful book 'Morning by Morning,' a gift that will never grow old to me; while as for mother, nothing else could have been like it; all the books were joy and gladness to me, but this was the best food for mother —brief, plain portions, full of the living Word, just as much as she could bear at a time when the pain was a little better. If you think of mother's condition, you will understand what a boon the books were to me; they are real company as well as comfort. Why, last year we had a very rough winter, and oftentimes the wind was fearfully high, and moaned and shrieked round our house, and then, as I sat through the long dark night, sick and weary in body, watching my suffering mother, and the only sounds I could hear were the roaring of the tempest and her cries of pain: at such times the company of a book was an unspeakable boon to me, and by God's blessing helped me to bear the heavy burden of care and sorrow which might otherwise have crushed me. At intervals, too, when the pain abated, and mother could listen to a sentence or two, I would playfully say, 'Now, I think, we will go and have a talk with Mr. Spurgeon,' and she would cheer up, and a few words from the portions would calm and comfort us both in those terrible 'night-watches.'"

"Did I receive some 'Sermons'? Yes, Mrs. Spurgeon sent me a good many in monthly parts, and some numbers of *The Sword and the Trowel*, and after reading them I was anxious to do all the good I possibly could with them, so I lent them to neighbours and friends; and when they brought back one they got another, till all had been thus used, and then I sent them to the other side of the island, for all the people are desperately eager to get anything of Mr. Spurgeon's. I can truly say that parcel of books was food, and company, and work, for me for more than twelve months!"

"Have I been made happy by another gift quite lately? Yes, indeed I have! and though I never danced in my life, I felt very much inclined to do so when the precious packages came to hand. But you see, my poor body is so worn, and so many pains prevail against me, I had just to sit down and let my heart dance, and my lips sing praises to God, while I looked at the riches so lovingly sent by Him through His messenger. Mother seemed to think that her eyes *must* be opened to see the good things that made me so glad; and when she knew that Mr. Spurgeon's son's likeness was in a small volume of his 'Sermons,' she insisted on having the bandages removed from her eyes, and while I supported her head with one hand, and held the book close to her poor face with the other, she tried her utmost to see the dear young preacher. But alas! all our efforts were in vain, the dim old eyes were fast closed, and might never more see earth's shade or sunshine. Blessed be God, their next vision will be the heavenly glory, and the face of Jesus Christ!"

"Did mother fret over the disappointment? Oh no, not in the least, she was quite content to hear of all the nice books and papers, and listen to a bit of one of the 'Sermons,' and then to enjoy the taste of the excellent tea, which I found so snugly wrapped up in the midst of all. *We did think it so wonderful that Mrs. Spurgeon should have thought of this for us;* and I am now rejoicing in the prospect of more delightful reading for myself, my mother, and my neighbours. I am especially glad to find some 'Illustrated Almanacks' in the parcel, and on looking for the first text in the year, how did my heart glow to find it was that wonderful question, 'Is not the Lord your God with you?' We had been talking over that very subject, mother and I, only a few days ago, and we could truly say, 'Yes, the Lord our God has been with us, and is with us still; not only that, He has come *very near* to us every day, and His blessed presence banishes our every fear, and we believe His promise that He will remain with us to the end, till He takes us to dwell with Him for ever.'"

"You are fearing to take up too much of my time, though you delight to hear of God's tender kindness to us? Well, I must soon go back to mother; but do tell Mr. Spurgeon how we thank him for the cheering words of his 'Sermons,' and the precious things he says to us. I saw one day in a paper that he had asked his friends to *pray for him, and spread abroad his 'Sermons'*; it made my heart glad to think that I could do both these things, though I am so poor and feeble. Good-bye, kind friends, do not weep for me; when my trials increase, then my Father multiplies His mercies—the deeper I sink into trouble, the more fully do I *feel* the support of the everlasting arms; and the more I suffer, the greater cause have I to praise and love the dear name of the Lord!"

What a glorious testimony to the truth and power of the love of Christ! What a blessed "Yes, Lord," to the Saviour's assurance, "My grace is sufficient for thee!" What a triumph of faith and hope over weakness, and poverty, and sore suffering! What rich clusters of fruit to reward the Husbandman's constant and careful pruning! We come away from that lowly cottage as from the suburbs of Heaven, we have surely been where the feet of God's ministering angels are wont to light softly and silently, as they bring succour and support to these heirs of salvation. Our tears for earth's sorrows are dried upon our cheeks by the felt nearness of "the glory which shall be revealed," and the sighs which might have risen to our lips are hushed as we hear "One" saying that His people *shall* obtain joy and gladness, and sorrow and sighing shall flee away.

* * * *

After this visit, so full of holy lessons and sweet teachings, we end our wanderings, and come back to our home, with softened, chastened spirit, pondering these things in our heart, praising God for all that He is to His people, and praying on our own behalf that more simple, child-like faith, and tender, trustful acquiescence in His loving will may henceforth distinguish our daily walk and conversation.

Back, in a flash of thought, to the arm-chair, and the cosy room where plenty of Book Fund work is awaiting us, feeling amply encouraged by all we have heard and seen, to continue with unabated zeal the labour which the Lord has made so abundantly successful and profitable.

* * * *

In the early part of this year, a friend brought under my notice a very precious little volume by Andrew Murray, entitled "Abide in Christ,"* and subsequently I made the acquaintance of its wonderful sequel, "Like Christ." Ever since then these two books have been held in dear and close companionship, and by God's blessing have been most helpful to me in my spiritual life. Feeling a strong desire to spread the good tidings, as did the lepers when they found the spoil, in the camp of the Syrians (2 Kings vii. 9), of riches and provision in abundance, I went and told "the King's household" by distributing a great number of copies of these admirable works among the ministers applying to the Book Fund, praying that they might first enrich themselves, and then bless their people with the priceless jewels of truth herein set forth ; and I believe God has answered my prayer.

Thomas à Kempis has said, "All men wish to be with Christ, and to belong to His people, but few are really willing to follow the life of Christ." I would fain believe, dear reader, that you are one of the "few"; and if you long to leave the lowlands of doubt and indifference, and to walk in the highway of holiness in the sunlight of God's countenance, I earnestly advise you to procure and prayerfully study these delightful daily portions, which, by God's Spirit, will surely guide you into close following of the Master's footsteps.

I think no true child of God, however dull or lifeless he may have become, could read these glowing, impassioned descriptions of the joy of abiding communion with the Lord Jesus without having his soul set on fire with longing after

---

*"Abide in Christ," "Like Christ," by Andrew Murray. James Nisbet and Co., Berners street, W.

it, without being re-enamoured of the glorious beauty and tender love of the Saviour who calls him to it. Note, these books do not teach the doctrine of that "sinless perfection" by which souls are puffed up with pride and boasting, their spiritual senses being deadened, if not destroyed, by the opiate of self-approval; but, keeping close to the direction of the living Word, they set forth the blessedness and beauty of a Christ-like life, giving "such a portrait as should make likeness to Him infinitely and mightily attractive, should rouse desire, awaken love, inspire hope, and strengthen faith in all who are seeking to imitate Jesus Christ." In the note to the 20th chapter, on page 154 in "Like Christ," we have so fine an illustration of the text, 2 Cor. iii. 18, that I must give it to my readers as a sample of the "precious things of Heaven" to be found in this earthly casket.

"What rich instruction in regard to the Divine photography of which the text speaks there is in what we see in the human art! In the practice of the photographer we see two things: faith in the power and effects of light, and the wise adjustment of everything in obedience to its laws. With what care the tenderly sensitive plate is prepared to receive the impression! With what precision its relative position to the object to be portrayed is adjusted! How still and undisturbed it is then held face to face with that object! Having done this, the photographer leaves the light to do its wonderful work; his work is indeed a work of faith.

"May we learn the precious lessons! Let us believe in the light, in the power of the light of God, to transcribe Christ's image on our heart. 'We are changed into the same image as by the Spirit of the Lord.' Let us not seek to do the work the Spirit must do; let us simply trust Him to do it. Our duty is to seek the prepared heart, waiting, longing, praying for the likeness; to take our place face to face with Jesus, studying, gazing, loving, worshipping, and believing that the wonderful vision of that crucified One is the sure promise of what we can be; and then, putting aside all that can distract, in stillness of soul, silent unto God, just to allow the Blessed Spirit, as the Light of God, to do the work. Not more surely or wonderfully than in the light-printing which is done here on earth, will our souls receive and show the impress of that wonderful likeness.

"What a solemn calling is that of ministers as the servants of this heavenly photography! To lead believers on and point them to Jesus, and every trait in that blessed face and life, as what they are to be changed to; to help them to that wistful longing, that deep thirsting, for conformity to Jesus, which is the true preparation of soul; to teach them how, both in public worship and private prayer, they have just to place themselves face to face with their Lord, and give Him time, as they unbare and expose their whole inner being to the beams of His love and His glory, to come in and take possession, by His Spirit to transform them into His own likeness."

Just one other short quotation will show how tenderly Mr. Murray seeks to put Christians on their guard against unworthy or selfish motives in seeking conformity to Christ, and how plainly he enforces the necessity of keeping God's commandments, and doing those things that are pleasing in his sight:—

"We have heard a good deal in these later years of full surrender and entire consecration, and thousands praise God for all the blessing He has given them through these words. Only let us beware that we be not led too much in connection with them to seek for a blessed experience to be enjoyed, or a state to be maintained, while the simple, downright doing of God's will, to which they point, is overlooked. Let us take hold of and use this word which God loves to use—obedience. 'To obey is better than sacrifice'; self-sacrifice is nothing without, is nothing but, obedience. It was the meek and lowly obedience of Christ, as of a servant and a son, that made His sacrifice such a sweet-smelling savour: it is humble, childlike obedience, first hearkening gently to the Father's voice, and then doing that which is right *in his sight*, that will bring us the witness that we please Him.

"Dear reader! shall not this be our life? so simple and sublime: obeying Jesus, and abiding in His love."

*   *   *   *

Swiftly as the months go by, Book Fund work keeps pace with them; and sometimes, as my daily post-bag can well testify, it even seems to outrun them in busy haste and eager impetuosity. If I were to allow an accumulation of letters for a few days, the result would be such an overwhelming mass of correspondence that I should shrink from the difficult task of giving each one due attention; my only chance of keeping the work at all within the boundary of my strength is to clear up all business every day, as the banking clerks do, and allow no putting off till to-morrow of what should be done to-day.

I confess that, very often, this persistent and steady labour taxes my energy to its utmost limit, and consumes all my little store of strength; and it is on this account that I have no new plans, or projects, or proceedings to announce in this year's "Diary," but am compelled to report only a steady onward plodding, a persevering discharge of existing obligations, and an earnest desire to "keep inching along"* till my Master bids me stop. Here, however, is the pity of it, for fresh ways of usefulness are continually opening up, and I could tell of many pleasant side-paths of sacred service, which I have been obliged to pass by from sheer lack of power to pursue them. Oh that some willing heart and able hand would undertake the blessed work which has in it such possibilities of exceeding increase and expansion, that it must to some extent suffer and groan under the limitations rendered necessary by my weakness!

By the way, I heard lately of a lady in Scotland, who, in queenly style, had made a splendid present of books to a newly-ordained minister; her gift utterly eclipsing, both in monetary value and the number of volumes, anything that' the Book Fund has been able to do *at one time* for its poor pastors. Here is a powerful rival in the little kingdom where I have hitherto reigned supreme! Yes, but I welcome her with all my heart, and pray that her work may be established, and glorious success crown all her endeavours to supply mental food to those who so painfully need it. Perhaps this is the beginning of the help I have so long and

---

* See pages 73, 74.

so earnestly desired ; perhaps in this way the Lord will entrust to *many hands* the labour which blesses, while it has burdened, this one feeble pair ; and fill *many hearts* with the sympathetic purpose which, till lately, has seemed to engage and gladden mine alone.

I do not know that I ought to be anxious, either for the present or the future of my work. It belongs to the Lord so manifestly ; He gave it, He has supported it, He has smiled upon it, ever since. Surely I need have no care as to what shall become of it when I leave it. No: yet sometimes the thought will intrude into quiet moments, "Who will carry this on ? Will the poor Pastors be able to write to some one else ? Will the beautiful ledgers and day-books, with their many thousands of entries all so carefully and lovingly kept,—will they be continued, or must they be laid aside on a shelf, disused and forgotten ?" Ah, foolish heart ! what needless vexation and anxiety these questions give thee, and how much of vanity and self-sufficiency do they reveal ! As if thy little bit of work were of consequence to the universe ! or thy morsel of ground in the vineyard brought forth all the fruit for the wine-press ! Why, the Lord has hundreds of servants, ready and waiting to do His bidding, and to do *thy* work far, far better than thou hast done it ; and if it pleases Him, He can enlarge its borders, and increase its strength, and make it a praise in the whole earth—without thee ! Hush thee, then ! wait, and watch, and work ; "rest in the Lord, and wait patiently for Him." He knows the end from the beginning, and thou mayest contentedly leave all in His dear hands, whether "for advance or retreat"—for life or death.

Give me, O Lord Jesus, a spirit of entire dependence on Thee, waiting to learn Thy will, looking for the "kindly light" which shall either lead me on, or give me blissful rest. All I can wish to know is known to Thee most perfectly ; teach me to trust Thee fully, and to say, without the shadow of a fear, in this and in all other matters,

"The Lord will perfect that which concerneth me."

* * * *

According to my usual custom, I have this year done some little business in encouraging the distribution of my dear husband's "Sermons" among the needy and neglected population of our towns and villages. I do not profess to enter fully into this service; it is one of the splendid opportunities offered by Book Fund work to its manager, which I am compelled to dismiss with but scanty attention and notice; nevertheless, I feel that if I cannot cast the good seed with ungrudging hand over the broad acres of expectant furrows, I must be content to sow a tiny corner of the field with loving care and watchfulness, knowing that the Lord will prosper the endeavour, and give the sheaves in harvest-time.

I think the first parcel of these soul-winners was sent to the canal boatmen in the Midland counties, and I know it was received with earnest prayer that God, by His Holy Spirit, would incline their hearts to hear the message. No class of persons more needs the loving efforts of Christian people to raise them from their degradation than these long-neglected toilers; and it is matter for great gratitude that of late years so many kind hands have been stretched out for their uplifting and deliverance. I believe that they will read Mr. Spurgeon's words with eagerness; and I was glad indeed to be able to send 300 of these messengers of mercy, which will gently and quietly talk with them by day or night of the love of Jesus, as they pursue their monotonous journeys along the watery thoroughfares of our land.

After this, a grant of 250 "Sermons" found its way into the hands of two young ladies belonging to the Church of England, who, nevertheless, are very earnest distributors of the Baptist Pastor's discourses. They have always kept their districts well supplied with tracts and papers; but since they commenced to furnish these "Sermons," the demand has been so great that their resources were crippled, and application was made to me for assistance in the emergency. With great joy I gave it, wishing them still greater success and delight in their work, and marvelling at the way in which God's loving purposes are sometimes carried out by most unlikely persons.

A fervent petition from the Black Country constrained a gift of 300 copies of "The Metropolitan Tabernacle Pulpit," to form the nucleus of a "Loan Tract Society." "Mr. Spurgeon's 'Sermons,'" wrote the applying pastor, "are anxiously looked for and highly appreciated in this part of the country, and when any are discovered in the religious papers, they are eagerly devoured. It would be practically impossible for us to furnish the funds to start the Society, and yet the church is so hopeful of the work that the members could not endure the idea of giving it up." My little gift just started them, and cheered their hearts; and they have been working on ever since, I hope, with success and pleasure.

Of another parcel, sent to a large seaport town, the distributor says, "I am so glad you have sent 'Sermons' for sailors. I meet with many here, and try to point them to Jesus. I shall divide the 'Sermons' into sixteen parts, and distribute them at the sixteen railway stations where I visit, and who knows what widespread blessing may follow; for they will be read and passed on to all parts of the world from this place?"

A good Primitive Methodist brother, who labours as a voluntary home missionary in a distant county, going about from house to house, and trying to lead sinners to the Saviour, received a grant of "Sermons" and tracts some five years since, and now pleads for more. He is poor and in infirm health; but his heart yearns to do his neighbours good, and the Lord has given him much success in his modest mission; so another parcel was despatched to him, and it is good to think how busy he will be for many weeks to come, arranging and sorting, and giving away the precious pages. He is sure to "steep the seed" in tears and prayers, so we may know assuredly what the reaping will be.

A country pastor writes: "The villages and hamlets surrounding our own village are dependent entirely on the light received from us. Open-air and cottage meetings are held from place to place; and on leaving, each person is provided with a tract; but I find it very difficult to procure a fresh supply, and should be exceedingly grateful if you could favour me with some of Mr. Spurgeon's 'Sermons.'" I sent 300 copies, and a nice lot in the form of little penny books, which are always welcomed most heartily, and perhaps are more highly prized on account of their neat covers, and somewhat superior appearance.

Two hundred sermons went to the very poor in one of the lowest parts of Glasgow, and two hundred more to a country village in Midlandshire, where, as the pastor writes, "there are many of our old people who cannot get out to the House of God, and I shall be glad indeed to take them a mouthful of such strengthening meat occasionally."

From a "Report" of the "Seamen and Boatmen's Friend Society" for 1885, I quote the following paragraph:— "March 31st. Boarded the ss. "S———," of West Hartlepool. On going into the cabin, was met by the steward, to whom I gave some tracts; he said, 'I beg pardon, sir, but have you any of Mr. Spurgeon's "Sermons"?' I said, 'Yes, through the kindness of Mrs. Spurgeon, I have, and I will give you some with pleasure.' He said, 'These will be treasured up, and read when we are at sea, I assure you, sir; many thanks for your visit and gifts.'"

But I should tire my dear readers if I kept on in this strain, telling them of the design and destination of the thirteen thousand "Sermons" which I have sent out during the past twelve months. I will just gratefully record the help in this direction which some kind friends have given me, and then pass to another subject. About half-a-dozen persons have volunteered to send the "Sermons" regularly to poor country ministers, and have faithfully performed their loving and self-imposed task. During the war in the Soudan, there was one who longed to do the soldiers good, and failed not to post every week some copies of the Sabbath "Sermon"; while the more extensive effort, of which I spoke last year—the supplying of all the Fire Brigade Stations in London with Mr. Spurgeon's discourses, is still patiently and perseveringly carried on by the faithful friend who first commenced it.

A fitting conclusion to this brief account of an earnest but fettered endeavour is found in the following sweet words from an aged lady—words so sweet, and pure, and precious, that comment or commendation would be equally out of place :—

> My dear Mrs. Spurgeon,—I shall feel greatly obliged and thankful if thou canst send me another parcel of "Sermons" on the same terms as before. They are so well received that I wish to extend my district. Thy husband's suggestion to look out for a fresh alabaster box of precious ointment to pour upon the Master's feet, as an expression of love, has led me to make this effort, which, in the opinion of some, might appear an unsuitable undertaking for one *in the last half of her 88th year*. But I hope to find a successor ; the " Sermons " are sure to be used, and a blessing is even now resting on the work.

* * * *

Pictures and Parables.

July 8.—A very pretty and suggestive picture is this week to be seen from the windows of my sitting-room. To the uninitiated observer there might appear to be nothing more extraordinary than a dense mass of shrubbery, overhung with a canopy of trees, and exhibiting in one corner a profusion of white flowers of unusually large size ; but I will tell the little story, and try to enlist your interest. This clump of evergreens has been allowed to luxuriate in unchecked growth during many years, and there is in consequence such an increase in their size and height that they are more like trees than shrubs, displaying a density and superabundance of foliage which is lovely, but undesirable in their position. Down in the heart of this miniature wood or forest, a small Syringa bush had its home, and disliking the darkness and lowliness of its dwelling-place, it took heart of grace, and for five years it has been endeavouring to gain access to the light, patiently pushing its way upward, growing through the laurels, and hollies, and briers, slowly ascending in spite of every obstacle, till now, in all the glory of eighteen or twenty feet of height, it overtops the surrounding trees, joyfully hangs out its snow-white garlands of perfumed blossoms, asserts its right to the lofty place it has attained, and seems to be making up in excessive beauty and luxuriance for the long years of repression and cruel hindrance it has suffered while struggling to reach this climax of growth.

"Are those white roses?" say our friends when their attention is called to the mass of blossom towering above the great arbutus trees. "No, not roses," we exclaim, "but something quite as well worth looking at"; and then the aspiring Syringa is duly admired and applauded, while its heavy bunches of flowers nod and quiver, giving forth their fragrance to every gentle breeze that stirs them, as joyful evidence of fulfilled desire and complete satisfaction.

Pretty, impetuous, ardent, living thing, I love to think how it persevered in its efforts to escape from the surrounding pressure and darkness, how patiently it forced its way through the fretting obstacles which barred its progress to the light; and it does my heart good to go and look at it, as now, revelling in the free and open air of heaven, and the blessed light of the sun, it blooms in unexampled beauty, and showers down its sparkling white petals in a very abandonment of joy.

What does the Syringa say to me as I stand far below it, gazing with pride and pleasure on its loveliness?

I think I hear a whisper from each little twig and spray, "Learn from us to be brave and patient, think no waiting too wearisome to win a blessing, no toil too great to obtain a triumph; ever turn from the darkness, and seek the light, though hindrances throng around you, and rankling cares, like thorns, would fain obstruct your progress; believe wholly in God, and trust in Him to bring you through all difficulties into the sunshine of His love and favour in His own good time. The days were very dark with us down there when we were growing, and sometimes we almost despaired of obtaining deliverance; yet inch by inch we advanced, the living sap within us enforcing our upward growth; and ever and anon, when the wind swayed the thick branches of the trees above us, we had such bright glimpses of blue sky and golden beams that the darkness became even more distasteful, and the imprisonment more intolerable, while our inward longing for the light lent us faith and courage to struggle bravely on! And see to what strength and beauty our Creator has brought us!"

Dear fellow-Christians,—the Syringa has a word for us all. "Go thou and do likewise," it says. By the power of Christ's life within you, *you can* rise above all your trials, and difficulties, and hindrances; *you can* get up above the darkness of any unhappy surroundings, and walk in the light of God's countenance. Be not content to dwell in the depths where the galling, grieving contact of doubts and fears will well-nigh choke your spiritual life, but, asking God "that He would grant you, *according to the riches of His glory*, to be strengthened with might by His Spirit in the inner man"; seek to "grow up into Him in all things," "forgetting those things which are behind, and *reaching forth* unto those things which are before," and glorifying His dear name by bearing, not merely the fine flowers of profession, but the blessed fruit of a holy, consistent, gracious life. Sweet Syringa, now I leave you, pondering, as I go, the apostle's words, which you have so well illustrated,— "Whereunto I also labour, striving according to His working, which worketh in me mightily."

* * * *

I think it must have been through the attention we bestowed upon the Syringa, and the enquiries we made concerning it, that our eyes were first opened to the folly of our mistaken forbearance in allowing the unrestrained growth of the trees and shrubs in the garden. For it was not *that* clump of evergreens only, of which I have spoken in the former paragraph, that had escaped the pruning-knife; but everywhere the plantations had grown at their own sweet will, and developed an enormous amount of life and vigour during the five years of our residence at "Westwood." When we came to look closely around, we found that these charming neighbours had completely surrounded and shut us in, and that the splendid view we had at first enjoyed and prized was now entirely hidden from us.

We awoke to the fact as from a dream. Where were the distant, but beautifully distinct, Surrey hills? Where was the lovely stretch of landscape? Where the ever-varying play of light and shade on all the nearer fields and meadows, and the changeful beauty of the far-off Downs and open country? They were all there truly, but we could not see them, they were effectually concealed from our eyes; and we went from window to window, vainly endeavouring to discover any opening in the leafy screen, through which we might once again gaze upon that glorious prospect which had hitherto so fascinated and delighted us. In the garden itself it was much the same. There were some charming nooks and corners where we had aforetime stood enraptured, watching the effect of every mood and variation of the atmosphere on the landscape; but these were now choked up by a dense mass of foliage, and tall trees waved their luxuriant branches in joyous defiance of the prying eyes which would fain look beyond them.

From the windows of the Pastor's study there had been most lovely peeps at the distant hills; Caterham, and Wallington, and Banstead, and Epsom Downs were all spread before the spectator as in a panorama; on a sunny summer's day quivering in a golden haze, or at night putting on a strange, solemn beauty, as one by one the lights in far-away villages and houses twinkled like stars come down to visit earth. Now one could see "nothing but leaves"; green and beautiful, it is true, but none the less embarrassing and mischievous, since they not only excluded some of the necessary light and air from the house, but did us the great wrong of concealing the loveliest of our lovely pictures.

"How could you have permitted this invasion of our once cherished privilege?" some reader asks. Well, the trees worked subtly, you see; they grew leaf by leaf, twig by twig, so noiselessly, so gradually, that we took no note of their encroachments till the thick barrier was formed, and our glorious view was hidden; and I must confess, also, that the Master of "Westwood," though a decided Liberal in politics, leans terribly to Conservatism in his own garden, and deems it almost a sacrilege to use knife or axe on any of the precious living things that have taken root in this favoured and fortunate spot.

So, even when we became aware of our enclosed condition, no small amount of coaxing and persuasion was required to induce him to allow the first gap to be made in the green barrier; and I verily think that the passage of the saw through those tree-trunks, and the down-crashing of the severed branches, brought for the moment positive physical pain to his tender, sensitive heart.

But, oh! when the sacrifice was once accomplished, and an exquisite gem of a picture was revealed through a framework of verdure, with what exclamations of delight did he welcome the beautiful result, and with what readiness did he admit the necessity for like painful but decisive measures throughout our small domain! This first grand and successful venture of mine, this onslaught against the aggressive vegetable kingdom, was made on the dear Pastor's birthday, and such a victory did I achieve, so charmed was he with the conqueror's spoils, that he thenceforth began to wage war on his own account, and became almost as enthusiastic for the subjugation of our persevering obstructionists as I had schooled myself to be. Since that day, decidedly Liberal, not to say Radical, views obtain on the "open space" question in our garden. Notable improvements are everywhere visible, pleasing prospects meet one at every turn; some of the trees that remain are taught to lend themselves to frame-making in the most charming manner, and through these lovely loop-holes we look across miles of hill and dale, while the larger part of our battlements of living green has been sufficiently demolished to throw open again the magnificent view which makes our Hill of Beulah into a true "Delectable Mountain."

Now this is a little bit of very common-place experience, but is there not a lesson here for a willing heart to learn?

Is it not just in this way that, by ignorance or unwatchfulness, we often allow earthly cares, perhaps worldly enjoyments, to grow up so thick and fast around our life that we are at last fatally surrounded by them, and the glorious outlook, which faith should keep and enjoy from the windows of our soul, is blocked and almost forgotten. I have said that the trees grew but slowly—it was only a leaf at a time—and so imperceptible was the increase that not until the landscape was quite hidden did we discover the forfeiture of our privilege—and I fear it is often thus that we let our spiritual enemies steal upon us. A *little* conformity to worldly ways and fashions, an occasional divergence from the narrow path which is the only safe road for Christ's followers, a small concession to that selfishness which so frequently urges disobedience to our Lord's commands, sinful habits unchecked, the hour of prayer neglected—ah! how these things grow, grow softly, stealthily, but, oh, so surely, with fearful vigour and awful speed, till the soul is shut in, and the light of God's countenance is shut out, and darkness and misery are the sure result!

Oh for an unsparing hand in the cutting down of all that dares to grow up between us and our God! It will not be enough to make only pleasant openings *here;* all must come down, every barrier must be swept away that hides the light of Heaven from our eyes, or intrudes itself before the fair vision of heavenly things which God's love has set in faith's sight; nothing must be allowed to cluster round our Christian life that can choke its power and spirituality, and intercept the sweet gales of the Spirit's breath, which, if unhindered, will "blow upon my garden, that the spices thereof may flow out."

How pitiful is the state of an encumbered and hedged-up Christian! How great is his loss! How sorrowful his indifference! How unhealthy his condition! You can imagine some one coming to see us when we were surrounded as I have tried to describe, and saying, "Do you know what folly you are guilty of in letting these trees grow so thickly? Are you insane, that you allow yourselves to be deprived of that prospect which is the chief joy of your residence on the hill? Do you not realize that you are every day disregarding a precious privilege, and perhaps growing content with these nearer delights with which the dwellers in a mere valley are able to solace themselves?" Ah, yes! we were indeed foolish. And all the time these barricades were closing around us, the fair landscape had been smiling in the sunshine, or veiling itself softly in the mist,—looking its loveliest at all seasons. Its glory and beauty were not lessened because it was hidden from our gaze, neither was its existence to be doubted because we could not see it; yet our joy in it was gone, and so far as our comfort and delight in it went, it might as well have been a parched and desolate wilderness. Ah, dear friend! cannot you see here some likeness to your own experience? I can to mine. You have seen other believers walking in the light, rejoicing in their God, steadfast in the faith, while you have felt gloomy, overshadowed, depressed, unable to lift up your eyes to the hills from whence cometh your help. And why? It cannot be that God's love has changed, or that His mercy is clean gone for ever? No, the precious promises are there still, like green pastures, and the sweet influences of the Spirit, like still waters; all the great and glorious things that accompany salvation are spread out before you in their fairest reality and truth; but, alas! you cannot see them, you cannot enjoy them; you are shut in, encompassed; you are well-nigh stifled by the luxuriant, deadly growth of some sin, or habit, or indulgence, which you have, through ignorance or sloth, spared to develop itself into a screen between your soul and heavenly joys; it is with you as the prophet so sternly says of the Jews: "Your iniquities have separated between you and your God, and your sins have hid His face from you."

Now, what are you going to do? Let the trees grow higher and denser, and your soul-domain become more darkened and desolate? Forget the lovely vision of the "things eternal" that your faith used to rejoice in, and content yourself with earthly shadow, in lieu of Heaven's sunshine? No—a thousand times, no—if you are indeed a child of God; but the rather will you arise, and utterly destroy and lay waste all that dares to exalt itself against God in your heart, and cry to the Strong for strength to make the clearance complete and enduring.

You will ask your Lord to show you all that is contrary

to His will in you, and then solemnly and honestly give it up, *whatever it may be;* you will take the axe of holy resolution, and cut the barrier altogether down; even though it be some darling sin which looks innocent and fair, some beautiful earthly thing which has woven its tendrils into your inmost nature: all, all must be torn away and uprooted, before the peace and joy which God's favour gives can shine into your heart again, or the eyes of your soul can look unhindered across the valley, and gaze upon the glory-land beyond.

And, dear friend, do not hesitate, DO IT NOW. "The Lord is able to give thee much more than this." Thou dost but cut down and surrender that which would harm thee, and work thee incalculable mischief; and while thou art thus engaged, behold! before thee opens a vista of "joy unspeakable and full of glory"; the sweet gales of grace refresh thy tired spirit, and thy emancipated soul suns itself in the Father's love, the Saviour's grace, and the Spirit's gentlest comfort;—the full light of "His reconciled countenance" falling on thee from the meridian of His love. Will not this entice thee? Doth not this suffice thee?

"'Giving up' this, that, and the other," says Frances Ridley Havergal, "is a downright *unfair* way of putting it; unless, indeed, the magnificent gain is distinctly set against the paltry loss. As well talk of an oak-tree 'giving up' the withered leaves which have clung to the dry twigs all the winter, when the sap begins to rise fresh and strong, and the promise of all the splendour of summer foliage is near! Over and above the unspeakable gift of eternal life, Jesus promises to those who leave anything for His sake that they shall receive 'an hundred-fold *now, in this time*'! Do you suppose He did not mean what He said?"

May I try to say just two little words of comfort to those who have *not* negligently and wilfully allowed their "trees" to grow up in their soul's garden, and yet can seldom get a glimpse of Canaan's fair and pleasant land, or "view the landscape o'er"? Well, dear souls, perhaps you *live in a valley*, where no prospect is possible, except by long and painful climbing! Or it may be with you as it is with us sometimes, when our lovely view from Beulah's Hill is obscured by cloud or mist, and we seem surrounded only by a dense white sea of vapour;—in both these cases God's hand is to be recognized, and you must be content if *He* put you in the low place, or if *His* fingers drew the curtains of the sky across your fair landscape.

But, supposing that you are one of the dale-folk, a dweller at the foot of the mountain, and that you can very seldom climb the heights which hem you in, yet you *know* of the grand prospect to be seen from those summits, and you can talk of it to others; you can cultivate, even in the lowlands, a spirit of cheerful confidence in God; you can look up to the stars at night, and you can sing, oh! surely you can always sing, that sweet "Song of Degrees," "I will lift up mine eyes unto the hills, from whence cometh my help. My help cometh from the Lord, which made Heaven and earth."

Or, assuming that it has pleased the Lord to bring the shadow of a cloud between you and your spiritual joys, that He has darkened your sun for a while, and blotted out your fair prospect by some mysterious dispensation of His providence, you have but to trust Him, and bide His time, and sing softly, " In the shadow of His hand hath He hid me;" and if the interposing veil be of *His* weaving, you will presently find that He will "blow with His wind" and scatter all clouds and fogs and mists, and once again reveal to your adoring eyes the bright vision of things beyond, which faith holds so dear and precious.

Oh, Blessed Lord! teach us by Thy Holy Spirit to rest satisfied with nothing short of whole-hearted consecration of body, soul, and spirit, to Thee, and Thy sweet service! Let everything that hinders or darkens our spiritual life be instantly and joyfully surrendered, that so we may know the blessedness of the apostle's assurance. "If we walk in the light, as He is in the light, we have fellowship one with another, and the blood of Jesus Christ His Son cleanseth us from all sin."

* * * *

I do not think that the dear soul whose loving act of self-denial I am now about to relate, and from whose letters

I intend to quote, would imagine she had done anything worthy of notice in the pages of even this unimportant chronicle; but, methinks, the angels carried the sweet story to the heavenly Father, and that there, in His "book of remembrance," this "thing that she hath done" is noted down in fairer characters than earth can trace. If I had passed by the little incident, her record still would have been on high; but I should have lost a beauteous flower, which fairly claims the right to grace and adorn my work, since the Report for last year was the seed from which grew this lovely thought and act of a loving heart.

A large parcel of nice, clean, strong clothes for women and children came to me the other day with this note enclosed:—

Honoured Madam,—Reading your Book Fund Report set me thinking if I could not in some way help you to send gladness to the homes of which you speak. I have to-day sent a small parcel of things which I thought might perhaps be put in with your books. They were given to me by kind friends, but I just give them again to Him, who "gave Himself for me." I wish so much that I could send more, and some money, but I cannot: I have five little ones, and my husband's wages are 26s. per week, but oh! we have so much to be thankful for.

Thus this noble woman gives out of her poverty the things which would have saved her many an hour's patching and darning for her own children, and consecrates to the Lord the comforts which she might most righteously have retained for herself.

In acknowledging her gift, I ventured a gentle remonstrance for her children's sake, but this is the reply I received:—

Honoured Madam,—When I first began to think if I had anything I could send you, I clapped my hands for very joy as I came upon one article after another which I felt I could do without; but when they were all together, they looked so poor and mean, I was tempted not to send them, fearing you might return them, but I had asked my Father to accept them, and like Jephthah, I *dared* not go back. Your kind note this morning has put a song in my mouth to Him who has so graciously allowed me to offer Him a mite, and has accepted it too! I did just once think how much I would like to keep this and that, but to give something to God which costs us a little, oh! this is a great delight.

Then, lest I should again plead against her self-sacrificing spirit, she adds,—

Please do not think we are needing what I sent ; neither myself nor mine want for anything. To the praise of my covenant-keeping God I can say, He supplieth all our needs, and for what He withholds, I praise Him also.

Is not this good woman's heavenly charity a rebuke to some of us, who have more than heart can wish, yet keep it all selfishly to ourselves! Ah, my poor Pastors! ye would be no longer poor if but a grain of the sweet compassion which filled the Saviour's heart could find a lodgment in some of our unpitying breasts! It is so easy to keep our stores to ourselves, so pleasant to lay up treasures on earth, and to enjoy the self-indulgence of forgetfulness of others' needs. There is a poor minister, in the next town or village, who is striving to bring up a large family on £60 or £70 per annum. What are we doing to help him? We go sometimes to hear him preach, and wonder at his careworn face and shabby coat, and very likely grumble at his dulness and want of energy in the pulpit, and say he is "a poor stick." But do we do anything to cheer, and comfort, and brighten him up a bit? "A poor stick!" Yes, very likely, with the biting wind of poverty always blowing upon him, and scarcely any nourishment, either mental or bodily, to invigorate him, and very little of the sunshine of human kindness to refresh him, how can he help being dwarfed, and stunted, and *dry* ?

Let us give him some books—real, first-rate ones—and a new suit of clothes, and a nice dress and a new bonnet for his wife, and some things for his children, and let us stock his larder and coal-cellar, and see what a change will come o'er the spirit of his dream! Would he not, think you, soon be stirred up, by the reading of those books, to fresh lines of thought, and greater diligence in his preparation of sermons? And would not the absence of dull care, and the bracing effect of a heart at ease, lead to a livelier and warmer manner in the delivery of them? Certainly it would. I only marvel how some men *can* preach at all with the awful pressure of poverty's grip upon head, and heart, and hand ; it must be that God pities them, and gives them compensating spiritual riches. Blessed be His name! He will not forsake His own; but He must be displeased with those who could help His servants if they would, and yet withhold "more than is meet."

If God had chosen to deliver to *angels* the charge of preaching His gospel of grace, how men would have hastened to load the heavenly visitants with marks of their favour and countenance! Would they not have offered fine salaries? Wealth and influence would have been laid ungrudgingly at the feet of those who needed it not. Could anything have been too good or precious to offer to such distinguished guests, bringing such good tidings of great joy?

But when God sees fit to ordain men "subject to like passions as we are" to be His ambassadors on earth, and to tell out the tale of His love and pity, the matter assumes a different aspect. These persons are bone of our bone, and flesh of our flesh; they must eat, and drink, and dress, and sleep as we do; to them the items of beef, and broadcloth, and boots, and beds, are a daily and inevitable necessity, and so we disesteem them, and, overlooking their high appointment, we treat them with scant courtesy, feed them on meanest fare, burden them with all possible earthly cares, and then listen to the message God has given them with an indifference bordering on contempt!

If I am speaking too strongly, I must ask pardon; but my soul is stirred up to a righteous indignation sometimes, when I see and know of the deep poverty in which some ministers have existed, year after year, while in the same village, or within a mile or two, reside professing Christians with ample means, who might easily help their poor brother, yet who stand aloof unpityingly, and withhold the succour which would bless and comfort the Lord's servant, and never make themselves a penny the poorer. Oh! what blindness hath happened unto them? How is it that they cannot see the dreadful mistake they are making in despising the opportunities given them of ministering to the Lord of glory? With what horror of conscious guilt will they hear this sentence from the Judge's lips: "Ye did it not to one of the least of these—YE DID IT NOT TO ME"!

December 17.—For some time past, I have been debating in my mind whether or not I should give to my readers the particulars of a pleasant circumstance, which has lately enlivened my quiet life with its interesting details. To-day has decided the question, for a donation of £5 to the Book Fund, the "First-fruits of the fishing-smack, 'Susie Spurgeon,'" supplies the link to my dear work, which seemed needful to justify the relation of the story.

To begin at the beginning—among the large fleet of vessels which regularly leave the port of Grimsby for the fishing-grounds in the North Sea, there has long been one which bears my husband's honoured name, and from time to time we have rejoiced to hear tidings of its voyagings and welfare, while mutual tokens of interest and goodwill have passed between the owner of the ship and the owner of the name. The "Charles Haddon Spurgeon" has done noble work, too; for not long ago it towed a *wreck* into port! The disabled schooner was a foreigner, and when the crew of the "C. H. S." saw her flying signals of distress, they boarded her, and found her full of water; but they bravely agreed to tow her into Grimsby! This took them three days and nights. During this time, the second and third hands had to remain on board the water-logged vessel, at the risk of her going to pieces any moment, and sinking under them! The good friend who gave me these details feelingly adds, "I like to think of the 'C. H. S.' doing this! It is so suggestive! How many wrecked and storm-tossed souls has the Pastor, C. H. Spurgeon, been the means of bringing into the haven of rest! How has he toiled to win them to the only place of safety!"

In this last summer, there was another vessel built for the same owner, and it was decided to call her the "Susie Spurgeon," to my intense gratification and delight. While she was building, Mr. E. greatly desired that I should be the first to see the "burgee," a large flag with the ship's name in; so it was sent up for my inspection, and, on unpacking it, I found to my great surprise a huge "colour," eight yards long, and two and a-half yards wide, with the smack's name, "𝕾𝖚𝖘𝖎𝖊 𝕾𝖕𝖚𝖗𝖌𝖊𝖔𝖓," in great letters a foot long, marvellously fashioned, and inlaid in the bunting. It was too large to go up anywhere but in the largest room in the house, and there, though it wound itself gracefully round the book-cases, and dropped in voluminous folds from the curtain-rods, it looked as if it pined for the bright blue sea, and felt out of place in a parson's library! As it hung there day after day, waiting till the ship was fitted, a strong desire took possession of me to use it in some way to show my appreciation of the honour done me. But how should I set about this? I lay awake at night, pondering by what means I could make it my messenger to carry a word to captain and crew, of good cheer and good wishes, and give a little evidence of my interest in *my ship!* At last a "happy thought" visited me, and I caught it, and cherished it with much care! It occurred to me that it would be a delightful task to work some few words on the flag, which should not only embody my best desires for the brave men who would serve under it, but should also set always before them the only way of safe sailing over the stormy sea of life, something which should not only attract the eye, but find an entrance into the heart! So far, so good; but how to bring my "happy thought" to a happier interpretation was another embarrassment. What should the few words be? How I puzzled over that question! How many things my mind suggested and then "declined with thanks," I cannot tell you. Then, one wakeful night, some rhymes popped into my head, and I cried "Eureka!" But I have no gift for rhyming, and it took me an inconveniently long time to arrange my undisciplined numbers into the following lines:—

> This flag shall bear
> On high my prayer,
> While playful winds enwreath it:
> God save the crew,
> Good men and true,
> Who worship God beneath it!

Now, I must confess I thought this rather good, and was a little bit proud of it, after all the trouble I had expended on it; but my dear husband, being an editor, is also a critic, and rather hard on "poets," as a good many people know to their cost; and so, when I, with meekness and fear, showed him this production, he smiled, and shook his dear head, and said it was "very nice, but it would not do." The rhymes of the third and sixth lines he could not pass—I must try again. I did so, with this result :—

> This flag shall bear
> Aloft my prayer
> As it floats in the heavenly blue :
> God bless the "S.S.,"
> Give good success,
> And save every one of the crew!"

This time I was not surprised when I found my dear Mentor could not give his unqualified approval; but I had done my best, and could do no better, so he tenderly undertook to revise the lines, and put them into proper shape for me, and from his unfettered pen they flowed forth thus :—

> This flag shall bear
> Aloft my prayer,
> That good success attend you ;
> God save each one,
> Through Christ His Son,
> And from all ill defend you.

Hurrah! This was just what I wanted, good wishes and the gospel of the grace of God combined! Thanks to the dear writer, and blessings on his words!

Then I began to work the lines on the great flag, and many tender little prayers were interwoven with the stitches, as one by one the letters were formed in white and gold silk on the bunting! The labour of love was accomplished in about three weeks, Book Fund work not allowing me to spend more than an hour each day upon it, and the large size of the canvas preventing rapid progress. But at last it was finished and forwarded, and most enthusiastically received at Grimsby, giving great delight to all concerned in the matter. "I have seen almost all kinds of things in flags," wrote my correspondent, "but never before an *inscription* of any kind. I can assure you this is a real novelty ; but it is splendidly in keeping with the name on the 'burgee.' The owner and captain, together with a great number of friends, have seen it this morning, and all are highly delighted with it, and are deeply gratified by the fact that you have yourself expended this labour on it. Nothing I could have suggested would have given the pleasure that this has done. Please thank Mr. Spurgeon for the lines you have worked on the flag. All our friends say there is a hearty ring in them—*just like him !*"

In the cabin of the " S. S.," which is fitted up with unusual taste and cost, the verse has been carved on the main beam, so that, as long as the ship lives, her crew may know of our interest in them, and our prayers for their welfare; and over the brass stove a large embossed plate of the same metal is set, with these quaint words engraved thereon—

"𝔄ll 𝔊od sends we take,"

which it is hoped may prove a message, or a word in season, to all who come on board. Medallions of Pastor C. H. S., and the ship's namesake, are also fixed in the cabin; and Mr. D., in one of his many kind letters, says, " The 'S. S.' is a noble ship. About thirty-five of us had tea on board the day before she sailed, and we had a good time. The cabin looked beautiful, the medallions in their cases on the sides giving it quite a home-like appearance. I can assure you the crew are all very proud of your notice and kindness." Later on, in another letter, my friend says, "You cannot imagine the interest that the ordinary labourers on our fish-market take in the 'S. S.'; it is really quite amusing. When she came into dock last time, I was passing by, and just for a minute I joined a group of men who were giving their opinion on her, and, as if 1 knew nothing of the ship, I asked one or two questions, and was told that *you* had put a verse on the flag. 'Oh!' said I, 'what was the verse?' and, to my great surprise, the man repeated every word of it."

My friends can imagine what a freshness and novelty these details have introduced into my somewhat monotonous life. Pleasant sea-breezes these, blowing briskly round the house at "Westwood," sweeping away the dust that gathers on an undisturbed existence, and bringing an invigorating ozone into the mental atmosphere! And now that the " Susie Spurgeon" on the sea has sent part of her earnings to her namesake on the land, to help to cheer the hearts of poor ministers, what can this " S. S." do less than record her gratitude, and tell of her delight and pride in the other " S. S.?" God speed her!

The Bethel Flag is hoisted on board the "C. H. S.," when at sea, and services are held on board. I need scarcely say that we have provided the crews of both vessels with books, " Sermons," etc.; and since the captains are Christian men, we may hope that the good influences surrounding the sailors will, by God's blessing, result in an abundant answer to the prayer on the flag:

> " God save each one
> Through Christ His Son."

Distribution of Sermons to Missionaries in Foreign Lands.

This good work goes on steadily and prosperously, rejoicing the hearts of many labourers in distant lands, and helping, so we have reason to hope, in the spread of Christ's kingdom on earth. What urgent need there is for the extension of God's truth in this wicked world, we at home have only too sorrowful evidence; while abroad, error, superstition, ignorance, fanaticism, and gross sensuality are all ranged against God and His Christ.

Perhaps this service is more essentially a " work of *faith*" than the home-labour can be, because the fields are so far away that we cannot walk in them, and pluck the ears of corn which have sprung from the seed we have sown; but lacking this, we have abundant assurance that God has given a harvest, and that it continues to be a very blessed and glorious one. Most of my foreign correspondents speak touchingly of the aid given by the "Sermons" to their own spiritual life, and the help they are to their daily walk with

God. Doubtless this is one of the chief reasons that they are so desired and longed for, because they feed the soul with the rich dainties of covenant love, and strengthen the heart "unto all patience and long suffering with joyfulness" in the cause and for the sake of so blessed a Master.

I give a few quotations from the letters lately received, as they will illustrate the nature of the work far better than any description from my pen.

From New Guinea, a missionary writes:—

Dear Mrs. Spurgeon,—A word or two of thanks comes to you from this land, as I know they will do from "all along the line," all round the globe. Many years have your beloved husband's "Sermons" been to us a feast in seasons of poverty of means of grace. We have been blessed, strengthened, fitted for new work through them, and now to be regularly supplied with the source of such great blessings is a boon, the result of which only the glorious future can unfold.

From that land of fire and fever which has been the "Gate of Heaven" to so many of our brave men, from "Afric's burning strand," I have this encouraging word:—

I must express my most hearty thanks for the "Sermons" you have sent me so regularly. After having read them to my own soul's profit, I forward them to my brethren on the Congo, so that they have been read at Stanley Pool, and, perhaps, further up than that, and wherever they have gone they have been a blessing.

A missionary in Almora, North West Province of India, writes:—

Allow me to assure you, and that very heartily, that the "Sermons" you send are most welcome. In such a land as this, with a constant and heavy drain on faith, hope, patience, and love, any help is welcome, and these "Sermons" are especially precious. The cry here is constantly, "Give, give"; and though it is undoubtedly "more blessed to give than to receive," still there are times when the soul grows very hungry, and is very glad of even the crumbs from the Master's table, to say nothing of such good fat loaves as those you have so kindly sent.

I have a very interesting letter from the martyr land of Madagascar, giving particulars of two native gentlemen, father and son, who are specially interested in Mr. Spurgeon and his work, and to whom the "Sermons" are sent by the missionary who receives them from me. The younger of the two—Dr. Rajonah—received his education in Edinburgh, and is of course a highly intelligent and cultured man. Some time since he gave an interesting lecture on "Mr. Spurgeon," which was printed in a monthly magazine, and has secured a large circulation.

"I thought you would be pleased to know," says my correspondent, "that even in this remote region Mr. Spurgeon's name and work are well known. When the 'Sermons' began to arrive, I thought I could not do better than forward them to Dr. Rajonah and his father; and should you continue to send them, I purpose to continue the practice, as I believe good use will be made of them in this way. Though I do not think any of Mr. Spurgeon's discourses have been translated into Malagasy, some of our educated natives are said to make great use of them, and to borrow from them pretty freely. This kind of plagiarism will not, I think, incur your censure, but rather will you rejoice that even here Mr. Spurgeon may, though indirectly, make his voice heard. May God long spare him to lift up that voice in making known the glorious gospel of the blessed God!"

Time would fail me to tell of all the interest which letters bring to me from Northern and Southern India, Jamaica, Newfoundland, Rio de Janeiro, Eastern Roumelia, Texas, Cape Verd Islands, Natal, West Indies, Smyrna, Turkey, Palestine, Morocco, Samoa, Colorado, Dacota; and, nearer home, France, Italy, Belgium, Prussia, and Sardinia! I wish I could transcribe them all; they would make a most effective all-round-the-world Missionary Record! In China, the "Sermons" are likewise received with great joy, and are carried far into the interior, for the comfort and cheer of the lonely workers. I send nearly 200 "Sermons" there every month, and the "Father" alone knows how His exiled children are helped by them. "Surely the Lord has led you to undertake this important service," writes a missionary from Ta-li-fu. "We who are buried among the heathen do so enjoy something fresh from home, especially when isolated as I am, my nearest neighbours being forty days away. How I do *enjoy* Mr. Spurgeon's 'Sermons,' and what a help they are to me!" "I was led to devote my life to mission-work," says a young preacher at Gan-king, "through reading Mr. Spurgeon's sermon, 'A Divine Call for Missionaries,' and therefore I need scarcely tell you how delighted I shall be to receive every utterance of the 'beloved preacher' which you are able to send me." Another missionary, from the North-west of China, sends similar testimony. He says, "It was the sermon, 'A Young Man's Vision,' read on a packsaddle, during a drizzling rain, among the mountains of the Kokonor border, that moved me to desire to circulate God's Word throughout all Eastern Central Asia, Mongolia, Turkestan, and Thibet. The same sermon suggested to Mr. King, of Shense, his appeal for fifteen hundred missionaries for this vast and needy field. I always take a packet of these treasures with me on distant itinerations, and many a Sabbath evening has our little company been refreshed by a sermon that has previously stirred my own heart in my lonely travels."

I have space for only one more letter, though it grieves me to crowd out others which equal, if they do not excel, in interest those already given. From North China comes the following:—

Dear Mrs. Spurgeon,—The arrival of your kind letter and the copies of Mr. Spurgeon's "Sermons" has made me more deeply in debt than ever. Before they arrived I was in doubt as to how much of my sermons were my own, and how far they belonged to your husband, but now, with the prospect of such a continual supply of his good things, I think my doubts will be resolved. Ever since I arrived in China, his works have been my storehouse, my armoury. If I may be allowed the figure, his productions have been the mine from whence have come the lumps of ore, and I have sought to pass them through the mint of my own mind, and so give them currency. His books have supplied the wheat, and I have sought to grind it down to flour, and so dispense food to the hungry. I have filled my little water-skin from his ever-springing well, to give the thirsty ones drink. Dropping all figures, however, I do thank you most heartily for sending me the "Sermons." I have already read two of them in public, and hope to use them, in one way or another, to a far larger extent; and they will be, I am sure, the means of great blessing.

I have thus given you, dear friends, just a taste of the sweet wine of grateful joy which has been poured out from the hearts of many weary toilers in heathen lands. As you read of their loneliness and need, breathe a prayer for them, that they may be sustained and strengthened in their noble, self-sacrificing work, and then help me to be one of God's ways of answering your petitions, by continuing to send them the blessed food upon which their souls may fatten and grow strong.

To those dear helpers in this part of my service, whose faithful devotion has stood the test of years, and whose love does not grow cold, or their zeal diminish, I tender my warm and fervent thanks. My God shall reward you.

* * * *

THE PASTORS' AID FUND has again this year rendered loving service to many needy brethren, whose scanty stipends have known no augmentation, even though, in many cases, their families and consequent expenses have increased. It is said that "agricultural depression" is at the root of all their sorrows. One feels a little tired of hearing this cuckoo-note year after year, and the high-sounding syllables may cover as much pretence as possible truth. I know not, but the pitiful fact remains that, from some cause or other, poverty in its deepest and darkest aspects is overshadowing our villages and hamlets, and our Pastors are sharing to the full in the universal discouragement. Only to-day, a letter from a country pastor reveals a sorrowful state of things, which, alas! is not peculiar to the place from which he writes. He says he never before witnessed so much poverty and distress in his district; yet, at the same time, he speaks with holy enthusiasm of the trust in God and resignation to His will manifested by the suffering people. "It is no easy work," he writes, "to live in a place like this, where one sees 'trouble' written on every face. I could not go into the homes of my people, and see shoeless feet and empty cupboards, without doing something to help them. Many must have gone to the poorhouse, or have died without medical aid, if I had not paid the cost." This pastor, dear friends, so ready and willing to help others, has a wife and five children, and only a few pounds over £100 per annum to live upon, and in his own household has experienced a large share of the prevalent sickness and sorrow. With noble self-forgetfulness, he chooses to remain with his flock. "I cannot leave the post of danger," he says; "God has helped me, and greatly blessed my ministry. There is suffering to be borne, but He suffered the shame of the cross for me, and when He putteth forth His own sheep, He goeth before them."

To such a true under-shepherd the Pastors' Aid Fund delights to stretch out a helping hand, and though its grants are small, they many a time tide over a season of trouble, and heal with tender touch the festering wounds which Poverty's barbed stings produce.

"I have been afflicted in body these many years," writes a veteran minister. "I am straitened in circumstances, affected by the general depression, and I am hungering after knowledge: so that I can hardly say which is my greatest sorrow—my lack of health, money, or books." Is not this a sad story to have to tell after a ministry of nearly forty years? Yet this is but one out of many, many cases, all of which present some special claim to tender and helpful sympathy.

The gratitude of some of these tried servants of God, when a little relief does reach them, is often very touching. A minister wrote the other day: "My wife has *never before* had a book or a dress-piece given to her; she can scarcely believe that your generous present is meant for her;" and then, thanks for all I sent are poured forth from their full hearts, overflowing with the joy of escape from the burden of care and anxiety.

"I feel I must join my dear husband," writes a pastor's wife, "in thanking you for the books you so kindly sent him, and for all the other things the parcel contained. Our hearts are so full of thankfulness to our heavenly Father, and to you, His servant, that we do not know how to express it. My husband feels too much overcome by your kindness to write more just now. We can only say, 'Thank you, and God bless you!'"

The gifts of the Pastors' Aid Fund are limited to poor *Baptist* ministers, necessarily, for I could not undertake so immense a work as the relieving those of all other denominations; yet my heart often grieves over this inability, and I wish that I had strength enough and means sufficient to help all the Lord's servants, not to books only, but to the money which never seems to find its way wisely to the empty, waiting pockets, where it is so deeply needed.

You will not wonder that sometimes I cannot keep my rule. I *must* break the barriers down. Here is a case in point. In a respectably-sized city there lives a minister, his denomination I will not divulge, but he is *not* a Baptist, and in a letter which now lies before me, he gives these pitiful facts: He has a wife and four children to keep, clothe, and educate; his salary is £70 per annum, and a rent of £17 10s. to pay out of that. "I need hardly say," so he writes, "that we are in a very reduced state. My wife and two girls have but one dress each for week-day and Sunday. None of us have more than one pair of boots, and these are in bad repair. The pinching and contriving to which I and my wife are put, in order to make things straight, is very trying, and detracts much from our home comfort and happiness. I am serving on the Relief Committee, and, really, I frequently feel I am myself needing the help given to others; but very few know of our troubles."

I am hotly indignant as I quote his words; I have scarcely the patience to write them out! What can his people be thinking about? Are they blind, and deaf, and altogether foolish? But "indignation" will not help him, and a £5 note *will;* so the money, and a parcel of clothes, will be despatched, and while they make a large gap in the hedge set around my little Fund, they will carry so much joy and blessing with them, that who could say me nay? Certainly not you, dear friends, who so generously entrust me with the means wherewith to bless these needy ones!

What I should do without this power to supplement, in a small degree, the meagre pittances on which some of our Pastors contrive to live, I do not know; but the Lord has inclined so many loving hearts to help me in this matter, that I am generally spared the sorrow of seeing misery which I cannot relieve. God reward you, dear friends, you, whose noble generosity keeps my treasury ever full and open! The Lord will deliver you in time of trouble, and the blessings of many grateful hearts shall rest on your heads. I have given away £317 17s. 9d. during the past twelve months, and I wish it had been in my power to have doubled or trebled the amount sent to each case, so sadly urgent and distressing have been the needs and privations which have come under my notice.

* * * *

The Sword and the Trowel is still sent out to the very poorest ministers month by month, and appears to give great help and comfort to them in their work. There is generally a chorus of thanksgiving at the end of the year from the recipients, and a very hearty *encore* to the twelvemonth's *pastorale* from all the auditors. They say it helps them in their labours among the people, profits their own minds and hearts, instructs, suggests, and inspires them with fresh faith and courage, and is so very welcome a visitor at their homes that they "really couldn't do without it." I think this is one of the little things that give great pleasure; and I should be very grateful if many friends would follow the example of some, who regularly despatch a copy of the magazine to a poor country minister, rejoicing in the thought that, though he might be able to afford threepence a month for it, it is better for him to receive it from them in this kindly and gracious fashion.

* * * *

THE GIFTS OF STATIONERY have been continued on the most liberal and extensive scale by my munificent friend, who is as wholesale in his generosities as in his commercial transactions.

The present of writing-material to a poor minister is so useful that one expects it to be valued, and almost invariably grateful mention of the writing-paper mingles with the glowing thanks for paper already written on in the shape of books. "The first use I make of the stationery enclosed in your most welcome parcel," writes a pastor, "is to send a sheet and an envelope back to you bearing my most thankful acknowledgments."

A serious item in a poor minister's expenditure must be this same letter-paper when he has to buy it all himself; and thus we find one saying, " The stationery will be very useful, for while I am writing hundreds of letters for all sorts of objects, and to all sorts of persons, somehow I fail to get a special fund from which to draw expenses." Very often my friend's gifts are received in a tender, loving way, which is most pleasant. "The envelopes and note-paper touched me as a gift of thoughtful kindness most unexpected," says one; and again: "When we came to the paper and envelopes, we could not help exclaiming, 'This is like a parcel from *home*, it is so full of kindly thought and consideration." It was indeed a happy thought, as well as a devising of liberal things, when my good friend undertook to provide thus bountifully for the enrichment of my parcels. The pastors do not know to whom they are indebted for this increase in their stores, but none the less surely will the blessing of the Lord follow the gifts given in His name, and the deed of kindness done for His sake.

* * * *

THE LEMON TREE must have a word of remembrance in this closing record of my work. How it has grown! And what a sturdy, healthy tree it is! Yet it has never borne fruit, and in this respect has greatly disappointed me, though it is foolish to be impatient at Nature's dignified deliberation. If it had been grafted, the fruit would have been forced; now it awaits the time of perfection as God ordered it, and as it was arranged when He pronounced all to be "very good." So it stands in the green-house, flourishing, and extending its branches year by year, and I still hold it in tender estimation as the emblem of my Book Fund, blessing the Lord that He has allowed the spiritual work to outstrip the leisure of Nature, and come into full fruit-bearing so soon and so happily, to feed and refresh His fainting servants. It is to me a tree of tender memories, for not only has its simple story won sympathy and help for my Fund, and interested friends in my work, but, whenever I look at it, I seem to see again the sick chamber which was my pleasant prison in Nightingale Lane; the couch where I lay suffering so many months and years; the sunlit window where the little flower-pot was placed, and where the "pip" grew slowly into a feeble plant; then, looking round upon myself and my present circumstances, I am amazed at the gracious contrast which the Lord's loving hand has wrought. "Can that fine tree, of eight feet six inches high, be the same tiny thing that began its frail life under such unusual conditions?" "Can I, with this unexpected measure of health and activity, be the same person who then seemed to be passing quickly through the Valley of the Shadow of Death?" 'Tis even so. Then do you wonder that often, as I stand gazing upon this lemon tree, happy tears of thankfulness for God's great tenderness to me should gently blot out the details of that *past* experience; and then that they should magnify the beauty and brightness of the present blessings?

New Year's Eve.

December 31.—Once again the Lord has brought us within sight of the closed door of another year; in a short hour or two we shall stand upon the threshold, its solemn portals will open wide before us, and passing through, our feet will tread the vestibule of the year of grace 1886.

What awaits us within this unexplored palace, which, like the Heavenly City, hath twelve fair gates of pearl? Shall we be allowed an entrance into the King's chambers? Will He bless us with a time of feasting in the banqueting-hall of His love? May we look for an active part in the work and service of His household? Or shall we find that our appointment is to make close acquaintance with gloomy corridors, and dark places, and shadowy corners in the house?

It may be we shall be called upon to wait and watch by the sick-bed of one of the inhabitants of the place, letting the light of our faith, and love, and patience, cheer and gladden the heart of the suffering one; or again, this

"House of God" may prove to *some of us* to be the very "Gate of Heaven," where the King's messenger awaits us with the glad summons to the Royal Presence!

What say you, dear friend? Would you rejoice to pass quickly through the lower rooms, and, ascending by "the secret places of the stairs," come upon a quiet, shadowed chamber, set apart and made ready for you by your loving Lord, with its " window open toward Jerusalem," and the attendant angels waiting on outstretched wings for your ransomed spirit's flight, "coming to carry you home"? Oh! methinks, if we did but realize the bliss of LIFE FOR EVER WITH CHRIST, the disrobing room of death could have no terrors for us. Rather should we enter it with glad surprise, and expectant haste, and with this sweet password upon our lips: "My beloved spake, and said unto me, Rise up, my love, my fair one, and come away."

* * * *

Let us stay a moment, and ask ourselves this question, "Am I ready and prepared for *anything* that my God may appoint for me during the coming year? Have I so truly proved His faithfulness in the past, that with joyful unconcern I can rest in the Lord, and wait patiently for Him?" It is well for us, if from the depths of our heart we can say, "I have no fear, or foreboding of evil; I know whom I have believed, all I have is in His dear hand, and I myself am in Him; if He bring me into bright and glorious places, it will be His smile, and the light of His countenance, which alone can make my blessedness, and with these, what matters it even if He should see fit to guide my feet where the shadows fall, and the night draws on?"

> "Christ leads me through no darker rooms
> Than He went through before,"

and the sure confidence in His presence and His love makes it blessed to go with Him anywhere.

This is "Watch-night," and in a few hours, God's people everywhere will be meeting together to praise and bless His name for mercies past, present, and to come, and to welcome this New Year's Gift of His with the voice of joy and melody. Though I can only join them in spirit, lifting up my heart to the same God and Father, this quiet study shall not be a place of silence, for a tender little song of thanksgiving shall go up from my "solitary place" unto Him, who, throughout all this year, throughout all the ten years of my work,—ay, and throughout all my life, hath "done all things well" for me.

On such a night, one can hardly help indulging in a renewed retrospection of the "eternal mercies" which have compassed one's path so long and so faithfully. The history of my unknown and sheltered life repeats itself as strangely and constantly as does that of the great tumultuous world outside, only with this difference, that my record can tell of naught but a repetition of pleasant things, a very tautology of tenderness, a sweet rhythm of gracious remembrance; and when for a moment I look back on the many "Ebenezers" I have had to raise to the lovingkindness of my God, I feel an ardent desire that this additional "stone of witness" shall rise as high, and be inscribed with as glad a song as any that have preceded it.

I am reminded by my present surroundings of the many times that, in this very room, and under almost exactly similar circumstances, I have prepared this Report for the press, and bid you and the Old Year—"Good-bye." I have before told you how I come into this great, solemn study when the dear master is away, bringing all the belongings of my work, because I somehow feel nearer to him, and the shadows cannot gather in the corners, or the room look desolate while Punchie and I are here. So again I am sitting in my husband's lonely study, yet I am not alone; once more he is in the sunshine, and I in the snow, yet both united in heart, with sea and land bridged by love; and again, as aforetime, I have to say to you what I have so many times repeated, that the Lord's goodness has been so wonderful, His love so tender, His mercies so manifold, His gentleness so great, His arm so ready to save, His pity so swift to succour, and His grace so abundant to forgive, that though I should write on for ever, the half would not be told you.

The Lord has made my time of loneliness to be a season of such intensely busy labour, that the days have not been long enough to enable me to finish all my work; and there has not been a crevice of time into which a dreary, cheerless feeling could intrude itself. Then the news from Mentone has been so encouraging and hopeful, that were it only for that mercy, I ought to sing the Old Year out with a "Jubilate." There came this sweet message to me this morning, and it will not be difficult for my readers to imagine that it has made music in my heart all the day :—

> "From sunny lands my spirit flies to thee,
>   And doth salute thee in the chilly day :
> Long hast thou been a summer's sun to me,
>   Fain would I chase thy every cloud away.
> Though dark thy skies, I would thy light increase
>   By one short message which my pen can tell,
> It brings thy love some little light of peace
>   To know that with thy husband—ALL IS WELL."

Perhaps I ought not to give my "love-letters" in the Book Fund Report, but this one came *on a post card*, and by this fact proclaimed itself *pro bono publico;* besides which, my few previous home confidences have been so tenderly welcomed and cherished, that I could not refrain from sharing with my readers on this last day of the Old Year the "little bit of sunshine" which has gilded every hour of it for me. Oh, blessed wedded love! that has grown brighter and clearer after shining on for thirty happy years ! Thanks be to God for a love that " Fonder grows with age, and charms, and charms for ever."

Very soon, if the Lord will, there will be again the joy of the home-coming, when the happiness of re-union will efface all the heartache of separation, and the two lives which, like mountain streams parted for a while by some ponderous impediment, having passed it, meet again with tumultuous current, shall flow on once more in deep and abounding bliss. Then all the routine of the dear happy home-life will begin afresh, and the days, so full of work and service, will fly swiftly on their busy rounds, and the sweet Saturday nights—my Sabbaths—will again crown the week's labour with blessing and holy peace.

Seeing that we began this year with a long account of the doings and the duties of its first twelve hours, I might have asked my dear readers to "assist" in the same way at its close; for the letters of to-day have been, to the full, as many and as interesting as those we opened on January 1st, 1885. Do they not say that, in a well-concerted piece of music, the final note should correspond to that on which the air commences? Even so, in composing this unpretending little tune of mine, I ought doubtless to have tried to harmonize it rightly, and have played the "finale" on the same chords as the opening "aria." But I spare you and myself.

The hand that holds this pen is very weary; and the brain, which tries to think the thoughts that guide it, is jaded and overstrained. Soon the midnight chimes will be ringing, and "each breeze that rises from the earth be loaded with a song of Heaven." It is meet and wise to say ADIEU now, softly and tenderly, to those who have for so many years been partakers with me of the joy of this sweet service, and then to go alone before the Lord, and bless Him for the immeasurable love and goodness which have ensured so blessed an ending to a year of blessing.

* * * *

> "Oh! tired heart—
> God knows!
> Not you nor I,
> Who reach our hands for gifts
> That wise love must deny—
> *We blunder*, where we fain would do our best—
> Until a-weary, then we cry, 'Do Thou the rest';
> And in His hands the tangled skein we place
> Of our poor blind weaving with a shaméd face—
> All trust of *ours* He sacredly will keep;
> So tired heart—
> God knows!
> Go thou to work or sleep."

Epilogue.

DEAR Helpers, Givers, and Loving Friends,—So many of you have, for the ten years of my service, gladly and steadfastly served with me, and rejoiced in the goodness of the Lord to me, that I long to give you *all* a very sweet and special word of thanks, now that these records are gathered together in one volume. Your part of the business is not so heavy, but neither is it so joyful, as mine; for though you experience some of the blessedness of giving, you have to use me as your deputy, and I consequently secure the very essence of the bliss. I would, therefore, that you should realize how happy the service makes me, how bright are the mercies that cluster around the work, and shine into my heart, how inexpressibly tender are the dealings of the Lord with me, that thus some of the gladness may be reflected from my life on to yours, and you may bless God for the joy which has increased through being scattered abroad. Truly the Book Fund is the blessing, as well as the business, of my life; I should be discontented and sad indeed without it, I cannot imagine myself deprived altogether of the sweet work, engrossing, as it now does, my time, my strength, my thoughts, and a very large share of my affections.

That I must somewhat curtail its operations, and in part relax the strain of my own efforts, is, I think, an inevitable conclusion. My dear husband, in the preface to this book, has truly and tenderly set forth a fact which I am reluctantly compelled to endorse. I feel very weary sometimes, am often burdened with an overwhelming amount of correspondence, fatigued with long hours of sedentary labour, and chiefly do I mourn my inaptitude and inability to write worthily the Annual Records of my work ; but I dare not say this without also adding that never have I cried to my Lord for help in vain, and often in my time of greatest weakness and emptiness, have I been enabled to say, " I can do all things through Christ which strengtheneth me;" I can even "glory in my infirmities, that the power of Christ may rest upon me."

Yes! with the blessed experience of these ten happy, laborious years to justify me, I can indeed speak rapturously of the dear Master's service. See how gracious He has been to one so weak and unworthy; note how my feebleness has but magnified His power, my ignorance and foolishness but solicited His heavenly wisdom, my urgent need but allured a supply "according to His riches in glory by Christ Jesus"!

Oh, that this true story of His love and help, given so graciously to me, may win some heart, hitherto at a distance from Him, to come and "taste and see that the Lord is good," or stimulate others, who already know Him, to a firmer faith in His tenderness, and a more distinct and deliberate dependence on Him for everything!

Dear friends, who have been so good to me, when you are helping the Book Fund, I pray you always to remember that the blessing you bestow is *fourfold*. You greatly enrich the minds of many poor Pastors; you lovingly help to feed the Lord's sheep in the wilderness; you graciously adorn my life with the beauty of service ; and, doubtless, you lay up for yourselves treasure in Heaven! Eternity alone can reveal all the blessing and spiritual help afforded *by you*, through the Book Fund, to those who are working for God and His kingdom under great and cruel disadvantages.

Would that I could put into the hearty THANK YOU with which I conclude my closing speech a thousand sparkles of loving gratitude! It looks so tame and prosy in these dull, black letters, but it bears all my heart in it ; and if you look with loving eyes upon it, you will see that it enshrines also a fervent

God bless you!

"WESTWOOD," BEULAH HILL, UPPER NORWOOD,
    March, 1886.

Alabaster, Passmore, and Sons, Printers, Fann Street, E.C.

WORKS BY C. H. SPURGEON,

AND OTHER AUTHORS,

PUBLISHED BY PASSMORE & ALABASTER,

PATERNOSTER BUILDINGS, E.C.

Expository.

TREASURY OF DAVID: Containing an Original Exposition of the Book of Psalms; a collection of illustrative Extracts from the whole range of Literature; a series of Homiletical Hints upon almost every verse; and list of Writers upon each Psalm. By C. H. SPURGEON. Cloth, 8s. each vol. May also be had in half-calf and calf bindings.

Vol.	I., containing Psalms	I. to	XXVI.—Twenty-fourth Thousand.
" II.,	"	" XXVII. "	LII.—Twentieth Thousand.
" III.,	"	" LIII. "	LXXVIII.—Nineteenth Thousand.
" IV.,	"	" LXXIX. "	CIII.—Seventeenth Thousand.
" V.,	"	" CIV. "	CXVIII.—Thirteenth Thousand.
" VI.,	"	" CXIX. "	CXXIV.—Ninth Thousand.
" VII.,	"	" CXXV. "	CL.—Fifth Thousand.

"If the eloquent Baptist preacher of the Metropolitan Tabernacle had produced nothing but these volumes he would certainly be entitled to the thanks of all Bible readers."—*The Rock.*

THE INTERPRETER; or, Scripture for Family Worship; being selected passages of the Word of God for every morning and evening throughout the year, accompanied by a running comment and suitable Hymns. By C. H. SPURGEON. Cloth 25s., Persian Morocco 32s, Turkey Morocco 42s. Hymn Book, 1s.

"The impress of Mr. Spurgeon's genius is observable in the very felicitous arrangement of the passages of Scripture as well as in the characteristic running comments, in which latter, by the way, Mr. Spurgeon's theological views come prominently to the front."—*The Christian Family.*

Homiletical.

THE METROPOLITAN TABERNACLE PULPIT, Containing the Sermons of C. H. SPURGEON, preached during the past thirty-one years. Vols. I. and II., 6s. 6d. each. Vols. III. to VI., 7s. each. Vol. VII., 8s. 6d. Vols. VIII. to XXXI., 7s. each. Whole calf 17s. 6d. and 21s., and half-calf, 12s. per vol. The Sermons are published every Thursday at 1d.; and will be sent weekly by the Publishers, post free, to any address in the United Kingdom:—Three months, 1s. 11d.; Six months, 3s. 9d.; Twelve months, 7s. 6d.

TWELVE SERMONS ON VARIOUS SUBJECTS. By C. H. SPURGEON. With a Portrait, Views of Cottage where Mr. Spurgeon first preached, and of the Metropolitan Tabernacle. Limp Cloth, 1s. Post free 14 stamps.

TWELVE SELECTED SOUL-WINNING SERMONS. Bound in Limp Cloth, 1s. Post free 14 stamps.

TWELVE STRIKING SERMONS. Bound in Limp Cloth, 1s. Post free 14 stamps.

TYPES AND EMBLEMS: A Collection of Sermons preached on Sunday and Thursday Evenings at the Metropolitan Tabernacle. By C. H. SPURGEON. 3s.

"'Types and Emblems' are attractive themes, and in Mr. Spurgeon's hands they neither lack suggestiveness nor power. All his well-known qualities as a preacher are in great force throughout this volume."—*Gen. Baptist Mag.*

TRUMPET CALLS TO CHRISTIAN ENERGY, A Second Series of Mr. SPURGEON's Sunday and Thursday Evening Sermons. Price 3s. 6d.

"The aim in each of these addresses is the simple one of rousing Christian men and women to renewed activity for God. Believing them to be eminently calculated to do good, we wish them a wide circulation."—*Rock.*

THE PRESENT TRUTH: A Third Series of Mr. Spurgeon's Sunday and Thursday Evening Sermons, 3s. 6d.

"Thank God for such mighty discourses! . . . No better gift-book could be suggested for an unconverted or backsliding friend."—*The Christian.*

STORM SIGNALS: A Fourth Series of Sermons preached on Sunday and Thursday Evenings at the Metropolitan Tabernacle. By C. H. SPURGEON. Price 3s. 6d.

FARM SERMONS. Nineteen Discourses on Farming. By C. H. SPURGEON. Crown 8vo. 3s. 6d. cloth gilt. Illustrated.

"These sermons are fresh and as fragrant as the newly-ploughed soil, or the new-mown hay, and ought to be perused with pleasure and profit by many who know little or nothing of agricultural pursuits."—*The Christian.*

Illustrative.

FEATHERS FOR ARROWS; or, Illustrations for Preachers and Teachers, from my Note Book. By C. H. SPURGEON. Price 2s. 6d.

"The collection is very varied, but all bearing on the highest themes, and fitted to help the highest purpose of the Christian ministry. There is an admirable index of subjects, and another of texts, which greatly add to the practical usefulness of the book: we cordially recommend it."—*Evangelical Magazine.*

ILLUSTRATIONS AND MEDITATIONS; or, Flowers from a Puritan's Garden. Distilled and Dispensed by C. H. SPURGEON. Price 2s. 6d.

"It is a Garden full of beautiful and useful things, which will yield its delights to many classes of readers."—*Christian World.*

Extracts.

FLASHES OF THOUGHT; being one Thousand Choice Extracts from the Works of C. H. SPURGEON. Alphabetically arranged, and with a copious Index. Price 5s.

"A thousand extracts, bright with the light of heaven, sparkling with wit, rich in imagery, beautiful in their setting, forcible in style, and devoutly stimulating in tone, make up a volume of unique merit."—*General Baptist Magazine.*

SPURGEON'S GEMS: being Brilliant Passages Selected from the Discourses of C. H. SPURGEON. Large Type, 4s.

GLEANINGS AMONG THE SHEAVES. By C. H. SPURGEON. Cloth Antique, Price 1s.

"These extracts are quite Spurgeonic—racy, rich, and rare, both as to style and matter—full of exquisite consolation—faithful advice—clear analogies—poetic touches—and glorious old gospel."—*Weekly Review.*

SPURGEON'S BIRTHDAY BOOK. Cloth, 2s. 6d.; Calf or Morocco, 5s; Russia, with Photograph, 10s. 6d.

"A metaphor, simile, allegory, or illustration for every day in the year, compiled from the works of C. H. SPURGEON. For thirty pence our readers may possess a book which is as useful as it is handsomely got up."—*Christian Age.*

Devotional.

MORNING BY MORNING; or, Daily Readings for the Family or the Closet. By C. H. SPURGEON. 3s. 6d. Morocco, 7s. 6d.

"Those who have learned the value of morning devotion, will highly prize these helps. All who love a full-orbed gospel, vigorous, varied thought, and a racy style, will appreciate this volume."—*Rev. J. Angus, D.D.*

EVENING BY EVENING; or, Readings at Eventide for the Family or the Closet. By C. H. SPURGEON. 3s. 6d. Morocco, 7s. 6d.

"On learning that 'Evening by Evening' was published, how gladly I bade it welcome! And I can humbly commend it in no higher terms than by simply saying that it will be found a fit companion, every way, for its forerunner of the morning."—*Charles J. Brown, D.D., Edinburgh.*

For Students.

LECTURES TO MY STUDENTS; A Selection from Addresses delivered to the Students of the Pastors' College, Metropolitan Tabernacle. By C. H. SPURGEON, President. First and Second Series. Price 2s. 6d. each.

"We have read this work with a feeling very nearly approaching to delight. Nothing that Mr. Spurgeon has printed has so thoroughly pleased us, and few of his works are calculated to be of greater practical service. It abounds in words of wisdom; it is rich in humour, but richer in human and spiritual experience."—*Nonconformist.*

COMMENTING AND COMMENTARIES: Two Lectures addressed to the Students of the Pastors' College, together with a Catalogue of Bible Commentaries and Expositions. Price 2s. 6d.

"Every candid reader will admit that, in impartiality, in terse and telling brevity, in wisdom sharpened into wit, in unaffected zeal for Christ's cause, and, above all, in robust common sense, this volume has few equals, if any."—*Literary World.*

MY SERMON-NOTES. A Selection from Outlines of Discourses delivered at the Metropolitan Tabernacle. By C. H. SPURGEON. Part I. Genesis to Proverbs—I. to LXIV. Part II. Ecclesiastes to Malachi—LXV. to CXXIX. Cloth, 2s. 6d. each, or bound together in one volume, 5s. Part III. Matthew to Acts, 2s. 6d.

"'My Sermon Notes' will be as heartily welcomed by the clergy of the Establishment as by Nonconformist pastors. In point of freshness, the work is such a contrast to many books of the same order, that preachers of every grade will find something suggestive under every head."—*The Christian World.*

SPEECHES by C. H. SPURGEON AT HOME and Abroad. 2s. 6d.

The pieces are in the main given as they originally appeared; in the majority of instances the author is made to speak in the first person; but this is not the case throughout. The reader will also find that the principal subjects are admirably reported.

Periodical.

THE SWORD AND THE TROWEL: A Monthly Magazine, Price 3d. Yearly vols., 5s. Cases for binding, 1s. 4d.

It is an accurate record of the religious movements which emanate from the Metropolitan Tabernacle, but its advocacy is far from being confined within that area. No pains will be spared to render the Magazine growingly worthy of the widest circulation.—Editor, C. H. SPURGEON.

Historical.

THE METROPOLITAN TABERNACLE: its History and Work. With 83 Illustrations. By C. H. SPURGEON. Price, in paper covers, 1s. Bound in cloth, 2s.

"Profusely illustrated with portraits, fac-similes of forgotten caricatures, and other engravings, quaint and otherwise, is likely to rival 'John Ploughman' in popularity."—*Christian World.*

MEMORIAL VOLUME. Containing Sermons and Addresses delivered on the completion of the Twenty-fifth year of the Pastorate of C. H. SPURGEON. Price 1s., cloth.

THE SPURGEON PHOTOGRAPH ALBUM, in Hand-some Binding, Royal 4to, gilt edges. Containing a brief sketch of Mr. SPURGEON's Life and his numerous Institutions, with Photographic Views, and Portraits of Mr. and Mrs. SPURGEON. 10s. 6d.

"This is a very worthy memorial of the Jubilee. A work of art for the drawing-room table, and at the same time a historical document of an event which has been a joy to many. The price is moderate for such a production."—C. H. SPURGEON.

Popular.

JOHN PLOUGHMAN'S TALK; or, Plain Advice for Plain People. Illustrated. By C. H. SPURGEON. In stiff covers, 1s. Cloth, gilt edges, 2s. 340th Thousand.

"Racy and pungent; very plain, and to the purpose. No fear as to whether it will be read or not by those into whose hands it may fall. If Mr. Spurgeon goes on at this rate in his multiform publications, he will leave nothing racy unsaid."—*Watchman.*

JOHN PLOUGHMAN'S PICTURES; or, More of his Plain Talk for Plain People. In stiff covers, 1s.; cloth, gilt edges, 2s. 110th Thousand.

SPURGEON'S SHILLING SERIES. Bound in Cloth.

No. 1.—Christ's Glorious Achievements.	No. 4.—The Mourner's Comforter.
,, 2.—Seven Wonders of Grace.	,, 5.—The Bible and the Newspaper.
,, 3.—The Spare Half-Hour.	,, 6.—Eccentric Preachers.

No. 7.—Good Cheer.

ALL OF GRACE. An earnest word with those who are seeking salvation by the Lord Jesus Christ. By C. H. SPURGEON. Cloth, 1s.

THE CLUE OF THE MAZE. By C. H. Spurgeon. Cloth Gilt, 1s.

"A seasonable as well as characteristic little book for doubters."—*The Christian Leader.*

Just out, handsomely bound, 3s. 6d.

TEN YEARS OF MY LIFE in the Service of the Book Fund: Being a Grateful Record of my Experience of the Lord's Ways, and Work, and Wages. By Mrs. C. H. SPURGEON.

"A deeply interesting narrative of a beneficent and courageously sustained effort. Mrs. Spurgeon has much of the style of her husband's writing, and this autobiographic sketch might in many respects have proceeded from his pen."—*Daily Telegraph.*

ONE PENNY EACH. By C. H. SPURGEON.

Specially adapted for gratuitous distribution.

- A DOUBLE KNOCK AT THE DOOR OF THE YOUNG.
- A GOOD SOLDIER OF JESUS CHRIST.
- A VERY EARLY BIBLE SOCIETY.
- AN ANXIOUS ENQUIRY FOR A BELOVED SON.
- APOSTOLIC EXHORTATION.
- A SILLY DOVE.
- A SPUR FOR A FREE HORSE.
- A WORD FOR THE PERSECUTED.
- BAPTISMAL REGENERATION.
- BELLS FOR THE HORSES.
- CALL TO THE UNCONVERTED.
- CHASTISEMENT.
- CONFESSION OF SIN.
- EXETER HALL SERMON TO YOUNG MEN.
- FAITH: WHAT IS IT? HOW CAN IT BE OBTAINED.
- FEAR NOT.
- FEED MY LAMBS.
- GOD'S JEWELS.
- HELPS TO FULL ASSURANCE.
- HIGH DOCTRINE AND BROAD DOCTRINE.
- HOW TO OBTAIN FAITH.
- HOW TO RAISE THE DEAD.
- INFANT SALVATION.
- IS CONVERSION NECESSARY?
- IS IT NOTHING TO YOU!
- JESUS AND THE LAMBS.
- LANDLORD AND TENANT.
- LET US PRAY.
- LOVING ADVICE FOR ANXIOUS SEEKERS.
- MAY I?
- NONE BUT JESUS.
- NUMBER 1,500; OR, LIFTING UP THE BRAZEN SERPENT.
- ONLY TRUST HIM!
- RECEIVING THE KINGDOM OF GOD AS A LITTLE CHILD.
- SERMON FOR EVERYBODY.
- "SUPPOSING HIM TO BE THE GARDENER."
- THE ANXIOUS ENQUIRER.
- THE BEST BURDEN FOR YOUNG SHOULDERS.
- THE CHILDREN AND THEIR HOSANNAS.
- THE DROPPING WELL OF KNARESBOROUGH.
- THE ESSENCE OF SIMPLICITY.
- THE LUTHER SERMON AT EXETER HALL.
- THE HOLD FAST.
- THE LITTLE DOGS.
- THE PEARL OF PATIENCE.
- THE PERPETUITY OF THE LAW OF GOD.
- THE PRIEST DISPENSED WITH.
- THERE GO THE SHIPS.
- THE SEA! THE SEA! THE WIDE AND OPEN SEA.
- THE SILVER TRUMPET.
- THE SUNDAY SCHOOL AND THE SCRIPTURES.
- THE TURNING POINT.
- THE UPPER HAND.
- THE WAY OF SALVATION.
- THE WAR HORSE.
- TOKEN FOR THE BEREAVED.

THE GOSPEL OF THE GRACE OF GOD: being Sermons delivered at the Metropolitan Tabernacle, by THOMAS SPURGEON, during his father's illness. With Preface by C. H. SPURGEON. Cloth, 1s. 6d.

WORKS BY OTHER AUTHORS.

A BODY OF DIVINITY, contained in Sermons upon the Assembly's Catechism. By the Rev. THOMAS WATSON, Rector of St. Stephen's, Walbrook. A new and complete edition, revised and adapted to modern readers by the Rev. GEORGE ROGERS, Camberwell. With a Preface and Appendix by Pastor C. H. SPURGEON. Price 6s.

"Every divine of Calvinistic views should read it, and every private Christian also. We can heartily recommend it to all lovers of sound doctrine, among whom we hope for a large sale."—C. H. SPURGEON.

ELISHA COLES ON DIVINE SOVEREIGNTY. With Preface by C. H. SPURGEON. 2s. 6d.

Romaine says of this book: "The doctrines of grace, of which this book treats, are the truths of God: our author has defended them in a masterly manner. He has not only proved them to be plainly revealed in the Scriptures, but has also shown that they are of such constant use to the children of God, that without the steadfast belief of them, they cannot go on their way rejoicing. In the practical view of these points Elisha Coles is singularly excellent."

HENRY'S OUTLINES OF CHURCH HISTORY: A Brief Sketch of the Christian Church from the First Century. By JOSEPH FERNANDEZ, LL.D. 2s. 6d.

"The Church Histories hitherto in vogue are too cumbersome, too verbose, too involved to be used in schools and colleges, and we entertain the hope that the present work will remedy that evil, and supply a work which all our friends who are tutors can use with pleasure and safety. Every young Christian should be acquainted with ecclesiastical history; it should be taught in every school of a high grade, to young ladies as well as to their brothers."—C. H. Spurgeon.

GLIMPSES OF JESUS; or, Christ Exalted in the Affections of his People. By W. P. BALFERN. Eighth Thousand. Fcp. 8vo. Cloth 3s.

"I hailed with pleasure the advent of this precious volume. I sat down to read it, and soon discovered its beauty; it was a feast of fat things, a season long to be remembered. I have read it again and again, and would desire to adore the Holy Spirit for that gracious unction which rested on me in its perusal."—C. H. Spurgeon.

LESSONS FROM JESUS; or, the Teachings of Divine Love. By W. P. BALFERN. Second Edition. 3s.

"This is a worthy sequel to 'Glimpses of Jesus,' by the same author. Every book is valuable that fixes our attention upon Jesus, and revives our perception of his beauty; and especially when it discovers new beauties, and brings his whole character more vividly before us. Such will be the effect of these 'Lessons from the life of Jesus.'"—C. H. Spurgeon.

THE BEAUTY OF THE GREAT KING, and other Poems for the Heart and Home. By W. P. BALFERN, Author of "Glimpses of Jesus." Second Edition. 2s. 6d.

"We strongly recommend this book to the attention of our readers. No child of God can read it without pleasure and profit. It has been written in the furnace, and will comfort such as are in it. The Author has seen some of 'The Beauty of the Great King,' and has well uttered the joy of that great sight. We hope that many will have equal delight with ourselves as they read this book."—C. H. Spurgeon.

Pastor C. H. SPURGEON: his Life and Work to his Fiftieth Birthday; with an Account of his Ancestors for 300 Years. By GEORGE J. STEVENSON, M.A. Paper covers, 1s., cloth, 2s.

BOOTH OF THE BLUE RIBBON MOVEMENT; or, The Factory Boy who became a Temperance Evangelist.

By ERNEST BLACKWELL. With Preface by CANON WILBERFORCE. Crown 8vo, 328 pages, handsomely bound in cloth, with illustrations. Price 3s. 6d.

"Very well written. A singular life, revealing the greatness of divine grace. R. T. Booth is one of the truest and most devoted of Temperance Evangelists. It has been our lot to see him near at hand, and to have fellowship with him, and the result is genuine Christian love to him, and esteem for him. The book is so prettily got up, that it ought to run to a hundred thousand at the least. It must be popular, or else we are greatly out of our reckoning."

C. H. SPURGEON.

THE PATHOS OF LIFE; or, Touching Incidents Illustrative of the Truth of the Gospel.

By W. POOLE BALFERN. Second Edition. 2s. 6d.

"Sensitive, refined, and tender, suited to contact with the highest class of mind, he yet seeks to reach the finer feelings of those who externally too often exhibit a rough, hard, and unimpressible aspect. The young, we venture to say, will be charmed by the fatherly tenderness characteristic of many of these poems."—*Literary World.*

BOOKSELLERS AND BOOKBUYERS in Byeways and Highways.

By C. H. SPURGEON, SAMUEL MANNING, LL.D., and G. HOLDEN PIKE. With a Preface by the Right Hon. the EARL OF SHAFTESBURY, K.G. Cloth, gilt edges, 1s. 6d.

"Externally this is an attractive book. It is brought out with the view of creating and increasing public interest in Colportage. It remains a mystery with us that we cannot obtain support for Colportage in as liberal a measure as so good a work demands. It does not say much for the wisdom and prudence of Christian people. If they gave most where the best return might legitimately be expected, we may say of our religious societies—these are last which would be first. If these addresses, papers, and reports should bring us in a revenue of sympathy, it will soon be followed by substantial help. To reach the villages and hamlets by means of sound literature taken to the cottagers' doors, is a most worthy work."—C. H. SPURGEON.

CONFERENCE ADDRESSES, being a Selection from Addresses delivered at the Annual Conferences of the Pastors' College,

by the Rev. GEORGE ROGERS. With a recommendation by C. H. SPURGEON. Cloth 2s. 6d.

"Our honoured friend, the Rev. George Rogers, has given an address at each gathering of our College conference, and on each occasion he has been singularly happy in his theme and in his mode of handling it. It would have been a pity and a sin to allow these racy addresses to be forgotten: and, accordingly, we are glad to see them preserved in print. Twelve such addresses it would be very hard to find anywhere else. We firmly believe that every student and minister who heard them will be anxious at once to possess a copy, and we shall be greatly surprised if the volume does not command a host of readers. Mother-wit is blended with fatherly wisdom, and the whole is sanctified by zeal for the cause of God. We cannot too heartily commend the volume to our subscribers."—C. H. SPURGEON.

A COLLECTION OF RARE JEWELS. From the Mines of WILLIAM GURNALL.

(1680.) Dug up and deposited in a Casket, by ARTHUR AUGUSTUS REES (1853). Second Edition. Price 2s.

"Of all the Puritans, Gurnall is the best adapted for quoting. He is sententious, and withal pictorial, and both in a high degree. Mr. Rees has made his selections with a discerning eye; they are not mere clippings at random, but extracts chosen with judgment."—*C. H. Spurgeon.*

STRAY LEAVES FROM MY LIFE STORY. By J. Manton Smith. Illustrated. Price 2s. 6d.

FRONDED PALMS. A Collection of Pointed Papers on a wide range of subjects. By W. Y. Fullerton. With over one hundred Illustrations. Cloth gilt, bevelled boards, 2s. 6d.

WAYMARKS FOR WANDERERS. Being Five Addresses on the Prodigal Son. By W. Y. Fullerton, Evangelist. Price 1s.

THE PULPIT BY THE HEARTH. Being Plain Chapters for Sabbath Reading. By Arthur Mursell. Price 2s. 6d.

FOUR LETTERS TO THE CHRISTIANS CALLED "BRETHREN" on the subject of Ministry. By Arthur Augustus Rees. Price Sixpence.

BUNYAN'S WATER OF LIFE. Preface by C. H. Spurgeon. 1s.

UPTON CHAPEL SERMONS. By W. Williams. With Three Potographs, and Preface by C. H. Spurgeon. Price 6s.

SOME OF THE GREAT PREACHERS OF WALES. By Owen Jones, M.A. Price 6s. 6d.

BAPTIST CONFESSION OF FAITH. Thirty-two Articles on Christian Faith and Practice, with Scripture Proofs, adopted by the Ministers and Messengers of the General Assembly, which met in London in 1689. Preface by C. H. Spurgeon. Paper covers, 4d. Post free, 5 stamps.

BAPTISM DISCOVERED PLAINLY AND FAITH-fully according to the Word of God. By John Norcott. A New Edition, corrected and somewhat altered by C. H. Spurgeon. Price, *paper covers*, 6d.; cloth, 1s.

LECTURES ON BAPTISM. By the Rev. W. Shirreff. With Preface by C. H. Spurgeon. Price 2s. 6d.

FOR EVER AND EVER. A College Lecture upon the Duration of Future Punishment. By Rev. George Rogers. Price 2d.

FUTURE PUNISHMENT. A Lecture Delivered to the Students of the Metropolitan Tabernacle College, in reply to a series of letters in "The Christian World," from the Rev. Edward White. By the Rev. George Rogers. Price 1d.

MURSELL'S LECTURES TO WORKING MEN. Delivered at the Lambeth Baths, Westminster Bridge Road. Price One Penny each; or 10d. the series in wrapper. Post free.

WHAT'S YOUR NAME?	COLOURS OF THE RAINBOW.
TEMPLE BAR.	RIPPLES ON THE RIVER.
THE CRYSTAL PALACE.	FACES IN THE FIRE.
SUGAR-COATED PILLS.	CRIES FROM THE CRADLE.

WASHED AWAY.

PASSMORE & ALABASTER, PATERNOSTER BUILDINGS.

www.ingramcontent.com/pod-product-compliance
Lightning Source LLC
Chambersburg PA
CBHW051722300426
44115CB00007B/432